C000001668

Reflective Practice in English Language Teaching growing literature on reflective practice in Engl outlines an empirical, data-led approach to refle examples of real data along with reflexive vignettes from a range of contexts in order to help teachers reflect on their practices. Mann and Walsh also note the importance of dialogue as crucial for reflection, as it allows for clarification, questioning and enhanced understanding. This is a superb book and a must-read for novice teachers as well as teacher educators and moves the scholarship on this complex concept to a new level.

Thomas S.C. Farrell, Brock University, Canada

This unique book demonstrates the vital importance of principled reflective activity on teaching experiences to inform and improve English language teaching practices. One of its main contributions is its use of vignettes and other data to foreground a range of voices, insights and opinions from teachers and teacher educators to demonstrate what reflection actually looks like in practice. *Reflective Practice in English Language Teaching* is a valuable resource for the professional development of L2 teachers at all levels of experience.

Joan Kelly Hall, Pennsylvania State University, USA

Mann and Walsh bring together in this book three core elements of reflective practice (real data, teachers' voices and investigative tools) and weave them into a coherent and compelling system. Teachers' own data, written and spoken, is at the heart of the book and we are presented with an abundance of authentic voices from around the world. Those voices interact and collaborate, bringing to the reader the personal and universal meanings of reflection for teachers actively researching their classrooms and contexts. The many voices are held together by the thread of scholarly commentary and discussion by Mann and Walsh, respected authorities in the world of English language teacher education. The book is a challenge to the field of reflective practice to reassess its own activities and to examine critically the tools it offers to both the trainee and the in-service teacher.

Michael McCarthy, University of Nottingham, UK

Reflective Practice in English Language Teaching

Offering a unique, data-led, evidence-based approach to reflective practice in English language teaching, this book brings together theory, research and practice in an accessible way to demonstrate what reflective practice looks like and how it is undertaken in a range of contexts. Readers learn how to do and to research reflective practice in their own settings. Through the use of data, dialogue and appropriate tools, the authors show how reflective practice can be used as an ongoing teaching tool that supports professional self-development.

Steve Mann is Associate Professor, Centre for Applied Linguistics, University of Warwick, UK.

Steve Walsh is Professor of Applied Linguistics, Newcastle University, UK.

ESL & Applied Linguistics Professional Series
Eli Hinkel, Series Editor

Visit **www.routledge.com/education** for additional information on titles in the ESL & Applied Linguistics Professional Series

Reflective Practice in English Language Teaching

Research-Based Principles and Practices

Steve Mann and Steve Walsh

Routledge
Taylor & Francis Group

NEW YORK AND LONDON

First published 2017
by Routledge
711 Third Avenue, New York, NY 10017

and by Routledge
2 Park Square, Milton Park, Abingdon, Oxon, OX14 4RN

Routledge is an imprint of the Taylor & Francis Group, an informa business

Library of Congress Cataloging in Publication Data
Names: Mann, Steve, 1960- author. | Walsh, Steve, 1959- author.
Title: Reflective practice in English language teaching : research-based
principles and practices / Steve Mann and Steve Walsh.
Description: New York : Routledge, 2017. |
Series: ESL & applied linguistics series | Includes bibliographical
references and index.
Identifiers: LCCN 2016056827 | ISBN 9781138839489 (hbk) |
ISBN 9781138839496 (pbk) | ISBN 9781315733395 (ebk)
Subjects: LCSH: Reflective teaching. | English language—Study and
teaching.
Classification: LCC LB1025.3. M37113 2017 | DDC 428.0071—dc23
LC record available at https://lccn.loc.gov/2016056827

ISBN: 978-1-138-83948-9 (hbk)
ISBN: 978-1-138-83949-6 (pbk)
ISBN: 978-1-315-73339-5 (ebk)

Typeset in Minion
by Keystroke, Neville Lodge, Tettenhall, Wolverhampton

Dedication

For our children: Aine, Ciaran, Lara, Rob, Rosie and in loving memory of Nick.

Contents

Acknowledgements

We have a number of people to thank in relation to this book. We'd like to thank them for their feedback and encouragement and for influencing our thinking. Keith Richards has always been a source of great support and inspiration. Tom Farrell has always been very generous with his time and encouragement. Tom Morton and John Gray have inspired and encouraged us, even if they do not always agree with some of our thinking. Others to whom we owe a great deal of gratitude include Tony Young, Fiona Copland, Graham Hall, Anne O'Keeffe and Mike McCarthy. In addition, Julian Edge has always been a source of inspiration and his book *The Reflexive Teacher Educator in TESOL* has been insightful in showing how a series of reflexive episodes can reveal a great deal about being a committed practitioner. We hope we have brought this spirit to our book.

Many of the insights in this book have arisen from engagement with some excellent MA and PhD students in recent years, and a good number of them have contributed to the book and its rationale in various ways. Some of them have provided data or vignettes and some have offered feedback. As we have published more on RP and attended various conferences and seminars, we have made contact with other teachers and teacher educators who are interested in RP. The following is a list that recognizes the debt we owe these people. There would be no book without them. There are too many to make clear the precise nature of their contribution, but many of them are cited in the following chapters. And so, we would like to thank Jane Spinola, Joan Sim, Jennifer Heo, Samiah Ghounaim, Timi Hyacinth, Flori Dzay-Chulim, Wayne Trotman, George Skuse, Mohammad Manasreh, Manuel Herrera Montoya, Shefali Kulkarni, Bulara Monyaki, Reem Doukmak, Bushra Ahmed Khurram, Jose Alberto Fajardo Castañeda, Amir Hamidi, Andrea Luci, Keith Richards, Andy Boon, Sue Garton, Andy Harris, Audrey O'Grady, Bede McCormack, Dario Banegas, Ezra Ora, Fiona Copland, Tom Farrell, Fiona Farr, Gokce Kurt, Hansung Waring, Heather Buchanan, Ivor Timmis, Ian Nakamura, Jade Blue, Jo Ann Delaney, Jo Gakonga, Julian Edge, Lara Walsh, Li Li, Marisela (Brasil), Mark Brooke, Mark Wyatt, Mike Chick, Mohammad Aldhaen, Olcay Sert, Hatice Ergul, Olly Beddall, Paul Slater, Phillip Saxon, Rana Yildirim, Rezvan Rashidi, Richard Pinner, Russell Stannard, Sandra Morales, Sarah Banks, Sue Wharton, Jane Willis, Sarah Haas,

Natalia Dura Gatti, Wimansha Abeyawickrama, Saleha Mersin, Abdou Dieng, Suzuki Koda Fuentes, Jennifer Joshua, Ema Ushioda, Jingli Jiang, Andrew Davidson, Annamaria Pinter, Mala Palini, Sukhbir Atwal, Teti Dragas, John Gray, Tom Morton, Tony Wright, Christine Tudor Jones, Jiamei Chen, Mohammed Bashir, Allwyn D'Costa, Larissa Goulart Da Silva, Urmila Khaled, Sol Loutayf, Vuyokazi Makubalo, Erkin Mukhammedov, Alireza Safar, Sefalane Shaike, Pipit Suharto, Aom Wongchaiwa, Betelhem taye Tsehayu and Abdalla Yousif.

In truth, there are many other students we have worked with at Aston University, Queen's University Belfast, the University of Birmingham, Newcastle University and the University of Warwick who have helped shape many of these ideas. In all these institutions, we have learned a great deal from working with such committed teachers and researchers.

We are grateful for Routledge's support in publishing this book and we would particularly like to thank Naomi Silverman for her advice, patience, good humour and commitment. Special thanks too to Rosie Copland-Mann and Lara Walsh, who helped enormously with checking and formatting references.

STEVE MANN
Alrewas, Staffordshire

STEVE WALSH
Ovingham, Northumberland

Introduction

'The Two Steves' met on a flight from London to Hong Kong in 1987. It is 30 years since that initial meeting, but we have often been in touch, sharing ideas about teaching and teacher development, and more latterly about research. It has been a real collaboration over time. We would say that a great deal of our talk when we get together is reflective. There are lots of well worn ways of expressing this ('two heads are better than one'; 'it's good to talk'; 'collaboration is better than competition'). The ideas for this book have, then, emerged over a very long period of time, through much discussion and debate, and the sharing of professional experiences.

The central argument of this book is that reflective practice (RP) is an important element in learning to be a competent teacher. While we, like many practitioners, accept that it is both necessary and positive, we also feel that it has become a little 'tired' and in need of revitalizing; in particular, it needs to be theorized and researched much more through more sustained and appropriate use of data. In the ten chapters of this book, we demonstrate how a data-led approach to RP can be revealing and might be made more accessible to practitioners, especially in the early stages of their career. We argue that, in the tradition of action research, professionals need appropriate tools, their own data, and preferably some kind of collaborative dialogue in order to reflect on – and ultimately improve – their practices. By using actual data as empirical evidence, we demonstrate how RP 'gets done' in a range of contexts. We offer an approach with specific spoken and written tools that will help readers learn how to do RP in their own context. We also show how teacher educators encourage and foster RP.

Key Themes and Organization of the Book

A perusal of the contents page (p. vii) shows that the book begins with a consideration of reflective practice (RP) in the first two chapters. In Chapter 1 we review important literature and ideas related to reflective practice, and present some critical positions with regard to the nature and status of RP. Chapter 2 provides our response to these challenges and sets out what we believe are important ways forward that we investigate in the remainder of the book; these two chapters provide the backdrop to the remainder of the book. The focus then switches to various contexts for training, education and development. Chapter 3 concentrates on pre-service teaching contexts, while Chapter 4 provides different perspectives on in-service teacher education. Chapter 5 looks at the role of reflective practice beyond formal education and in CPD contexts. The focus of the book then switches to the medium of reflection. Chapter 6 investigates aspects of written reflection and then Chapter 7 considers aspects of spoken reflection. We are keen to show that this distinction is simplistic and that practices associated with written and spoken reflection often have a mutually supporting relationship. This is made explicit in Chapter 8, where we explore the notion of dialogic reflection, which we believe is essential to establishing a revitalized perspective on RP. The final two chapters then provide two different positions on reflection and research: Chapter 9 considers practitioner research and Chapter 10 presents an agenda for further research into RP.

Who Are You?

We have written this book to be usable by a wide range of teachers and teacher educators. We hope it will appeal to novice teachers as they embark on their careers. For them, having a more robust sense of RP will help sustain and nurture their careers. However, we have also written the book for more experienced teachers and those tasked with organizing and supporting pre-service teacher training, in-service teacher education and more long-term CPD. The book might be used as a self-study guide, as a reference or as a set text on taught higher education courses.

The Role of Reflexive Vignettes in the Book

Most chapters have three or four reflexive vignettes. They are a key part of our data-led approach to RP. These vignettes usually have three parts. They:

1. make clear important elements in the interactional context;
2. provide a piece of reflective data or perspective on RP;
3. comment on key issues in the extract.

For us, these vignettes are the heart of the book. Not only do they foreground the voices and experience of teachers and teacher trainers (both novices and more expert practitioners), they also show the importance of reflecting on and learning from interactional experience (through transcripts and vignettes). Unless otherwise indicated, the researchers' real names are used in the introduction to each vignette. We have tried to integrate the vignettes into the main commentary and our own thinking. We are extremely grateful to everyone who has contributed to this book and enriched it with their thinking; any omissions, errors or misrepresentations of the vignettes are entirely our responsibility.

Transcription

If you are unfamiliar with transcription conventions, we would recommend Atkinson and Heritage's *Structures of Social Action* (1984: ix–xvi). Alternatively, you could consult a web resource. The following offers a useful one-page summary: www.esourceresearch.org/eSourceBook/ConversationAnalysis/ 10TranscriptionSymbols/tabid/531/Default.aspx

Feedback

In the spirit of reflexivity and professional development, we welcome your comments, questions and suggestions on this publication. Please contact us by email at:

Steve.mann@warwick.ac.uk

Steve.walsh@ncl.ac.uk

1
Reflective Practice Reviewed

1.1 Introduction

This book is about the value and importance of reflective practice. Reflection and reflective practice continue to have a central position in professional education. As Grayling argues 'the best thing any education can bequeath is the habit of reflection and questioning' (2003: 179). The importance of reflective practice has been established; it is widespread and a ubiquitous part of the teacher education landscape. However, we believe that our book adds something distinctive and original to discussions and debates around reflective practice. The book highlights the importance of data and evidence with regard to reflective practice. This is important in two ways. First, we want to highlight the role data and evidence play in triggering and fostering reflection. Second, we want to demonstrate what reflection looks like in practice, by using data and evidence to show reflection actually happening. In addition, we want to give a platform to a range of voices, insights and opinions. In order to do this, we integrate data and viewpoints from a range of teachers and trainers about the nature and importance of reflective practice. According to Dewey (1933: 8) 'reflection is something that is believed in, not on its own account, but through something else which stands as evidence'. This is our starting point. What is helpful as evidence or data to sustain reflection? What tools or procedures are useful for teachers in fostering and supporting reflection through the gathering of evidence and data?

In what follows we briefly review the early work of Dewey (1933) and then Schön (1983), and connect this to more recent work (e.g. Farrell, 2004). In addition to offering a theoretical perspective of the field, we show how these positions have resulted in a range of models, practices and tools for implementing reflective practice. Chapter 1 aims to provide an overview of the origins of reflective practice (RP) and trace its developments over time. In providing a review of the conceptualization and operationalization of reflection, we establish that there is a great variety in its treatment (e.g. El-Dib, 2007; Farrell, 2004). In addition, we consider the value of alternative ways of depicting RP, including a number of frameworks (e.g. Stanley, 1998), levels (El-Dib, 2007), typologies (e.g. Jay and Johnson, 2002) and phases (e.g. Zeichner and

Liston, 1996). Our summary and discussion of different critiques of RP in 1.4 provide us with the backdrop to the critical perspective we are taking on RP.

One of the central aims of Chapter 1 is to provide a critical review of reflective practice, drawing attention to particular problems with its representation, as well as proposing a more evidence-based and data-led approach. We reconsider some of the arguments made in Mann and Walsh (2013) that RP in the fields of applied linguistics, TESOL and education has achieved a status of orthodoxy without a corresponding evidence-led description of its value, processes and impact. Our concern is that RP is often described in ways that are elusive, general and vague, which may not be particularly helpful for practitioners. This is largely due to the lack of concrete, data-led and linguistic detail of RP in practice and to its institutional nature, lack of specificity, and reliance on written forms. However, there are a growing number of data-led accounts of reflective practice (see Farrell, 2016) and we hope this book will add to this literature in demonstrating how reflective practice can be and needs to be operationalized in systematic ways (Korthagen and Wubbels, 1995).

This chapter argues that applied linguistics needs to champion a description of RP's processes and impact by drawing on data-led accounts of reflective practice across a range of contexts. Too many RP accounts rely on general summaries and so are not critical, transparent or usable by other practitioners. Such accounts do not engage with data or evidence from teachers or teacher education practitioners. Our aim in this book is to share examples of 'reflection-in-action' through the data and vignettes in order for the nature and value of reflective practice to be better understood. We propose here that RP needs to be rebalanced, away from a reliance on written forms and taking more account of spoken, collaborative forms of reflection; in sum, we argue for a more dialogic, data-led and collaborative approach to reflective practice.

In Mann and Walsh (2013) we argued that while RP has considerable merit in professional education, it is:

- dominated by models and writing 'about' reflection and lacks precision about 'how to'
- not sufficiently data-led
- too often presented as an individual process and fails to foreground collaboration, how it can be scaffolded, or how it might result from participation in a community of practice
- dominated by written forms of reflection at the expense of potentially more beneficial spoken forms
- dogged by inconsistencies and concerns about whether assessment of reflection is desirable
- faced with issues about the nature and variety of reflective tools
- undermined by professional educators who do not always practise what they preach.

In the first part of this chapter, we trace the origins and developments of RP as a means of providing a context for the critical position we are adopting. In subsequent sections, we offer an overview of the theoretical underpinnings and approaches to RP, before returning to the seven problems listed above. In the final section of the chapter, we provide a critical perspective of RP as the backdrop to Chapter 2 that explains how we consider RP should be revitalized.

1.2 Origins and Developments

A number of theorists (in particular Dewey, Schön and Kolb) have been influential in the development of the concept of reflection. Dewey is widely credited for turning attention to the importance of experiential learning and reflective thought as the 'sole method of escape from the purely impulsive or purely routine action' (1933: 15). He provided the impetus for establishing the notion that teachers need to be reflective. He argued that teachers should not be passive recipients of knowledge but should play an active role in materials design and curriculum reform and innovation (Dewey, 1933). His concerns focus principally on the relationship between experience, interaction and reflection. It could be argued that the key messages of this chapter (albeit with a linguistic twist) are consistent with Dewey's original formulations of reflection. In particular, our position has resonance with Dewey's concerns about linear models of thinking misrepresenting the nature of reflection. Reflection is a highly complex process in which thinking, interaction, knowledge and learning have a reflexive relationship (see Semetsky, 2008).

Dewey's work in teacher education, emphasizing a pragmatic and scientific rationality, is widely held to be instrumental in establishing reflection as a driver for moving away from routinization (e.g. Osterman and Kottkamp, 2004) and encouraging active and ongoing consideration of beliefs and possible action. Dewey's contribution (1933), followed by others such as Habermas (1972), Stenhouse (1975), van Manen (1977), Schön (1983) and Kolb (1984), consolidated the notion of reflection in relation to action, even though this is not always an easy process. In many ways the process can be 'troublesome' because it involves 'overcoming the inertia that inclines one to accept suggestions at their face value'. It can involve reconsidering beliefs and practices and can involve willingness to 'endure a condition of mental unrest and disturbance' (Dewey, 1933: 13).

Dewey drew attention to particular values (open-mindedness, responsibility and whole-heartedness) that are pre-requisites for successful reflection. Farrell confirms the continuing importance of these qualities (Farrell, 2008) and they continue to be important in recent research on reflective practice (e.g. Dzay Chulim, 2015). Open-mindedness is a desire to listen to more than one side of an issue, fully embrace, and give attention to alternative options. Responsibility involves the disposition to carefully consider the consequences of actions and willingness to accept those consequences, and whole-heartedness 'implies that teachers can overcome fears and doubts to critically evaluate their practice in order to make meaningful change' (Farrell, 2008: 1).

Although it is important to recognize the enduring influence of Dewey, it is certainly possible to trace reflection in education back to Descartes (rationality) and further back to Plato and Socrates. The works of Kant and Wittgenstein (see Cornford, 2002) have also been key contributions in the way reflection is seen as fundamental to individual education and personal growth. We do not intend to provide a comprehensive history here, but in the chapters that follow we will return to some of these philosophic positions in considering ways that reflection is defined and positioned.

For us, Dewey is particularly influential and we would recommend reading some of his initial formulations (1933). Dewey's notions of continuously challenging and re-visiting current educational practices provide both the impetus and spirit of this book and our work on reflective practice to date (e.g. Mann and Walsh, 2013; Walsh and Mann, 2015). Partly because of the value put on autonomy and reflection by Dewey and his followers, there has been a general trend away from the notion of teacher training towards one of teacher education. This is often characterized as a movement from transmission to constructivism. The emphasis of second language teacher *education*, as distinct from second language teacher *training* (Richards and Nunan, 1990; Wallace, 1991), means that the focus of attention is much more on the realization that teachers need to develop themselves and that this is a life-time CPD (continuing professional development) process. Mann (2005: 8–9) provides a detailed consideration of the terms 'education', 'development' and 'training'. Here, we simply recognize the possible negative connotations of the term 'training' (leading to greater adoption of the term 'teacher preparation') but we consider that some skills, tools and strategies can be trained, and indeed in Chapters 3 and 4 we consider specific ways in which reflective practice might be modelled and demonstrated.

There is clearly more to teacher preparation than skills training; teachers need to be equipped with the tools that will enable them to find out about their own classrooms and make adjustments (Bartlett, 1990). In short, it is helpful for teachers to be able to adapt their role from teacher to that of teacher-researcher, a logical extension of what Wallace (1991: 8) terms 'the applied science model' of teacher education, first proposed by the American sociologist Schön (1983, 1987). Dewey's ideas were further developed by Schön, who argued for the importance of teachers as 'reflective practitioners' (1983: 332). Schön argued that teachers could come to new understandings of their professional practice through processes of reflection and reframing. The influence of Schön's ideas is clear in the way reflection has developed within teacher education (e.g. Stanley, 1998; Zeichner and Liston, 1996; Farrell, 2004). In particular, Schön put forward a model of 'reflection-in-action', according to which teachers are involved in critical thought, questioning and re-appraising their actions (1983). Habermas (1972) was also influential in the development of Schön's arguments for a critical/reflective form of reasoning (based on a fundamental mode of enquiry in social sciences). Habermas and Schön are also important in the development of more 'critical' forms of reflection.

Schön was particularly influential in distinguishing between reflection-in-action and 'reflection-on-action'. Reflection-in-action is synchronous with the professional act (thinking on your feet) and reflection-on-action is asynchronous (a reflection after the professional action or incident). Killion and Todnem (1991) added 'reflection-for-action', which is prospective and identifies steps or guidelines to follow to succeed in a given task in the future. 'For-action' pushes the process in more sustained and systematic directions and so overlaps with notions of research (e.g. action research, exploratory practice) and we return to this aspect of RP in Chapter 9.

Reflecting on past actions is an endeavour that increases understanding of the teaching/learning process (Wallace, 1998). Competencies are acquired by participants who have an active role in their own development, which in turn is based on two types of knowledge: received knowledge and experiential knowledge. Received knowledge is 'the intellectual content of the profession' (Wallace, 1991: 14), including the specific knowledge (linguistic and pedagogic) that language teachers need in order to perform their role. Experiential knowledge is based on experience gained in the classroom and reflection on that experience. Both types of knowledge are important and often interrelated, but it is the second which is of most concern to the present discussion, since it rests on the assumption that teachers can and should reflect on their practices and learn from them. Central to the notion of experiential knowledge is collaborative discussion, where thoughts and ideas about classroom practice can be articulated and shaped.

Hobson and Malderez (2013) argue that by the 1980s, teacher educators in the UK increasingly foregrounded the provision of a 'reflective practitioner' model of professional learning (Furlong et al., 2000). There was a great deal of variety in the way that reflective practice was conceptualized (see Calderhead, 1989; Furlong and Maynard, 1995) but its inclusion in some form became orthodox. A great deal of teacher education literature foregrounded reflection as an important aspect of professional practice (Smyth, 1989; Hatton and Smith, 1995; Jay and Johnson, 2002; Harkin, 2005; Pollard, 2005; Alger, 2006; Farrell, 2008).

One of the challenges facing both participants in, and commentators on, RP is that there is no commonly agreed definition. Hatton and Smith (1995) feel that both reflection and critical reflection are often ill-defined. While most definitions highlight the importance of experience, they vary in the extent to which they foreground interaction or action. Most include the intellectual and the affective (what you think and how you feel). Two other elements of many definitions are 'action' and 'critical', though, again, there are huge variations in emphasis. Some writers foreground a critical element (e.g. Brookfield, 1997; Bailin et al., 2007), while others, like Mezirow (1991), put the emphasis on critical self-awareness and critical reflection of presuppositions (on which learning is based). Given this range of use and emphasis, we would not expect much agreement in definition. For the purposes of this chapter and in previous articles, we adopt the definition put forward by Boud et al. (1985: 3), '[reflection is] a generic term for those intellectual and affective activities in which individuals engage to explore their experiences in order to lead to new understandings and appreciation'. However, we argue in this book that those 'activities' vary greatly depending on context (Chapters 3 to 5). We also want to focus on what reflection is possible with others and so we focus particular attention on an under-represented subset of reflective activity (spoken and collaborative reflection) in Chapters 7 and 8.

The articulation of phases suggested by Zeichner and Liston (1996) in their model for reflection have been influential. They suggest the following five reflection phases:

1. *Rapid reaction* which occurs instinctively and immediately (rapid and private);
2. *Repair* that may entail reflection-in-action but with a brief pause for thought;
3. *Review* which involves interpersonal and collaborative elements and happens after the teacher's work day (reflection-on-action);
4. *Research* which may take place over weeks or months and is more systematic and focuses on particular issues;
5. *Retheorize and reformulate* that takes place over months or years and is more abstract and rigorous, critical examination (in relation to public academic theories).

Stanley (1998) also articulates five levels of reflection for the individual, moving from basic engagement and awareness of reflection to actual reflective thinking. She also differentiates various forms of using reflection in order for these forms to be understood and integrated into ongoing teaching. Although there are some differences in emphasis, most of the literature identifies three levels of reflection (Day, 1993; Farrell, 2004; Jay and Johnson, 2002; Larrivee, 2004). The work from an initial level, sometimes called descriptive, focuses on specific actions, techniques and issues. The second level is concerned with rationale, justification and evaluation. The most prized form of reflection is usually described at the moral, social and political level and is often characterized as 'critical'.

In the chapters that follow, we use data to consider the value of various ways of seeing reflection (models, phases, steps and levels). Although we believe that there is value in various models and typologies, they need to facilitate reflection, rather than obstruct it, which, we suggest, may sometimes occur. We take a similar position to Burns (2005) in her consideration of models, phases, steps and levels of action research. It may be more helpful to see models, phases, steps and levels as interrelated practices (rather than fixed, linear or hierarchical). In this regard, we see our work as congruent with Dewey's concerns about the imposition of linear models of thinking.

1.3 Theoretical Perspectives

One of the most influential perspectives on learning and professional development which has relevance to the process of reflective practice is the socio-cultural learning perspective. Socio-cultural theories (SCT) of learning emphasize their social nature, which takes place as learners interact with the 'expert' 'in a context of social interactions leading to understanding' (Röhler and Cantlon, 1996: 2). The core notion of this view is that learners collectively and actively construct their own knowledge and understanding by making connections, building mental schemata and concepts through collaborative meaning-making. Although we do not think it is the case that there always needs to be an 'expert' or facilitator, it is the case that, especially in the early stages of training and development, teachers might benefit from such help. SCT and the overlapping perspective of constructivism provide the basis for the reconceptualized perspective on RP we advocate in Chapter 2; it is also dealt with more fully in Chapter 8 with a focus on dialogic reflection. We believe that socio-cultural theory has much to offer in terms of advancing our understandings of the theoretical underpinnings of RP. Although it is certainly true that Vygotskian perspectives have been most influential in considering children's learning, this is beginning to change, and Lantolf and Poehner (2008: 2) see it as unfortunate that Vygotskian educational thinking has been 'virtually ignored in adult educational settings'. Nearly all the data featured in this book are from adult educational settings, and one of the aims of our work is to consider a Vygotskian perspective to RP.

In addition to the social nature of learning, socio-cultural theory emphasizes the fact that the mind is *mediated* by symbolic tools, such as language, to both interpret and regulate the world we live in and our relationships with each other (Vygotsky, 1978). Lantolf explains mediation as follows (2000: 1):

> . . . we use symbolic tools or signs to mediate and regulate our relationships with others and with ourselves and thus change the nature of these relationships.

Our relationship with the world is an indirect, or *mediated*, one, which is established through the use of symbolic tools (Lantolf, ibid.). Understanding the ways in which human social and mental activity are organized through symbolic tools is the role of psychology, according to a Vygotskian perspective. While thought and speech are separate, they are 'tightly interrelated in a dialectic unity in which publicly derived speech completes privately initiated thought' (Lantolf, 2000: 7). In other words, understanding and knowledge are 'publicly derived' but privately internalized. Again, this view of learning and professional development resonates strongly with reflective processes: new understandings might be derived first through discussion with another professional and then internalized following reflection and consideration at a slight distance. Through this process of experience, dialogue and reflection, professionals gain owner-ship by integrating new knowledge and understanding with prior experience. Consider, for example, how a conversation with a colleague about a feature of teaching practice such as eliciting might result in reflection, further discussion, changes to practice, further reflection and so on. The outcomes of the process – new knowledge or new understandings – are derived in both public and private contexts, entailing dialogue and reflection.

Three principles of socio-cultural theory have direct relevance to RP:

1. Professional development is fundamentally a *social* process.
2. Teachers need to *appropriate* new understandings (make them their own).
3. Development may be assisted by *scaffolding*.

Professional Development Is Fundamentally a Social Process

The dynamism of social interaction and its effects on development are central to Vygotsky's work. Unlike many other theories of self-development, or ontogenesis, which consider the individual as an enclosed unit, Vygotsky stresses the importance of social interaction to an individual's development. In this book we see the perspective we take on RP as falling under socio-cultural theory, particularly as we see learning as essentially social and cultural in nature, and not an individual and solitary phenomenon (Lantolf, 2005; Lantolf and Thorne, 2006). Socio-cultural theory is concerned with learning and develop-ment over time, and Vygotsky (1978) is central to this paradigm in its emphasis on the social, dynamic and developmental nature of learning where an indivi-dual's learning potential depends on mediation. In this respect we are interested in the support, tools and techniques (scaffolds) that might help foster develop-ment. We also draw on the overlapping/related field of social constructivism (e.g. Wells, 1999) in recognizing the social and dialogic nature of cognitive development. Téllez (2007) tells us that the 'importance of constructivism in educational theory and research cannot be underestimated' (2007: 553). Wood (1995) and Tatto (1998) offered early support for constructivist programs and demonstrated that they were more successful and more influential on PRESET (pre-service education and training) teachers than conventional programs.

Wideen et al. (1998) also support a constructivist shift away from traditional transmission programmes.

Socio-cultural learning theory emphasizes the social, dynamic and collaborative dimensions of learning; both Vygotsky (e.g. 1978) and Bruner (1990) stress its 'transactional' nature, whereby learning occurs in the first instance through interaction with others who are more experienced and in a position to guide and support the actions of the novice. During this part of the process, language is used as a 'symbolic tool' to clarify and make sense of new knowledge, with learners often relying heavily on discussions with the 'expert knower'. As new ideas and knowledge are internalized, learners use language to comment on what they have learnt; oral communication is the 'organising function' (Hickman, 1990: 236) used to both transmit and clarify new information and then to reflect on and rationalize what has been learnt – a gradual process of self-regulation, explained by Ahmed (1994: 158):

> a linguistically constituted mental process [. . .] through which the locus of control of mental activity shifts from the external context [. . .] to the internal mind.

In sum, drawing on SCT, we can say that for professional development to occur, three elements are usually involved: a focus, dialogue with another professional, and reflection. Essentially, through dialogue, professional development is mediated by language; new understandings emerge through conversations with other professionals, through experience and reflection on that experience. This entire process entails not only the acquisition of new knowledge but also the appropriation or ownership of that knowledge. This is the second of our theoretical principles discussed here.

Teachers Need to Appropriate New Understandings (Make Them Their Own)

Through discussion, dialogue and reflection, new understandings are appropriated, or made one's own. Ownership is a key aspect of any learning or development process since we all learn in different ways and the actual understandings we achieve will vary from one individual to another. By way of illustration, spend a minute re-reading the previous section in this chapter and summarize it for a colleague: it is almost certain that you will both summarize it in different ways and demonstrate different degrees and levels of understanding. In a professional context, appropriation is even more important since we are applying what we have learnt or understood and using that new knowledge to benefit our learners. We return to this important theoretical construct in later chapters.

To summarize this section, we are proposing that professional talk is far from a one-way process from a more experienced to a less experienced colleague; it is a co-constructed series of encounters in which interlocutors may offer support and guidance through scaffolding, the third principle of socio-cultural theories considered in this section.

Development May Be Assisted by Scaffolding

The term 'scaffolding' was originally used to refer to the linguistic support given by a more experienced 'knower' (parent, teacher, tutor) to a less experienced individual (child, pupil, student) (Bruner, 1990). Support is given up to the point where a learner can 'internalise external knowledge and convert it into a tool for conscious control' (ibid.: 25). Scaffolding is 'an instructional tool that reduces learning ambiguity' (Doyle, 1986: 3). Central to the notion are the important polar concepts of challenge and support. Learners are led to an understanding of a task by, on the one hand, a teacher's provision of appropriate amounts of challenge to maintain interest and involvement, and, on the other, support to ensure understanding.

Clearly, the amount of scaffolded support given will depend very much on the perceived evaluation by the 'expert' of what is needed by the 'novice'. In a classroom context, where so much is happening at once, such fine judgments can be difficult to make. Deciding to intervene or withdraw in the moment by moment construction of classroom interaction requires great sensitivity and awareness on the part of the teacher, and inevitably teachers do not 'get it right' every time. In a professional teacher training or development context, tutors or colleagues may help an individual acquire new understandings by highlighting a particular teaching practice, by drawing attention to a specific phenomenon or by 'feeding in' a piece of terminology or metalanguage to facilitate discussion.

Consider the extract below in which a group of trainee teachers on a four-week TESOL course is receiving feedback from their teacher educator. We use this piece of data to provide an example of how a data-led discussion of scaffolding might help establish its relation to RP. In the extract, L is the teacher educator, D is the trainee who has just taught and A is another trainee who observed the teaching. The teacher educator (L) has invited D to reflect on and comment on his teaching performance; D describes the way in which he had to explain the word 'destination' before moving into the main activity.

Extract 1.1

```
1. D: And I had to (.) make it clea::r what des- destination meant

2. A: You >↑DID a good job< thou::gh (.) I mean

3. L: Yeah
```

```
 4. A: it was you said like one or two wo::rds and then it was like
 5.    (.) >got it<

 6. L: °Right°

 7. D: And then I (?) because I was thinking if they are confu::sed
 8.    (.) my topic it might be difficult (for them) go to next step
 9.    but if they still confused they (.) don't know what they maybe
10.    (one pla::ce) (or) (what they had to do actually)

11. L: Right

12. D: (Finding place one day or activities)

13. L: Yeah I I agree: with all of you I think that it was great to
14.    get them straight into the topic like that a::nd to pick up
15.    tha:t (0.4) they needed more (.) they didn't know >what
16.    destinations were< and that was very quickly and efficiently
17.    (.) [verified right]
```
Harris, 2013

Extract 1.1 opens with D explaining why he needed to check the meaning of the word 'destination' in line 1. His colleague A affirms his decision in lines 2 and 4, supporting his classroom practice and giving praise. The trainer (L) also adds support to D's practice in lines 3 and 6, before D goes on to further justify and rationalize his actions (lines 7 to 10). Essentially, his reflections, as spoken here, suggest that he knew why he had introduced this piece of vocabulary and how that decision related to the main activity which was to follow. In lines 13 to 17, the trainer L adds her support to his rationalization, summarizing for the group and adding her own appraisal of the actions taken. Importantly, in line 17, she feeds in, or scaffolds, the semi-technical term 'verified', used here to mean the checking of new language as part of a longer or larger activity. There are many possible explanations for this; one might be that she would like her group to begin using a more 'technical code' to describe their teaching. Learning to talk the talk of TESOL is, arguably, a key element in becoming a more proficient teacher – hence the need to scaffold the word 'verified' here. Other examples of scaffolding will be presented in later chapters; for our purposes here, we acknowledge its value in helping promote understanding, develop criticality and assist professionals as they gain ownership of new concepts.

In this section, we have presented a summary of the more important theoretical constructs underpinning the perspective on RP being advocated here. Our main argument is that socio-cultural theory has much to offer understandings not only of RP, but also of teaching and learning more generally (see, for example, Howe and Mercer (2012) on the value and potential of socio-cultural theory). Any reconceptualized perspective on RP (see Chapter 2) would be well advised to try and embed some of the constructs presented here as a way of making more explicit the relationship between practice, dialogue, interaction, reflection and action. We return to this argument in Chapter 2. In the next section, we offer a critique of RP by considering what we perceive as its major challenges.

1.4 A Critique of RP

There have been a number of concerns expressed related to reflection and RP. For example, Boud and Walker (1998: 191) assert that although they are essentially sympathetic to reflective practice within professional courses, they believe that 'there are now many examples of poor educational practices being implemented under the guise and rhetoric of reflection'. For others there is a sense that RP has run its course and there is a need to move 'beyond reflective practice' (Bradbury et al., 2010: 55) and consider new approaches to CPD. What follows takes a critical stance. This section extends previous criticisms and summarizes some of our own (Mann and Walsh, 2013; Walsh and Mann, 2015). The section works on a thematic basis to outline key challenges, presented under seven major themes: a dominance of models of RP; a lack of data-led accounts; a focus on the individual; an over-emphasis on written RP; problems of assessing RP; using the 'wrong' reflective tools; not 'practising what you preach'.

Dominance of Models of RP

We have said that we think problems of definition are inevitable. However, the preponderance of models, frameworks and ways of talking about reflection is a more serious issue and is partly to blame for the lack of data-led description which we tackle below. There are two aspects to this problem. The first is the impression that models and frameworks usually suggest a necessary order and linear progression. The second is simply the space that is routinely given to going through the various models, instead of providing exemplification and detail about 'how to'. Put simply, practitioners are frequently told about RP rather than being shown examples of how to do it or being shown practitioners' comments on RP's value for them.

Influential models include those of Kolb (1984), Gibbs (1988), Korthagen (1985), Johns (2000), Rolfe et al. (2001), Zwozdiak-Myers (2012) and Farrell (2016). Kolb's (1984) model of experiential learning works from concrete experience to reflective observation and then in the stage of abstract conceptualization the focus shifts to a theoretical perspective before moving into a phase of active experimentation.

Kolb (1984) sets out the four-stage cycle of learning shown below and underpins it with four distinct learning styles:

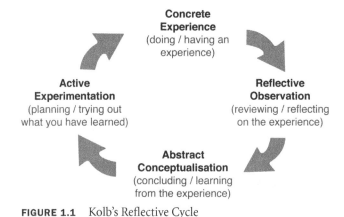

FIGURE 1.1 Kolb's Reflective Cycle

Zwozdiak-Myers (2009: 50) provides a useful summary of this cycle:

> The cycle can be summarised as: immediate or concrete experiences (1) that provide the basis for observations and reflections; observations and reflections (2) are distilled and assimilated into abstract concepts (3), which produce new possibilities for action, which can be actively tested (4) through experimentation, that in turn, create new experiences.

Although we would agree that this is a useful model, it does present a view of reflection as requiring 'abstract concepts' and leading to action ('experimentation'). We agree that reflection *can* lead to these stages. However, it may be unhelpful for novice teachers to insist on formulating 'abstract concepts' or theory. It may also be unhelpful to push them too quickly to further experimentation and further action. We return to this issue in Chapter 3.

Gibbs' (1988) 'reflective cycle' has an order of description, feelings, evaluations, analysis, conclusions, and then action planning. Other models have stages and steps. Our contention is that models of any kind need careful handling as they can be interpreted too literally. They are not derived from data in any empirical way and we need to guard against reflection becoming a series of steps or procedures rather than a reflexive enterprise. Any model advocating steps and procedures is faced with the problem that participants may simply go through the motions of RP rather than actually engage in RP. The same can be said of action research, which as Burns (2005) has pointed out should be seen as a series of interrelated practices *rather than a fixed series of cycles or steps*. If we foreground models, we are in danger of prioritizing the conceptual and theorized nature of reflection (about reflection) rather than focusing on data-led examples of reflection. One of the problems is that even when Kolb (1984) explicitly says there is no one entry point in four major stages (the concrete experience stage, the observation and reflection stage, the forming abstract concepts stage, and the stage of testing in a new situation), the model can still be unwittingly *taught* as a linear process.

In sum, while recognizing the value of models of RP in developing understandings of how the process might appear, we argue here that we need data-led accounts in order to actually experience RP in action and to facilitate the embedding of reflection in our professional practice.

Lack of Data-led Accounts

Mann and Walsh (2013) have provided an argument that RP in the fields of applied linguistics, TESOL and education (and undoubtedly wider afield) has achieved a status of orthodoxy without a corresponding data-led description of its value, processes and impact. There are too many accounts of reflection that contain models, checklists or series of questions to be used as prompts. Very few have examples of reflection and where data is included it is usually self-reported or short extracts from reflective journals. We are particularly worried about the lack of data about spoken reflective processes. For example, Farrell (2007), in an otherwise excellent introduction to reflective language teaching, has a chapter on collaborative teacher development in groups. However, there are no data extracts (although there is a summarized scenario late in the chapter).

We also think that where data is central to views of RP, there is a preoccupation with the identification of levels (and this is something that we consider further in Chapter 3). El-Dib, for example, develops both action research and reflective thinking (including 'levels of reflective thinking' (2007: 25)) during an Egyptian PRESET undergraduate programme. However, most of the article is concerned with establishing that his TLs were only capable of 'low-level reflection' because they have a lack of awareness of the complexity of the classroom. He makes useful arguments that reflective thinking cannot 'take care of itself' (ibid.: 33) and needs to be better supported. We would agree that 'scaffolding and mentoring are required in order to develop prospective teachers' reflective abilities' (ibid.: 33). However, we need more concrete and data-led accounts of how this might be managed.

Data-led accounts are essential since they provide the kind of evidence which promotes understandings of reflection. Data-led accounts help us to acquire the close-up understandings of our professional practice and, further, help to establish the knowledge base on which RP rests. By collecting data, we speak to both practitioner and research communities.

Focus on the Individual

RP is often presented as an individual process which does not foreground collaboration or participation in a community of practice. This is partly an issue relating to models where accounts of reflection (e.g. Brockbank and McGill, 1998) see reflection as an individual matter (the individual thinks about their intentions before teaching, conducts the class and then reflects on action). While independent and individual reflection does have its place, an over-emphasis on 'lone reflection' devalues the importance of reflection as a series of collaborative processes. Johns' model (2000) puts more emphasis on the act of sharing with a colleague or mentor, which enables the experience to be understood at a faster rate than reflection alone. We also find Zepke's (2003: 17) definition helpful in this regard. He says that reflection 'is a process to help us learn from our own or others' experiences and to turn that learning into action'. This process is dialogic and, especially in Chapter 8, we focus on the dialogic processes involved in more collaborative reflection. Hatton and Smith (1995) see dialogic reflection as involving discourse with self. We would agree with this, but the notion of dialogic reflection should also include discourse with others (in various collaborative and workplace processes) as well as between different forms of knowledge, particularly experiential and received knowledge at the level of the self (Wallace, 1991).

Dominance of Written Forms of Reflection

The dominance in the RP literature of written forms of reflection at the expense of possible spoken forms is a key issue in this book. While we recognize that there are varied approaches to written reflection, such as narratives, introspective journals and portfolios, there are many issues with the forms of writing which are typically required on pre- and in-service teacher education programmes. A common problem with written forms of RP is that the focus of attention becomes the actual writing itself, or rather the pro-forma, checklist or whatever is used as a stimulus to reflection. There are (at least) two outcomes of this problem. The first, as stated above, is that practitioners become concerned with completing the reflective task (whether this has any connection with their 'real' experience or not). At its worst this can result in inauthentic reflection (Roberts, 1998) and even 'faking it' (Hobbs, 2007), where the twin pressures of external course demands and a natural tendency to conceal weaknesses and concentrate on strengths and success stories combine to limit real reflection. Hobbs (2007: 410) talks about leading and repetitive writing prompts being used which can lead to the temptation to write 'strategic journal entries' in order to achieve a better response (and a better mark) from the tutors. Hobbs argues that written reflection is especially difficult for novice teachers (her context is an initial teacher certificate course), while McCabe et al. (2011) reported similar problems among trainees in Northern Ireland and Canada. The use of pro-formas on such initial teacher education courses may be counter-productive. If, after each teaching session, trainees are asked to describe what went well, what went badly and what to work on the next time they teach, over time, and with repeated enactments of this task, they can become disenchanted with the process and simply write the first things that come into their heads so that they can get the task finished. The consequence is that reflections operate, at best, at surface level and there is no real evidence of engagement or criticality.

The second problem with written forms of reflection is that there is no grading of the reflective task to the corresponding stage of development. Teachers in training, for example, would benefit greatly from completing a range of reflective tasks over time rather than completing the same task (a checklist or pro-forma) repeatedly. By using a variety of tasks, practitioners are encouraged to think more deeply and there is scope for progression in the tasks themselves.

With regard to reflective writing we need to think more about the distinction between 'reflection through writing' and 'writing as a record of reflection'. It is held that reflection can be 'slippery' (Moon, 2004: 4) and so it needs to be recorded while it is fresh in the mind. However, writing is not just a record of reflection. It is reflection in itself. The process of reflective articulation does not report pre-existing thought. It distils, clarifies or even reframes an experience, situation or event and increases awareness. It is ongoing and reflexive, a constant process of trying to 'get it right' in which 'saying it right' or 'thinking it right' are intermediary processes. There is also huge variety in the forms that written reflection can take and we will explore this further in Chapter 6.

Difficulty of Assessment

RP has been dogged by inconsistencies and worries about whether assessment of reflection is desirable (Hobbs, 2007; Akbari, 2007). Hargreaves captures this dilemma when she says that it is 'extremely difficult to make the development of reflective skills a core element of the curriculum design' without it being assessed. Despite her 'reservations regarding the ethics of assessing student reflections', she maintains that it is impossible 'to envision a curriculum where reflection was central to the learning strategy but absent in the design of assessment' (2009: 91). So RP remains stuck on the horns of this dilemma. Teacher learners do not know if they are to be rewarded for being confessional (revealing weaknesses) or constructing a version of themselves as resourceful (foregrounding pragmatism and innovation).

Whichever position is adopted, there are clearly tensions in assessing a process which is intended to be formative and enhance professional development. Yet, for many practitioners, their only experience of RP is as one assessed component of a teacher education programme. Our concern here is that not only are there tensions in assessing reflection, but the process of assessment may actually put people off doing RP later in their careers (McCabe et al., 2011). By only focusing on assessed RP, there is a danger that it will not become embedded in a teacher's future professional practice.

Lack of Appropriate Reflective Tools

There remain issues with the nature and timing of reflective tools used. First of all, there is the 'one-size fits all' problem where a particular tool (e.g. stimulated recall) is not sufficiently orientated to particular contextual needs. Many of the tools used in RP have their origins in applied linguistics research and may not always be appropriate for practitioners, especially when insufficient attention is paid to local context. There is also some disagreement on the nature of the term 'tool'. Beauchamp (2015: 137) referring to Danielowich (2007) says the following:

> ... reflection has too often been presented as a tool in teacher education, rather than as a complex concept that must be deeply understood. If this is the case, we may need to shift our focus from it as a required tool in programs of teacher education to the actual concept itself, and explore more fully its meaning and potential for enhancing professional practice in a myriad of contexts.

In this book, we take the position that RP is not reducible to particular tools but that the systematic use of tools and triggers can help. However, we do need more understanding of how such tools help in the process of theorizing practice. We also recognize that there can be a 'too much too soon' problem which is especially problematic in short pre-service courses (see Hobbs, 2007). Reflective tasks need to be introduced with care. If they are too complicated, they stifle budding reflection. If they become an 'increasing chore' and there is a lack of variety, the reflective task becomes an institutionalized requirement that then encourages superficial engagement or inauthentic reflection. In Chapter 2, we argue for a graded approach to reflection, where expectations regarding the amount and detail of the reflection vary according to the stage of the course, career, experience, etc. Novice teachers will reflect differently from more experienced colleagues; the tools used should acknowledge this and be designed with both context and expertise in mind. A related problem is lack of progression: if there is not a systematic progression in reflective tasks, practitioners may become disenchanted and engage with the reflective process at little more than a surface level. In addition to grading tasks according to level of experience and expertise, we suggest that an appropriate degree of challenge is also needed in order to maintain interest and stimulate thought.

We observe that many prompts for reflection are problem-based, which may be both limiting and oriented towards negativity; practitioners are actually directed towards looking for things they do 'wrong' or 'badly'. A more fruitful direction would be to encourage practitioners to focus more on puzzles or points of interest in their reflections (Allwright, 2003). Munby and Russell (1990), for example, suggest puzzles of practice and this is more in tune with Schön's view that attention should be brought to bear on 'some puzzling or troubling or interesting phenomenon' (1983: 50). Allwright also argues that the notion of puzzle avoids the negative connotations of problem (the admission of incompetence), and involves areas of professional life we might just 'want to try to understand better' (2003: 117).

There is then plenty of scope for the development of tools and procedures which are fit for purpose, which allow for 'timely reflection' according to a person's stage of development and which allow reflection to become embedded in our professional practice. By addressing these concerns, there is also the potential at least to move away from reflection as assessment.

Not Practising What You Preach

At its most worrying, reflective practice becomes so much part of the landscape that we forget to ask questions about why we are promoting it. We get what Bengtsson (2003: 295) sees as a 'paradoxical situation', that reflection is 'used in an unreflective manner'. This unreflecting status quo is partly an outcome of teacher educators not reflecting themselves with a corresponding lack of congruence between stated beliefs and beliefs-in-action. It is problematic that 'while teacher educators promote reflection among teachers' they 'seem to have less tendency to consider reflection as a method for their own practice' (Moon, 1999: 57).

Brockbank and McGill argue that academics can only facilitate reflective practice if they themselves use reflection in their own professional development, or as Akbari argues 'reflection itself also requires reflection' (2007: 205). Edge (2011: 20) talks of 'consistency' (the demand of teachers that they should be reflective must also apply to the teacher educator). Edge also quotes Argyris and Schön (1974: 196) that we need teacher educators who '... are strong enough to invite confrontation of their teaching and to make themselves vulnerable to inquiry into the incongruities in their teaching'. He then quotes Gore and Zeichner (1991: 271) in making the argument that we cannot simply claim lack of time because 'if we argue that we do not have time', how can we blame teachers for not adopting reflective practices 'as a regular part of their teaching?'

Our position is that, in order to promote reflective practice, teacher educators, university tutors and lecturers, and those running pre- and in-service teacher education programmes (such as CELTA and DELTA) ought also to engage with reflective processes. Perhaps more importantly, they should demonstrate their engagement with reflection through discussion and dialogue with less experienced colleagues as a means of opening and making visible the process of reflection and encouraging others to do the same. 'Talking the talk' of reflection is perhaps one of the easiest and quickest ways of making it accessible to others and of creating not only a genuine community of practice, but also a community of reflective practitioners.

1.5 Summary

In this chapter we have reviewed important influences in the history of the development of the notion of RP. It has achieved a ubiquitous status and has been widely drawn on by teacher educators as a mediational tool for teachers' professional learning (Zeichner and Liston, 1996; Golombek and Johnson, 2004; Burton, 2009). This chapter has also made evident reasons why RP is problematic in nature. We have provided a critical review of reflective practice (RP), concentrating on various problems with its representation. In 1.4 we have made explicit these various challenges and issues. Our response to these challenges forms the basis of Chapter 2 where we propose a more evidence-based and data-led approach. While we remain committed to RP and regard it as the fundamental bedrock of professional development and growth, we are also concerned that its current status and level of acceptance are not always matched by a corresponding degree of research, evidence and knowledge about reflective processes. It is this central concern which we propose to address in the subsequent chapters.

In Mann and Walsh (2013) we argued that working towards a better under-standing of reflective practice is a 'real-world' challenge for applied linguistics (AL). AL has already played an important role in revealing that the majority of professional practices are accomplished through various forms of workplace interaction (see, for example, Edwards and Westgate, 1992; Drew and Heritage, 1992) and that institutional practice is inextricably linked to language and communication. The role of RP too, as a process of professional development, is to understand and improve practice (Schön, 1991). Consequently, we believe that AL can play a stronger role not only in promoting understandings of 'real-world' workplace practice but also in supporting the goal of RP in achieving this understanding. By focusing on language as social action and considering the ways in which RP 'gets done' through human interaction, we are adopting a 'pragmatically motivated' (Bygate, 2005: 571) perspective on the situated real-world circumstances of reflective practice. We argue that there are two ele-ments of the potential role of AL in understanding RP. These can be expressed in the distinction between 'the language for reflection' and 'the language of reflection':

- (for reflection) the aim should be to produce tools and frameworks for fine-grained understanding of professional activities.
- (of reflection) the aim should be to produce systematic accounts of the language used in reflection (an analytic challenge for AL).

Chapters 3 to 9 focus on how procedures *for* reflection might encourage atten-tion to real-world linguistic and interactional features of professional practice. These chapters also exemplify a range of tools that foster reflection and show examples *of* reflection, as well as practitioners' perspectives on these examples.

References

Ahmed, M.K. (1994). Speaking as cognitive regulation: a Vygotskian perspective on dialogic communication. In J.P. Lantolf (ed.), *Vygotskian approaches to second language research.* Norwood, New Jersey: Ablex.

Akbari, R. (2007). Reflections on reflection: a critical appraisal of reflective practices in L2 teacher education. *System: An International Journal of Educational Technology and Applied Linguistics,* 35(2), 192–220.

Alger, C. (2006). 'What went well, what didn't go so well': growth of reflection in pre-service teachers. *Reflective Practice,* 7(3), 287–301.

Allwright, R. (2003). Exploratory practice: rethinking practitioner research in language teaching. *Language Teaching Research,* 7, 113–114.

Argyris, C. and Schon, D. (1974). *Theory into practice: increasing professional effectiveness.* San Francisco, CA: Jossey Bass.

Bailin, S., Case, R., Coombs, J. and Daniels, L. (2007). Conceptualizing critical thinking. *Journal of Curriculum Studies,* 31, 285–302.

Bartlett, L. (1990). Teacher development through reflective teaching. In J.C. Richards and D. Nunan (eds), *Second language teacher education.* Cambridge: Cambridge University Press.

Beauchamp, C. (2015). Reflection in teacher education: issues emerging from a review of current literature. *Reflective Practice,* 16(1), 123–141.

Bengtsson, J. (2003). Possibilities and limits of self-reflection in the teaching profession. *Studies in Philosophy and Education,* 22, 295–316.

Boud, D. and Walker, D. (1998). Promoting reflection in professional courses: the challenge of context. *Studies in Higher Education,* 23(2), 191–206.

Boud, D., Keogh, R. and Walker, D. (eds). (1985). *Reflection: turning experience into action.* London: Kogan-Page.

Bradbury H., Frost, N., Kilminster, S. and Zukas, M. (eds). (2010). *Beyond reflective practice; new approaches to professional lifelong learning.* Abingdon: Routledge.

Brockbank, A. and McGill, I. (1998). *Facilitating reflective learning in higher education.* Buckingham: Open University Press.

Brockbank, A. and McGill, I. (2007). *Facilitating reflective learning in higher education.* Buckingham: Society for Research into Higher Education.

Brookfield, S.D. (1997). Assessing critical thinking. *New Directions for Adult and Continuing Education,* 75, 7–29.

Bruner, J. (1990). Vygotsky: a historical and conceptual perspective. In L. C. Moll (ed.), *Vygotsky and education: instructional implications and applications of sociohistorical psychology.* Cambridge: Cambridge University Press.

Burns, A. (2005). Action research: an evolving paradigm? *Language Teaching,* 38(2), 57–74.

Burton, J. (2009). The scope of second language teacher education. In A. Burns and J. Richards (eds), *The Cambridge guide to second language teacher education* (pp. 298–308). New York: Cambridge University Press.

Bygate, M. (2005). Applied linguistics: A pragmatic discipline, a generic discipline? *Applied Linguistics,* 26(4), 568–581.

Calderhead, J. (1989). Reflective teaching and teacher education. *Teaching and Teacher Education,* 5(1), 43–51.

Cornford, I. (2002). Reflective teaching: Empirical research findings and some implications for teacher education. *Journal of Vocational Education and Training,* 54, 219–235.

Danielowich, R. (2007). Negotiating the conflicts: re-examining the structure and function of reflection in science teacher learning. *Science Education,* 91(4), 629–663.

Day, C. (1993). Reflection: a necessary but not sufficient condition for professional development. *British Educational Research Journal,* 19(1), 83–93.

Dewey, J. (1933). *How we think. A restatement of the relation of reflective thinking to the educative process* (Revised edn). Boston: D. C. Heath.

Doyle, W. (1986). Classroom organisation and management. In M.C. Wittrock (ed.), *Handbook of research on teaching* (3rd edn). New York: Macmillan.

Drew, P. and Heritage, J. (eds). (1992). *Talk at work: interaction in institutional settings.* Cambridge: Cambridge University Press.

Dzay Chulim, F.D. (2015). Pre-service teachers reflecting on their teaching practice: an action research study in a Mexican context (Unpublished doctoral dissertation). University of Warwick. Downloaded 10.10.15 at http://wrap.warwick.ac.uk/77716/

Edge, J. (2011). *The reflexive teacher educator in TESOL: roots and wings*. New York: Routledge.

Edwards, A. and Westgate, D. (1992). *Investigating classroom talk*. London: Falmer.

El-Dib, M.A.B. (2007). Levels of reflection in action research: An overview and an assessment tool. *Teaching and Teacher Education*, 23(1), 24–35.

Farrell, T.S.C. (2004). *Reflective practice in action*. Thousand Oaks, CA: Corwin Press.

Farrell, T.S.C. (2007). *Reflective language teaching: from research to practice*. London: Continuum.

Farrell, T.S.C. (2008). *Novice language teachers: insights and perspectives for the first year*. London: Equinox Publishing.

Farrell, T.S.C. (2016). The practices of encouraging TESOL teachers to engage in reflective practice: an appraisal of recent research contributions. *Language Teaching Research*, 20(2), 223–247.

Furlong, J. and Maynard, T. (1995). *Mentoring student teachers: the growth of professional knowledge*. London: Routledge.

Furlong, J., Barton, L., Miles, S., Whiting, C. and Whitty, G. (2000). *Teacher education in transition: re-forming professionalism*. Buckingham: Open University Press.

Gibbs, G. (1988). *Learning by doing: a guide to teaching and learning methods*. Birmingham: SCED.

Golombek, P.R. and Johnson, K.A. (2004). Narrative inquiry as a mediational space: examining emotional and cognitive dissonance in second-language teachers' development. *Teachers and Teaching: Theory and Practice*, 10(3), 307–327.

Gore, J. and Zeichner, K.M. (1991). Action research and reflective teaching. *Teaching and Teacher Education*, 7(2), 119–136.

Grayling, A. (2003). *Meditations for the humanist: ethics for a secular age*. Oxford: Oxford University Press.

Habermas, J. (1972). *Knowledge and human interests*. London: Heinemann.

Hargreaves, J. (2009). Voices from the past: professional discourse and reflective practice. In H. Bradbury, N. Frost, S. Kilminster and M. Zukas (eds), *Beyond reflective practice: new approaches to professional lifelong learning*. London: Routledge.

Harkin, J. (2005). Fragments stored against my ruin: the place of educational theory in the professional development of teachers in further education. *Journal of Vocational Education and Training*, 57(2), 165–179.

Harris, A.R. (2013). Professionals developing professionalism: the interactional organisation of reflective practice (Unpublished PhD thesis). University of Newcastle. Downloaded 10.10.15 at https://theses.ncl.ac.uk/dspace/bitstream/10443/2354/1/Harris,%20A.%2013.pdf

Hatton, N. and Smith, D. (1995). Reflection in teacher education: Towards definition and implementation. *Teacher and Teacher Education*, 11(1), 33–49.

Hickman, M.E. (1990). The implications of discourse skills in Vygotsky's developmental theory. In L.C. Moll (ed.), *Vygotsky and education: instructional implications and applications of sociohistorical psychology*. Cambridge: Cambridge University Press.

Hobbs, V. (2007). Faking it or hating it: can reflective practice be forced? *Reflective Practice*, 8(3), 405–417.

Hobson, A.J. and Malderez, A. (2013). Judgementoring and other threats to realizing the potential of school-based mentoring in teacher education. *International Journal of Mentoring and Coaching in Education*, 2(2), 89–108.

Howe, C. and Mercer, N. (2012). Explaining the dialogic processes of teaching and learning: the value and potential of sociocultural theory. *Learning, Culture and Social Interaction*, 1, 12–21.

Jay, J.K. and Johnson, K.L. (2002). Capturing complexity: a typology of reflective practice for teacher education. *Teaching and Teacher Education*, 18(1), 78–85.

Johns, C. (2000). *Becoming a reflective practitioner: a reflective and holistic approach to clinical nursing, practice development and clinical supervision*. Oxford: Blackwell Science.

Killion, J.P. and Todnem, G.R. (1991). A process for personal theory building. *Educational Leadership*, 48(6), 14–16.

Kolb, D.A. (1984). *Experiential learning: experience as the source of learning and development*. New Jersey: Prentice-Hall.

Korthagen, F.A. (1985). Reflective teaching and preservice teacher education in the Netherlands. *Journal of Teacher Education*, 36(5), 11–15.

Korthagen, F.A.J. and Wubbels, T. (1995). Characteristics of reflective practitioners: towards an operationalization of the concept of reflection. *Teachers and Teaching*, 1, 51–72.

Lantolf, J.P. (2000). *Sociocultural theory and second language learning*. Oxford: Oxford University Press.

Lantolf, J.P. (2005). Sociocultural and second language learning research: an exegesis. In E. Hinkel (ed.), *Handbook of research in second language teaching and learning* (Vol. 2, pp. 335–354). New York: Routledge.

Lantolf, J.P. and Poehner, M.E. (2008). Introduction to sociocultural theory and the teaching of second languages. In J. P. Lantolf and M. E. Poehner (eds), *Sociocultural theory and the teaching of second languages* (pp. 1–30). London: Equinox.

Lantolf, J.P. and Thorne, S. (2006). *Sociocultural theory and the genesis of second language development.* Oxford: Oxford University Press.

Larrivee, B. (2004). Assessing teachers' level of reflective practice as a tool for change. Paper presented at the Third International Conference on Reflective Practice, Gloucester, UK.

Mann S. (2005). The language teacher's development. *Language Teaching*, 38, 103–18.

Mann, S. and Walsh, S. (2013). RP or 'RIP': a critical perspective on reflective practice. *Applied Linguistics Review*, 4(2), 291–315.

McCabe, M., Walsh, S., Wideman, R. and Winter, E. (2011). The R word in teacher education: understanding the teaching and learning of critical reflective practice. *International Electronic Journal for Leadership in Learning.*

Mezirow, J. (1991). *Transformative dimensions of adult learning.* San Francisco: Jossey-Bass Inc.

Moon, J.A. (1999). *Reflection in learning and professional development: theory and practice.* London: Kogan Page.

Moon, J.A. (2004). *A handbook of reflective and experiential learning.* London: Routledge.

Munby, H. and Russell, T. (1990). Metaphor in the study of teachers' professional knowledge. *Theory into Practice*, 29(2), 116–121.

Osterman, K.P. and Kottkamp, R.B. (1993/2004). *Reflective practice for educators: improving schooling through professional development.* Thousand Oaks, CA: Corwin Press.

Pollard, A. (2005, 2nd edn). *Reflective teaching.* London: Continuum.

Richards, J.C. and Nunan, D. (1990). *Second language teacher education.* Cambridge: Cambridge University Press.

Roberts, J. (1998). *Language teacher education.* London: Arnold.

Röhler, L.R. and Cantlon, D.J. (1996). Scaffolding: a powerful tool in social constructivist class-rooms. Available at <http://edeb3.educ.msu.edu./Literacy/papers/paperlr2.html> (last accessed 24 June 2005).

Rolfe, G., Freshwater, D. and Jasper, M. (2001). *Helping professions: a user's guide.* London: Palgrave Macmillan.

Schön, D.A. (1983). *The reflective practitioner.* London: Temple Smith.

Schön, D.A. (1987). *Educating the reflective practitioner: toward a design for teaching and learning in the professionals.* San Francisco: Jossey-Bass.

Schön, D.A. (1991). *The reflective practitioner: how professionals think in action.* Aldershot: Arena.

Semetsky, E. (2008). On the creative logic of education, or: re-reading Dewey through the lens of complexity science. *Educational Philosophy and Theory*, 40(1), 83–95.

Smyth, J. (1989). Developing and sustaining critical reflection in teacher education. *Journal of Teacher Education*, 40(2), 2–8.

Stanley, C. (1998). A framework for teacher reflectivity. *TESOL Quarterly*, 32(3), 584–591.

Stenhouse, L. (1975). An introduction to curriculum research: the contribution of classroom teachers. In J. Edge and K. Richards (eds), *Teachers develop, teachers research: papers on classroom research and teacher development* (pp. 26–38). Oxford: Heinemann International.

Tatto, M. (1998). The influence of teacher education on teachers' beliefs about purposes of education, roles, and practice. *Journal of Teacher Education*, 49, 66–77.

Téllez, K. (2007). Have conceptual reforms in pre-service teacher education improved the education of multicultural, multilingual children and youth? *Teachers and Teaching: Theory and Practice*, 13, 543–564.

van Manen, M. (1977). Linking ways of knowing with ways of being practical. *Curriculum Inquiry*, 6(3), 205–228.

Vygotsky, L.S. (1978). *Mind in society: the development of higher psychological processes*, Cambridge, MA: Harvard University Press.

Wallace, M.J. (1991). *Training foreign language teachers: a reflective approach.* Cambridge: CUP.

Wallace, M.J. (1998). *Action research for language teachers.* Cambridge: Cambridge University Press.

Walsh, S. and Mann, S. (2015). Doing reflective practice: a data-led way forward. *ELT Journal*, 69(4), 351–362.

Wells, G. (1999). *Dialogic inquiry: towards a sociocultural practice and theory of education*. London: Routledge.

Wideen, M. F., Mayer-Smith, J. and Moon, B. (1998). A critical analysis of the research on learning-to-teach. *Review of Education Research*, 68(2), 130–178.

Wood, T. (1995). From alternative epistemologies to practice in education: rethinking what it means to teach and learn. In L. Steffe and J. Gale (eds), *Constructivism in education* (pp. 331–340). Hillsdale, NJ: Lawrence Erlbaum Associates.

Zeichner, K.M. and Liston, D.P. (1996). *Reflective teaching: an introduction*. Mahwah, NJ: Lawrence Erlbaum Associates.

Zepke, N. (2003). Reflecting-learning-teaching. In N. Zepke, D. Nugent and L. Leach (eds), *Reflection to transformation: a self-help book for teachers* (pp. 17–33). Palmerston North, New Zealand: Dunmore Press Ltd.

Zwozdiak-Myers, P. (2009). An analysis of the concept reflective practice and an investigation into the development of student teachers' reflective practice within the context of action research (Unpublished PhD thesis). Brunel University.

Zwozdiak-Myers, P. (2012). *The teacher's reflective practice handbook. Becoming an extended professional through capturing evidence-informed practice*. London and New York: Routledge.

2
Reflective Practice Revisited

2.1 Introduction

We start this chapter with examples of what we mean by reflective practice (RP) and highlight its centrality for teacher development and professional practice. To better understand RP, we argue that we need data and evidence to show how it is perceived and accomplished in context. Using this data-led approach, we demonstrate how RP can be revisited and revitalized by focusing on a number of key elements. These include the importance of a reflexive relationship with context, a more systematic and appropriate approach, the use of reflective tools and a recognition that RP is most effective when it is dialogic. We also recognize that RP needs to take account of developments in other related fields such as teacher cognition, teacher learning, educational technology and teacher identity. (See Li Li's vignette in Appendix 8 for a perspective on reflection and teacher cognition.)

Essentially, Chapter 2 provides an overview of the book; each of the sections which follow will be dealt with in much greater depth in subsequent chapters. In section 2.2, we present our perspective on the relationship between RP and teacher development. Section 2.3 explains why we give so much attention to context, while 2.4 describes and exemplifies what we mean by data and evidence, key elements of our take on RP. In 2.5, we offer examples of how RP might be approached in a more structured and systematic way. A key theme in this book is the importance of dialogue and collaboration in reflection, presented in 2.6. Finally, in 2.7, we outline the overall structure of the remainder of the book.

2.2 Reflective Practice and Teacher Development

In Chapter 1, we highlighted some of the main concerns that we have about current approaches to reflective practice. Among these concerns, we commented on the fact that for many professionals, RP is regarded as an institutional requirement, either as a central element of a teacher education programme or as a means of evaluating professional performance. Put simply, the issue is that RP is predominantly viewed in these cases as an evaluative tool which is used for assessing competence.

Our aim in this chapter is to consider how RP might be embedded in a teacher's professional life. In other words, how might RP be viewed less as a tool for assessing or evaluating performance and more as a means for improving teaching and aiding professional development? The focus of attention is clearly on enabling teachers to develop themselves (Edge, 2011), based on a recognition that there is far more to teacher preparation than skills training; teachers need to be equipped with the tools that will enable them to both find out about their own classrooms and make adjustments (Bartlett, 1990).

While we acknowledge that RP is positive, necessary and key to teacher development, we are proposing that it needs to be refocused if it is to survive (Mann and Walsh, 2013). We will argue in the sections which follow that for teachers to become researchers of their own practice they need detailed understandings of their local context, appropriate tools, data, and dialogue with other or more experienced professionals. If RP is to assist teacher development, it needs to be taught on pre-service teacher education programmes, a position adopted elsewhere (see, for example, McCabe et al., 2011; Walsh, 2011). Other pre-requisites include the desirability for more appropriate tools to facilitate reflection; the importance of recognizing that RP should be evidence-based, using data taken from classrooms; the need for RP to be removed from the constraints of institutional requirements so that it might become a career-long practice; and recognition of the value of spoken, dialogic practices in addition to the more commonly found written forms of reflection.

In Chapter 1, we pointed out that in most contexts where RP is practised, teachers adopt a retrospective stance and reflect on past actions in an endeavour to increase their understanding of the teaching/learning process (Wallace, 1998). By developing understandings of both received and experiential knowledge, new competencies are acquired by participants who play an active role in their own development. Again, in Chapter 1, we highlighted the importance of experiential knowledge which is gained through reflecting on and learning from 'ordinary' classroom practices. Central to this process are professional dialogue and data, both of which are discussed at length below.

One possibility within the frame of reflective practice is for teachers to identify and address issues which are specific to their own context. This is also a central concern of action research, which rests on the premise that teachers can and should investigate their own classrooms. The starting point for action research is the identification of a puzzle or issue; the process continues with data collection, data analysis and finally possible outcomes. The value and relevance of this approach are self-evident: helping teachers to focus on puzzles in their own classrooms and to identify solutions is desirable from the position of both professional development and student learning. As Johnson puts it (1995: 29) 'the more research-driven knowledge teachers have, the better their teaching performances will be'.

Because teacher-researchers are both the producers and consumers of their research (Kumaravadivelu, 1999), since they both own the data and are responsible for effecting changes to classroom practices, the process is more private and, arguably, less intimidating. The concern is to enhance understanding of local context rather than generalize to a broader one, though this may also occur. Developing understandings of local context and adopting a more context-led approach (Bax, 2003) to promoting effective learning are central to our reconfigured notion of RP. Following Wallace (1998), developing understandings of local context lies at the heart of this book and is, we suggest, central to both professional development and enhanced learning.

In summary, we make the following observations about the relationship between RP and teacher development:

- The relationship is a reflexive one; reflections inform teacher development that in turn promotes further reflection. Reflection and development are inextricably entwined in a professional dialectic.
- For professional development to work in a more meaningful way, and for it to operate at a level which is not merely 'surface', we need evidence in the form of data. Data are anything which inform practice and may include, for example, audio and video recordings of a segment of teaching, feedback from a peer, a conversation with a group of students, a piece of material or a journal extract. Essentially, data provide a focus for reflection.
- Similarly, data-led discussions of practice are a means of promoting deep (as opposed to surface) reflection. By working collaboratively and by using data, we argue that reflection can be more meaningful, more fruitful and have longer-lasting consequences. Dialogue lies at the heart of this process.
- Reflection leads to a better understanding of local context, something that we believe to be critical if learners are to be the main beneficiaries of a teacher's reflective practices. Understandings of local context at a micro level are central to this enterprise.

In the sections which follow, we propose a revitalized perspective on RP, presented through a number of interrelated, yet independent, visions. In the discussion which follows, we address the concerns and challenges presented in Chapter 1 and suggest how RP might be repositioned.

2.3 A Reflexive Relationship with Context

For many practitioners, 'context' simply refers to the precise place or educational setting in which teaching and learning occur. At its most basic, any educational context could include a teacher, learners and materials. Typical definitions will include words like classroom, teacher and learner roles, curriculum, assessment, perceptions and expectations. While we acknowledge that these factors all affect what goes on in any educational setting and are all aspects of context, our concern here is a much more detailed understanding of context as a flexible, dynamic construct which is created by participants and which is constantly shifting (Seedhouse, 2004; Walsh, 2006). Under this *variable* perspective, a number of important features emerge and have consequence for the kinds of understanding which might be developed through reflective practice. Essentially, what we are saying is that if one of the aims of reflection is to develop closer understandings of context, we need to be clear about what we mean by context. This point is developed below. First, let us consider why a more static view of context has prevailed.

According to Drew and Heritage (1992), much of the research on second language classrooms has adopted an approach whereby context is viewed as something static, fixed and concrete. The majority of studies have had one of two central goals, attempting to account for either the nature of verbal exchanges or the relationship between SLA and interaction (Wu, 1998). Whatever their focus, most studies have referred to *the* L2 classroom context (singular), implying that there exists such an entity and that it has fixed and describable features. There are a number of possible explanations for this uni-directional and static view.

Firstly, there has been an overriding concern to compare L2 classroom interaction with 'real' communication, whereby 'authentic' features of 'genuine' communication occurring in the 'real' world are somehow imported into the L2 classroom setting (Nunan, 1987; Cullen, 1998; Gilmore, 2007). By following this line of enquiry, many researchers have failed to acknowledge that the classroom is as much a 'real' context as any other situation in which people come together and interact. As van Lier says (1988: 267):

> The classroom is in principle and in potential just as communicative or uncommunicative as any other speech setting, no more, no less. Nor should the 'real world' stop at the classroom door; the classroom is part of the real world, just as much as the airport, the interviewing room, the chemical laboratory, the beach and so on.

Blanket interpretations of the L2 classroom as either 'communicative' or 'uncommunicative' (Nunan, 1987; Kumaravadivelu, 1993), adopting an invariant view of context, have failed to take account of the relationship between language use and pedagogic purpose (van Lier, 1988; Seedhouse, 2004; Walsh, 2006). When language use and pedagogic purpose are considered together, different contexts emerge, making it possible to analyze the ensuing discourse more fairly and more objectively. According to this variable view of contexts (plural), learner and teacher patterns of verbal behaviour can be seen as more or less *appropriate*, depending on a particular pedagogic aim or in response to an emerging agenda. So, for example, teachers' language should not be regarded as 'uncommunicative' if their pedagogic goal is to provide a detailed grammar explanation (see Seedhouse, 2004).

Secondly, in a quest to pursue 'rigorous' modes of scientific enquiry usually reserved for 'hard' disciplines such as physics and chemistry, there has been a tendency to use reductionist research tools which have ignored the important (often small) details of interaction in the L2 classroom; a position summarized by van Lier (1988: iv):

> Research into second language classrooms is to date ... still very much concerned with the aim of finding cause-effect relationships between certain actions and their outcomes. [...] At the risk of over-simplification, research can be divided into a type which wants to obtain proof and a type which wants to understand. So far, research into foreign language classrooms leans overwhelmingly towards the former type of research.

The kind of research we are describing here is small-scale, localized, context-specific and private, conducted by teachers for their own ends. Typically, this process is situated and concerned with the development of an appropriate methodology (Holliday, 1994).

The point we are making here, then, is that up-close, detailed and 'ecological' (van Lier, 2000) understandings of local context are needed if professional development is to occur. A reflexive relationship with context is one in which teachers develop fine-grained understandings of their local situation and, in response to this knowledge, make changes to their professional practice. Professional practices both shape and are shaped by up-close and detailed understandings of local context (Heritage, 2007).

Understandings of local context, where teachers act as researchers of their practice (see Chapter 9), will be best achieved when the following conditions are met:

- Condition 1: the research takes place in the classroom.
- Condition 2: teacher-researchers reflect and act on what they observe.
- Condition 3: understandings emerge through dialogue.

Research Takes Place in the Classroom

There have been a number of debates about what constitutes legitimate research and these can produce very different views (e.g. Jarvis, 2001, and Borg's 2002 response). According to Nunan, much of the research which goes on in second language teaching is deemed irrelevant, resulting in a 'wedge between researcher and practitioner' (1996: 42). There are a number of barriers to the 'teacher as researcher', not least enduring post-positivist views that research is best conducted under experimental conditions in classrooms created for research purposes. The division between research and practice articulated by Clarke (1994) remains a divisive one and Borg (2003) usefully highlights various teachers' difficulties with engaging with TESOL research. However, it is also true that such practitioner inquiry and action research detailed in Burns (2005) has gone some way to bridging the gap. The Teachers Develop Teachers Research (TDTR) series of conferences is also a good example of a substantial platform for teacher research projects (see De Decker and Vanderheiden, 1999; Edge and Richards, 1993; Field et al., 1997; Head, 1998). We return to this literature in Chapter 9.

In the same way that much of the body of research established under TDTR has its origins in 'ordinary' classrooms, we are proposing here a need for small 'r' research, conducted by teachers for their own ends; understanding and professional development can only be enhanced when the process of inquiry is carried out *in situ*, in the teacher's natural environment. Van Lier terms this 'ecological research' (2000: 11):

> Ecological research pays a great deal of attention to the smallest detail of the interaction, since within these details maybe contained the seeds of learning. The reflective teacher can learn to 'read' the environment to notice such details. An organism 'resonates' with its environment, picking up affordances in its activities. This is a different level of understanding than the one based in explicit knowledge or studied facts. It is a deeper sense of reflection in action.

The main attraction of this view of 'reflection-in-action' is that teachers work very closely with the data they collect in their own context, their own 'environment', to use van Lier's word. The understanding they gain from working with the detail of their data is very much their own – personal, private and internal – enabling teachers to read the interactional processes and interactive signals as they arise. Sharing this research with a wider community is voluntary, and the teacher does not necessarily have to worry about generalizability; research is a process of inquiry, conducted by the teacher for the teacher. Other researchers have called for class-based research which is conducted in the teacher's own classroom, preferably by the teacher (see, for example, Bailey and Nunan, 1996; Wallace, 1998). One of the main advantages of action research is that there is a unification of theory and practice since the smallest details can be studied, and changes implemented and then evaluated (van Lier, 2000). The main reason for the potential for such micro-level analysis is the fact that the research is located in a context which is both clearly defined and familiar to the teacher-researcher.

Teacher-Researchers Reflect and Act on What They Observe

The second condition is very much in tune with the broad philosophy of action research: research plus action, not just research for research's sake (Cohen et al.,

2007); when participants 'do something' based on their self-observation, the ultimate benefactors will be their students. In the words of Kemmis and McTaggart (2000: 21–2):

> Action research involves problem-posing, not just problem-solving. It does not start from a view of 'problems' as pathologies. It is motivated by a quest to improve and understand the world by changing it and learning how to improve it from the effects of the changes made.

The suggestion here is that the very act of 'posing problems' and coming to understand them is, in itself, developmental. We would go a little further, replacing 'problems' (which have negative connotations) with 'puzzles' (which are more closely connected to issues or foci of interest) as suggested by Allwright (1992). Puzzles may or may not be solved; the real value lies in discussing options and considering possibilities, a process of 'exploratory practice' (Allwright and Lenzuen, 1997). Reflection and action result in a kind of 'emergent understanding', an ongoing process of enhanced awareness.

For most second language teachers, this vision of class-based research might appear somewhat daunting – teachers are not automatically equipped with classroom observation skills and may know even less about how to process and analyze data (Nunan, 1990). Not only are L2 teachers normally too busy to take on such a commitment, most have not been trained in class-based research techniques. Furthermore, if action research is regarded as something that is imposed, it loses its 'emancipatory' (Zuber-Skerritt, 1996) or 'empowering' (Wallace, 1998) function. In other words, the research has to be carried out following a *desire* to learn more about a particular aspect of a teacher's professional life. Teachers have to have ownership of their research and, perhaps after collaborative dialogue, take actions which they deem appropriate.

Understanding Requires Dialogue

Our third condition is that reflection benefits from dialogue with a peer or more experienced colleague, mentor or teacher educator. Dialogue is a crucial part of the reflection–action–further action cycle, since it allows for clarification, questioning and ultimately enhanced understanding. Conversation is the means by which new ideas are expressed, doubts aired and concerns raised (Wells, 1999). Extending a socio-cultural view of learning to teacher education (Lantolf and Thorne, 2006; Johnson, 2009), it becomes very quickly apparent that professional development and professional learning need dialogue, which can establish 'proximal processes' or contexts which create opportunities for learning potential (Bruner, 1990). There are parallels here too in the place of 'dialogic teaching' advocated by mainstream education practitioners and researchers (see, for example, Alexander, 2008; Mortimer and Scott, 2003;

Mercer, 2000). Essentially, the argument advocated by this group of researchers is that, through dialogue and discussion, children learn to think and develop together. Based on socio-cultural theories of learning and development, where learning is mediated by language, the central claim of researchers like Robin Alexander and Neil Mercer is that learning occurs primarily through dialogue. We are making the same argument in a teacher education setting.

In a teacher education/development context, and from a socio-cultural perspective, teachers are 'scaffolded' through their 'zones of proximal development' (ZPD) to a higher plane of understanding through the dialogues they have with other professionals (van Lier, 1996). Under this perspective, reflection and action alone are insufficient means of allowing professional development – scaffolded dialogues, where issues are clarified and new levels of understanding attained, are central to reflective practice. This discussion is taken up in section 2.5 below (and see Chapter 8).

2.4 Data and Evidence

One of the key ways in which RP practices and procedures can be made more principled and objective is to make the whole process data-led. In light of the fact that teaching is a hugely complex process, involving multi-party talk and any number of agendas occurring simultaneously, it is, we suggest, difficult to reflect without some kind of evidence. Put simply, data is a key form of evidence and evidence-based decision-making lies at the heart of good practice in any professional endeavour. Richards and Lockhart (1994: 1) were among the first to put emphasis on the importance of data. Through collecting 'data about their teaching' teachers could examine 'their attitudes, beliefs, assumptions, and teaching practices'.

If we accept that data is central to reflection, the question then becomes 'whose data'? We can take the position that any form of data can be helpful in providing opportunities for reflection. However, our argument is that a teacher's own data is a particularly rich resource. This is partly a question of ownership, and where there is ownership of the data there is more likely to be a change in teaching behaviour, since teachers are more engaged when they use data from their own context and experience. They are both the producers and consumers of their research (Kumaravadivelu, 1999).

Of course, research for many involves the collection and analysis of data and the publication of findings. As we have said above, any form of data can be useful (e.g. narrative accounts, critical incidents), but later in this book we make a particular argument for the value of recorded data and transcripts of these recordings (see Chapters 7 and 8). We see this kind of use of data as different from data in 'big R' research (large-scale, public, generalizable). The kind of research we are describing here is small-scale, localized, context-specific and private, conducted by teachers for their own ends. Typically, this process is situated and concerned with the development of an appropriate methodology (Holliday, 1994).

Greater understanding of professional practice is made more possible when a process of inquiry is carried out in the teacher's natural environment, using a teacher's own data. This is consistent with the kind of reflexive relationship (between interaction, language, learning and knowledge) that we emphasized earlier.

It is also valuable to note that the value of this kind of data-led reflective process is just as important for teacher trainers as for novice teachers. As we argued in Chapter 1 (1.3) a teacher educator who practises what he or she preaches is more likely to show commitment to and therefore promote reflective practice. We argued that this is a question of congruence or 'consistency' (Edge, 2011: 20). By way of exemplification, consider extract 2.1 below, in which we see an example of two teacher trainers using transcripts of their feedback sessions as an impetus for reflection:

Extract 2.1

```
A:  It was really interesting looking closely at this one (.) I'm
    beginning to think it might be useful to look again at the way
    we use observation and discussion tasks (.) th- (.) sometimes
    think they get in the way of the trainees (.) too much our
    agenda maybe=

B:  =you mean in the actual feedback sessions?

A:  yeah (.) the focus needs to come from them more often (.)
    if they were more involved in choosing the focus of the
    observations they'd get more out of it (.) I might suggest
    that they use some of Pebblepad discussions to choose an
    observation focus (.)
```

Mann and Walsh, 2013

What is interesting about this piece of data is that it not only shows how the teacher trainer is considering how best to promote engagement and reflection (through integrating PebblePad discussions), but it also gives an insight into how a data-led process (the use of transcripts) can lead to new possibilities in practice.

Although, as we have argued above, the 'big R' research model may not be appropriate here, more informal traditions do resonate with the position we are adopting. For example, exploratory practice (EP) (see Allwright, 2003) and action research (AR) rest on the premise that teachers can and should investigate their own classrooms and have reflection at their core (see Chapter 9).

2.5 A Systematic and Appropriate Approach

The previous two sections established arguments for a more data-led approach to RP. In this section, we demonstrate how the approach may be made more systematic and more appropriate through the use of appropriate tools. A small 'r' approach to data collection entails the use of instruments or procedures which are tailored to a particular context and which have the potential to uncover the smallest details of that context. So, for example, if we want to address the puzzle of why students sometimes code switch and use L1 it helps to collect evidence (for example, in the form of recordings, a conversation with students, observation by a peer) in order to reflect. Data also has the enormous advantage of aiding dialogue and discussion with another professional and may lead to further collaboration.

The extracts presented above already, to some extent, exemplify the kinds of tools we are advocating (for example, the use of teachers' own transcripts and the use of video recordings). Below, we present two further examples of tools that teachers might use to facilitate a process of RP and make it more data-led. These are illustrative of the approach we want to take in subsequent chapters where we want to concentrate on 'reflection-in-action'.

'Ad hoc' *Self-observation*

In Chapter 1, we argued against the wholesale adoption of frameworks or models for RP. This said, there is a case to be made for the use of '*ad hoc*' instruments, designed for specific tasks in specific contexts (Wallace, 1998). Such an approach permits up-close self-observation and allows for the emergence of detailed understanding of professional practice, without the need for a transcription or recording. An *ad hoc*-based approach to self-observation responds to the issue of standardization that Gray and Block (2012) raise. In this paper, Gray and Block present a critique of:

> a McDonaldised system designed to produce teachers capable of using basic tools of the trade such as textbooks in ways which are efficient, calculable and predictable and which guarantee the delivery of a standardized product into the educational marketplace.
>
> *2012: 127*

Ad hoc tools are designed by and for teachers in a local context and so, to some extent at least, avoid issues of standardization. One example of such an instrument was devised by Walsh (2006). The SETT (Self Evaluation of Teacher Talk) framework was designed in collaboration with a group of university TESOL teachers and used to help teachers gain closer understandings of the complex relationship between language, interaction and learning. Essentially, it is an adaptable instrument comprising four micro-contexts (called modes) and 14 interactional features (such as clarification request, display question, teacher echo). By recording their classes and then completing the SETT grid, teachers establish a 'snapshot' of their verbal behaviour while teaching. It has been used and adapted to a range of contexts globally and is now employed on initial teacher education courses in, for example, Singapore, Ireland and Taiwan (see Walsh, 2011). Similar tools have been advocated by other researchers with an overall goal of making classrooms more dialogic and more engaging for learners (see, for example, Mortimer and Scott, 2003; Alexander, 2008).

In extract 2.2 below, the teacher, Joy, has analyzed her teaching using the SETT framework and is talking about her evaluation with a colleague, Mike. The focus of the reflection is scaffolding.

Extract 2.2

Mike: Is scaffolding something you think you do more of in that
        type of mode for example you're in a skills and systems
        mode here. Do you think it's something that happens more in
        some modes than others or is it maybe too difficult to say
        at this stage?

Joy: My first feeling would be yes because it's so focused on
        language that anything they give me that might not be
        correct and not clear then I'm going to re-formulate it or
        anything they don't understand I'm going to give them a lot
        of examples so that's all scaffolding isn't it?

Walsh, 2013: 48

This is perhaps the first time that Joy has had an opportunity to reflect on her use of scaffolding. Her comments indicate that she is trying to both understand for herself and explain to Mike how scaffolding occurs in practice (*I'm going to re-formulate it [. . .] I'm going to give them a lot of examples so that's all scaffolding isn't it?*). Joy explains that scaffolding occurs more in skills and systems mode because this is the mode where the main focus is the language itself (*it's so focused on language*). Mike plays a key role in withholding suggestions or his evaluative position and posing reflective questions. They help Joy to clarify her own reflections, understand when a particular practice occurs, and explain why.

What we are witnessing here is that this teacher is reflecting *through* dialogue, based on an earlier analysis of her own interactions with students. Not only are teachers able to discuss particular aspects of their teaching, they are also able to give reasons for a particular strategy and make observations about its appropriacy at a given moment. One of the aims of this book is to exemplify and consider the ways in which reflection 'gets done' by presenting illustrative data such as that found in extract 2.2.

Stimulated Recall

One of the most powerful means of promoting reflective practice is to get teachers to make a video recording of their teaching and then discuss it with a critical friend or colleague. This procedure, known as *stimulated recall* (see, for example, Lyle, 2003), has the immediate advantage of allowing both parties to watch something and comment on it together. It is a very useful tool and an excellent means of raising awareness about specific features of a teacher's professional practice. In its purest form, it is used to get practitioners to actually recall specific incidents and comment on them, but it can also be used as a stimulus to provide 'talking-points' and promote discussion.

In extract 2.3 below, for example, the teacher, Mary, is explaining to the trainer, Paul, how she clarified a piece of vocabulary which had been elicited (note that the classroom interaction is presented on the left, then Mary's commentary on the right).

Extract 2.3

(The teacher is eliciting vocab items and collecting them on the board. Learner 1 is trying to explain a word)

```
1. L1: discographics=
2. M: =ooh what do you mean?
3. L1: the people who not the
people the (4) the business
about music record series and=
4. M: =is this a word you're
thinking of in Basque or
Spanish in English I don't
know this word 'disco-
graphics' what I would say is
er (writes on board) like you
said 'the music business'=
5. L1: =the music business?
what is the name of of er
industry?=
6. M: =the music industry as
well it's actually better
```

I was going to say it's a false friend but I decided not to because I thought that might confuse her . . . maybe I misunderstood her now when I look back at it . . . I understood at the time that she meant that this was a particular industry but maybe she meant a business. . . . but I wasn't prepared to spend a long time on that because it didn't seem important even though there was still a doubt in my mind . . . .

Mann and Walsh, 2013

A number of observations can be made about the interaction:

- In 1, L1 comes up with an 'invented' piece of vocabulary, 'discographics', which is immediately met with surprise by Mary in 2.
- L1 tries to explain (in 3) and encounters some perturbation, indicated by self-initiated self-repair and a 4-second pause, which Mary ignores, preferring to let L1 struggle a little longer.
- In 4, Mary interrupts L1 (indicated =) and seeks clarification, offering an acknowledgement of L1's previous contribution ('like you said'). Mary

also scaffolds a more 'precise' term, offering 'the music business' as a more appropriate phrase for 'discographics'.

- In 5, it is apparent that L1 is not satisfied with this attempted clarification, as indicated by her two questions, both suggesting some doubt and confusion.
- Mary again interrupts (in 6), possibly preventing a fuller explanation from L1 and possibly causing further confusion.

It is clear, from this extract, that stimulated recall is a useful data-led reflective tool, offering as it does an opportunity for teachers to use data to inform their reflections and then engage in dialogue to fine-tune their thinking. By using video recordings and talking with a colleague, much can be learned by participants. It is a methodology which brings together very nicely the various elements which, we have argued, are necessary for RP to work effectively: tools, data and dialogue. Stimulated recall is relatively easy to organize, inexpensive and unobtrusive, and has considerable potential for influencing professional development. We return to this procedure in Chapter 5.

2.6 Dialogic Reflection

This section combines two concerns outlined in Chapter 1: (a) reflective practice is often conducted in a written form and (b) it is often an individual enterprise. Our argument is that we should be embracing a dialogic/collaborative view of reflection that allows potentially richer articulation and analysis (see also McCabe et al., 2011). In this section, we consider how any future repositioning of RP should emphasize dialogic collaboration and constructivist views of professional development. Developing experiential knowledge, we suggest, is supported by collaborative discussion where thoughts and ideas about classroom practice are first articulated and then reformulated in a progression towards enhanced understanding. In this approach, reflection on practice does not occur in isolation, but in discussion with another practitioner. An example of such a process would be cooperative development, which involves a 'Speaker' and an 'Understander' (Edge, 2002). We explore this further in 7.4.

Socio-cultural and constructivist views of learning are helpful here, emphasizing as they do the fact that all human development is underpinned by language, often talk. Quite simply, if we wish to develop, understand or improve in any aspect of our lives, one of the first steps is usually to talk about it. It is especially important for novice teachers to have opportunities for reflection through talk so that they articulate current understanding but also experience 'the forms of inquiry by which competent practitioners reason their way, in problematic instances, to clear connections between general knowledge and particular cases' (Schön, 1987: 39). Socio-cultural theories of learning emphasize its social nature; learning often takes place as learners interact with an 'expert knower' in 'a context of social interactions leading to understanding' (Röhler and Cantlon, 1996: 2). In addition, learners collectively and actively construct their own knowledge and understanding by making connections, building mental schemata and concepts through collaborative meaning-making.

Conversation is the essence of all professional dialogue, the prime force through which meanings are negotiated, concepts explained and understood, and exchanges of opinion given. Instructional conversations have been trialled in a number of contexts (see, for example, Goldenberg, 1992). They are essentially discussion-based lessons in which linguistic and conceptual understanding of key areas are affected through teacher-led discussion based on student contributions. Instructional situations are highly complex and for scaffolding to work, learners need to be given opportunities to ask and answer questions according to Sternberg's principle of question and comment generation (1994: 137):

> The single most helpful thing a teacher can do is to take [learners'] questions and comments seriously and turn those questions and comments into learning opportunities.

As a way of exemplifying how dialogue might enhance reflection, consider this extract in which two teachers (Ann and Beth) on an in-service teacher education programme are discussing their use of 'teacher echo' (repetitions) in an ESL context involving a group of multilingual adult learners. Both teachers had agreed to focus on teacher echo before they taught. They then individually made a short (15-minute) video recording of their teaching. The next step was to watch both recordings together and use this as a basis for discussion, part of which is shown in extract 2.4 below:

Extract 2.4

```
Ann:    I was struck by how much echoing I did before and sometimes
        there was a justification for it . . . . but a LOT of the
        time. . . . it was just echo for the sake of echo so I was
        fairly consciously trying NOT to echo this time

Beth:   And what effect did that (reduced echo) have on the
        interaction patterns or the involvement of learners in the
        class, did it have any effect that you noticed?

Ann:    I think that it made them more confident perhaps in giving
        me words because it was only going to come back to them if
        the pronunciation WASn't right rather than just getting
        ((1)) straight back to them. When you're eliciting
        vocabulary if they're coming out with the vocabulary and
        it's adequate and it's clear, there's no need for you to
```

```
echo it back to the other students . . . . you're wasting
a lot of time by echoing stuff back.
```
Walsh, 2013

Here we see very clearly the value of dialogue in promoting closer under-standings. Ann is reflecting on her use of 'echo', the repetition of student contributions – a common feature of classroom discourse. Her realization that echo can become a kind of habit ('echo for echo's sake') is probed by Beth who asks about the effect of echo on learner involvement. Ann's response is quite revealing: she says that reduced echo makes learners more confident and that a lot of echo is unnecessary. Arguably, this realization may not have occurred without an opportunity to discuss echo and reflect on its effects. Beth's contribution allows her to think about her language use and give reasons, possibly for the first time. It is this kind of 'light-bulb moment' which pro-fessional dialogue can create. Through talk, new realizations and greater insights come about and get their first airing before becoming internalized.

A dialogic approach to reflective practice, we suggest, addresses the need for more spoken forms of reflection and for a collaborative, rather than individual, approach. We deal with this more fully in Chapter 8. In the next section we consider the implications for RP of the ideas and arguments proposed in this chapter.

2.7 Summary

Our main argument in this chapter is that reflective practice needs to be repositioned and revitalized if it is to prosper and play a full and important role in teacher education. Through this book, we aim to show how RP can be more evidence-based, data-led, dialogic and collaborative. The importance of 'talk' in the workplace has already been highlighted elsewhere (see, for example, Edwards and Westgate, 1992; Drew and Heritage, 1992). We adopt the position that RP can greatly enhance professional practice by focusing on both the *what* and the *how* of teacher development. In terms of the 'what', we are proposing a more reflexive relationship with context, one which promotes fine-grained understandings of the ways in which a local classroom context emerges through co-constructed interaction. This view of context highlights its variability, dynamism and constantly shifting focus. It also emphasizes the fact that any one lesson is made up of a series of micro-contexts which will shift according to the teacher's pedagogic goals of the moment and according to local agendas and circumstances. The focus of RP should, therefore, be on multiple contexts, not on a singular context.

Having made a case for repositioning the 'what' of RP, we went on to detail the 'how': what practices or procedures might result in enhanced understandings of professional actions and how might changes to practice be brought about?

Specifically, we argue that RP needs to be data-led, evidence-based and dialogic, and utilize tools and procedures which are fit for purpose – that is, which are appropriate to the context(s). Such a repositioning of RP might contribute to deeper understandings of 'real-world' workplace practice. As well as descriptions of reflective practice, we need more accounts of reflective tools which consider their nature and appropriacy at particular stages of professional development. It is fair to say, for example, that the reflections of CELTA trainees during week 1 of their four-week course will be very different from their reflections in week 4, which, in turn, will differ markedly from the reflections of teachers on a DELTA programme or an MA programme. The tools which are used to aid reflection must, we suggest, be appropriate for the context (and stage of development); we will explore this further in Chapters 3 and 4.

A more data-led treatment of RP will help in achieving greater understanding of professional practice, especially if the data involves those doing the reflecting. This might help avoid the situation prevailing on many teacher education programmes where reflection is left to the individual who lacks clarity about what reflection might look like. In avoiding vague understandings, we need to design teacher education materials which integrate data-led examples of reflective practice so that choices, decisions, puzzles and scenarios are foregrounded. This not only gives a more concrete idea of what reflection looks like, but it encourages a view that teachers are always in a process of becoming a better teacher. Considerations of appropriacy and fit with context are always and necessarily in a state of flux and accommodation. This is why reflection is important.

In the final section of the chapter, we highlighted the importance of dialogue and collaboration. That is not to say that we do not recognize the importance of self-reflection and autonomy. As Heron (1996: 3) remarks, in any professional development process, collaboration and autonomy are both essential ingredients:

> Self-directing persons develop most fully through fully reciprocal relations with other self-directing persons. Autonomy and co-operation are necessary and enhancing values of human life.

The first two chapters of the book have highlighted the concerns we have towards RP as it is presently being used and offered a perspective which revitalizes and repositions RP. In the remainder of the book, we extend and exemplify this position by demonstrating how reflection gets done in a range of contexts and by considering how it might be researched.

In part 2 of the book, Chapters 3 to 5 evaluate RP in a range of professional development settings, including pre-service teacher education, in-service teacher education and contexts which are less tightly prescribed, such as self-development and teachers' groups. We consider a number of issues relating to the institutionalized nature of many forms of RP, the opportunities and challenges posed when working with teachers with varying levels of experience and the need to actually teach RP if it is to succeed.

Part 3 (Chapters 6 to 8) considers the different approaches to actually doing RP and looks in a critical way at some of the tools available for conducting written reflection (Chapter 6) and spoken reflection (Chapter 7), before looking in more detail at dialogic approaches to reflection (Chapter 8). Data-based forms of RP are considered in depth and we present our own data of professionals actually performing RP from settings around the world. We consider how, with some adjustments to roles, reflection can be made to operate at a more meaningful level and examine ways of embedding the practice in regular classroom procedures.

Finally, in part 4 (Chapters 9 to 10), we offer a perspective on researching RP, first (in Chapter 9) by considering the relationship between reflection and research and providing examples of how opportunities for reflection are integral to various versions of practitioner research. In the final chapter of the book (10), we pave the way for a fuller data-led understanding of what forms reflection takes, how various stakeholders value it, and whether it has any impact. This chapter provides suggestions for a range of research questions that need further attention and clarifies the research opportunities that exist.

References

Alexander, R.J. (2008). *Towards dialogic teaching: rethinking classroom talk* (4th edn). York: Dialogos.

Allwright, D. (1992). Exploratory teaching: bringing research and pedagogy together in the language classroom. *Revue de Phonétique Appliquée*, 103, 101–117.

Allwright, R. (2003). Exploratory practice: rethinking practitioner research in language teaching. *Language Teaching Research*, 7, 113–114.

Allwright, R.L. and Lenzuen, R. (1997). Exploratory practice: work at the Cultura Inglesa, Rio de Janeiro, Brazil. *Language Teaching Research*, 1, 73–79.

Bailey, K.M. and Nunan, D. (eds). (1996). *Voices from the language classroom*. Cambridge: Cambridge University Press.

Bartlett, L. (1990). Teacher development through reflective teaching. In J.C. Richards and D. Nunan (eds), *Second Language Teacher Education*. Cambridge: Cambridge University Press.

Bax, S. (2003). The end of ELT: a context-based approach to language teaching. *English Language Teaching Journal*, 53, 278–289.

Borg, S. (2002). Research in the lives of TESOL professionals. *TESOL Matters*, 13(1), 1–5.

Borg, S. (2003). Teachers' involvement in TESOL research. *TESOL Matters*, 13(3), 1–5.

Bruner, J. (1990). Vygotsky: a historical and conceptual perspective. In L. C. Moll (ed.), *Vygotsky and education: instructional implications and applications of sociohistorical psychology*. Cambridge: Cambridge University Press.

Burns, A. (2005). Action research: an evolving paradigm? *Language Teaching*, 38(2), 57–74.

Clarke, M.A. (1994). The dysfunctions of the theory/practice discourse. *TESOL Quarterly*, 28, 10–27.

Cohen, L., Lawrence, M. and Morrison, K. (2007). *Research methods in education*. New York: Routledge.

Cullen, R. (1998). Teacher talk and the classroom context. *English Language Teaching Journal*, 52, 179–187.

De Decker, B. and Vanderheiden, M. (eds). (1999). In *Proceedings of the TDTR4 conference*. CD-ROM, available from Centrum voor Levende Talen, Dekenstraat, B-3000 Leuven, Belgium.

Drew, P. and Heritage, J. (eds). (1992). *Talk at work: interaction in institutional settings*. Cambridge: Cambridge University Press.

Edge, J. (2002). *Continuing cooperative development*. Ann Arbor, MI: University of Michigan Press.

Edge, J. (2011). *The reflexive teacher educator: roots and wings*. New York: Routledge.

Edge, J. and Richards, K. (eds). (1993). *Teachers develop teachers' research*. Oxford: Heinemann.

Edwards, A. and Westgate, D. (1992). *Investigating classroom talk*. London: Falmer.

Field, J., Graham, A., Griffiths, E. and Head, K. (eds). (1997). *Teachers develop teachers' research 2*. Whitstable, UK: International Association of Teachers of English as a Foreign Language (IATEFL).

Gilmore, A. (2007). Authentic materials and authenticity in foreign language learning. *Language Teaching*, 40(2), 97–118.

Goldenberg, C. (1992). Instructional conversation: promoting comprehension through discussion. *The Reading Teacher*, 46, 316–326.

Gray, J. and Block, D. (2012). The marketization of language teacher education and neoliberalism. In D. Block, J. Gray and M. Holborow (eds), *Neoliberalism and applied linguistics* (pp. 114–143). London: Routledge.

Head, K. (ed.). (1998). *Teachers develop teachers' research 3*. Whitstable, UK: International Association of Teachers of English as a Foreign Language (IATEFL).

Heritage, J. (2007). Intersubjectivity and progressivity in references to persons (and places). In T. Stivers and N.J. Enfield (eds), *Person reference in interaction: linguistic, cultural and social perspectives* (pp. 255–280). Cambridge: Cambridge University Press.

Heron, J. (1996). *Co-operative inquiry: research into the human condition*. London: Sage Publications.

Holliday, A. (1994). *Appropriate methodology and social context*. Cambridge: Cambridge University Press.

Jarvis, S. (2001). Research in TESOL: sunset or a new dawn? *TESOL Research Interest Section Newsletter*, 8(2), 1–7.

Johnson, K.E. (1995). *Understanding communication in second language classrooms*. Cambridge: Cambridge University Press.

Johnson, K.E. (2009). *Second language teacher education: a sociocultural perspective*. London and New York: Routledge.

Kemmis, S. and McTaggart, R. (2000). Participatory action research. In N. K. Denzin and Y. S. Lincoln (eds), *Handbook of qualitative research* (pp. 567–605). Thousand Oaks, CA: Sage.

Kumaravadivelu, B. (1993). Maximising learning potential in the communicative classroom. *English Language Teaching Journal*, 47, 12–21.

Kumaravadivelu, B. (1999). Critical classroom discourse analysis. *TESOL Quarterly*, 33(3), 453–484.

Lantolf, J.P. and Thorne, S. (2006). *Sociocultural theory and the genesis of second language development*. Oxford: Oxford University Press.

Lyle, J. (2003). Stimulated recall: a report on its use in naturalistic research. *British Educational Research Journal*, 29(6), 861–878.

Mann, S. and Walsh, S. (2013). RP or 'RIP': a critical perspective on reflective practice. *Applied Linguistics Review*, 4(2), 291–315.

McCabe, M., Walsh, S., Wideman, R. and Winter, E. (2011). The R word in teacher education: understanding the teaching and learning of critical reflective practice. *International Electronic Journal for Leadership in Learning*, 13(7), 271–283.

Mercer, N. (2000). *Words and minds: how we use language to think together*. London: Routledge.

Mortimer, E. and Scott, P. (2003). *Meaning making in secondary science classrooms*. Oxford: Oxford University Press.

Nunan, D. (1987). Communicative Language Teaching: making it work. *English Language Teaching Journal*, 41, 136–145.

Nunan, D. (1990). Action research in the language classroom. In J. Richards and D. Nunan (eds), *Second language teacher education* (pp. 62–81). New York: Cambridge University Press.

Nunan, D. (1996). Hidden voices: insiders' perspectives on classroom interaction. In K.M. Bailey and D. Nunan (eds), *Voices from the language classroom*. Cambridge: Cambridge University Press.

Richards, J.C. and Lockhart, C. (1994). *Reflective teaching in second language classrooms*. Cambridge: Cambridge University Press.

Röhler, L.R. and Cantlon, D.J. (1996). *Scaffolding: a powerful tool in social constructivist classrooms*. Available at <http://edeb3.educ.msu.edu./Literacy/papers/paperlr2.html> (last accessed 24 June 2005).

Schön, D.A. (1987). *Educating the reflective practitioner*. San Francisco: Jossey Bass.

Seedhouse, P. (2004). *The interactional architecture of the second language classroom: a conversational analysis perspective*. Oxford: Blackwell.

Sternberg, R. (1994). Answering questions and questioning answers: guiding children to intellectual excellence. *Phi Delta Kappan*, 76(2), 136–138.

van Lier, L. (1988). *The classroom and the language learner*. London: Longman.

van Lier, L. (1996). *Interaction in the language curriculum: awareness, autonomy and authenticity*. New York: Longman.

van Lier, L. (2000). From input to affordance: social-interactive learning from an ecological perspective. In J.P. Lantolf (ed.), *Sociocultural theory and second language learning*. Oxford: Oxford University Press.

Wallace, M.J. (1998). *Action research for language teachers*. Cambridge: Cambridge University Press.

Walsh, S. (2006). *Investigating classroom discourse*. London: Routledge.

Walsh, S. (2011). *Exploring classroom discourse: language in action*. London and New York: Routledge.

Walsh, S. (2013). *Classroom discourse and teacher development*. Edinburgh, UK: Edinburgh University Press.

Wells, G. (1999). *Dialogic inquiry: towards a sociocultural practice and theory of education*. London: Routledge.

Wu, B. (1998). Towards an understanding of the dynamic process of L2 classroom interaction. *System*, 26, 525–540.

Zuber-Skerritt, O. (1996). Emancipatory action research for organisational change and management development. In O. Zuber-Skerritt (ed.), *New Directions in Action Research*. London: Falmer.

3

Pre-service Teacher Training

3.1 Introduction

The next two chapters consider issues of context and factors affecting the appropriate development of reflective practice. Putting context early in the book reinforces our view that, above all, we need to consider what is appropriate in each context and avoid 'one size fits all' models and views of reflective practice; striving for appropriate methodology is necessarily bound up with context-sensitive reflective practice (Holliday, 1994). In simple terms, Chapter 3 is concerned with different PRESET (pre-service education and training of English language teachers) contexts and Chapter 4 is concerned with INSET (in-service education and training of English language teachers) contexts. Although there is a well-established distinction between PRESET and INSET, it is not always possible to sustain this distinction. Of course, we can say that PRESET is the training and education received before starting to work as a teacher and INSET is the training and education received during a teacher's career, and for many teacher trainers this distinction is unproblematic. However, for others it is not that simple. In some contexts the norm is for groups of participants with and without experience to be trained and educated together (see Mann and Edge, 2013).

This chapter covers well recognized but very different forms of PRESET. It begins with the CELTA (officially now called 'Certificate in Teaching English to Speakers of Other Languages') and then goes onto BA and MA programmes. The chapter ends by considering contexts that offer alternative forms of training for novice teachers. In focusing on teachers with no or at least little experience of teaching (novice teachers), the chapter considers the range of options available in promoting and supporting reflection. Especially in PRESET contexts, it is important that we pay more attention to the potential for reflection and sharing of experience to 'bridge the gap' from training input to the realities of classroom teaching (Farrell, 2012).

The data, vignettes and accompanying commentaries in this chapter enable us to consider the extent to which RP is both accessible and achievable in pre-service contexts, by highlighting the range of ways in which reflection 'gets done'. This chapter builds on existing accounts and revisits some of the arguments made in Mann and Walsh (2013) and Walsh and Mann (2015).

3.2 CELTA: A Challenging Context for Reflection

The first context we consider is that of the CELTA. We focus on CELTA as an example of the range of initial teacher training courses that are typically completed in four weeks full-time or some equivalent in a part-time version. Thousands of people each year take some kind of certificate course; indeed, for many, a CELTA or equivalent is the only professional qualification attained. In the UK most people take a 'CELTA' type course validated by one of two UK-based examination bodies; Cambridge ESOL validates the 'Certificate in English Language Teaching to Adults' and Trinity College, London validates the 'Certificate in TESOL'. Time constraints, rigorous standards and criteria-led assessment can mean there is little time for reflection (Brandt, 2006). This is despite the fact that reflection is usually an explicit syllabus requirement and that there have been a number of arguments for the process of reflection to start as soon as possible in initial teacher training (e.g. Braun and Crumpler, 2004; Lee, 2007). However, it has long been recognized that it is not easy to handle these two competing pressures. Roberts argues that the most difficult balance for a coach/tutor/supervisor to strike is 'to build the most open and supportive relationship possible while also applying course criteria and challenging students' (1998: 161). One of the key elements of CELTA type courses are POCs (post-observation conferences). POCs are usually small group discussions where the tutor and peers provide feedback shortly after the practicum/teaching practice. We will look closely at what happens in this interactive space in Chapter 7. Certainly there is evidence that feedback practices (including POCs) are often 'at variance with reflective components of the course' where 'a technical rational world view with a focus on the technical means of achieving predetermined objectives' is then 'evaluated by experts' (Brandt, 2008: 45). Although it is generally held to be crucial to give trainees the opportunity to reflect during the course (Farr, 2006), Copland shows how trainees put a great deal of energy into negotiating face (2011) and trying to determine what is legitimate in terms of roles and speaking rights (2012). All this can mean a mismatch between the stated reflective aims of the programme and the nature of the interaction that trainees experience.

It is well recognized then that CELTA courses are a challenging environment to support reflection. Moore and Ash (2003) identify a number of factors that helped their teachers' reflections as well as a number of factors that inhibited them. Inhibiting factors included the presence of anxiety and stress, a lack of time, and an overwhelming volume of new experiences. They also found that students were aware of the contrived or ritualistic nature of some of their reflective practice, particularly when this was subject to formal assessment or evaluation. Harford and MacRuairc also make clear that assessment can be problematic for teachers:

> Students were strongly of the view that any form of assessment of this particular activity would have negatively impacted on their engagement with the whole process, reducing the quality and value of the reflective dialogue.
>
> *2008: 1887*

Despite the fact that this is a challenging context, in terms of enabling and promoting reflection it is important to avoid simply promoting 'ready-made solutions to problems of instruction' (2008: 1887). With this in mind, there are two identifiable positions in the literature. The first is that as teacher educators we should be engaging in more co-constructed and dialogic relationships. For example, Morton and Gray (2010: 315) argue that teacher learners (TLs) should be 'apprenticed into a co-constructed model of planning (and therefore teaching) that may better equip them for the uncertainties and complexities of their future professional lives'. The other position is evident in the arguments of Brandt (2006) who suggests that reflective learning is not possible in the instrumental and judgmental ethos of tutor-led POC feedback.

We are fully aware that time is always pressing and that relatively short courses (like CELTA) mean that this is necessarily a challenge. Also, tutors may feel that, under time pressure, it is necessary to 'cut to the chase' and be relatively directive and authoritative. We recognize the challenge but do not take the position that reflection is not possible. We would argue for a middle ground. Harris (2013), for example, shows convincing evidence that reflection is possible in POCs. His study is valuable in detailing how POCs are organized into different phases orienting to different 'types' of feedback (e.g. positive, critical, self and group). His conversation analytic (CA) study reveals evidence that trainees engage in a progression as they reflect on their practices; they describe their experiences, draw interpretations and theories from descriptions and then use these reflections to make plans for future actions.

Another reason that, in this context, reflection is felt to be limited is that novice teachers may not be ready to do more than simply *describe* what has happened. Watts and Lawson (2009: 610) argue that 'beginning teachers find difficulty in evaluating their lessons effectively' and that their 'emphasis remains descriptive rather than analytical, and superficial rather than critical'. However, rather than worrying that our novice teachers are too descriptive and not critical enough, we need more accounts of the extent to which reflection can be encouraged (or indeed how it is constrained) in sessions on input, lesson planning and feedback. How do beginning teachers progress from description to critical reflection? In order for this to happen, PRESET reflective practice will probably need to be taught or demonstrated in a systematic way. It is unlikely to emerge without help. Although we share Clarà's (2015) suspicion that the very spontaneous and essentially natural process of reflection is not reducible to formulas or frameworks, there is no doubt in our mind that teachers' competencies in reflecting can be 'guided' or 'developed' (see Husu et al., 2007, 2008).

Turning now to data from a specific CELTA context, we focus here on the most important elements: teaching practice (TP) and POCs. The teacher learner (TL) typically undertakes six hours of supervised teaching practice in total. TP has a number of elements but the TL usually has opportunities to reflect-on-action. The overriding purpose of most course artefacts is evaluative, as the document below demonstrates:

Extract 3.1

CELTA Teaching Practice Feedback	**19th November**

Comments on plan
Your plan is fine and shows logical staging.

Strengths
You seem much more confident this week and you set up the listening well. When asked, you were able to explain 'altar' and your modelling of the conversation with Michael was good fun.

Areas for development
Overall, this was a nice skills lesson. It's a shame that you didn't use the opportunity to teach some vocabulary related to the topic. Think about how you can use time most effectively in class.
Make sure that you have sufficient material in your plan for purposeful learning and keep an ear open so that learners are on-task even when you are not near them.
This was a much stronger lesson than last week – well done. Aim to teach some grammar in your next lesson.

The text is a familiar mix of positive evaluation, specific criticism and prompts for reflection and action. However, in addition to such documents, there are usually opportunities too for some kind of self-evaluation (usually written). There might be reflective prompts such as 'what things were you pleased with in this lesson?' or 'what would you do differently if you taught this lesson again?' TLs therefore have an opportunity to reflect on their teaching and receive some kind of response to their written reflections.

Such comments often justify or warrant the provision of an overall grade (where the lesson is judged as 'not to standard', 'to standard' or 'above standard').

This does not necessarily negate a reflective process and can be, at least in a limited way, dialogic. However, there is a clear sense of 'endorsement' of these contributions too and this gets us to the heart of the challenge for CELTA courses. Such template-based feedback is overridingly and inescapably evaluative in nature, and although we can point to features in this extract which might act as a prompt for further reflection (for example, 'think about how you can use time most effectively in class'), it would be difficult for participants to deviate far from the real-world set of activities that lead to being able to get the certificate (with its ultimate label of competence). Ferguson and Donno (2003) go further and argue that short CELTA courses might inhibit the growth of reflective thinking in their drive to assess and evaluate TLs through standard criteria. This is true but it is perhaps in the feedback meeting or conference (usually conducted in groups) that there is the greatest opportunity for at least some reflection. We turn now to consider a data-set featuring a trainer working with a group in a POC.

In extracts 3.2(a) and 3.2(b) below, we witness Christine, a teacher trainer working with a CELTA group. She has been consciously working on promoting more reflective interaction. In the data extracts we see her specific focus on the nature and functions of questions she uses to deliver feedback to a group of trainees. She reviewed a number of audio recordings and selected extract 3.2(b) for transcription. The extract is taken from quite early in the course when the TLs are still getting considerable support with lesson planning. At the start of this excerpt, Sarah is briefly describing a follow-up activity from her listening lesson.

Extract 3.2(a)

```
01   Sarah   I thought that just maybe might introduce them to (.)
02           the:: concept of a routine. What they do each day of the
03           week and whether they share similarities with the person
04           next to them.
05→  Chris   OK. Anybody spot the purpose of that activity? What's the
06           idea behind it? Why do we do that with our students?
07   Fred    Which one?
08   Chris   (x)You describe it.
09   Sarah   Oh, erm, yeah, the listening activity, I- I-=
10   Chris   =After the listening.=
11   Sarah   =After the listening I asked them to talk to their
12           partner about what they do in the week, what kind of
13           routine they have- and that wasn't actually in my
14           lesson plan.
15   Chris   mhm
16   Sarah   I just added that,
17   Chris   mhm
```

```
18  Sarah  erm to discuss and maybe whether they share any
19         similarities about activities they do, with each other,
20         each day. Most of them said that they come to college
21         every single day with the English lessons.
22  Chris  °mhm°
23  Elly   °So what was the purpose?°
24  Nick   Practise the language to see if they can use what they've
25         heard in the listening, they can use that and can
26         practise that and then they can incorporate it and
27         elaborate on it and use it in their own knowledge of
28         whatever vocab they have.
29  Elly   Share ideas.
30  Nick   Yeah.
31  Chris  Mhm.
32  Sarah  [Work out similarities and differences]
33  Olly   [They get to use their grammar,] I mean their- their
34         sentences, I- one of them was saying I- weekend I go
35         shopping. I think it was Fu, she was saying, I go- I go
36         you know weekends shopping. So, I mean, she's using
37         vocabulary.
38  Sarah  They were talking about tenses as well, about what they
39         have done and what they usually do, what they do daily or
40         usually or what they do sometimes.
41  Chris  mhm.
42  Elly   Well it's a fluency activity so they are more free to use
43         whatever language they really want. They are not
44         constrained.
45→ Chris  So was it a fluency?
```

Following Sarah's initial explanation for the follow-up task after the listening activity, Christine asks the group about the purpose of this activity, which wasn't mentioned in Sarah's plan (lines 5–6). Sarah describes her activity in more detail, after which three trainees in turn identify what they think was happening in terms of language learning. This process is very typical of what happens during feedback on many CELTA courses and is designed to promote group reflection and discussion.

In extract 3.2(b) below, the trainer, Christine, offers a reflexive commentary on her interactions with the TLs. She identifies four questioning strategies and realizes that they play significantly different roles in opening up discussions amongst the whole group, sharing knowledge, developing reflective talk and learning.

Extract 3.2(b)

COMMENT FROM TRAINER (CHRISTINE)

This shows an example of where I've used three linked questions (05) to introduce the topic of 'learning aims' and get students exchanging ideas. It doesn't go well immediately. I notice first of all my pronoun choices – ('why do we do that with our students?'). There's a shift in 'footing': the inclusive pronouns align me to their professional selves as teachers, co-members of a group that shares classroom practices and routines.

There are two trainer question turns in this excerpt. The first group of three are hinting questions, highly inexplicit, implying knowledge accessible to practitioners if they look beneath the surface of a speaking activity for a pedagogic purpose. The ensuing interaction has something of the feel of 'a shared endeavour' (Mercer and Howe, 2012). Each trainee is trying to articulate an understanding of language learning with a limited degree of control over the metalanguage (this is only the fifth day of the course). They seem to be listening to each other and responding to gaps in each other's accounts, and attempting greater explicitness.

This kind of interaction can usefully draw on the notion of exploratory talk, 'in which a speaker articulates half-formed thoughts so that they can be tested out in the telling, and so that others can hear them, and comment'(Mercer and Howe, 2012: 1). I'm conscious in my questions of attempting to 'encourage students to put knowledge into their own words (while also offering them new vocabulary to accommodate new ideas)' (Mercer and Howe, 2012: 1).

I have been wondering for some while why we don't have a session on SLA? Trainees do need a metalanguage and frameworks for understanding language learning. It is implied but not made explicit enough in the course although the Learner Focus assignment does nod in that direction. Many centres seem to interpret this part of the assignment in terms of 'learning styles'. Mmm.

What is apparent in Christine's commentary is the trainer's awareness of the importance of the role of dialogue in promoting understanding and in particular subtle language choices (like use of pronouns) that may contribute to a more collaborative POC. A fuller account of her work can be found in Tudor Jones (2012). There she demonstrates the value of a trainer becoming more aware of interactions with trainees, especially of the ways in which turns are designed and the consequences for more dialogic possibilities. Tudor Jones (2012) shows that it is possible to make POCs more reflective in nature and that students value opportunities for reflective talk. McCabe et al. (2009) also found that many student teachers on initial teacher education programmes felt that they benefited more, in terms of learning, from discussions about their teaching with peers and teacher educators than they did from completing written report forms.

While extract 3.2(a) exemplifies the kind of interaction that can take place during TP feedback sessions, we do not wish to underplay the inherently asymmetrical power relations in CELTA feedback. Analysis of pre- and post-observation conferences shows that the supervisor has more turns and control of what is judged 'legitimate talk' (Copland, 2011). We need to give more attention to the potential role of opportunities for reflection, whether it is with a tutor, coach, supervisor or mentor. Just to re-iterate the point, we recognize that a number of studies have pointed to the relative lack of opportunities for reflection in the teacher preparation process and argued that this affects positive outcomes. Our argument is also that increasing opportunities for talk, dialogue and reflection is crucial to teachers' long-term development.

CELTA interaction and exchange can take place in a congested and contested space. If this is the case, then there is a danger that exchanges fall back on a view that a teaching episode is either good or bad and something of a black and white matter. It is important, even in CELTAs, to recognize that there are grey areas. The promotion of reflection is not best served by classifying things into 'good' and 'bad' categories. It has long been recognized that feedback conferences work better when there is a 'positive/negative/positive sandwich' (e.g. Edge, 1993). However, our suggestion here would be that we make space for the discussion of intermediate, interesting, puzzling and less clear-cut issues and decisions. This is what Edge and Richards called 'dialogues of doubt' (1998). We are reminded of de Bono (1992) and his PMI (Plus-Minus-Interesting) thinking tool. This opens up the important third space (the 'interesting' category) in a discussion that builds trust, openness and inquiry. We believe that this can lead participants to a more open-ended discussion (see also de Bono's six coloured thinking hats in Appendix 2). We also note that some CELTA course trainers organize their feedback notes in three columns (positive, negative, interesting), and when running peer observation, ask participants to structure their own feedback in this way (for more detail see Tudor Jones (2012)).

We also believe that video has an important role in making the feedback less of a black and white affair and bringing out the complexity and nuances of teaching. Video is increasingly being used in PRESET, and we come back to this topic in Chapter 7. Of particular value is Harford and MacRuairc's (2008) study where teachers use video recordings to promote group discussion of teachers' classroom performance. They found that this process led pre-service teachers to a range of diverse teaching methodologies and a deeper level of reflection. Zottmann et al. (2012) also show how video encourages detailed reflections and the development of analytical skills in PRESET teachers.

One study which has highlighted the importance of dialogue between TLs and tutors is that of Lee (2007: 321), who claims that 'reflection is a skill that has to be fostered from the beginning of the learning-to-teach process' and consequently PRESET has 'shifted its emphasis from a transmission-oriented to a constructivist approach' where TLs 'focus on prior knowledge and personal experience'. She argues for reflective journals that require dialogue between the tutor and the trainee, and provides evidence of trainees working beyond superficial description and considering more critical perspectives (including cultural and affective factors in language teaching).

She quotes Kitty, for example, who, in her journal, comments on the question of 'innovation' in relation to ELT methodology:

> Very often, people tend to support 'new' ideas blindly. They think that everything 'new' is 'creative', 'up-to-date' and 'better'. However, this is absolutely not true. I strongly believe that the existing language teaching methodology could be improved. But this does not mean that any change or any new methodology would help . . . We have to think carefully if the new methodology is better than the existing one or not. . . . Then it's the idea of suitability. When this idea is from the West, it may not suit the cultural background of Hong Kong students.
>
> *Lee, 2007: 327*

What is evident in the example above is that the journal is allowing a space for reflection on issues of both identity and context-appropriate methodology. By providing space and time to reflect through a written journal entry, Kitty has come to a realization that innovation in education is not always a 'good thing' and that adapting to local culture and context is more important.

In a third example from the CELTA context below, we see a TL reflecting on his identity and how this impacts on his teaching (extract 3.3(a)). This is followed by the trainer's (Tom's) comment on the data (extract 3.3(b)). In extract 3.3(a), taken from a lesson-planning session, the teaching practice group of six TLs is preparing with the tutor for an upcoming lesson. For each teaching practice lesson, three of the TLs are asked to prepare some activities from the course-book. The student teacher here, Bill, has been asked to do some work on the definite article. Just before this extract, he has made a suggestion for a practice activity (students talk about their holiday plans) and this has been rejected by the tutor for being too 'wide-ranging' (i.e. not enough focus on the article). Here, we witness Bill's response to this rejection:

Extract 3.3(a)

```
01  Bill   I think that- I think personally I feel burdened by being
02         a native speaker and the fact that I pay little attention
03         to the way I speak <you know> and a lot of those erm sort of
04         a lot of that laziness can come out in my speech you know
```

```
05 Tutor  mmm    .
06 Bill   you don't over analyse everything you say but when
07        yo(h)u d(h)o
08 Tutor             [mmm
09 Bill   you definitely do
```

Bill comments on a common issue for native-speaker TLs on CELTA courses; native speakers feel that they are less aware of their use of language than non-native-speaker TLs because they have not studied the language in the same way that non-native-speaker TLs have. They simply say what comes into their heads and this is not always suited to a particular task or activity. Here, Bill describes the 'burden' of being a native speaker in terms of learning to become an EFL teacher.

In extract 3.3(b), we witness Tom's (the trainer) reaction to Bill's reflections:

Extract 3.3(b)

COMMENT FROM TRAINER (TOM)

Bill is not just 'reflecting' on what it means to be a native speaker in the context of teaching English. If we take an 'action-oriented' perspective on discourse (Hepburn and Wiggins, 2007), we can see that Bill is carrying out certain actions, and that his turns both construct a certain version of reality, and are themselves constructed out of sets of symbolic resources.

Bill is claiming an identity for himself. He claims membership of the category 'native speaker'. His reflection in talk explores the negative attribute for the category 'native speaker' (that he is 'burdened' by belonging to). Perhaps he is warding off the (always lurking) opposite assumption that belonging to this category is an advantage in TESOL.

In a context where Bill is being constantly evaluated as regards his growing competence as a novice teacher (with language awareness being one criterion), such a statement could ward off another failing, with perhaps graver consequences for his final outcome on the course, that is, a lack of self-awareness, or 'reflection'. He designs the final part of his turn as an explicit contrast between everyday uses of language and teaching, thus constructing himself as knowledgeable of this distinction, and, by implication, as being on the way to becoming a language-aware TESOL practitioner.

What is interesting about Tom's reflexive comment is that it raises the question about the extent to which Bill's reflections may seem to align themselves with a 'critical' position current in TESOL discourse, that of the attack on 'nativespeakerism' (e.g. Rampton, 1990; Medğyes, 1992; Piller, 2001; Matsuda,

2014) which critiques what it claims are unquestioned assumptions about the superiority of the native speaking teacher. The interactional evidence cannot confirm that Bill is indexing these critical discourses, however tempting it may be to claim that he did so. Thus, positively evaluating Bill for such a reflection would be unwarranted, at least solely from this interactional data.

In making claims about the status and importance of such a piece of 'reflection' we need to bear in mind that it is a co-constructed interactional accomplishment. Bill knows that the tutor is constantly evaluating not only specific teaching performances, but also his capacity for 'reflection' (as this is a course requirement). This leaves us with the inevitable dilemma that the co-constructed interactional performance is one where the TL wants to be seen as 'doing reflection', and highlights the issue of evaluation which we now discuss in more detail.

The Problem of Evaluation

Short courses like CELTA have a particular problem with the pervasive nature of evaluation and assessment. Being seen to 'do reflection' can easily turn into 'faking it' (Atkinson, 2012) and when a teacher 'is asked to reflect on his/her strengths and weaknesses as part of a required, graded course assignment' it may be that 'genuine examination of self is already a lost cause' (Hobbs, 2007: 410). Whether we agree that the graded, assessed evaluative context means that reflection is possible or not, evaluation is certainly dominant, and trainees spend most of their energy negotiating the best way to handle this (to advance the cause of their success on the course). Interactive routines are built up during the course, as the following data extracts suggest:

Extract 3.4

```
. . . people in my feedback group tend to stick with positive
things to say (.) I sometimes feel it's not all sincere (.)
you kinda feel like you're expected to say something (.) you
go round in turns (.) first its self-evaluation then its peer
and then the tutor comes in with the final word (Gemma)
```

In extract 3.4, Gemma comments on the feedback process, making the point that most TLs tend to provide positive feedback on each other's performance, and commenting on the order of feedback: self, peer and tutor. Without more detail in the transcript, it is difficult to ascertain whether or not Gemma feels dissatisfaction with this procedure, though she does point to a lack of sincerity. McCabe et al. (2009) make similar observations concerning the need for more variable approaches to the reflective feedback procedure.

In the second extract (3.5), the researcher (Joan) is commenting on the kind of feedback available in the CELTA she has just finished.

Extract 3.5

```
1. Joan:  OK. What sorts of feedback have you found the most helpful and
2.        the least helpful?
3. Carla: Mmm
4. Ruby:  For me things which are activities which are designed to draw
5.        people out actually I personally find a bit tedious and time
6.        wasting and I (.) I- I would rather have somebody particularly the
7.        assessor say "this is what I felt about it."
8. Joan:            [Mm
9. Ruby:  Bish bash bosh.
```

(from Copland and Mann, 2010: 188)

Ruby clearly has a preference for a knowledge transmission approach even though some of the trainers on this CELTA were aiming for a more elicitation/reflective style of working. In this group, the other TLs agree that they are much more interested in what the trainer has to say than their peers. Akbari (2007) argues that a reflective model might not always be in the best interests of novice teachers. He suggests that trainees in the beginning stages of their careers are more concerned with self-image and approbation than they are with improving students' or their own learning. Although there are many aspects of Akbari's indictment of RP that we would disagree with, it is undoubtedly true that, particularly on short courses, TLs can get locked into a promotion of a positive self-image.

Roberts (1998: 59) also worries that the combined demands of formal assessment and the 'disguise of personal weakness' combine to make RP impossible. One paper that is particularly jaundiced in positioning teachers as inauthentic producers of reflective texts is Thomas and Liu (2012: 215). They look at evidence in their students' written reflections:

> Results indicate that prospective teachers tend to showcase or 'sunshine' their teaching and learning experiences rather than reflect on them analytically and critically. This 'sunshining' is accomplished by carelessly using academic buzzwords, whitewashing negative experiences by using downtoners and blaming others for problems in their classrooms as expressed in their online reflections.

Although they offer reasonably self-explanatory inductive codes (sunshining, buzzwording, blameshifting and downtoning) there is a failure to acknowledge their own involvement in the co-construction of an evaluative context. Instead, the article adopts what we would describe as a rather 'haughty tone' where they see the teachers as tending to 'blame others for their mistakes even when they clearly feel guilty' (2012: 315). It is probably better to value the small steps that novice teachers are able to take at this stage of their career than to fall further into a discourse of blame and guilt. It might be better to see these reflective efforts as playing with the language of reflection just as they try things and experiment with teaching practice. There are clearly frustrations and potential for disappointment on both sides.

Before we leave the CELTA type context, we finish with a reflexive vignette from Jo-Ann Delaney. We think this raises issues beyond feedback forms, CELTA criteria and standards, and POCs. It stresses the importance in reflective terms of what happens between peers and between 'knowledgeable others':

JO-ANN'S VIGNETTE

Context

The participant ('O') was attending a pre-service introductory ELT teacher education course (CELTA) delivered part-time over 20 weeks. The participant had no previous teaching experience before starting the course. The data below features an interview. This was the second of three carried out over the duration of the CELTA course and took place at approximately 14 weeks. The participant was asked to describe key learning moments that had taken place since the previous interview.

Data

J-A: And when you, when you get feedback from your peers
       and from the tutor, can you think of any particular
       in (.) particular bit of feedback that's been very
       valuable and you've implemented in your next lesson
       or something that's moved you on in terms of your
       teaching?

O: One thing that comes up time and time again for me and
       I think for J as well is the language grading thing.
       That's a really big (.) big deal. So that's helping me
       thinking about that. Just in terms of the instructions
       I give and just making sure that students understand
       me. Because I think when I'm thinking about my
       instructions I'm then (.) I'm just making sure that
       they are engaged and like, completely understand
       everything that I'm saying. So that's been really
       helpful.

J-A: So in the feedback these things are pointed out to
       you (.) that you need to work on your grading and
       instruction?

O: Yeah.

J-A: How do you go about then transforming what you do in
       the lesson? Where do you get that knowledge from?

O: Well that's hard isn't it? That's something that I've
       struggled with for the last four weeks and then

actually this (.) I mean I know this is outside of the realms of the course but I had a discussion with my mentor this week on Friday and he gave us a really sort of useful practical advice on how to implement these things. And that's something that we haven't really had in the course. There's a (.) it's a lot of like conceptual ideas. And I don't think that's (.) I'm not saying that as a criticism but it's quite hard to (.) I don't know, perhaps he just phrased it in a way that I really sort of understood.

J-A: What did he say to you? (.) Did he say (.)

O: He gave us some (.) he just gave us some practical examples of, you know, "this is something that you do. What you could do instead is this." "This is some . . . a way you present this material, but what you could do instead is this." So that, it was really sort of specific to me and what I'd done in the past and what ways that I kind of (.) tendencies that I had towards certain (.) you know (.) methods in the classroom. So that was really useful.

J-A: And did you find then that the next lesson (.) that actually helped what you had been doing?

O: Yeah, massively. So I taught a lesson on the (.) my first observation for the other course I am doing and I got some good feedback but I also got some bad feed-back. Well not bad feedback but things to improve on and, and then D (.) and sat down and we talked and then I had another lesson almost directly after it, after this discussion and I think he was a lot more happy about where I was at. And I was a lot more happy about the learning that went on in the classroom.

J-A: Yeah. And in between those two lessons it was about getting feedback and the reflection?

O: In between those two lessons it was about thinking about what D said to me. I got the feedback from him and then I really kind of tried to think about ways that I could be more creative with what I was doing, so yeah, that was really useful.

In the extract above a trainee on an initial ESOL teacher training course is describing the way feedback from his tutor on the course and his mentor in the workplace have helped him learn. His account illustrates the value of reflection with a 'knowledgeable other'; it refers to inter-action between the teacher who is thinking about their practice and the instructional input from a more experienced teacher (D).

The description of the reflective process reveals that the trainee (O) is aware of the impact of his actions on his learners. In particular he is conscious that the lack of clarity in his instructions is having a negative effect on the learners' understanding and this motivates him to change. On teacher education programmes it is often the case that tutors and trainees reflect on and evaluate teaching, but the learners can be neglected. The extract suggests that O's learners' responses are initiating some of his reflection and that he is motivated to learn and change because of them.

The most useful contribution from O's mentor seems to be feedback that provides procedural knowledge, and O values the practical advice on how to implement strategies in the classroom. He contrasts this with conceptual knowledge gained on his course and which he appreciates, but which is not as helpful in supporting his understanding of his practice. This procedural knowledge is not simply a recipe which O follows without thinking. He uses the practical advice to reflect and then generate more creative ways to implement changes in his classroom. In other words, having a procedural framework seems to generate a creative response, rather than binding the trainee to a prescribed formula.

Finally, O's reflection is a mix of his own thinking and what his mentor said. He is using input from the 'knowledgeable other' to generate his reflections. This would suggest the value of formal, instructional feedback for trainees, but also that ongoing professional development is enhanced by opportunities to discuss practice with other teachers and peers.

Jo-Ann's vignette reveals the value of novice teachers having conversations with and input from mentors in schools (not just CELTA tutors). The interview reveals the complex relationship between reflecting over time, drawing on responses from language learners in TP and using practical advice from mentors such as 'D' as a resource. It is especially important to note Jo-Ann's confirmation that more practical or procedural advice can generate creative responses and is not just a case of following a recipe (see also Delaney, 2015). In addition, the vignette demonstrates the potential value of interviewing (or at least talking to) novice teachers. Appendix 6 features another vignette (Rana Yildirim and Esra Orsdemir in Turkey) that also demonstrates how much a tutor can learn by talking to novice teachers about their reflective processes.

3.3 BA and MA Courses

Our discussion so far has highlighted some of the issues relating to RP on CELTA courses. We now consider longer, and sometimes more advanced, programmes such as those offered on BA and MA degrees. These courses have more time and potential to foster reflection as a lifelong professional practice, as opposed to a tool for assessment (although constraints still remain). Although BA students tend to take three or four years and MAs one year to complete their courses, we treat these contexts within the same section. However, in doing so, we are talking about MA students with no or very little teaching experience. Often MA programmes actually have teachers with very different levels of experience. Chapter 4 is more concerned with working with experienced teachers on MA programmes. In what follows, we develop two themes which will be taken up in subsequent chapters. These are space (for reflection) and online or blended approaches to reflection.

Space for Reflection

BA and MA students have more available time and space to 'bridge the gap' to the realities of classroom teaching (Farrell, 2012). They are usually able to incorporate a wider range of opportunities than CELTA courses. As we said above, many of the challenges are still there (especially the problem of assessment and evaluation) but, in addition to the ubiquitous teaching practice, a number of recent accounts in BA contexts have shown how reflection can be fostered through school-based processes of teaching shadowing (Erkmen, 2013) and ethnographic observation (Lengeling, 2013). The particular strength of Erkmen's innovation is the way in which she scaffolds the shadowing experience in order to enable trainees to make informed and reflective judgments about just what to 'copy'. The value of Lengeling's work lies in the ways that an ethnographic approach builds 'objectivity' through 'estrangement'. This ethnographic approach provides a new basis for awareness-raising and the building of reflective capacities.

One of the ways in which reflection can be maximized and optimized is through the establishment of a school-based relationship, such as a mentor or critical friend. In extracts 3.6(a) and (b) below, we present data to illustrate the value of this approach. Eline is a trainer on a PRESET programme that prepares students for teaching English as a second language to learners at elementary pre-intermediate and intermediate levels. The following data-set is from a PRESET undergraduate course in the Netherlands. The IDEE (International Degree in English and Education) is a four-year undergraduate degree programme offered by the Amsterdam University of Applied Sciences. During the first year, the students work with a school-based mentor. Here, we see the trainer (Eline) engaging her first year TLs in an exploration of the principles that underlie their particular mentor's teaching.

Extract 3.6(a)

```
6     M      . . . and this article said that reading for concept
7            information is important (.) it gives information about
8            authentic reading material and an authentic purpose for
9            reading (.) and my link teacher agreed with this(.)
10           she said it was important for their tertiary education to
```

```
11              read other things than English reading(.)
12   Eline      Can you give an example of an authentic purpose for reading?
13   M          Yes (.) if you look at Biology <for example> they have
14              to look at different texts (.) It's not about
15              the English use but it's about the subject
16              that you're studying (1.0) My link teacher, she talks about
17              concepts which is a specific thing that she does
18              before they are going to read a text (.) this
19              is part of pre-teaching (.) If the text is really detailed
20              it helps the learner to activate appropriate schema
21              is what I found out
```

(lines missing)

```
81   M          And I read about this in another article which
82              says it's important to help them combine skills
83              which is the same as a real life situation where
84              they do the same thing (.) combining it with speaking or
85              writing for example(.) This is a better way of assessing
86              them than solely answering questions for their exam (.)
87   Eline      So it seems that you made a move <if I might rephrase >
88              from "the way to teach students to read is to have them
89              read lots of texts and then answering questions on
90              those which are similar to the exam" to
91              "you should teach them how to read"(.)
92   M          Yes I think it's important to do both (.)because you
93              still need to be able to answer those questions (.) but
94              then they are able to be independent when they move
95              to tertiary education or work (.) I think that's
96              important as well(.)
97   Eline      So this whole idea that it's about them being independent
98              of you also automatically changes the way that you can
99              teach them, or should teach them?
100  M          Yes
```

The TLs have been introduced to concept mapping as a technique to first make explicit their own knowledge and beliefs (about the teaching and learning of reading, speaking or vocabulary) and then asked to uncover their mentor's practical knowledge about these same aspects. Students analyze both maps with the use of an article about the same topic. In an oral evaluation, students commented on the key issues they had uncovered, on possible (dis)agreements between the various sources and on new insights they had developed as a result of the project. In the extract above, we see how M has developed a close understanding both of the value of teaching students how to read and of the importance of recognizing key concepts in academic texts. She demonstrates a high level of awareness about reading as a process and uses metalanguage to talk about her teaching (pre-teaching, schema, etc.).

Eline's reflexive commentary on extract 3.6(a) is presented below in extract 3.6(b):

Extract 3.6(b)

COMMENT FROM TRAINER (ELINE)

Asking students to compare and contrast multiple sources seems to have several effects. First, it seems to add depth to the discussion that can be had with the mentor. M and her mentor agree that learners should read as much as possible. However, M has read in the article that authenticity is important too. She puts this idea to her mentor, who is thus encouraged to consider this issue and to comment on it.

Significantly, M herself is pushed to consider different viewpoints. This becomes evident when the article studied does not substantiate her mentor's belief that learners should be read to. What's more, where M cannot envisage the practical implications of what she reads (as is the case when she considers assessment of reading), she branches out and reads around the topic of her own accord. As such, this approach seems to add depth to the student's internal dialogue, too.

M has developed a much more informed and rich view on developing reading comprehension than she had when the project began four weeks earlier. At this point, no formal course input had been given on teaching reading comprehension. Yet M shows understanding of some complex concepts and has developed the linguistic tools to express these concepts, too.

From extract 3.6(b), we make a number of observations which add weight to the arguments we put forward in Chapters 1 and 2. In the first instance, we note the value of this dialogic and collaborative approach to reflection, both in the comments of the trainer Eline and in the reflections of the TL, 'M'. Eline refers to the 'internal dialogue' of M, a suggestion that M is appropriating new understandings from her own experience teaching reading and from her reflections on that process. Eline also comments on the extent to which M demonstrates a sound understanding of new concepts and has the metalanguage ('linguistic tools') to talk about them. Also apparent in both sets of data is the realization of the importance of authenticity in teaching reading and of the value in reading around a particular topic. Both extracts 3.6(a) and (b) demonstrate the value of reflections which are dialogic and collaborative and which allow ownership of new understandings to emerge. These points will be developed and exemplified further in Chapter 8. Appendix 4 also presents Wallace and Woolger's (1991) four-stage process for establishing a more collaborative style of feedback and distinguishes different levels of 'authority' in intervention types and more 'facilitative' intervention types.

It is clear from Eline's data above that the space for school-based processes creates important affordances for reflection. These spaces allow for greater capacity for novice teachers to reflect on their teaching experiences. This is partly an opportunity to 'bridge the gap' to the realities of classroom teaching (Farrell, 2012), but it also presents a chance to reflect on what it means to actually be a teacher and to come to terms with aspects of an emerging teacher identity. The following vignette demonstrates aspects of this 'journey' through school-based training, as we see teachers negotiating their 'novice' identity. In important ways, the longer time and space that BA courses often have allows for reflecting on changes in identity.

FLORI'S VIGNETTE

Context

Data included in this vignette are from a study that aimed at observing the effects of an intervention to foster reflective practice (RP) among a group of eight pre-service teachers (PSTs) in a Mexican university. The participants were registered in the teaching practice module of the English Language undergraduate programme. The PSTs had to teach at least one hour a week in a public or a private school as a requirement. They had to co-teach with an in-service teacher (or lead teacher) and with a peer. The intervention was designed to include the use of various tools (especially a reflective journal and reflective group sessions) to trigger reflection. The tools also promoted specific values in order to engage the PSTs in the practice (collaborative and dialogic reflection, enquiry and a non-threatening environment). All the aforementioned components (tools, strategies and values) were deployed throughout five cycles of the action research project. One of the main themes that emerged in the study was shifts in the 'teacher-self'. The data below reveals details of how the PSTs reflected on their practicum and how they identified themselves as teachers. Each data extract is tagged (i.e. GR1 is Group Reflection 1 and JC4 is Journal Cycle 4) and they appear in different fonts, depending on whether they were spoken or written:

Data

Extract 1:
(GR1/
Chicharito/T43)

```
Students are usually late and out of
control during the class (.) I think this
is because I am not the real teacher of the
subject
```

Extract 2: (JC1/August/ R1/ll57–58)	My students are about my age; some of them cannot simply take the teacher seriously if he/she looks like them.
Extract 3: (JC2/August/ R2/ll134–156)	The thing is that now I am in that struggle of changing what I used to believe [. . .]. I used to be like "I want to have an easy life", "I don't want to stress", etc. This last semester I have started thinking differently. It is not only about earning a lot of money. Doing a good job as a teacher is also important. I need to think more of the students, whether they are learning or not. [. . .] now I think that I have to put more effort because of the children, not because of my grades [for the teaching practice]
Extract 4: (JC3/Laura/ R2/ll16–33)	According to the text you [the researcher] shared with us on Facebook (by Brown), constant preparation is a quality that good language teachers must have. I want to be good; thus, looking for solutions will allow me to improve my performance, which in the long run will benefit the students. [. . .] I want to be the kind of teacher that students get excited when they come to the classroom. I want them to enjoy my class and show them that learning the English language is not always boring. And last but not least, I want to be a role model for them (I want I lot of things, don't I?)
Extract 5: (JC4/August/ R1/ll1–20)	One of the most important things of this process is that I have built more confidence. [. . .] I have had the opportunity to get to know how children work. I know how to discipline them. I know some games and activities to make the class less boring and more dynamic, I have an idea of what topics they like and, most importantly, I know how they can react to all of these actions.
Extract 6: (JC4/Luna/R1/ ll39–44)	[. . .] most of the times the classes don't go as we expect but I still feel good because I have tried something new and I have gained the knowledge that maybe that activity doesn't work, or I could think of a different way to present it or perform it.
Extract 7: (GR5/Lea/T66)	At the end (.) it was good to know that we were able to help students [. . .] you notice that you were in the school for a month and you observe good results (.) as a teacher, you know you didn't waste your time(.) it was worth it

Extract 8:
(JC5/Luna/
II28–35)

In my teaching experience so far the most valuable thing I have learned about myself is that I have capability to be a good teacher. At first I wasn't sure if I would make a good teacher even if I really wanted to [. . .]. I know that there will be ups and downs but I have found a passion for this profession and I hope to keep it alive throughout the years.

Commentary

The sample data above illustrates how the PSTs saw themselves at the beginning of the intervention and how they identified themselves towards the end of it. For instance, in extract 1, the participant referred to himself as not being a real teacher, partly because the group he was teaching was not his group but someone else's. Similarly, in extract 2, it is apparent that the PST's concern is with not being taken seriously due to his relative youth. Miller (2009: 177) argues that PSTs 'often face identity crises in their search to be accepted as legitimate teachers'. There was a great deal of similar data showing the teachers' struggle to accept themselves as actual/legitimate teachers. They saw themselves as 'temporary' teachers, lacking power to make important decisions in the classroom (mainly concerning decisions about discipline problems).

As the intervention progressed, the participants started negotiating and reflecting on their priorities, looking for a balance between what they wanted as students of the teaching practice module and as teachers. They started analyzing what was more important to them: their students or themselves (e.g. extract 3). They also showed evidence that they were trying to improve their teaching practice by reflecting on the type of teacher they wanted to become, by learning how to be a good teacher, and giving priority to their students' learning (extract 4). As Miller (2009: 175) argues, identity is constantly 'co-constructed in situ' and the PSTs have a range of resources they assess as they negotiate and develop their 'identities in social and institutional context'. As they gained more experience, learned more about their students, and trialled new activities (see extracts 5 and 6), the PSTs consolidated their identities based on their own feeling of achievement, improvement and confidence in their teaching performance and classroom management. Evidence showed that some of the PSTs were able to express that they identified themselves as real and committed teachers at the final stage of the intervention. Despite feeling more confident, they are aware of the fact that they will continue facing problems and learning from them (extracts 6, 7 and 8). This is understandable, as a teacher's identity should be viewed as a never-ending process of forming, changing and becoming (Fottland, 2004) and 'is something that develops gradually over time as a teacher's own education and later teaching experiences begin to accumulate' (Furness, 2008: 151).

The data in Flori's study shows the various aspects of the teaching practice that the PSTs focused on. Her data is an illuminating insight into both the nature of their practical concerns and also how, through opportunities for reflection, some changes of perspective were apparent. Her data supports the view of Farrell (2009: 183) that the first year of teaching can be 'an anxiety-provoking experience that involves attempting to take on the identity of a "real" teacher'. However, her data also shows that over time and with supported reflection, teachers start to feel more comfortable and confident, as they document their achievement and improvement. Her PhD thesis (Dzay Chulim, 2015) shows the value in allowing novice teachers time to come to terms with practical concerns and identity negotiation before pushing them to so-called 'higher levels of reflection'. We all probably share Larrivee's (2008: 358) desire to 'facilitate movement towards higher levels of reflection'. However, we doubt whether novice teachers necessarily move through level 1 (pre-reflection) to level 2 (surface reflection) to level 3 (pedagogical reflection) to level 4 (critical reflection). For Dzay Chulim the difficulty is that this hierarchical order of reflection thinking is essentially a top-down construct and is not derived from data. In addition, it values one kind of reflection more than another. Larrivee suggests that a potential value of 'assessing development as a reflective practitioner' could be in a collaborative dialogue format. This can jointly set goals that would 'facilitate movement towards becoming a reflective practitioner' (Larrivee, 2008: 358). It could, but it could just as easily get in the way. It may be that teacher learners (TLs) would benefit from talking about reflection and even seeing different peer reflections, but it is also possible that a hierarchical model might push TLs to try to display reflections they think are more prized.

Jay and Johnson also provide a justification for a pedagogy for reflection which aims to move teachers from 'superficial reflection' to the goal of 'deep reflection' (2002: 2). In fact, most models and descriptions of reflection move from a descriptive kind of reflection to a more critical reflection. Watts and Lawson (2009) is another example of a study designed to make critical reflection more explicit. Although we would agree that critical reflection is important and that teachers should 'recognize and value the importance of reflecting on frames, biases, assumptions, or social, moral, and political aspects of schooling' (Jay and Johnson, 2002: 76), we would question whether this is necessarily a higher level. Reflection is important for more utilitarian, instrumental and problem-solving situations and there at least needs to be a balance struck between a macro-level critical engagement and a more micro-level class- and interaction-based engagement. Gilpin (1997) offers a useful counterpoint to the two models above and has reflective elements such as noticing, reasoning, analysis, questioning, affective involvement and change.

Online Reflection

Our argument throughout this chapter (and the book) is that we need to give more attention to how the process of working with TLs promotes reflection. For example, does the use of web-based portfolios for developing pre-service teachers' reflective skills work in different ways from keeping paper-based versions? Oner and Adadan (2011) argue that a set of reflection-based tasks can enrich PRESET teachers' internship experiences. They detail an increase in the number of 'high-level reflective indicators' over time, but they also provide useful detail about the implementation of the web-based platform, including evidence from participants who collectively appreciate the easy access to portfolio artefacts. The primary purpose of the portfolios may be to assess teacher performance (Watson and Doolittle, 2011), but they may also prove useful for showcasing their work to prospective employers (Kimball, 2003).

Portfolio assessment can also build insight over time. Novice teachers can look back on their development as teachers as well as make connections between different experiences by revisiting their portfolios. Both Tanner et al. (2000) and Mansvelder-Longayroux et al. (2007) show how portfolio assessment can support the reflective process in this way. Tanner et al. (2000) suggest specific training ideas to help students acquire the necessary skills to compile portfolios, which allows awareness of the development of their teaching competencies. Mansvelder-Longayroux et al. (2007) also found that guidance on the production of portfolios seemed to be essential.

Whatever the medium (paper based, online, face-to-face), there needs to be a balance between a pedagogy for the development of reflection and its assessment. We have established that there are difficulties in assessing reflection and also dangers (Larrivee, 2008). Especially where RP takes the form of a checklist, a desire to both raise and assess the level of reflection may actually inhibit RP development. It may well be useful to assess levels of reflection, but this needs to be clearly differentiated from its promotion. Mann and Tang (2012) show how an unwieldy checklist approach to mentoring may well get in the way of engagement, interaction and reflection.

3.4 Contexts without PRESET

We said above that, although we have chosen to treat these two contexts (INSET and PRESET) separately, we are aware that this distinction is sometimes difficult to sustain. The last short section of this chapter considers contexts where teachers may have little or no PRESET training at all and have to learn as they go. Leo Mercado works in Peru, where the lack of qualified professionals in the job market often obliges language teaching institutions to hire and work with people who do not have pre-service training. He is responsible for teacher development at the Instituto Cultural Peruano Norteamericano (ICPNA) in

Lima, Peru. Within Leo's context, the team have developed a project called IMMERSE. This is a multi-tiered, comprehensive professional development model that allows novice teachers without training to develop their professional competence in a relatively short period of time. The following extract is typical of the kinds of comments expressed by teachers on the programme.

Extract 3.7

> *My first experience as an English teacher was terrible and quite disheartening. I almost gave up on it altogether. But I tried once more at ICPNA, and it's been completely different. They gave me the training I needed to succeed in the classroom from the very beginning. Now I am really happy with what I do*
>
> *Gabriel Dawling (1st year teacher)*

One of the key elements of the IMMERSE project is the reflective and collaborative style of group meetings. In addition, reflective practice is embedded in the various elements of the project, particularly in lesson planning, microteaching, class observation, group meetings and opportunities for reflective writing.

In extract 3.8 below, we experience some of the frustrations of Leo, a trainer, during the early stages of his career. We have included this extract to highlight the need for teacher professional groups and in order to emphasize the importance of collaboration in teacher professional development, especially in contexts where there is no structured, formal PRESET.

Extract 3.8

COMMENT FROM TRAINER (LEO)

I look back to January 1997, which is when I began my career at the Institute. I was an *expat* from another field who had just started working as an English teacher less than a year and half before, with no formal education or previous training in the field worth mentioning. I found several initiatives that are still in place today: the pre-service seminar, teacher development (TD) meetings, and teacher-supervisor orientation sessions. When I began, I immediately noticed the enormous difference compared to my previous work experiences. Even before my first month, I had already been invited to a previously arranged teacher development (TD) meeting, where we celebrated the arrival of Christmas with carols, hot chocolate and much cheer. Needless to say, this alone was enough to make me feel like I had become a part of something very special.

Once I actually began working at the Institute, I met with the academic supervisors, much as a new teacher still does today. They gave me the guidance I needed to make it through that first month,

> which was a trial period that could have just as easily resulted in a quick farewell. Over the next few months, I began to look forward to the TD meetings. By the time I finished my first year, I realized – unlike any other time before it – that English language teaching was the field in which I wanted to stay. That end result was something I would seek to replicate years later with new teachers in the various positions to which I would be promoted: academic supervisor, academic branch manager, assistant academic director and finally academic director.

One of the key development elements for Leo is the group meetings. Overall, the feeling of belonging to a group/community of practice is evident in both Leo's experience and the experience of teachers who follow the IMMERSE programme. The programme is born out of necessity but offers an alternative way of bridging the gap between the training process and the school environment. In Chapters 6 and 7, we present a range of tools for reflection which might be used by teachers working in relatively unsupported environments like those we have featured in 3.4.

3.5 Summary

In this chapter, we have outlined some of the issues pertaining to RP in a range of PRESET contexts. It is probably fair to say that PRESET is simultaneously the most challenging and the most important context in terms of the development of reflective practice. There needs to be a 'start as you mean to go on' attitude to RP. If there is no encouragement of RP in this context, it is much less likely to happen later. We would make the argument that RP should not simply be an institutional requirement that is 'tagged on' to a teaching practice/practicum in the form of a journal. Rather, it should be more systematically embedded in the whole process and especially in feedback conferences. In later chapters, we will consider how this might occur through the use of more systematic procedures and appropriate tools.

Although RP is apparently 'done' on PRESET programmes and appears in policy and curriculum documents, we argue that, despite a few exceptions (e.g. Korthagen and Wubbels, 1995) it is not operationalized. The operationalization of RP requires a more systematic approach using appropriate tools and approaches which promote understanding and awareness and focus less on problem-solving (Allwright and Hanks, 2009). This systematic approach needs to cope with the demands of assessment but not be determined by it. It needs to value different forms of reflection without rushing to more prized forms (i.e. critical reflection). Perhaps even more important is the need to disenfranchise RP from the demands of the course or institution where it is taking place. Through the examples presented in this chapter, we have tried to demonstrate how RP is often constrained by an institutional or assessment agenda.

Only by embedding RP as a key element of professional practice can this agenda be modified. This discussion is taken up in Chapters 6 to 8.

References

Akbari, R. (2007). Reflections on reflection: a critical appraisal of reflective practices in L2 teacher education. *System: An International Journal of Educational Technology and Applied Linguistics*, 35(2), 192–220.

Allwright, D. and Hanks, J. (2009). *The developing language learner: an introduction to exploratory practice*. Basingstoke: Palgrave Macmillan.

Atkinson, B.M. (2012). Strategic compliance: silence, 'Faking it,' and confession in teacher reflection. *JCT (Online)*, 28(1), 74.

Brandt, C. (2006). Allowing for practice: a critical issue in TESOL teacher preparation. *ELT Journal*, 60(4), 355–364.

Brandt, C. (2008). Integrating feedback and reflection in teacher preparation. *ELT Journal*, 62(1), 37–46.

Braun, J. A. and Crumpler, T.P. (2004). The social memoir: an analysis of developing reflective ability in a pre-service methods course. *Teaching and Teacher Education*, 20(1), 59–75.

Clarà, M. (2015). What is reflection? Looking for clarity in an ambiguous notion. *Journal of Teacher Education*, 66(3), 261–271.

Copland, F. (2011). Negotiating face in the feedback conference: a linguistic ethnographic approach. *Journal of Pragmatics*, 43(15), 3832–3843.

Copland, F. (2012). Legitimate talk in feedback conferences. *Applied Linguistics*, 33(1), 1–20.

Copland, F. and Mann, S. (2010). Dialogic talk in the post-observation conference: an investment in reflection. In G. Park (ed), *Observation of teaching: bridging theory and practice through research on teaching*. Lincom Europa Publishing.

De Bono, E. (1992). *Serious creativity: using the power of lateral thinking to create new ideas*. New York: Harper Collins.

Delaney, J. (2015). The 'dirty mirror' of reflective practice: assessing self- and peer- evaluation on a CELTA course. In R. Wilson and M. Poulter (eds), *Assessing language teachers' professional skills and knowledge* (pp. 91–112). Cambridge: Cambridge University Press.

Dzay Chulim, F.D. (2015). Pre-service teachers reflecting on their teaching practice: an action research study in a Mexican context (Unpublished doctoral dissertation). University of Warwick. Downloaded 10.10.15 at http://wrap.warwick.ac.uk/77716/

Edge, J. (1993). A framework for feedback on observation. *IATEFL TT SIG Newsletter*, 10, 3–4.

Edge, J. and Richards, K. (1998). May I see your warrant, please?: justifying outcomes in qualitative research. *Applied Linguistics*, 19(3), 334–356.

Erkmen, B. (2013). A shadowing experience for TEFL student-teachers. In J. Edge, and S. Mann (eds), *Innovations in pre-service education and training for English language teachers* (pp. 163–180). London: British Council.

Farr, F. (2006). Reflecting on reflections: the spoken word as a professional development tool in language teacher education. In R. Hughes (ed.), *Spoken English, TESOL and Applied Linguistics*. Basingstoke: Palgrave Macmillan.

Farrell, T.S.C. (2009). *Teaching reading to English language learners: a reflective guide*. Thousand Oaks, CA: Corwin.

Farrell, T.S.C. (2012). Reflecting on reflective practice: (re)visiting Dewey and Schön. *TESOL Journal*, 3(1), 7–16.

Ferguson, G. and Donno, S. (2003). One-month teacher training courses: time for a change? *ELT Journal*, 57(1), 26–33.

Fottland, H. (2004). Memories of a fledgling teacher: a beginning teacher's autobiography. *Teachers and Teaching*, 10(6), 639–662.

Furness, A. (2008). Formation of ESL teacher identity during the first year: an introspective study. In T.S.C. Farrell (ed.), *Novice language teachers, insights and perspectives for the first year* (pp. 150–158). Equinox Publishing Ltd.

Gilpin, A. (1997). Cascade training: sustainability or dilution? In I. McGrath (ed.), *Learning to train: perspectives on the development of language teacher trainers* (pp. 8–9). Hemel Hempstead: Prentice Hall.

Harford, J. and MacRuairc, G. (2008). Engaging student teachers in meaningful reflective practice. *Teaching and Teacher Education*, 24(7), 1884–1892.

Harris, A.R. (2013). Professionals developing professionalism: the interactional organisation of reflective practice (Unpublished PhD thesis). University of Newcastle. Downloaded 10.10.15 at https://theses.ncl.ac.uk/dspace/bitstream/10443/2354/1/Harris,%20A.%2013.pdf

Hepburn, A. and Wiggins, S. (2007). *Discursive research in practice: new approaches to psychology and interaction*. Cambridge: Cambridge University Press.

Hobbs, V. (2007). Faking it or hating it: can reflective practice be forced? *Reflective Practice*, 8(3), 405–417.

Holliday, A. (1994). *Appropriate methodology and social context*. Cambridge: Cambridge University Press.

Husu, J., Patrikainen, S. and Toom, A. (2007). Developing teachers' competencies in reflecting on teaching. In J. Butcher and L. McDonald (eds), *Making a difference: challenges for teachers, teaching and teacher education* (pp. 127–140). Amsterdam: Sense Publishers.

Husu, J., Toom, A. and Patrikainen, S. (2008). Guided reflection as a means to demonstrate and develop student teachers' reflective competencies. *Reflective Practice: International and Multidisciplinary Perspectives*, 9(1), 37–51.

Jay, J.K. and Johnson, K.L. (2002). Capturing complexity: a typology of reflective practice for teacher education. *Teaching and Teacher Education*, 18(1), 78–85.

Kimball, M.A. (2003). *The web portfolio guide: creating electronic portfolios for the web*. New York: Longman.

Korthagen, F.A.J. and Wubbels, T. (1995). Characteristics of reflective practitioners: towards an operationalization of the concept of reflection. *Teachers and Teaching*, 1, 51–72.

Larrivee, B. (2008). Development of a tool to assess teachers' level of reflective practice. *Reflective Practice: International and Multidisciplinary Perspectives*, 9(3), 341–360.

Lee, I. (2007). Preparing pre-service English teachers for reflective practice. *ELT Journal*, 61, 321–329.

Lengeling, M. (2013). Borrowing the use of ethnographic notes from the social sciences for classroom observation in central Mexico. In J. Edge and S. Mann (eds), *Innovation in pre-service teacher education and training* (pp. 66–88). London: British Council.

Mann, S. and Edge, J. (2013). Innovation as action new-in-context: an introduction to the PRESETT collection. In J. Edge and S. Mann (eds), *Innovations in pre-service education and training for English language teachers* (pp. 5–13). London: British Council.

Mann, S. and Tang, H.H. (2012). The role of mentoring in supporting novice English teachers in Hong Kong. *TESOL Quarterly*, 46, 472–495.

Mann, S. and Walsh, S. (2013). RP or 'RIP': a critical perspective on reflective practice. *Applied Linguistics Review*, 4(2), 291–315.

Mansvelder-Longayroux, D.D., Beijard, D. and Verloop, N. (2007). The portfolio as a tool for stimulating reflection by student teachers. *Teaching and Teacher Education*, 23, 47–62.

Matsuda, A. (2014). Beyond the native speaker: my life as an NJS, NNES, and bilingual user of Japanese and English. NNESTNewsletter: The Newsletter of the TESOL NNEST Interest Section. Available at http://newsmanager.commpartners.com/tesolnnest/issues/2014-09-09/2.html

McCabe, M., Walsh, S., Wideman, R. and Winter, E. (2009). The R word in teacher education: understanding the teaching and learning of critical reflective practice. *International Electronic Journal for Leadership in Learning*, 13(7), 271–283.

Medgyes, P. (1992). Native or non-native: who's worth more? *ELT Journal*, 46(4), 340–349.

Mercer, N. and Howe, C. (2012). Explaining the dialogic processes of teaching and learning: the value and potential of sociocultural theory. *Learning, Culture and Social Interaction*, 1(1), 12–21.

Miller, J. (2009). Teacher identity. In A. Burns and J. Richards (eds), *The Cambridge guide to second language teacher education* (pp. 172–181). New York: Cambridge University Press.

Moore, A. and Ash, A. (2003). Reflective practice in beginning teachers: helps, hindrances and the role of the critical other. Paper presented at the Annual Conference of the British Educational Research Association, University of Exeter, England, 12–14 September 2002. Downloaded on 12.12.15 at www.leeds.ac.uk/educol/documents/00002531.htm

Morton, T. and Gray, J. (2010). Personal practical knowledge and identity in lesson planning conferences on a pre-service TESOL course. *Language Teaching Research*, 14(3), 297–317.

Oner, D. and Adadan, E. (2011). Use of web-based portfolios as tools for reflection in preservice teacher education. *Journal of Teacher Education*, 62(5), 477–492.

Piller, I. (2001). Who, if anyone, is a native speaker? *Anglistik*, 12(2), 109–121.

Rampton, B. (1990). Displacing the 'native speaker': expertise, affiliation, and inheritance. *ELT Journal*, 44(2), 97–101.

Roberts, J. (1998). *Language teacher education*. London: Arnold.

Tanner, R., Longayroux, D., Beijaard, D. and Verloop, N. (2000). Piloting portfolios: using portfolios in pre-service teacher education. *ELT Journal*, 54(1), 20–30.

Thomas, M. and Liu, K. (2012). The performance of reflection: a grounded analysis of prospective teachers' eportfolios. *Journal of Technology and Teacher Education*, 20(3), 305–330.

Tudor Jones, C. (2012). A reflective inquiry into post-observation multiparty feedback (Unpublished dissertation). University of Warwick.

Wallace, M.J. and Woolger, D. (1991). Improving the ELT supervisory dialogue: the Sri Lankan experience. *ELT Journal*, 45(4), 320–327.

Walsh, S. and Mann, S. (2015). Doing reflective practice: a data-led way forward. *ELT Journal*, 69(4), 351–362.

Watson, C.E. and Doolittle, P.E. (2011). ePortfolio pedagogy, technology, and scholarship: now and in the future. *Educational Technology*, 51(5), 29–33.

Watts, M. and Lawson, M. (2009). Using a meta-analysis activity to make critical reflection explicit in teacher education. *Teaching and Teacher Education*, 25(5), 609–616.

Zottmann, J. M., Goeze, A., Frank, C., Zentner, U., Fischer, F. and Schrader, J. (2012). Fostering the analytical competency of pre-service teachers in a computer-supported case-based learning environment: a matter of perspective? *Interactive Learning Environments*, 20(6), 513–532.

4

In-service Teacher Education

4.1 Introduction

This chapter turns our attention to in-service teacher education. We consider some of the major challenges for in-service teacher education (INSET) and ways of overcoming them. We also concentrate on ways of making RP systematic and data-led. In doing so, we integrate viewpoints from both teacher trainers and student teachers. In reviewing the literature, we have found that accounts of in-service teacher education (INSET) vary considerably. They vary from the positively rosy and optimistic:

> In-service education is the elixir of life for teachers. It protects their professional health and often lends a golden touch to their activities.
>
> *Yadav, 2012: xv*

to much bleaker perspectives:

> The findings of this research showed that there is an urgent need for rebuilding and redesigning INSET programs regarding certain important factors that may help in producing better and more effective programs than the current ones.
>
> *Aldhaen, 2012: 226*

In this chapter we ask two main questions. What makes a good INSET programme? How can reflection be fostered within an INSET course? These interrelated questions form the basis of this chapter. The evidence presented in Chapters 1 and 2 suggests that a contextually appropriate and systematic approach to embedding reflection in teacher education is likely to help achieve effective INSET, but how is this best done? As in Chapter 3, Chapter 4 will demonstrate how working towards a systematic approach to reflective practice involves integrating specific tasks and procedures. In doing so, we will also consider various options and challenges in promoting reflection.

Chapter 4 integrates views from practitioners who have experience of delivering successful courses. It also integrates views from teachers taking the courses. Of course, reflective practice is not the only successful ingredient in appropriate INSET provision. However, a good course is more likely to provide a platform for teacher reflection, both during the course and beyond it. What factors do teachers value in describing 'a good course'? As well as considering the aspects of course design that are more likely to promote reflection, we will also discuss various constraints and difficulties that limit the effectiveness of INSET.

In Chapter 3, we concentrated on PRESET. There are obviously important differences between the nature of PRESET and INSET and the profile of the participants, most importantly because INSET teachers have teaching experience. However, in-service training also varies considerably in the length and nature of courses. INSET courses range from one-year or two-year MA courses to a relatively short training course which, although typically one to four weeks, can be as short as one day. Chapter 4 covers a range of course types and focuses on several contexts, because this will help show that reflection is conceived and co-constructed in particular and sometimes systematic ways depending on the nature of the course and who the participants are. We start by considering university-based Masters level programmes, and then look at other professional qualifications (in this case DELTA). We finish the chapter by considering shorter INSET courses.

4.2 A Systematic Approach to INSET

This section considers options for embedding reflective practice in in-service teacher education. It concentrates on Masters level INSET. As we have seen in Chapter 1, there is no shortage of books and articles that argue that reflective practice is important for teachers. This is the orthodox position. There is, however, a lack of detail regarding systematic attempts to operationalize reflective practice in teacher education. Nelson and Sadler (2013: 54) argue that if we agree that the development of reflection within teacher education programs is an important outcome, then we need to:

> increase our awareness of our own ideas with respect to both (a) the meaning, value, and purpose of reflection; and (b) the deliberate experiences through which that development is meant to occur.

This chapter is concerned primarily with raising awareness of (b). If we want to develop teachers' understanding, sharing and experience of reflection, we need to consider how it can be operationalized. How then can educators make the experience and development of reflective practice 'deliberate'?

The following list presents some of the choices that we have at MA level in terms of operationalizing reflective practice. These are not 'either/or' choices and might best be seen as 'blend elements':

- having a *discrete module* called 'Reflective Practice' within the programme;
- providing opportunities for *reflective writing across different modules,* perhaps in the form of a reflective portfolio;

- incorporating *reflective tasks and discussion* across different modules. Modules might involve tasks which encourage the sharing and articulation of learning and teaching experiences. They might also include reflection grids to bring out the significance of tasks;
- enabling teachers and tutors to interact online through wikis, VLEs (virtual learning environments) and other online tools;
- evaluating reflection as part of an assignment, either as one of the marking criteria or by requiring a section of the assignment to perhaps reflect on the learning in the module as a whole;
- giving feedback in a form which encourages reflection (i.e. formative and dialogic).

In reference to the list above, our experience suggests that the way reflective practice is treated in in-service language teacher education varies considerably across different institutions. For this reason, we think it is a good idea to start this chapter with an account of a deliberate and sustained attempt to place reflective practice at the heart of a Masters programme. Tony Wright, formerly of 'Marjon' (University of St Mark & St John, Plymouth), has written a vignette below which looks back on his experience of postgraduate student reflective writing and feedback. We asked Tony because he led a programme with a very good reputation, established over many years. We have broken up his vignette into different sections so that we can make further comment. Some of the students come from the MEd programme and some are from postgraduate certificates consisting of two modules from the MEd list. Tony's data extracts and comments introduce a number of specific aspects of the postgraduate programmes and detail the ways in which reflection was made visible and concrete within that programme. Another strength of this vignette is that it includes both his comments and some examples of reflection from individual students.

TONY WRIGHT VIGNETTE (PART 1)

A postgraduate course provides multiple opportunities for reflection, and it would be rare for a professional on such a programme not to reflect on their previous experience of both practice and learning at some time during or after the course. When Rod Bolitho and myself worked together on the Masters programmes at Marjon in the 1990s and 2000s, the process of reflection was consciously built in to the course we ran for teacher educators in two main ways:

1. As an integral part of the learning processes initiated by formal sessions on the programme, using, for example, reflective 'grids' (Bolitho and Wright, 1993) as the basis for learning from experience, and 'thinking questions' (Wright and Bolitho, 2007).

2. As part of the feedback process on different course components, either orally or in writing. For a brief period we recorded our own reflections in 'course diaries' and shared extracts with participants to stimulate further reflective conversations. Eventually, however, we found maintaining our journals too time-consuming and stopped doing it. Such a process was a course in itself. We did, however, persist with requesting written feedback on course components we taught, and encouraged students to write whatever they wanted to write and in whatever form they chose. Many of the 'student voices' in *Trainer Development* (Wright and Bolitho, 2007) were extracted from written feedback.

As the programme developed and evolved over the years, and in response to what was seen as a strong trend in thinking in the field, reflective writing became a more integral part of our programmes at Marjon, and became embedded in the written assignments that the taught part of the course (by the early 2000s, 'modules') required. Our experience up to that time seemed to indicate that participants appreciated the opportunity to write about their experiences as a means of trying to make deeper sense and meaning out of them. The inclusion of reflective writing in assessment provided a spur to devising a more coherent approach.

Course participants were prepared for the reflective component of assessment through a series of short writing tasks. This happened during the different modules on a weekly basis and also on completion (or daily in intensively taught modules). The main reason for this was to provide opportunities to practise what was, for many, a novel type of writing. They were also exposed to anonymous samples of written reflection from previous students, from the professional literature, and our own reflections (my own log from the 1990s proved a rich source). The aim was to initiate their response to their own and the group's learning processes during a module, using reflective writing as a tool. The element became known as the 'portfolio' and required participants to select 'items' from the module that they considered significant in their own learning in the module, and which they saw influencing their future practice. The items were selected from the participants' own private learning logs and reading logs, and learning activities and experiences on the course. It might also include incidents from their working lives during the course (if the course was being followed part-time by working professionals). They even commented on the other assignments they were required to do. Some extracts from postgraduate portfolios follow, illustrating some of the many directions reflective writing by professionals can take.

In this first part of the vignette, we can see that this systematic approach was built up over several years. The portfolio was a space in which teachers had a great deal of choice about what to include (logs, incidents, comments on reading, etc.). For many students, reflective writing is a new form of expression and it does not necessarily come easily. It needs practice and the portfolio provides plenty of scope for exploration. There is also a strong sense that this all establishes a safe and secure environment for the expression of different and sometimes critical viewpoints. Feeling 'safe' has to be a pre-requisite for reflection to work well.

In what follows, Tony chooses extracts from different teacher educator portfolios to bring out different aspects of teachers' reflective writing. The first data extract (Gerald) makes clear that reflective writing is a process. Drafting and redrafting takes time, but at the same time opens up new ideas.

TONY WRIGHT VIGNETTE (PART 2)

Gerald's Extract

> The process of writing the assignments and the portfolios (this included!) has given me the opportunity to verbalise my thoughts and to refine my thinking (Behrens et al., 2002). Writing also forces me to ask questions about my practice. Generally, I am a slow writer as I have to write draft . . . after draft . . . after draft. However, I found that the time between my drafts allowed me ample time to think through an idea or a problem because by writing a draft I had begun to put my thoughts into tangible words (Nagin, 2006). During this 'time-between-drafts', I would suddenly think of a better word or a more appropriate phrase, I would suddenly realise that I have a better idea, I would suddenly obtain a solution to a problem. I felt that because I used writing as a thinking tool, it was easier for me to stay focussed on the task. As far as professional development is concerned, this is certainly true for me – nothing really existed until I began to write about it. (Ross, B. 1995 cited in Hancock, 2001). I am now determined to write more!
>
> Gerald

Tony's Comment

It is noticeable that in his reflection on elements of this writing process, Gerald repeatedly uses the word 'suddenly'. Reflective writing is a process which takes time to develop, but it also produces moments of insight as it proceeds. Thoughts take shape and become more 'tangible', sometimes leading to new ideas and even 'a solution to a problem'.

Through drafting and re-drafting, practitioners have time to revisit their thinking and, possibly, look at well-established practices in a new way. These reflective episodes may result in 'light-bulb moments' where, as Tony suggests in his vignette, sudden insights emerge, resulting in new understandings or solutions to old problems. Light-bulb moments may be the emergent realizations of extended periods of reflection, or sudden 'I've got it' moments which occur as the result of a stimulus (such as a piece of reflective writing or dialogue with a colleague); they may also occur in new situations where old issues are seen in a different light.

In the next extract, Basil makes clear how the experiential and reflective space that the MA programme provides highlighted a desire to take such reflective practice back into his professional life (his 'lecture rooms') and his CPD. He uses his portfolio to identify and discuss various difficulties he faces in his daily working life, and which have been highlighted by the course.

TONY WRIGHT VIGNETTE (PART 3)

Basil's Extract

> Amidst all these, it is I who have to decide to make a little difference in my own professional development. I would like to continue in the state of learning that I have experienced in the last twelve months by thinking of ways of experimenting with and introducing more experiential and reflective learning opportunities in my lecture rooms. All these years, I have gone about teaching in a more transmissive manner where I am in control of student learning. I would like to explore experiential learning and reflective learning which Moon (2004:74) says are 'forms of learning relatively independent of mediation.' Experiential learning and reflective learning allow for 'learning (to extend) beyond formal education and becomes very important in self-managed continuous professional development' (Moon, 2004:74).

In this next data extract, Kathleen picks out two comments from her own learning and reading logs. This is an interesting extract, because Kathleen not only feels able to be honest but also reveals what at least a substantial minority may secretly think about reflection. She draws on Hobbs to open up a discussion on reflection and its value for her.

TONY WRIGHT VIGNETTE (PART 4)

Kathleen's Extract

REFLECTION! REFLECTION! REFLECTION!

> • *Why is there no end to reflection? So much has been said but what exactly have we achieved in schools/ITEs? How many of us really know what it is? How serious are we about it?* (Learning Log)

> • *I seem to agree with Hobbs quite a lot. It's like she knows what I/many teachers feel. It's like, she's describing me!* (Reading Log)

I also identify with another observation of Hobbs, which is that reflective practice should be introduced slowly and in a 'non-threatening atmosphere' (Hobbs: 2007: 415). When reflection was introduced to the teachers in our context, we were given little conceptual understanding of it. The briefings that were given were mere gestures to show that some kind of conceptual understanding had been given. It was assumed that everyone knows the whats and the hows of reflection. From then, teachers were forced to write their reflection after every lesson. In a magical moment, all teachers were expected to be reflective practitioners. We were also given samples of how the reflection sentences would be phrased. The sentences were simple, stating how many percent of the students were able to do the task or meet the objectives set by the teacher at the beginning of the lesson . . . (that constituted reflection?!)

Amidst this backdrop, I was curious, and had wanted to do a study on reflection practice. My inquiry led me to Schön's reflective practice. After reading the book, I was even more puzzled. What the teachers were forced to do was rather different from what was said in the book. I also wondered why there was only one chapter on reflection-on-action. Without a platform and time to discuss and define my (or rather, lack of) understanding at that time, I dropped this topic and forgot about it.

Tony's Comment

In this example, Kathleen cites two 'items' from her learning and reading logs, and uses them to open up a discussion on reflection. Her data demonstrates challenges for reflective practice. One challenge is that, even on a course which has a strong rationale for requiring reflective writing and that makes an effort to establish the requisite rationale and atmosphere, not everyone will buy into and relish the process. However, this 'reflection about reflection' does at least reveal a dimension of trust within the MA programme. In other words, at least Kathleen feels comfortable enough to offer such a critique.

Tony Wright has said above that they 'encouraged students to write whatever they wanted to write and in whatever form they chose'. This allows for critical and dissenting voices (like Kathleen's). The view of reflective practice and its value is much less positive than in Gerald's above, but its engagement with Hobbs and Schön makes it equally valuable as a reflective text.

The last data extract gives an insight into an example where the reflective process is very successful. Although Hee Hee sees herself as a relative novice in terms of reflective practice, there are signs that the teacher education process ('my actions and practice in class') is feeding into her long-term development. In fact, the last extract from her portfolio assignment shows her consideration of various dimensions of reflective practice. Here, she is able to make progress in her own thinking regarding the use of reflection with her own students.

TONY WRIGHT VIGNETTE (PART 5)

Tony's Introduction to Hee Hee's Extract

Students are encouraged to revisit their 'learning logs' and 'reading logs' to promote deeper reflection. In this example, Hee Hee is reflecting further on her reading log. She uses the quote to examine her own assumptions. You can also see her considering to what extent she has become a reflective practitioner herself and whether there is more opportunity for passing on this way of being to her language learners. The extract immediately below is from her reading log. This is followed by her learning log (commenting on the reading log).

Hee Hee's Extract

Reflective practice has an allure that is seductive in nature because it rings true for most people as something useful and informing. However, for reflection to genuinely be a lens into the world of practice, it is important that the nature of reflection be identified in such a way as to offer ways of questioning taken-for-granted assumptions and encouraging one to see his or her practice through others' eyes. The relationship between time, experience, and expectations of learning through reflection is an important element of reflection, and to teach about reflection requires contextual anchors to make learning episodes meaningful.

Loughran, 2002: 33

. . . . for reflections to lead to valuable learning outcomes for student teachers and teacher educators, I believe it must be meaningful reflective practice.

Loughran, 2002: 33, Reading Log: 28/9/2011

The above quote by Loughran from his article 'Effective Reflective Practice: In search of Meaning of Learning about Teaching' is indeed enlightening and thought-provoking. Through my engagement with this article, I was inevitably lured into deep thinking about my own practice in teaching. A few inherent questions lingered in my mind: Can I call myself a reflective practitioner? If so, do I usually question taken-for-granted assumptions? Do I find opportunities to allow others to see my practice? Do I give my students opportunities to engage in reflections and learn from reflections? Do I teach them to reflect? Can I teach them to reflect? How do I do it? Do they have the attitudes as pre-requisites to reflections?

As I appraise myself, I could sense I still have so much to learn . . . I am still at the 'pre-mature' stage of a reflective practitioner. . . . though I think I do practise reflective teaching to a certain extent in terms of reflecting on my actions and practice in class. However, to pay heed to Loughran's second quote above, I need to constantly make a conscious effort to give my students opportunities to reflect and learn from their strengths and weaknesses so that their awareness will lead to taking actions to improve. As for my role, the challenge is to make my reflections available to my student teachers, or in other words as Loughran asserts . . . 'making the tacit explicit' which according to him, 'for teacher educators, ways of acting and the reasons that direct that action are made explicit when attempting to help others see what it is that matters in one's own practice.' (Loughran, 2002: 34). More importantly, I need to ensure that they have the attitudes as pre-requisites towards reflections. This means they are whole-hearted, responsible and open-minded as addressed in my research. Having said that, I believe that it is meaningless in articulating all those words unless we are able to WALK THE TALK and as such, I must make sure all those preaching do not elude me! (Hee Hee)

ISSUES STILL OUTSTANDING

I strongly feel that the journey of learning and discovery is one that is filled with many 'light-bulb moments' like what I am experiencing now. As this course comes to an end, there are yet some important outstanding issues noted below that I find need constant attention in ensuring that my journey of professional development continues to grow and progress smoothly.

- Complacency can stifle our professional development and so does the danger of treading way from the 'comfort zone'.
- There must be sheer persistence to develop in me and others, self-criticism skills and reflective attitude. To be reflective, I need to be open-minded, responsible and whole-hearted. (Dewey, 1933).
- To uphold and live up to what is expected of a 'reflective practitioner'. One of which is that we need to make our reflective self available to our students and how do we do that ? . . . (risky and challenging!)

Tony's Comment

Experience has shown that, with support in the form of 'training' (involving the examination of samples of reflective writing, tutor feedback on reflective comments and exercises, discussion in training room sessions on the role of reflection in professional life and learning, for example), participants not only write cogently and expressively

> about their experiences as learners, they make connections with their own practice, past, present and projected. They report that they enjoy this type of writing more than the traditional 'paper' form, and find it more relevant to their professional work. Initially reflective writing is seen as yet another burden, but with supportive feedback and a willingness to share one's own practice and reflective writing, most participants report real benefits from the experience, despite the inevitable tensions created by assessment (both for tutors and students). (Tony Wright, May 2016)

Taken as whole, Tony's vignette brings into focus several priorities for dealing systematically with RP:

- By making systematic use of tasks, thinking questions and grids, experiential and reflective spaces in INSET are created.
- There is an important 'training' dimension as tutors seek to build up familiarity with the practice of writing reflectively. One way this occurs is by recycling examples of other course participants' reflective writing.
- Reflective writing is a process which takes time and support from tutors, but which can produce moments of insight and real development.
- Portfolio writing gives teachers the chance to revisit learning and reading logs.
- Not all teachers value opportunities for reflection, and critical/sceptical voices need to be encouraged too. Reflective writing can also be a vehicle for challenging norms and authorities peddled by courses! Therefore, it is important to establish a trusting atmosphere where critical voices are equally valued.
- It can be useful to share the trainer's reflections too. This is partly a case of 'practising what you preach'.

Chapters 6 and 7 return to many of these themes. In particular, Chapter 6 picks up the vexed question of whether reflective writing should be assessed. As Tony says above, there are 'inevitable tensions' and there are undoubtedly both advantages and disadvantages in assessing reflective writing.

4.3 Connecting Theory to Practice

One of the problems for INSET is what Clarke (1994) has conceptualized as the theory–practice dysfunction. This is where theories (typically put forward by academics) are meant to be 'applied' in classrooms by teachers. Clarke argues that we should address this dysfunction in teacher education, and this chapter focuses on a particular course that tries to establish more equitable connections between practice and theory and make these as evident as possible.

In Chapter 9 we argue for the importance of practitioner research in challenging the theory–practice dysfunction. In this chapter we are considering how a teacher education programme can challenge this dysfunction.

There has been a general shift away from reliance on theory as input (a transmission model of teacher education) to a more constructivist model (Roberts, 1998). This trend has intensified in recent years in light of the increased attention and greater focus which have been given to socio-cultural theories of language learning and second language teacher education (e.g. Johnson, 2009). Despite this general movement, input is still deemed valuable and desirable on both pre- and in-service teacher education programmes. In the same way that CELTA candidates may expect clear pointers for improvement in their teaching, so some MA students may still expect high levels of input. This said, connections between theory and practice are much more likely to occur if, alongside input, there is collaborative discussion, where students are given opportunities to relate theories to both their own context and classroom practices.

The next vignette features an MA programme at Leeds Beckett University in the UK. This course is distinctive because it allows candidates the option of completing a Cambridge DELTA (Diploma in English Language Teaching to Adults) while working towards completion of an MA in TESOL. The Cambridge DELTA is a well known and highly regarded professional qualification which stresses the importance of reflection in its documentation. According to their website, it is one of the

> ... best-known and most popular advanced TEFL/TESOL qualifications in the world. It is a flexible way for experienced English language teachers to progress further in their careers. DELTA can be taken at any stage in a teacher's career and is ideal for those wanting to update their teaching knowledge and improve their practice.

One of the four key outcomes at the heart of the Cambridge DELTA is that teachers will be able to show employers that they 'can reflect on' their 'current beliefs and practices as a teacher'. The Cambridge DELTA aims to connect theory and practice through an assessed teaching practice (TP) which is an integral part of the course design.

HEATHER BUCHANAN'S VIGNETTE

Route One of the MA English Language Teaching at Leeds Beckett University has been designed to cater for the needs of experienced English language teachers who are interested in pursuing both an academic qualification and a professional one. In the first semester, students work towards the Cambridge DELTA, whilst also completing related assessments for MA modules. One of these modules is

Developing Professional Practice/DELTA module 2. In this module, students complete a series of action research cycles where they identify areas of strength and weakness, devise an action plan to work on their weaknesses and then reflect on their progress and the usefulness of the action plan (Professional Development Assignment, Part A). Students often find it useful to work with others to identify their strengths and weaknesses rather than reflecting in isolation; talking through techniques and experiences with peers and tutors often helps them to crystallize their ideas.

Teaching is also assessed as part of the module. Students are observed by tutors four times, and the following three assessment criteria relate to reflection:

a. Reflecting on and evaluating their own planning, teaching and the learners' progress as evidenced in this lesson
b. Identifying key strengths and weaknesses in planning and execution
c. Explaining how they will consolidate/follow on from the learning achieved in the lesson.

The opportunities for reflection in this module constitute a valuable opportunity for students to take stock and to think about their beliefs with regard to teaching and learning and the extent to which their practice and beliefs are consistent with each other. Students try out different techniques to work on their identified weaknesses and are encouraged to be critical in the way they view their practice and the success of their action plan.

One of the interesting details of this vignette is that students usually find it useful to work collaboratively with others to identify their strengths and weaknesses 'rather than reflecting in isolation' and this is a theme that we will come back to in Chapters 7 and 8.

We interviewed Heather Buchanan (H) and her colleague Ivor Timmis (V) to get more detail about some of the content of the vignette above. We were particularly interested in how they felt the course promoted reflection. During the interview they emphasized a number of points related to what they regard as successful reflection. The first was a balance between the negative and the positive where they look for 'a sense of proportion and balance'. This balance means some retrospective comment, but also some forward-looking plans and speculation. In simple terms they want 'I was really pleased with the way this went but I'm not so happy about that' rather than the 'hairshirt' or 'it all went brilliantly'. They also value 'specific' comment on incidents:

```
31  I:  what would indicate to you that something
32      was reflective
```

```
33 H:  errm
34 V:  I think if there's an element of looking forward
35     something about what I'm going to do next time
36 I:                                    [mmm
37 H:  I think look- identifying specific things that
38     have happened in the lesson (.) Whether I did the
39     right thing there (.) or I could have done that
40     (.)I could have done this
```

This data highlights the notion that there are choices to be made at specific points in a lesson. We might characterize these as better choices and worse choices (rather than falling into a 'right thing to do' discourse). It also exemplifies 'online decision-making' that can be talked about and brought into focus. Effective teaching is not all about 'planfulness', but rather about making the right choice at a given moment. Reflection is often centred on different options (I could have done this or I could have done that). In INSET especially, this might be one of the most valuable aspects of reflection – to create opportunities to explore and discuss such specific moments and options.

They value reflection that refers to evidence from the classroom (rather than general comments):

```
37 V:  We try to get them to look at actual evidence, things
38     like getting them to record a little bit of that
39     class and then go back and do something analytical
40     with it (.) something like go back and listen to the
41     instructions that you gave (.) we try to make it as
42     evidence-based as we can
```

The interview with Heather and Ivor confirmed that their values (particularly as to what 'counts' as reflection) determine what they ask teachers to do. This is not surprising, and each teacher education programme will develop a sense of what constitutes successful reflection. This undoubtedly socializes novice teachers into particular ways of enacting or in some cases 'performing' reflection. Watton et al. (2001: 9) compare several pieces of reflective writing in a resource guide for their students. They identify various characteristics of reflective writing and in this summary they refer to Marianne (one of the students whose reflective writing they feature as an example which shows 'evidence' of reflection):

1. Self questioning is evident (an 'internal dialogue' is set up at times) deliberating between different views of her own behaviour (different views of her own and others).
2. Marianne takes into account the views and motives of others and considers these against her own.

3. She recognizes how prior experience and thoughts (own and others') interact with the production of her own behaviour.
4. There is clear evidence of standing back from an event.
5. She helps herself to learn from the experience by splitting off the reflective processes from the points she wants to learn (by asterisk system).
6. There is recognition that the personal frame of reference can change according to the emotional state in which it is written, the acquisition of new information, the review of ideas and the effect of time passing.

This list is consistent with many of the things that Ivor and Heather said about their approach to reflection and will undoubtedly establish generic features of 'desirable' reflection. It is helpful to form a consensus within a team about what counts as successful reflection. In addition, these views and consensus can be fed back into new groups, as they are introduced into the requirements and expectations of the programme. It certainly helps to have a consistent view within the team, and the systematic use of tools can help. In what follows we consider the value of three tools in particular: reflection grids, narrative texts and loop input.

Reflection Grids

Malderez and Bodóczky (1999) show examples of 'reflection grids' and these are an important part of systematizing opportunities for reflection (Wright and Bolitho, 2007). They give teachers the opportunity to analyze and reflect on tasks during each INSET session. In other words, reflection grids provide a systematic vehicle for allowing time at the end of each activity to make notes. Headings such as 'name of activity', 'feelings during activity' and 'implications for teaching' provide a grid or structure for reflection and thereby a point of reference in follow-up discussion. This opportunity for individual and then often collaborative discussion helps in securing further understandings through the articulating of ideas arising from tasks. Incorporating regular use of reflection grids provides a course with an inbuilt 'systematic review' that can be helpful not only for bringing out course, session and activity objectives but also for developing constructs and practising articulation skills.

Encouraging teachers to reflect orally after activities can be beneficial, as is inviting teachers to construct a 'future scenario' in which they imagine 'implementing a new idea they have learnt on a course' (Wright and Bolitho, 2007: 167). This last practice can encourage teachers to explore implications of taught elements at a deeper level. Pohl and Révész (2014: 120) explain how they use reflection grids to systematically review opportunities for reflection:

Reflection on shared experience was another key element of the training process. For example, video recordings of beginning teachers' classes, as well as real and role-played mentoring scenarios, were analysed and discussed. In the same way the systematic review of training activities with the help of reflection grids (Bolitho and Wright, 1993), processing tasks for course readings and the writing of two development reports ensured that the participants engaged in different modes of reflection as a matter of routine. These reports required participants to review and make explicit their learning half-way through and towards the end of the course. All of this provided opportunities for thoughtful deliberation, created a shared language to talk about mentoring and a social-professional space or 'community of practice' (Wenger, 1998: 48).

As the writers make clear, reflection grids can be used in a variety of different ways. We now turn our attention to the use of narrative texts. This is another tool that can help bridge the gap between theory and practice (see also Chapter 6).

Narrative Texts

Norton in a foreword to Nunan and Choi (2010) says that providing narrative texts has consequences for students' engagement. There are two points to make. The first is that narrative texts are more likely to foreground the voice of practitioners. The second is that they are sometimes easier texts for teachers to relate to, reflect on and draw meaning from. Norton (2010: x) explains this in the following way:

> ... in adopting a narrative style, authors have written in the first person, and the voice of the writer is highly visible to the reader. Most of the texts that students read in the course of their studies are written in expository, third person style, and as Angel Lin has pointed out in earlier work (Lin, 2004), students frequently struggle to construct meaning from these disembodied texts. Scholars such as Fairclough (2003) and Janks (1997) remind us that texts written in the passive voice frequently conceal the agency of the writer, and reinforce inequitable relations of power between writers and readers.

Consequently, decisions about what gets included on reading lists at MA level have implications for how teachers will engage and reflect. Making sure that there are at least some narrative texts as input (e.g. Johnson and Golombek, 2002; Nunan and Choi, 2010; Barkhuizen, 2011) as well as providing opportunities for the production of narrative texts is helpful. Narrative texts that are produced by the teachers can also become objects of analysis and discussion at a later date in the programme. This develops what Barkhuizen (2011) has called 'narrative knowledging', where the analysis of narrative texts is a reflective activity in itself.

Loop Input

Another way to keep a closer connection between theory and practice is to use at least an element of 'loop input' (Woodward, 1988) in INSET. Loop input provides an experiential and collaborative approach to the reflective enterprise. At one level, trainees are completing a task similar to that completed by language learners. However, at a meta-level, they are able to discuss and reflect on the task. In this way, teachers can get an insight into what it is like to be a language learner and use this experience to fuel discussion.

In loop input, the content (e.g. jigsaw reading) is mirrored in the processes (e.g. a jigsaw reading on learners' motivation). Learning points are then made more explicit through discussion. This is particularly helpful in dealing with areas of language teaching like task-based teaching where it is particularly nonsensical to simply lecture on the topic.

As well as in face-to-face training, loop input can be useful in blended approaches, as Peachey explains:

> Overall the course is a form of 'loop input', a 'style of experiential teacher training process that involves an alignment of the process and content of learning' (Woodward, 2003), in that a blended learning course is being used to develop understanding of blended learning approaches and methods based around content focused on blended learning methodology. This gives participants experiences similar to those their students will have as learners.
>
> *2013: 70*

At this point in the chapter, we have looked at two Masters level courses (Marjon and Leeds Beckett) to get teacher-education-practitioner perspectives on fostering reflective practice and what kinds of reflection are particularly valued. The next section looks more closely at good practice in INSET in order to consider how this might impact on reflective practice. We then look closely at the main challenges of INSET.

Established Good Practice in INSET

After having reviewed the literature in this area, the following is a list of what is considered good practice in embedding reflective practice in INSET and connecting theory and practice. INSET should be:

- *sustained after the event.* Avoid a one-off design and build in opportunities for follow-up reflection and communication (Wedell, 2009) This also involves giving thought to 'disbanding' where if groups split up in an unplanned way, it can leave a feeling of 'emptiness and incompleteness' (Wright and Bolitho, 2007: 180).

- *followed up* (Lamb, 1995). This is why follow-up opportunities to engage further and reflect on the promoted pedagogy are emphasized for any teacher education to have meaningful impact (Lamb, 1995; Tomlinson, 1988; Waters, 2006; Sim, 2011).
- *participant-centred.* Build on and acknowledge teachers' existing knowledge and experiences. Value teachers' opinions (Wolter, 2000). The trainer should connect new knowledge to existing beliefs and 'personal theories' (James, 2001). What trainees already know and believe will filter new information and so needs to be acknowledged, otherwise it will form the basis of resistance. Value different kinds of teacher knowledge (Freeman, 2002). Emphasis is on refining, strengthening and extending teachers' current practices. They need opportunities to develop skills.
- *positive.* Establish a positive atmosphere and concentrate on growth and development rather than deficit views of training when planning for educational change (Wedell, 2009); providing opportunities to practise skills in a positive environment can help establish a fuller understanding of an innovation (Hayes, 2014).
- *an interactive social experience.* Create varied opportunities for peer collaboration and talk. A group where a social environment is established and where group dynamics are fostered and interaction is central is more likely to be a positive experience (Moon, 2001; Hadfield, 1992); the group 'norming' stage (i.e. storming, forming, norming, performing) is particularly important and a 'lack of attention' to the group formation activities (e.g. icebreakers/warmers) 'is likely to diminish the effectiveness of the course as a whole' (Wright and Bolitho, 2007: 35).
- *connecting.* Connect input and tasks to teachers' context (Moon, 2001); try to connect practice and theory. Do not present theory and expect teachers to apply it to their practice (Edge and Richards, 1993).
- *congruent.* Practise what you preach. Use loop learning and be a good model.

After having reviewed what we see as important elements of course design and management, the next section (4.4) considers various challenges and difficulties in INSET course design and delivery. At the same time, the section considers appropriate options and solutions.

4.4 Overcoming the Challenges of INSET

There is plenty of literature about the challenges and difficulties of INSET courses, especially short ones (e.g. Tomlinson, 1988). However, there are also useful accounts of how to overcome some of the difficulties in facilitating successful INSET courses (e.g. Lamb, 1995; Waters, 2006). This section further clarifies some of the difficulties and draws on data to suggest some possible solutions.

Short Course Difficulties

Clearly, the design of the INSET course has important implications regarding whether teachers are able to reflect during and after the course. Sim (2011: 241) comments on the cultural island of the INSET programme (a 'holiday resort' atmosphere, where even though 'the teachers are working hard under the palm trees' they are divorced from the school's 'cloudy, rainy, and windy weather conditions'). Waters and Vilches (2000: 127) also talk about the difficulties teachers have in travelling back to their real practice. This difficulty limits any insights or benefits that they may have gained during the INSET course.

One problem with short courses is that teachers might naturally be sceptical about new ideas being introduced. Often, for good reasons, they may feel uncomfortable with new ideas that are unfamiliar in their existing context and practice. Having invested time and effort, they are inclined to reject innovation and change if they are not convinced of the rationale. Hayes (1995) suggests that resistance to change can be addressed if a 'sense of plausibility' is established (see also Prabhu, 1990). In other words, they may be more inclined to accept change and take ownership of new ideas if they can develop such a sense of 'plausibility' (what seems to the individual teacher justified and appropriate in relation to their actions and procedures).

One of the most important barriers to reflection is if the course leader is simply seen as an 'expert' and the purpose of the training to transmit expertise of some kind to its recipients. It will limit what can be achieved on the course if a deficit view of participants is foregrounded (Bell and Day, 1991). Of course, it is important for course leaders to have expertise. However, if they have no experience or knowledge of the specific local situation, it is particularly important to position participants as experts and encourage them to evaluate how new approaches, materials or techniques might transfer appropriately to the teaching context. Hayes (2012), in this case in South Korea, shows how such a discourse of deficit is readily internalized by teachers and this then affects their ability to engage and reflect.

Tomlinson (1988) also argues that isolated, one-shot workshops are ineffective in promoting long-term change. The table below summarizes the main points from Tomlinson's article and adds the voices of school-based heads of department from Mohammad Aldhaen's PhD data in Kuwait that resonate with Tomlinson's points:

TABLE 4.1

Tomlinson (1988)	Aldhaen (2012)
Courses designed by ministries without consultation	'I believe that what you have found is what we suffer from ... I think that these programs will not feed our real needs because such programs are designed as I said earlier by the Ministry and without any consideration of schools' or teachers' needs' (p. 109)

Tomlinson (1988)	Aldhaen (2012)
Participants have had limited input to policy and objectives that the course is designed to realize.	'the problem with INSET programmes lies in unclear goals and policies by the MOE and if these goals and policies were clear I believe that these programmes would be beneficial'. (p. 186)
Teacher needs are not addressed.	'the current programs miss the link with the actual needs teachers and school' (p. 188)
Follow-up support for using ideas and practices experienced on INSET courses is not considered.	'Unfortunately, I can't see that there is clear policy for follow up and evaluation of INSET programmes' (p. 186)
Not enough time for trainees to discuss relevance of new approaches to actual classrooms.	'. . . those who deliver INSET programs do not give enough time to trainees during the programme to discuss practically what we learn' (p. 188)
Too much is packed into a short time.	'INSET programmes loaded in content compared with time given for the programme and I can say that mostly time is not enough to present effectively to trainees.' (p. 185)
In general terms, not enough provision of training opportunities	'these programmes are very infrequent and not enough to cater for all teachers' (p. 186)

Unless addressed, these issues are most likely to severely limit the effectiveness of INSET. In what follows we pick out what we feel are the three major challenges from the table above to be overcome. The first is connecting to teachers' contexts, the second is establishing a collaborative course and the third is two-way feedback.

Connecting to Context

In terms of responding to these challenges, connecting to the teachers' context seems to be key. Participants may fail to connect with the training if it seems to be far removed from their teaching realities. Alternatively, they may become initially very enthusiastic about a new approach, but find it difficult to adopt on return to the classroom because they have not been able to reflect on the appropriateness to the teaching context. Opportunities for collaborative reflection during the course can help to bridge this gap (Waters and Vilches, 2000). Short courses are particularly problematic. If the course provides lots of recipes for the participants to follow but does not help them to develop ideas and materials of their own, there will be a disconnect. If the course is far too ambitious and attempts to effect a radical change in teacher behaviour (in a few short weeks), it is likely to fail (Guskey, 2000). In Sim's data (2011: 44), Vicky wrote the following:

> As for the INSET course, it should provide teachers (trainees) with time to practice and reflect what they learnt, not only aiming at giving or introducing teachers a list of newer activities.

Often when a course is too ambitious, it may end up with too many new ideas and not enough time to reflect on how they might be appropriate to the teachers' context.

If INSET provides opportunities for practice and reflection, is activity based, and tries to place trainee teachers and their realities at the centre of the process, the INSET is much more likely to be effective and help teachers achieve a sense of ownership (Bax, 1997). Ideally, teachers will be involved in the planning of an INSET course, at least through some form of needs analysis. Of course, the shorter the in-service course, the greater the pressure on trainers to pack in as much as possible. However, if the training aims to produce long-lasting changes in teacher practices, then trainees need to connect their current beliefs and behaviours to any new approaches, skills and strategies (see Hayes, 2000).

Collaboration

Teachers usually value collaboration and this is a theme that we will return to in Chapter 7. It has been claimed that teachers have a higher regard for their peers' views than for the views of university professors or researchers (Sandholtz, 2002). Beddall (2014) also confirms that teachers desire more collaboration on a specific course. His data comes from a project investigating reflective practice in a training course for young learner teachers in Doha. In terms of developing collaboration, participants' primary suggestion was to have shorter, more regular, gatherings, or even a 'buddy' system, to provide the opportunity for ongoing dialogue. The following exchange with the tutor and two teachers (Anna and Jane) demonstrates this point:

```
Anna:   Maybe, if you had a shorter session, so you said: 'Right,
        in two weeks, you are going to get together for twenty
        minutes and discuss how far you've come', I would have
        been more inclined to have kept a journal after having
        listened to everyone else. But make it short, or ten
        minutes, or even just pair up
Jane:   Like you said . . . have a buddy with it, particularly
        if you know someone's got the same questions, or even if
```

```
             you've got someone to share what you're going through,
             even if it's just a completely different question.
Tutor:   And that makes complete sense because, just like those of
             you who wrote in the journal quite frequently had a big
             record to look back on, I guess it works exactly the same.
             Like, you were talking about how your journal, in a way,
             was conversations. So, if that was more structured and you
             had more regular meetings about it, it would have had the
             same effect as if you'd been keeping the journal."
Jane:    Yes, exactly.
Anna:    Better, yeah.
```

Beddall suggests that this kind of innovation would better support teachers through giving them the opportunity to 'check-in' from time to time and not be working entirely alone. There is strong evidence of desire for more collaboration in his teachers' data. Anna said:

```
Anna:    I found what worked really well was having the little
             conversations in the staffroom, like I had to come back and
             vent to Penny and Maryam. And Maryam, as well, was really
             helpful 'cause we had the same level. So, I think that
             process – reflecting, but speaking with people, and using
             them as a sounding board – I found that was more useful.
```

Interestingly, Beddall reports that Anna had neglected the reflective journal (virtually from the start of the course), but found that her regular conversations with colleagues in the staffroom served as a better option for her. Again, this is a theme we will explore further in Chapters 7 and 8.

Two-way Feedback and Reflection

Feedback on assignments is seen as an essential component in the learning cycle for teachers in INSET. Feedback often aims at providing both formative and summative perspectives, although it appears that studies support the view that it is formative feedback that is both valued and that promotes reflection (e.g. Ferris, 2007; Ravand, 2011). It communicates to teachers their strengths and weaknesses, and it can also provide the basis for them to assess their performance, reflect and make improvements to future work. Feedback provides both grade and comment. One student in Monyaki's (2015) study says that:

> a grade is psychological while the tutor's comments are empowering and lead to self-reflection and self-evaluation.
>
> *2015: 29*

While earlier studies suggest that students do not pay attention to teacher comments given at the end of writing (Jollands et al., 2009), Monyaki's study in an INSET course found that teachers did engage with their feedback. In interviews, participants were able to say/describe in detail what they had reflected on from the feedback and in many cases how they had incorporated the feedback into subsequent assignments.

It is worth making the point that in a course which is designed to be reflective, feedback is not one way. Most courses have opportunities for participants to give feedback at the end of the module, but it is important to integrate opportunities for feedback in a more ongoing way. Getting reflections and feedback at the end of the session provides the opportunity of forming a bridge to the next session. This creates what Malderez and Bodóczky (1999: 34) call the 'feedback dialogue'. It reminds the group what happened in the last session, but, more importantly, it establishes that the course is collaborative and the group agrees on some things but not on others.

In the following vignette, Richard Pinner is talking about the value of a 'reflective paper' at the end of a teacher education workshop on authenticity and motivation in Japan. It shows that even on a very short INSET course, it is possible to make feedback more reflective. In revisiting the purposes of the course (and the 'reflective paper') he has managed to make it more meaningful and relevant to the teachers:

RICHARD PINNER VIGNETTE (JAPAN)

Every year since 2012, I have run a teacher education workshop which is part of the Japanese Ministry of Education (MEXT) requirements for teaching. Every 10 years, Japanese teachers must obtain a certain amount of credits in order to renew their licence, by attending sponsored workshops which are offered by accredited tertiary institutions such as Sophia University where I work. The course is basically a one-day INSET consisting of 4 x 90-minute sessions and a one-hour assessment. The assessment is mandatory because of the MEXT accreditation and licence renewal. All of the participants are Japanese and have at least 10 years' experience teaching English at Japanese high schools or junior high schools. I felt odd at first, as a relatively inexperienced teacher myself, in setting an assessment for these very experienced teachers. Some of the workshop participants have as much as 30 or 40 years of teaching experience. Therefore, I wanted to make the assessment a truly meaningful activity, and one which allows the participants the chance not only to reflect but also to provide me with some feedback as well.

The course I run is entitled *Using and Adapting Authentic Materials to Motivate Students*. The focus is on materials and understanding the concept of authenticity from the perspective of English as an International Language (EIL). Most teachers come to the class with the idea that authenticity is the product of 'native speakers' and I quickly do what I can to dispel this misconception by explaining that authenticity should be seen as a continuum with both social and contextual axes.

A large majority of the Japanese English teachers have an inferiority complex about not being 'native speakers' of English and therefore not being 'authentic' speakers or being able to provide an 'authentic model':

> My idea about authenticity has changed dramatically by participating in this workshop. [. . .] Now, I have learned what really makes materials and lessons authentic is how we teachers use it.
>
> *Aiko, Tokyo*

Also, some teachers express a renewed confidence in teaching English as an international language, as a result of the broader definition of authenticity which we discuss in the workshop:

> I will choose more materials from World Englishes. Before this class, I sometimes hesitated to use those kinds of materials, because they may not be accepted as 'authentic'. Now, I will choose world English materials more flexibly if the content is appropriate for my class.
>
> *Takako, Osaka*

The reflective paper, although initially a compulsory piece of bureaucracy that nobody (including myself) felt particularly excited about, has become a central part of the workshop and a way for the participants to organize and reflect on their experiences. It also became a vital way for me to get feedback from the participants about the workshop. I think, in this way, reflection papers are a very *authentic* form of assessment, because they offer a two-way channel of discourse which is highly meaningful. In constructing the reflection papers, I felt the participants were constructing a deeper understanding of their own experiences of the workshop, which they were then able to share with me.

Like many pieces of writing that are obligatory, it may be initially difficult to shift perceptions that this is a case of 'going through the motions'. Especially where the reflective writing is compulsory (in the case above because it is part of licence renewal), it may be necessary to breathe new life into the task. In Richard's case, the reflective paper has become both a more useful exercise and a source of valuable feedback.

4.5 Summary

In what we have covered in this chapter, we have established the importance of a systematic approach to reflection. We are not suggesting that this is the only aspect of designing successful INSET. Neither are we suggesting that it is easy to make INSET relevant for all the participants. We are conscious that trying to do so involves a great deal of commitment, discussion and 'ongoing reflection':

> This has been a long process of learning to co-create a programme that is relevant and responsive to the needs of all stakeholders – ministries of education, universities, teachers, learners, schools, parents in Uzbekistan and that is in line with modern thinking and international best practice. It required a lot of discussion at all levels, thinking together, ongoing reflection, identifying challenges and blockages, trying things out, re-visiting approaches and strategies and doing things differently as a result. This has been a huge learning and development experience..
>
> *Gulyamova et al., 2014: 50*

Reflection can be embedded in in-service teacher training in a number of ways. This ranges from fairly *ad hoc* opportunities for individual or group reflection in training sessions to more systematic attempts to make sure that reflection is an integral part of the teachers' INSET experience. The purpose of this chapter has not been to argue that there is necessarily a best way to approach this. Instead the chapter has aimed to open up choices that teacher educators have.

In the end, however, there is no point in teacher educators banging on about reflective practice if they show no evidence of it themselves. This is an argument we have made elsewhere:

> It is also worth saying that the value of this kind of data-led reflective process is just as important for teacher-trainers as for novice teachers. Indeed, a teacher educator who practices what he or she preaches is more likely show commitment to and therefore promote reflective practice. Edge (2011: 20) talks of 'consistency' (the demand of teachers that they should be reflective must also apply to the teacher educator).
>
> *Mann and Walsh, 2013: 302*

Farr and Riordan (2015) is a good example of this commitment to reflection on teacher training practice. They gain insights into their teaching context and see their research into reflective discourse as 'a type of reflective practice activity of our own' which will continue to 'impact on the ways we personally conduct ourselves verbally in our own teacher education processes'. In the following chapters we will add more detail of how teacher educators have demonstrated such commitment.

References

Aldhaen, M. (2012). INSET programmes in Kuwait: a national survey of stakeholder perception (Doctoral dissertation). University of Southampton. Downloaded on 1.1.15 at http://eprints.soton.ac.uk/345956/

Barkhuizen, G. (2011). Narrative knowledging in TESOL. *TESOL Quarterly*, 45(3), 391–414.

Bax, S. (1997). Roles for a teacher educator in context-sensitive teacher education. *ELT Journal*, 51(3), 232–241.

Beddall, O. (2014). Investigating reflective practice in a training course for young learner teachers (Unpublished dissertation). Aston University, Birmingham. Downloaded 4.4.16 at http://englishagenda.britishcouncil.org/

Bell, L. and Day, C. (1991). *Managing the professional development of teachers*. Buckingham: Open University Press.

Bolitho, R. and Wright, T. (1993). Grids as a reflective training tool on trainer-training courses. *The Teacher Trainer*, 7(2), 32–35. Canterbury: Pilgrims.

Clarke, M. A. (1994). The dysfunctions of the theory–practice discourse. *TESOL Quarterly*, 28(1), 9–26.

Dewey, J. (1933). *How we think. A restatement of the relation of reflective thinking to the educative process* (Revised edn). Boston: D. C. Heath.

Edge, J. (2011). *The reflexive teacher educator in TESOL: roots and wings*. New York: Routledge.

Edge, J. and Richards, K. (eds). (1993). *Teachers develop teachers' research*. Oxford: Heinemann.

Fairclough, N. (2003). *Analysing discourse: textual analysis for social research*. London: Routledge.

Farr, F. and Riordan, E. (2015). Turn initiators in professional encounters: teacher education discourse in an Irish university setting. Downloaded at https://ulir.ul.ie/bitstream/handle/10344/4577/Farr_2015_initiators.pdf?sequence=1

Ferris, D. (2007). Preparing teachers to respond to student writing. *Journal of Second Language*, 16, 165–193.

Freeman, D. (2002). The hidden side of the work: teacher knowledge and learning to teach. a perspective from North American educational research on teacher education in English language teaching. *Language Teaching*, 35, 1–13.

Gulyamova, J., Irgasheva, S. and Bolitho, R. (2014). Professional development through curriculum reform: the Uzbekistan experience. In D. Hayes (ed.), *Innovations in the continuing professional development of English language teachers* (pp. 45–64). London: British Council.

Guskey, T.R. (2000). *Evaluating professional development*. Thousand Oaks, CA: SAGE.

Hadfield, J. (1992). *Classroom dynamics*. Oxford: Oxford University Press.

Hayes, D. (1995). In-service teacher development: some basic principles. *ELT Journal*, 49(3), 251–261.

Hayes, D. (2000). Cascade training and teachers' professional development. *ELT Journal*, 54(2), 135–145.

Hayes, D. (2012). Planning for success: culture, engagement and power in English language education innovation. In C. Tribble (ed.), *Managing change in English language teaching: lessons from experience* (pp. 47–60). London: British Council.

Hayes, D. (ed.). (2014). *Innovations in the continuing professional development of English language teachers*. London: British Council.

James, P. (2001). *Teachers in action: tasks for in-service language teacher education and development*. Cambridge: Cambridge University Press.

Janks, H. (1997). Critical discourse analysis as a research tool. *Discourse: Studies in the Cultural Politics of Education*, 18(3), 329–342.

Johnson, K.E. (2009). *Second language teacher education: a sociocultural perspective*. London: Routledge.

Johnson, K.E. and Golombek, P.R. (2002). *Teachers' narrative inquiry as professional development*. Cambridge: Cambridge University Press.

Jollands, M., McCallum, N. and Bondy, J. (2009). If students want feedback why don't they collect their assignments? 20th Australasian Association for Engineering Education Conference. University of Adelaide.

Lamb, M. (1995). The consequences of INSET. *ELT Journal*, 49(1), 72–80.

Lin, A.M. (2004). Introducing a critical pedagogical curriculum: a feminist, reflexive account. In B. Norton and K. Toohey (eds), *Critical pedagogies and language learning* (pp. 271–290). Cambridge: Cambridge University Press.

Loughran, J. (2002). Effective reflective practice: in search of meaning in learning about teaching. *Journal of Teacher Education*, 53(1), 33–43.

Malderez, A. and Bodóczky, C. (1999). *Mentor courses: a resource book for trainer-trainers*. Cambridge: Cambridge University Press.

Mann, S. and Walsh, S. (2013). RP or 'RIP': a critical perspective on reflective practice. *Applied Linguistics Review*, 4(2), 291–315.

Monyaki, B. (2015). Feedback. Do MA in ELT students feed from tutor feedback on their writing? (Unpublished dissertation). University of Warwick.

Moon, J.A. (2001). *Short courses and workshops: improving the impact of learning, training and professional development*. London: Kogan Page.

Nelson, F.L. and Sadler, T. (2013). A third space for reflection by teacher educators: a heuristic for understanding orientations to and components of reflection. *Reflective Practice*, 14(1), 43–57.

Norton, B. (2010). Foreword. In D. Nunan and J. Choi (eds), *Language and culture: reflective narratives and the emergence of identity* (pp. x–xiii). New York: Routledge.

Nunan, D. and Choi, J. (eds). (2010). *Language and culture: reflective narratives and the emergence of identity*. London: Routledge.

Peachey, N. (2013). A blended learning teacher development course for the development of blended learning in English language teaching. In B. Tomlinson and C. Whittaker (eds), *Blended learning in English language teaching: course design and implementation* (pp. 65–74). London: British Council.

Pohl, U. and Révész, J. (2014). Training to become a mentor: Hungarian EFL teachers' personal discoveries. *Working Papers in Language Pedagogy* (School of English and American Studies, Eötvös Loránd University), 8, 116–131. Downloaded on 25.03.16 at http://langped.elte.hu/WoPaLParticles/W8Pohl%26Revesz.pdf

Prabhu, N.S. (1990). There is no best method – Why? *TESOL Quarterly*, 24(2), 161–176.

Ravand, H. (2011). Feedback in ESL writing: toward an interactional approach. *Journal of Language Teaching and Research*, 2(5), 1136–1145.

Roberts, J. (1998). *Language Teacher Education*. London: Arnold.

Sandholtz, J.H. (2002). In-service training or professional development: contrasting opportunities in a school/university partnership. *Teaching and Teacher Education*, 18(7), 815–830.

Sim, J.Y. (2011). The impact of in-service teacher training: a case study of teachers' classroom practice and perception change (Unpublished thesis). University of Warwick. Downloaded 3.3.14 at https://core.ac.uk/download/pdf/1384103.pdf

Tomlinson, B. (1988). In-service TEFL: is it worth the risk? *The Teacher Trainer*, 2(2), 17–19.

Waters, A. (2006). Facilitating follow-up in ELT INSET. *Language Teaching Research*, 10(1), 32–52.

Waters, A. and Vilches, M.L.C. (2000). Integrating teacher learning: the school-based follow-up development activity. *ELT Journal*, 54(2), 126–134.

Watton, P., Collings, J. and Moon, J. (2001). Reflective writing. The University of Sheffield. Downloaded 01.01.15 at www.learnhigher.ac.uk/wp-content/uploads/Reflective_writing_The_Park_WattonCollingsMoon.pdf

Wedell, M. (2009). *Planning for educational change: putting people and their contexts first*. London: Bloomsbury Publishing.

Wenger, E. (1998). *Communities of practice: learning, meaning, and identity*. Cambridge, MA: Cambridge University Press.

Wolter, B. (2000). A participant-centred approach to INSET course design. *ELT Journal*, 54(4), 311–318.

Woodward, T. (1988). Loop-input: a new strategy for trainees. *System*, 16(1), 23–28.

Woodward, T. (2003). Loop Input. *ELT Journal*, 57(3), 301–304.

Wright, T. and Bolitho, R. (2007). *Trainer development*. Lulu.com.

Yadav, S. K. (2012). *Impact of in-service teacher training on classroom transaction*. New Delhi: NCERT.

5

Reflection 'in the wild'

5.1 Introduction

This chapter functions as a bridge to part 3 of the book, where we consider the range of tools and procedures which can be used for RP. In this chapter, we highlight the fact that once practitioners complete a pre- or in-service teacher education programme, they need to find an alternative means of sustaining reflection and professional development, given that, potentially at least, reflection is a career-long practice. The chapter considers what can be achieved by individuals working alone, as part of a professional group or by using technology to interact in a wider community of practice. Our discussion centres on the balance between reflection for achieving a fine-grained understanding of local context and reflection for improving practice. That is, we make the case for teachers to gain detailed up-close understanding of their contexts as a means of appropriating – or gaining ownership of – professional knowledge.

The focus of this chapter, then, is what we are calling 'reflection in the wild', where teachers use RP as part of their professional practice, working alone or with other colleagues, rather than when they are taking part in a course or attending some kind of INSET event. We use the term 'in the wild' to capture the idea that reflection is not something which is restricted to pre- or in-service teacher education programmes. Indeed, we believe that the ultimate goal for teachers and teacher educators is to integrate and embed reflection in their daily professional lives. Essentially, we are saying that reflection is a practice which teachers might like to develop in the same way they develop expertise in other classroom practices, such as giving instructions, providing feedback or explaining a language point.

For many teachers, the notion of doing reflection might be seen as another demand on their time, or yet another yardstick to measure their performance and evaluate practice. While this sentiment is certainly understandable (and, indeed, is probably one of the main reasons why RP is not more widespread beyond the confines of a course), our counter argument is that RP can easily be embedded in the everyday professional practices which underpin teaching and classroom life. Essentially, we argue that RP needs to be integrated in teachers' professional practices in such a way that it does not feel like a burden or additional chore. The challenge, then, is to identify tools and procedures which can be used alongside existing pedagogical practices to promote reflection and enhance professional development. We will say more about that in part 3 of the book.

Although Keith Richards' vignette below seems to be adopting a pretty negative perspective on reflection, a closer reading reveals that he is actually making a strong case for reflection to be embedded in teachers' daily practice. He argues convincingly that there is a strong and pressing need to respect the reflections of teachers as they go about their business, chatting in the staffroom, for example – as Keith puts it, this is where professional development really happens.

KEITH RICHARDS' VIGNETTE (UK)

It seems to me that reflection represents one of the subtlest threats to successful teacher education and development. This is part of the price it has had to pay for its success, a consequence to some extent of its widespread adoption, but there are deeper issues that we should perhaps be considering and I should like to highlight some of those here.

I first became aware of the rich potential of reflection when I was fortunate enough to work with Julian Edge, in my view its most eloquent and persuasive advocate in our field. Collaborating with him on the first *Teachers Develop Teachers Research* conference and subsequent publication opened my eyes to the importance and the potential of reflection in the context of teacher development – when properly facilitated. That still holds true, but in the meantime what once represented an exciting and liberating opportunity has become for many a necessary and almost routine element in the teacher education curriculum, in some cases serving more as an evaluative tool than a key to deeper understanding and professional growth.

Thinking back to that first conference, I am struck by a comment made by a teacher in the concluding open discussion. She challenged the academics present to justify what she saw as their appropriation of an agenda that properly belonged to those engaging with it in the context of their daily professional challenges. Neither the charge nor the subsequent defence was new, but the relevance of professional embeddedness was brought home to me when I spent 15 months recording and analyzing staffroom conversation in a small language school. Far from avoiding shoptalk, the teachers involved were constantly reflecting on and collaboratively analyzing (often via stories) their professional performance. They were modest in their ambitions and local in their range, the word 'little' featuring often in their reflective exchanges ('That's a very interesting little awareness raising thing for the students'; 'It was quite another interesting little technique' etc.), but these exchanges enabled them to hone their professional skills and develop as teachers.

> This small staffroom is a world away from the institutional context in which reflection so often features, but it is where development happens. The focus has perhaps for too long been on the process of facilitating and refining reflective technique at the expense of finding out how reflection actually gets done so that we can understand how it might be done to greater effect. I have seen it held out as a panacea in situations where teachers are desperate to survive with some shred of professional dignity in contexts where they are driven to the point of exhaustion and tears. Such parodic distortions are mercifully rare, but panaceas inhibit deep development and the temptation to valorize reflection can be avoided only if in the spirit of postmethod engagement we recognize the importance of locality and seek to understand varieties of embedded reflective practice.

Keith's comments chime with much of what we will be discussing in this chapter: we advocate the use of embedded reflective practice in whatever form that may take; essentially, reflection should be something which teachers do naturally, as part of their daily professional lives. Similarly, we agree that reflection should not be an evaluative tool, used to assess professional development or manage teachers.

In the remainder of this chapter, we exemplify the ways in which reflection might get done 'in the wild', presenting data and commentaries from a range of contexts. In 5.2, we look at CPD (continuing professional development) and consider how teachers might use reflection as part of their own CPD programme. In contrast, section 5.3 examines ways of doing reflection when working alone: teacher self-development. Section 5.4 is concerned with professional groups, while 5.5 presents some thoughts around social networks and communities of practice.

5.2 Continuing Professional Development (CPD)

Current Issues

Continuing professional development (CPD) has been a facet of teacher education and teacher development for more than 40 years. According to Hayes (2014: 5), CPD is 'a multi-faceted, lifelong experience, which can take place inside or outside the workplace and which often moves beyond the professional and into the realm of a teacher's personal life too'. Put like this, it would seem that CPD can include almost anything which teachers (and other professionals) engage in over the lifetime of their careers. Of course, teachers do not simply engage in CPD for the love of it; there has to be a reason, a purpose, a goal, an innovation, something driving what essentially might well result in a change to practice. In this sense, CPD comprises a number of key elements:

- It is emergent and responsive to a perceived issue, problem or intended outcome.
- It entails change; participants are therefore change agents, working towards a particular goal.
- Change will normally involve learning: a new skill, better use of technology, classroom management practices, and so on.
- Change requires innovation or improvement; the extent of the innovation will very much be dependent on local conditions.
- Innovations do not have to be large scale – they can be small and incremental, but they must be rooted in and responsive to local context.
- Understanding of local context is a key component of CPD; in this book, we would go as far as to say that an understanding of local context lies at the heart of both CPD and effective teaching.

Some years ago, Day offered this definition of CPD:

> Professional development consists of all natural learning experiences and those conscious and planned activities which are intended to be of direct or indirect benefit to the individual, group or school, which contribute, through these, to the quality of education in the classroom. It is the process by which, alone and with others, teachers review, renew and extend their commitment as change agents to the moral purpose of teaching; and by which they acquire and develop critically the knowledge, skills and emotional intelligence essential to good professional thinking, planning and practice with children, young people and colleagues throughout each phase of their teaching lives.
>
> *Day, 1999: 4*

Day's definition is certainly all encompassing in much the same way that Hayes' (2014) is. Essentially CPD can be equated with lifelong learning, whereby learning might occur in both formal and informal settings and where learning needs vary according to a person's stage of career. While the nature of CPD and its extent will certainly vary from one context to another, the global trend is for an increase in CPD, following what Hargreaves (1994) calls 'the intensification of teaching', a phenomenon in which 'rapid shifts in the nature of work ensue from, among other factors, government-driven waves of "reform" and "restructuring"' (Zipin, 2002: 2). Such initiatives by government education authorities have not always been welcomed by teachers and this 'intensification of teaching' has certainly impacted on CPD, often in rather negative ways. Day et al. (2006: 123), in a study of more than 45,000 teachers, found that teachers felt less and less inclined to participate in CPD:

> Teachers across all professional life phases felt that heavy workload, a lack of time and financial constraints were important inhibitors in their pursuit of professional development.

We do not have the space here to engage in a full evaluation of current debates concerning CPD. Suffice it to say that there are many tensions: educational change is occurring at an increasingly rapid rate as education systems struggle to cope with the demands of rapidly evolving societies (OECD, 2011). Concomitant with these demands, teachers are facing increasing pressure to take part in CPD activities, while feeling less and less inclined to do so. At the level of policy, CPD is regarded as a key factor in improvements to teaching and learning and to the overall 'student experience' (Ingvarson et al., 2005; Muijs and Lindsay, 2008). At a personal level, CPD is crucial in supporting teachers and enabling them to cope with externally imposed forces, while taking control of their own teaching and professional growth.

A CPD Framework

One organization which has attempted to offer a more individualistic, tailor-made approach to CPD for teachers is the British Council. According to the Council's CPD Framework document (see Fig. 5.1 below):

> The British Council's Continuing Professional Development (CPD) Framework for teachers is for teachers of all subjects. It enables you to understand and plan your own professional development.
>
> *British Council (2015: 2)*

The CPD Framework is organized around four stages of professional development, each demonstrating an increasing level of competence and knowledge:

- **Awareness**: You have heard of this professional practice.
- **Understanding**: You know what the professional practice means and why it is important.
- **Engagement**: You demonstrate competency in this professional practice at work.
- **Integration**: You demonstrate a high level of competency in this professional practice and this consistently informs what you do at work.

In addition, the framework uses a range of professional practices:

- Planning lessons and courses
- Understanding learners
- Managing the lesson
- Knowing the subject
- Managing resources
- Assessing learning
- Integrating ICT

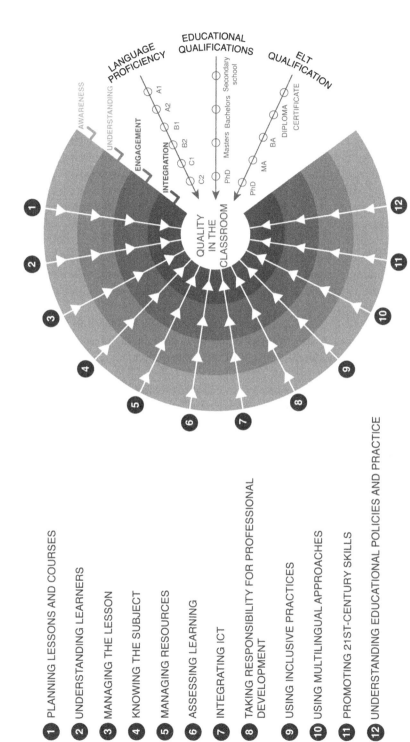

FIGURE 5.1 The British Council's Continuing Professional Development (CPD) Framework for Teachers

1 PLANNING LESSONS AND COURSES

2 UNDERSTANDING LEARNERS

3 MANAGING THE LESSON

4 KNOWING THE SUBJECT

5 MANAGING RESOURCES

6 ASSESSING LEARNING

7 INTEGRATING ICT

8 TAKING RESPONSIBILITY FOR PROFESSIONAL DEVELOPMENT

9 USING INCLUSIVE PRACTICES

10 USING MULTILINGUAL APPROACHES

11 PROMOTING 21ST-CENTURY SKILLS

12 UNDERSTANDING EDUCATIONAL POLICIES AND PRACTICE

- Taking responsibility for professional development
- Using inclusive practices
- Using multilingual approaches
- Promoting 21st-century skills
- Understanding educational policies and practice.

The thinking behind the framework is that users may have different levels of competence in each of the 12 areas of professional practice. For example, while you might regard yourself as having reached the stage of 'engagement' in 'knowing the subject', you may be at the stage of 'awareness' for 'understanding educational policies and practice'. The advantage of the CPD Framework is that it recognizes that most teachers have what we might call a 'jagged profile' in terms of their CPD: they may excel in one area, but be almost a novice in another. Another key element of this approach is that it promotes autonomy by encouraging teachers to plan and implement their own approach to CPD. By having 'ownership' of a professional development programme, it is much more likely that teachers will engage and commit to change (see also Nunan and Lamb, 1996).

Each of the 12 professional practices is further subdivided into a range of competencies, using descriptors. For example, under 'taking responsibility for professional development', we find the following elements:

- Understanding my professional needs, interests and learning preferences in order to identify areas for development;
- Defining my short-, medium- and long-term career goals;
- Understanding the developmental pathways available to reach my specific career goals;
- Using technology to facilitate my professional development;
- Staying up to date with developments in education in teaching and learning;
- Being aware of, selecting and engaging in appropriate professional development opportunities and resources to inform my classroom practice, including:

  collaborating with colleagues and other professionals
  reflective practice
  teacher research and other forms of classroom inquiry
  attending and presenting at conferences
  participating in training
  reading and publishing
  joining teachers' associations
  observing other teachers and being observed.

- Reflecting on and evaluating the benefit of my continuing professional development and its impact on my classroom practice and my learners' achievements.

There are several features of the British Council's CPD Framework which resonate with the main message of this section and, indeed, with this book as a whole. First, there is an obvious emphasis on reflection and its likely impact on practice. Second, teachers are encouraged, at least implicitly, to engage in action research and use classroom data to inform and guide their CPD. Third, working with colleagues, collaboration and communication are all given some attention. Fourth, there is more than a suggestion that CPD is a lifelong process for which teachers have responsibility.

Further details of the CPD Framework and how to use it can be found at: www.teachingenglish.org.uk/teacher-development/continuing-professional-development

Collaborative CPD

Throughout this book, we make the case for RP (and by definition, CPD) to be more collaborative, evidence-based and dialogic. By working with other teachers who are facing similar problems, by sharing concerns and issues and by adopting a less individualistic, more collectivist oriented approach to professional development, we believe that much can be done to overcome current frustrations and disillusionment with CPD. More importantly, the process can become more enjoyable and more beneficial when undertaken with others working in a similar context (see section 5.4 'Professional Groups').

It is certainly true to say that collaborative continuing professional development (CPD) is increasing in popularity (Kennedy, 2011). Recent studies have demonstrated its value, especially when undertaken over a longer period of time and with relatively small teacher groups (see, for example, Cordingley et al., 2005; Bolam and Weindling, 2006). The problem is, as outlined above, that many countries have standards-based CPD frameworks which measure teachers' competence against static and fixed descriptors. It is unlikely, as Kennedy (2011) points out, that such frameworks can adequately account for the value of collaborative CPD, whose main benefits accrue from the fact that it is relatively informal and relies heavily on interpersonal and communication skills.

Based on previous studies such as the ones cited here, and on the arguments we present throughout this book, we advocate a more collaborative approach to CPD which has the following features:

- Participating teachers work in relatively small (3–4), context-specific groups. On the one hand, there is an argument that the more specific the context and the more shared experience teachers have, the more beneficial will be the collaboration. On the other, it may well be the case that teachers from different contexts can benefit from collaborating, especially when the problem or issue they are reflecting on is shared.

- Understandings of local context are crucial to CPD. Any collaborative CPD activity should make this a key goal, its driving force. It is by gaining under-standing of context that practices will improve, especially when context is viewed as dynamic and variable, created through interactions between teacher and students (see, for example, Seedhouse, 2004; Walsh, 2013).

- The social element of professional learning (comprising mentoring, coach-ing and dialogue) is not in itself enough to achieve ownership of CPD. There is also a need to incorporate some kind of experimentation, an innovation, or change to practice, which all participants adopt, discuss and evaluate. This might be seen as an action research project (see Chapter 9). Other studies have shown this to be a particularly useful way of promoting collaborative CPD (see, for example, Bolam and Weindling, 2006).

- Collaborative CPD should take place over time and not simply be organized as a 'one-off'. Groups take time to form and adopt appropriate working practices. Educational change does not occur quickly – it takes time to introduce an innovation and to reflect on its usefulness.

- Much can be done through the use of VLEs and online resources (see Sandra Morales' vignette below). While we certainly advocate face-to-face dialogue in any professional development activity, we appreciate that this may not always be possible. Much can be done through the use of Skype, blogs, social media and so on.

- The use of video is a particularly appropriate means of sharing ideas and working collaboratively (see 5.3). Video has two immediate advantages: it provides evidence to focus the discussion while at the same time acting as a 'springboard' for discussion.

In the remainder of this chapter and throughout the next section of the book, we present tools, procedures and activities which are designed to promote collaborative CPD. In the final part of this section, we offer an example of a collaborative CPD project which took place in Chile. In Sandra Morales' study, eight English language teachers from Chile and Easter Island were invited to participate in an online CPD project concerning the use of technology in classroom teaching.

SANDRA MORALES' VIGNETTE (CHILE)

Context

These extracts were taken from the interactions of language teachers from Chile and Easter Island (eight teachers in total) in discussion forums and blogs that were part of an online teacher training and development course implemented on the virtual learning environment (VLE) *Moodle*. The aim of the online course was to develop teachers' technological and pedagogical skills to use technology with language learners. The duration of the course was eight weeks and the developmental cycle included theoretical aspects of technology for L2 teaching, practical activities and reflection, both individual (blogs) and collaborative (discussion forum).

Each week, the teachers learned about and discussed issues relating to the use of technology for language education such as digital literacy, computer mediated communication (CMC), computer assisted language learning (CALL), learning styles, mobile learning, culture and CALL, social networks and community building, and online teaching and learning. Data were analyzed using the Community of Inquiry model (Garrison, Anderson and Archer, 2000), which has been widely applied to examine the cognitive (i.e. critical thinking and reflection), social (i.e. group cohesion) and teaching (i.e. materials and tutor's role) development of online communities in educational contexts.

Procedure

Reflection in the online course was usually initiated by the online tutor (this researcher), but the teachers had the opportunity to do so as well. In addition to group reflection (see Sandra Morales' second vignette in Chapter 8), participating teachers provided individual reflections in the form of online blogs. Individual reflection was also part of the course as teachers had to implement a blog where they could keep a record of their experiences using technology. However, this kind of reflection seemed to be less prevalent amongst the teachers, as only five out of eight used individual blogs.

As we can see in the entry below, from Easter's blog, this space was useful for the teachers to write down ideas and plans for their future lessons, but not so much as a platform for dialogue. As seen in Andy's entry, sometimes the teachers included useful information (or questions) in their blogs which might have not been seen or shared in the online community. The reason for that is that teachers did not have time or the willingness to read their colleagues' individual blogs and/ or post in them. As they had the discussion forum, they preferred that channel to share and discuss with their peers. The findings in these data suggest that teachers can be reflective writers (as opposed to only thinking about their practices) if they have the appropriate tools to reflect. In this online course, group reflection seemed to have had greater impact on the development of the teachers' technological and pedagogical skills.

Online Posts

Easter's Blog

> My students are not digital natives like many children all over the world. Currently they are learning how to deal with technological resources applied to language education; for example, they have

learned how to use PowerPoint for oral presentations. They have also understood how to download and transport information, especially music and videos. However, their level of written English is poor and messy. Although they can follow linguistic models, completing with their own information, they aren't able to participate in more complex and advanced communicative situations. Therefore, choice of the most suitable technological resource depends on the dominant learners' styles as well as the development of linguistic and metacognitive abilities. In this decision-making process, I would like to work with Penzu, since it seems to be simple and appropriate for my students. They could attend the computer room once a week to practise different patterns adding images related to the weekly topic. I think this online tool could provide them with learning opportunities considering their language level and linguistic skills. As this is a process, I would like to see my students participating in project-based learning activities and being actively engaged and motivated.

Andy's Blog

I have mentioned in my previous posts that I have come to think and agree that the new literacy should be teaching to code: Mitch Resnick 'Let's teach children to code' and Professor Richard Nossin 'Technology Enhanced Learning: www.tel.ac.uk/'. With all that as a backup, I will say tonight, that if I am asked to teach tech or not to teach tech, I will go and teach tech in my class and will inspire others to do it, starting with my students. How am I going to do it? I am not sure yet, but I will. To finish I will quote Rt Hon Michael Gove: 'Almost every field of employment now depends on technology. From radio, to television, computers and the internet, each new technological advance has changed our world and changed us too. But there is one notable exception. Education has barely changed.' So, our mission as educators is to: Connect, Share, Analyse, Assess, Apply, Personalise, Engage, Streamline, Include, Know, Compute, Construct.

There are a number of observations to be made from this vignette:

- Interestingly, Sandra highlights two ways in which online reflections were created: individual reflections are used to 'write down ideas and plans for their future lessons', while the discussion forum was used 'to share and discuss with their peers'.
- Sandra also comments that there was a preference for the more dialogic, discussion-focused type of reflection involving peers (see also Kiely and Davis, 2010). From these observations, it seems that individual reflections

are useful as a means of planning *before* teaching, while group reflections are more concerned with discussion and dialogue *after* teaching. In addition to there being a preference for group reflection, it would appear that this mode was also more beneficial. As Sandra tells us: 'group reflection seemed to have had greater impact on the development of the teachers' technological and pedagogical skills'.

• Another comment which Sandra makes coincides with much of our thinking in this chapter: 'teachers can be reflective writers (as opposed to only thinking about their practices) if they have the appropriate tools to reflect with'. In this case, once teachers had been shown how to use online blogs and discussion forums as tools for reflection they were quite happy to use them, resulting in a sharing of ideas and issues.

• From the online blogs, we see how Easter makes a connection between language level and choice of technology; the higher the level, the more sophisticated the choice and use of software. This is an important observation and one which may be overlooked when teachers are selecting an appropriate technology to use with their students.

• Andy's blog highlights the fact that many teachers are not really sure how to integrate technology with their more 'normal' classroom practices, a point made by others, notably Li (2008). There is clearly much work to be done in this area: having access to software and online tools is not adequate in terms of technology enhanced learning. Teachers and learners need to be shown how to make the most of these materials by integrating them with their regular classroom procedures and practices. Online tutorials can be helpful here (see Stannard, 2016).

In this section, we have looked at the ways in which teachers might engage in CPD collaboratively, using online resources to reflect on their practices and give feedback to peers. In the next section, we consider how teachers might engage in self-development, again using a range of tools and practices.

5.3 Teacher Self-development

There now exist a number of tools and procedures which teachers can use to reflect on their practice. Rapid developments in technology mean that it is very easy to make classroom recordings and use those recordings to promote closer understandings of professional practice. In this section, we present a number of extracts which illustrate how teachers might use recordings and reflection as a means of self-development. The suggestion is that teachers can develop very close understandings of their practice through the use of 'snapshot' recordings, which allow them to build up a picture of their professional practice. Essentially, through repeated use of short recordings, reflection at a slight distance and perhaps a conversation with a 'critical friend', there is enormous scope for developing detailed and 'up-close' understandings of local context.

While it is evident that the current teacher education and professional development landscape promotes reflection which is integrated in pre- and in-service courses, the notion of teacher self-development has at least as much to offer. The benefits of undertaking reflection which is integrated into a course are paramount and have been highlighted elsewhere in this book. But the advantages of *teaching* reflection and embedding it in a teacher's practice are potentially limitless. Working independently of a teacher education course gives teachers unique opportunities to investigate their practice and gain closer understandings of local context. Professional *self*-development (i.e. outside the confines of a course) is likely to be longer-lasting, deeper and, ultimately, more fulfilling. For this to happen, time, energy and resources need to be invested in initial teacher education programmes so that reflection is actually *taught* and so that teachers are equipped with the necessary tools and procedures which will enable them to reflect independently, 'in the wild'.

In the remainder of this chapter, we consider how reflection in the wild gets done by considering a number of extracts from a range of contexts. Our focus is largely on the use of procedures which use video with reflection and dialogue, namely: stimulated recall, SETT (self-evaluation of teacher talk) and VEO (video-enhanced observation).

Stimulated Recall

The first extract, 5.1, is taken from a pre-sessional English language course in a UK university. Students on the course are adults and come from a range of international contexts, many from South East Asia, some from Europe and South America. A small group of teachers working on the pre-sessional pro-gramme has formed a professional self-help group to look at the dynamics of their classes, which often include fairly reticent students who are unwilling to participate.

In extract 5.1 a stimulated recall procedure is used to facilitate a teacher's reflections on his use of language while teaching. Stimulated recall entails making an audio or video recording of part of a lesson, selecting part of it for comment and discussing that extract with a colleague (for more detail see Richards, 2004; Walsh, 2011). The video extract may be very short and is selected by the teacher for whatever reason. It is designed to act as a 'springboard' for reflection and to highlight a particular feature or incident. In this extract, the teacher is reflecting on the importance of using appropriate feedback with a group of intermediate adult learners. The transcript of the classroom interaction is presented in the left hand column, while the teacher's, Neil's, reflections and comments on that interaction are in the right hand one.

Extract 5.1

```
L1: when I was a course at
night school=
T: when you were doing a
course right=
L1: we sometimes read Koran
and er but they say I don't
know every time when they were
reading Koran er I was
laughing (mispronounced) so
they said you should go out=
L1=I don't know why because
they had concentration to read
Koran so I haven't I didn't
have concentration so every
time I was laughing
(mispronounced) so they said no
you should go out they er were
they were reading Koran so I
don't know why after that in
our house my family my family
was reading Koran and again I
was laughing (mispronounced)=
T: =you were laughing
```

```
I gave it to them. I allow them
to do that (have long turns)
because I think it's the only
way they gain confidence. And
that's why I reinterpret because
then they think 'oh yes, now
everyone understands'. I think
they are acutely aware as
learners that they have
deficiencies in their delivery
and how articulate they are and
they're aware of this. If I
assist, a re-interpretation,
then everyone is aware of what
they are trying to say then it
gives them confidence.
This girl is willing now to
struggle, whereas 6 months ago
she wasn't.
```

Walsh, 2013: 64

In the extract, Neil has recorded part of a lesson and then is explaining to a colleague the need for the combined strategy of scaffolding and challenge when dealing with feedback. In the classroom interaction data (on the left), there is evidence of Neil 'shaping' learner contributions (Walsh, 2013) (*T: when you were doing a course right=)* in order to ensure that the lesson proceeds smoothly, with the whole class coming along together. 'Shaping' entails providing feedback to a learner contribution and improving it in some way. It combines the two strategies of scaffolding and error correction. Shaping is a very important skill for teachers to acquire since it helps learners 'notice' (Schmidt, 1990) features of their language and make improvements. It is not the same as error correction; the goal is not to correct but rather to help learners improve, possibly by offering a fuller contribution or one which is more appropriate. Essentially, the aim is to help learners produce better formulated and more considered responses.

In his reflective commentary (on the right), we see how Neil alludes to this (*And that's why I reinterpret because then they think 'oh yes, now everyone understands'*). He also makes the interesting observation that a 'reinterpretation' gives learners confidence and suggests that 'struggle' is an important phenomenon in learning a language. The level of awareness Neil demonstrates about his own language use is, arguably, greatly enhanced by the use of stimulated recall, a procedure which enables reflections to be based on actual data taken from the teacher's own context. Note too his reference to the importance of struggling while learning a language (*This girl is willing now to struggle, whereas 6 months ago she wasn't*). This is potentially a very important realization and one which may, directly or indirectly, influence his approach to feedback and error correction. Others have commented on the fact that learning is more effective when students are 'forced' to think for themselves and work things out (e.g. Bygate, 1987); this teacher is alluding to the same idea through the opportunity he has had to look at some evidence from his teaching and reflect on it.

It is clear from the stimulated recall reflective commentary that Neil is able to demonstrate a fairly sophisticated level of understanding of his role in supporting and scaffolding learners as they struggle to express themselves. Teacher interventions and feedback have the dual purpose (as stated here) of keeping the class together and helping learners grow in confidence. Not only is this teacher helping L1 produce a fuller, more appropriate and more clearly articulated response, he is helping the whole class who are, indirectly, participating in a *multilogue* (Schwab, 2011) – the kind of multi-party talk which is typified by almost all classroom discourse.

SETT: Self-evaluation of Teacher Talk

SETT is a framework which allows teachers to evaluate their communication in the classroom. Using SETT (Walsh, 2013) entails making a short recording of a lesson (10–15 minutes) and analyzing the recording (without transcribing it) using the SETT framework. The main goal of SETT is to promote understandings of classroom communication and help teachers improve their use of language and interaction. Its main advantage is that the emphasis is on 'Self'. Teachers simply make a short recording, replay it and make a note of the particular features of their talk which were used. It eliminates the need for wholesale transcription, focusing instead on specific features of talk, and allows the teacher to select which elements of their practice they would like to study. Perhaps most importantly, the SETT framework militates against more evaluative features of peer feedback by allowing teachers to set their own reflective agendas. The 'evaluation' stems from teachers' ability to notice specific features in their talk which are more or less appropriate to their pedagogic goal at that point in time. So, for example, if my goal is to promote discussion and debate, but my SETT evaluation reveals that I ask only display questions, I clearly need to change my questioning strategy. Arguably, self-evaluation is a more powerful means of achieving professional development and one that is more likely to have longer-lasting benefits.

In the next extract, 5.2 below, the teacher T1 (Nick) is using the SETT (self-evaluation of teacher talk) framework as a means of enhancing understandings of 'wait-time'. He is explaining his self-observations to a second teacher, Jane.

Extract 5.2

```
Nick:  I just found it was very enjoyable and the feedback, like
       extended wait-time. Lots of GAPS here where you think there's
       nobody replying and then they suddenly come in

Jane:  Was that conscious or was that just something. . . .?

Nick:  No I deliberately because I know that the far-easterners
       have problems speaking and therefore I gave them I just gave
       them whatever time they needed you know. In some cases
       they're processing the question and they're processing the
       information and they HAVE to literally look into their own
       minds and do they have an experience which relates to the
       question. And this is the case I think particularly with Roy
       with Yung rather and Jang who are Korean I think the wait-
       time is ALways more extensive for them.
```

Walsh, 2013: 85

For Nick, there is a growing realization of the value of wait-time in whole class open discussion (*I just gave them whatever time they needed*). He comments on what actually happens following a teacher prompt (*they're processing the question [. . .] and they HAVE to literally look into their own minds and do they have an experience which relates to the question*) and makes the interesting observation that for some students, this takes more time and they need to be given that time (*the wait-time is ALways more extensive for them*).

It seems from Nick's comments that the process of self-evaluation has helped him to clarify his thinking and develop a closer understanding of his interactional choices. As he says: 'I deliberately because I know that the far-easterners have problems speaking and therefore I gave them I just gave them whatever time they needed you know'. Arguably, using the SETT procedure allowed him to analyze this aspect of his teaching in far greater detail and make changes by increasing wait-time where necessary. A simple change in practice maybe, but it is one which is likely to have a huge impact on the kind of inter-action which occurs and a change which is likely to open up 'space for learning' (Walsh and Li, 2013. See also Chapter 7).

In extract 5.3 below, we can see how the same teacher actually incorporates extended wait-time into his teaching. Here, we see Nick trying to elicit a par-ticular piece of vocabulary (*shopping centre*). Note the three-second pauses between questions. This use of extended wait-time and the accompanying strategy of using a different question each time leads to an extended learner turn. Again, arguably, it is this use of extended wait-time which results in a longer response than the one which might be expected by the teacher. The learner not only provides the piece of vocabulary the teacher is seeking, she also comments on why people go to shopping centres (*it's very convenient*). The point is that Nick is not only able to articulate and discuss a particular aspect of his teaching (the use of extended wait time in extract 5.2), he is also able to demonstrate this practice while teaching.

Extract 5.3

```
T:  what are the things that we have today with shopping? what do
    we have today? (3) what do we call these places today? (3)
    what's the word we're talking about? (3)
L:  shopping centres because you just go the shopping centre you
    can buy everything (.) it's very convenient
```
Walsh, 2013

The SETT framework has been used in a range of educational settings since its publication in 2006 and 2013. These include initial teacher education programmes (PGCE) for English and drama teachers (Walsh and Lowing, 2008); INSET courses for experienced teachers; a study evaluating the value of classroom observation in the Middle East (Howard, 2010); CELTA programmes around the world; a primary science classroom; various secondary EFL contexts around the world; two university classroom contexts; and an Irish-medium secondary classroom. In short, the framework has been used extensively to promote awareness and understanding of the role of interaction in class-based learning and to help teachers improve their practice.

The SETT framework comprises four classroom micro-contexts (called *modes*) and thirteen interactional features (called *interactures*). Classroom discourse is portrayed as a series of complex and interrelated micro-contexts (called *modes*), where meanings are co-constructed by teachers and learners and where learning occurs through the ensuing talk of teachers and learners (Walsh, 2013). The key to developing good practice is for teachers to acquire detailed profiles of the interactions which take place in their classes as a means of understanding how learning opportunities are created and how 'space for learning' (Walsh and Li, 2011) can be opened up, and in order to create the kind of dialogic, engaged learning environments which are currently being advocated (see, for example, Mercer et al., 2009; Alexander, 2008). (See Walsh, 2013 for a full description of the framework.)

VEO: Video-enhanced Observation

There is no doubt that one of the most useful ways of encouraging self-development and facilitating reflection is through the use of video. With continuing improvements in technology, it is easy for anyone to make a video recording of their teaching and use that recording to identify particular aspects which they would like to improve, or, indeed, features which should be extended or developed as examples of good practice. Short recordings are often more valuable than recordings of whole lessons, which is why we advocate the use of 'snapshot' recordings: short (7–12 minute) lesson segments, taken from different stages of a class. Using this approach, it is possible to quickly identify features of a teacher's practice which could be improved or developed. In 7.3 we will return to the topic of how video fosters spoken reflection.

One piece of software which is being used more and more to enhance understandings of classroom life and facilitate the creation of profiles is VEO (video-enhanced observation, Haines and Miller, 2014 (see www.veo-group. com/)). VEO is a freely downloadable app (at the time of writing) which is used to tag video recordings of a teacher's performance. Tagging entails identifying specific interactional practices (either synchronously or asynchronously) and then evaluating them during playback to build up a profile of that teaching episode. The advantages of using video for reflecting on practice are well-established in the literature and have been promoted for some years now. According to Kong, for example, (2010: 1772), '(t)he use of these video systems is considered constructive in supporting (. . .) teachers to externalize their reflective thoughts, based on accurate video-recorded data from their teaching practice'. (See also, Borko et al., 2009; Hixon and So, 2009; Marsh, Mitchell and Adamczyk, 2010.)

By enabling the live-tagging of video, the VEO app goes further, generating data and evidence which is both quantitative and qualitative in nature. Predefined tags are used by practitioners to time-stamp video and jump to the exact instance of a particular feature. For example, by using VEO, it is possible during playback to move through all the examples of display questions, error correction, instructions, or whatever has been tagged. By engaging in dialogue with a peer or critical friend, it is possible, quickly and easily, to heighten awareness of particular features of a teacher's practice and build understanding of interaction for professional development.

The advantages that VEO brings to analyzing complex situations make it highly appropriate for studying interaction, where multiple perspectives are possible and where relevant frameworks can clarify and enhance its understanding. An important feature of VEO (and indeed, almost any professional development work using video) is the potential to create an online community of practice where short extracts can be displayed and discussed in a spirit of mutual self-help and professional development. A similar community has been built through WebCEF (www.webcef.eu/), where language teachers can benchmark their language evaluation skills with colleagues across Europe with reference to the Common European Framework of Reference (CEFR). On this site, language learners or language teachers can upload and assess video samples together with teachers and language learners across Europe. (Other examples of similar online sites are given in Appendix 10.)

Online communities such as VEO and WebCEF are formed between teachers sharing videos of interactions, with the potential for posting comments and offering feedback to teachers across the world or within a particular context. VEO enables practitioners to describe and discuss their teaching through online forums in the first instance. Through dialogue and discussion, however, it is possible to foster greater levels of understanding by classifying, aggregating, sharing, comparing and discussing practice, in an iterative, reflective process. Communicating via the VEO social/professional network, these processes and the communities involved may operate at a distance, thus exposing practitioners to a wider range of different interaction styles and offering a clearer view of their own practice.

In the vignette below, Paul Miller talks about the ways in which VEO has benefited teachers in a UK secondary school.

PAUL MILLER'S VIGNETTE (UK)

Investigating how teachers and trainers use the VEO system to support lesson observation and feedback has uncovered interesting insights into processes of reflection.

A Deputy Head Teacher of a large secondary school encouraged teacher colleagues to form small groups to share 'tagged' video using the VEO app and system. Lesson excerpts were recorded and time-stamped via the VEO app, before being shared. This enabled teachers to jump to categorized key moments according to predefined frameworks, such as examples of error correction or instructions.

Reflecting on the reflective process itself, it soon became clear to the Deputy Head that focus was critical to the quality of professional learning to emerge:

> The feedback part is really intertwined with the initial observation capture. If you can plan and agree a focus, then it helps the reflective conversation enormously.

For the conversation to be valuable to busy teachers it needed to be direct and to the point. As the same Deputy Head commented:

> Using VEO to jump to key moments was important for the teacher to know that the video would be relevant to their professional needs. It developed a confidence in the process, as teachers began to better understand what they actually do in the classroom.

Selecting key moments also allowed for focus on pedagogy and interaction, beyond self-conscious consideration of voice and appearance.

> Without focus, and with everything that happens in the class, it became too much. The teacher looked more at themselves as a teacher, what they look like and how they sound. That can be helpful, but it's important to get past that and look at the techniques you employ, the delivery and the learning.

> Selecting *critical* moments allowed the teacher to look past their personally held self-identities to analyze their actions, alongside impact on students. This was made possible by explicitly agreeing a professional focus, so that practice could be continuously adapted and improved over time.

A number of observations emerge from Paul's vignette:

1. The formation of small groups to share and comment on video extracts is something which seems to have considerable value, especially when there is a clear focus to the discussions. Such a practice helps to eliminate the typically judgmental comments which the sharing of videos might encourage. Focused observation helps to keep the discussion firmly centred on an issue or puzzle.
2. Having short episodes with the potential to jump through the video to the next example is an important feature of the process, as highlighted by the Deputy Head. The procedure means that all extraneous events may be ignored, allowing a focus to be maintained on repeated social actions, or classroom practices.
3. Even the process of agreeing a focus is likely to promote professional development. As Paul comments, the selection of *critical* moments is an important first step and one which is likely to generate a useful and reflective discussion.

A key to self-development in the use of VEO is the use of short, 'snapshot' recordings made over a period of time and involving different classes and a range of contexts in order to build up a profile of a teacher's practice. This in itself allows teachers to first describe and then understand their practice. More importantly, the procedures described in this section offer valuable insights into the ways in which classroom practices might be improved or extended. Through the use of tools like VEO, WebCEF and stimulated recall, and by creating online communities, we suggest that much more detailed understandings can be attained through discussion and dialogue which are evidence-based. In this way, 'self' development can be extended to involve other professionals, promoting a more 'social' perspective on learning which is (arguably) more enjoyable, more interesting and longer-lasting.

5.4 Professional Groups

Teachers' groups or professional networks can be a powerful means of self-help and support, offering a context in which professional development can occur in a non-threatening and collaborative way. There are many examples of such groups, including organizations such as TESOL, English UK, MLA, BAAL and

IATEFL, all of which hold an annual conference and offer other kinds of support, normally through membership and through the employment of newsletters, blogs and special interest groups. The main advantage of these groups is that they offer a structured and well-organized support network and make members aware of new developments, materials, publications and so on.

In terms of promoting reflection, it is probably fair to say that smaller, more localized networks offer more opportunities for professional development. The main reason is that teachers in such professional groups all work in the same context and share common problems, issues and frustrations, as well as being able to share successes and highlight achievements. One such group that has been working together since 2004 in the south west of Ireland around the Shannon area includes university teachers from Cork, Limerick and Ennis. This informal professional group works together to share examples of good practice, highlight common issues and engage in discussions about current debates in higher education in Ireland and beyond. Around eight higher education institutions (HEIs) are members, including colleges, regional training centres and institutes of technology. Participating members teach at both undergraduate and postgraduate levels and offer a full spectrum of courses across the whole curriculum. Every year this consortium holds a competition which results in a prestigious teaching excellence award, offered to the most deserving university teacher, as judged by a panel of experts from within and outside Ireland. The process involves candidates submitting a reflective portfolio of their teaching, including short video clips with accompanying reflective commentaries. (An example of one portfolio is presented in Chapter 6.)

The panel of experts, working independently, assesses the portfolios and accompanying video clips and draws up a shortlist of their top three candidates. In the final stage of the process, the panel comes together and a discussion ensues in order to identify the winner for that particular year.

There are many points of interest in this process which have direct relevance to our discussion here. First, there are no published criteria for making the award. The panel members use their own experience and expertise to identify (independently) their top three entries, based on the evidence presented in the portfolios and video recordings. Second, the discussions are heavily evidence-based: panel members must make use of written comments in the candidates' portfolios, or evidence taken from the video recordings. Third, in the years since its inception, there has never been any disagreement concerning the overall winner, despite the fact that there are no pre-determined descriptors or assessment criteria.

Many readers might find this entire process rather subjective and even unfair, given the very high stakes of the award. Some readers might even suggest that the criteria should be agreed in advance and the winning entry selected against those criteria. The counter argument to this is that there is obviously no one 'right' way to teach; imposing criteria might influence the ways in which the process is undertaken and even result in candidates teaching in a certain way in order to increase their chances of success.

In the extracts below, we see samples of comments taken from two panel members in the same year (2010–11). The panel comprised five highly experienced teacher educators, all of whom wrote a separate evaluation of each candidate's performance based on their submitted DVD and portfolio.

Extract 5.4

Panel member 1

1. The philosophy is good but relates to transmission approach.
2. Teaching performance on DVD does not closely match claimed philosophy – actually quite didactic and traditional.
3. Clearly very concerned about student development and responding to student needs and has changed teaching as a result of feedback.
4. Portfolio weak on discussion of assessment
5. Very reflective but there are gaps in this.
6. Range and breadth of teaching – offsite and online teaching environments explored.
7. Highly committed and keen.
8. Gaps in evidence with no student evaluations present.

A number of observations can be made on these comments by panel member 1, cited here verbatim. First, it is apparent that the espoused theory on learning and teaching of the panel member does not coincide with that of the candidate. Nor does the candidate's espoused theory appear to correspond to what they do in practice; there is (apparently) a mis-match between what this candidate claims in their portfolio and what they actually do in practice (comments 1 and 2). It is evident from these comments that both panel member and candidate have a clear sense of what constitutes good teaching in a higher education context; they reject 'transmission' style teaching in favour of a more student-centred approach (see also comment 3).

Second, the panel member highlights the need for consistency in providing evidence (comments 5 and 8). It is interesting that this panel member highlights the importance of student evaluations as evidence and also the need to talk about assessment in the portfolio (comment 4). This panel member also suggests that reflections need to be consistent and thorough in order to stand up to scrutiny (comment 5). Finally, note the importance attached to being able to teach in a range of contexts – here, both on- and off-site (comment 6).

We now turn to panel member 2's comments on the same candidate:

Extract 5.5

Panel member 2

1. Teaching philosophy not related to literature.
2. Wide range of evidence, including Head of Department report, but lacks evidence from student survey.
3. Wide range of teaching approaches: buzz groups, snowballing, online.
4. Student support and advice very strong. Inclusive learning and support but didn't elaborate on what he had changed as the result of feedback.
5. Sense that he is teaching individuals rather than a mass of students, and responsive to individual needs.
6. Empathetic, although weaker on evidence of student feedback and response to this.

Interestingly, this panel member's opening comment stresses the need for a candidate's teaching philosophy to relate to literature and they then underline the need for evidence and support from students (comments 2, 4 and 6). These comments suggest that for teaching in HE to be effective, university teachers should be aware of the knowledge base of their discipline (HE teaching and learning), as espoused in the literature, as well as the more subtle, less tangible experiential knowledge which can be gained through, for example, student feedback (see Johnson, 2009). In the comments above, panel member 2 highlights the need to connect espoused knowledge and experiential knowledge.

There is some allusion in panel member 2's comments to the importance of establishing good relationships in HE teaching and learning (comments 4, 5 and 6). In each of these comments, this panel member seems to be commending the candidate's empathy for and attention to their students, highlighting the importance of student support, inclusion and being responsive. Like panel member 1, however, panel member 2 also points to the need for more specific evidence from student feedback (comment 6). There is also an implicit suggestion in these comments that feedback from students and subsequent reflection should lead to a change in practice (comment 4). We return to the theme of reflecting on feedback from language learners in 9.3.

From this very brief discussion, a number of observations can be made about these two panel members' evaluations of candidate reflections. Both sets of comments indicate that teachers need to use both espoused theories of teaching and learning and a more experiential knowledge base derived from experience and introspection. Panel member 2 highlights the need for evidence from literature, while panel member 1 points to the need to be less 'traditional' and more inclusive.

There are, then, benefits to be gained from belonging to a professional group, where reflections are likely to be of interest to all involved and where there are opportunities for the sharing of good practice. The advantages are increased when there is a common purpose for the group and when the context is clearly defined.

In the final section of this chapter, we look a little more closely at social networks and communities of practice.

5.5 Social Networks and Communities of Practice

We have already seen in this chapter and elsewhere in this book how current developments in technology have resulted in an increase and improvement in opportunities to engage in more interactive and collaborative reflection. In this chapter, for example, we witnessed how the use of VEO can help teachers create communities, share video recordings and comment on both classroom practices and reflective commentaries. We saw an example of an online community of eight teachers in Chile looking at ways of integrating technology with their teaching and reflecting on their practice through the use of an online discussion forum and individual blogs.

We live in a highly networked world; most of us are associated with several professional networks such as LinkedIn or ResearchGate, while many readers will be on Facebook, Twitter and so on. It is, arguably, almost impossible to engage in any professional activity without some recourse to social networks – the act of finding or changing a job, for example, will often involve looking at people's profiles on social networks.

Attitudes towards social networks vary hugely, as we see in Sarah Silva-Banks' vignette below. In her vignette, Sarah describes the experiences of two students on a summer internship, reflecting on their approach to and use of professional networks.

SARAH SILVA-BANKS' VIGNETTE (UK)

Context

These extracts are taken from a study looking at how students use blogs for personal development and reflective practice whilst on a paid internship. The internships take place over the summer within a university department and usually last for eight weeks. The interns are selected after interview and one of the requirements is that they must use a blog to write reflectively about their experience. They are given guidelines to follow which have prompts for the interns to respond to. They also have regular meetings and communication with their mentor. These extracts are taken from two different blogs but both follow the prompt 'Networking and Marketing Yourself'. Students are asked to consider what they are doing to build a network and market themselves as well as think about the problems they are having with doing so.

Data Extracts

(Please note: to maintain anonymity, **recognizable** names have been replaced with a generic name in italics.)

Intern 2 – Networking and Marketing Yourself
In terms of actively building a network, I haven't had many opportunities. There are only a set number of people in my team, and virtually all of our work involves sitting at a desk. I have added people on my LinkedIn page, and have even been written a recommendation [sic], which is a big boost to my profile.

I guess my main difficulty with networking is that a lot of connections made this way feel quite superficial to me. This may be because I haven't been in this environment before, but having a loose connection to friends in high places isn't nearly as impressive as a few close people who know you really well, and can give a perfect recommendation. I would like to be more of a believer in the whole networking world, but it just doesn't feel right. Everyone has a friend on Facebook who has about 2000 'friends'.. that's how networking feels to me.

I am trying to build up a personal brand, thinking of what I can provide and what my USPs are. I have started working on a personal webpage, to show both my coding and digital art skills. I am also working on a portfolio, as an easy and direct way to show people what I have made.

When I was making my LinkedIn profile, I put as little information on there as possible. That sounds silly, doesn't it? Surely people would want to know about *everything* I have to offer? I realised that most people don't. Is a recruiter really going to care that I was form captain in Year 7? No, but they will care that I've had work experience in a certain field. **UX** has taught me that the less people have to read to get the point, the better.

Intern 4 – Week 6 blog – Networking and Marketing Yourself
(Sorry for the delay!)
The job market can be so highly competitive that it is imperative to **utilise** contacts in order to get ahead. Luckily I have a large network due to my parents, which has helped me gain experience at *various companies*. I have also met young professionals through my elder brother, which is how I built a tie with *a company*. When networking, never underestimate someone due to their age. The younger they are the more they remembered the struggle of finding a job after uni! The key skill I must now develop is how to turn existing experiences in to larger networks and possible jobs.

Although it is easier to gain work experience through contacts, it is harder to be offered a job! However it is often beneficial to have contacts read and edit your applications, as, if they are in the agency you're applying to, they know it best. Within the advertising industry I have made key contacts through my boyfriend as luckily he is an account executive at a London agency but also through my uni friend's parents – one of which used to headhunt for this industry and has become a kind of mentor to me. We e-mail regularly and she has suggested books for me to read, agencies to apply for and given me invaluable advice about the industry.

I use LinkedIn to build and record a network whilst promoting myself as a potential employee. In order to have a strong profile I have uploaded all of my qualifications and keep it updated regularly with my experience.

One thing I have been wondering recently is whether to upload examples of my work to LinkedIn (aka 'professional content')?! I have written an essay looking at creativity in advertising and how it conflicts with strategy, throughout the process of creative advertising. I have also produced material during this internship which I could upload consisting of social media reviews, infographics and other visuals. However I am hesitant to take the plunge – any advice?

Commentary

I chose these two extracts because even though the interns have different views on networking they approach the task similarly. Intern 2 describes his feelings towards networking and the reasons why he might feel this way. He gives details about what he is doing to try and 'market' himself and describes what he has done with his LinkedIn profile. It is interesting to me that he feels able to speak negatively about networking a) even though there is an expectation on him 'to network' and b) because he knows his blog posts are not private, that they will be read by his mentor. Intern 4's feelings towards networking are quite different to those of intern 2. To her, it seems that the more networking you do the better. She talks about the number of contacts she has, but she is keen to explain that she must now develop the skill of turning those network contacts into jobs. Similarly to intern 2, she explains what she is doing to 'promote' herself and how she has used LinkedIn.

What I find fascinating about both blog posts is the dialogic nature they have, something which I'm starting to consider as inherent of reflective writing in the blog form. Both seem to be engaging with the reader, as if they are having a conversation with the person reading their blog. The use of rhetorical questions shows this, for example, in intern 2's post: 'That sounds silly, doesn't it?' Intern 4 does something similar: 'One thing I have been wondering recently is whether to

upload examples of my work to LinkedIn (aka 'professional content')?!'
At the very start of intern 4's blog post there is an indirect address to
the reader with the "[s]orry for the delay". As a reader, I feel involved
in what the intern is going to tell me. Intern 4 even poses a direct
question to the reader at the end of her post asking for advice. She
seems to be opening up a channel for two-way communication.

This kind of two-way conversation is what we are often striving for
when encouraging students, trainees or employees to engage with
reflective practice; for them to consider their stance or what they
have done, and why they feel that way and to express that. Although
the rhetorical questions may not be considered two-way, they do
work to show what is concerning the intern and it demonstrates
that they are perhaps thinking a little deeper and questioning what
has been asked of them. Likewise, the interns do have access
to a mentor, and their mentors as well as other members of the
careers and skills team will be monitoring their blog and are able to
comment and strike up a conversation with the intern based on any
points that arise in the blog. The interns are well aware of this and
perhaps are using this indirect way of addressing the reader for this
purpose.

Of interest to our discussion here is the extent to which the students' attitudes
to networking differ: intern 2 seems to have an inherently negative attitude to
networking while intern 4 sees it as an essential process in finding a job. While
they both use networking, it is clear that they engage with the process in very
different ways: for intern 2, it seems rather like the process of having 'friends' on
Facebook, while intern 4 sees it as a key feature of her professional life.

We were particularly struck by the dialogic, almost conversational nature of
these reflections, a point also made by Sarah Silva-Banks, who comments,
'What I find fascinating about both blog posts is the dialogic nature they
have, something which I'm starting to consider as inherent of reflective writing
in the blog form'. This observation concurs with much of what has already been
said in this chapter relating to the value of dialogue and collaboration in online
reflection. Sarah points to a number of features of these posts which makes
them dialogic: the use of rhetorical questions; direct requests for help or advice;
apologies. She also comments on the importance of engaging the reader and
making the reader feel part of the reflective process, a point which has been
made elsewhere in this book. Interesting too is the point Sarah makes about
who reads these posts; here, and in many contexts, blog posts have multiple
audiences and may be written for more than one purpose, something for writers
to consider when writing their reflective commentaries.

5.6 Summary

In this chapter, we have discussed 'reflection in the wild', a context which arises when practitioners are working independently and not on a PRESET or INSET course. We considered what can be achieved by individuals working alone, as part of a professional group or by using technology to interact in a wider community of practice. We use the term 'in the wild' to capture the idea that reflection may become a lifelong practice which teachers develop in the same way they acquire expertise in other classroom practices.

For reflection to succeed over time, we argue that RP needs to be integrated into teachers' professional practices in such a way that it does not feel like a burden or additional chore. The challenge, then, is to identify tools and proce-dures which can be used alongside existing pedagogical practices to promote reflection and enhance professional development. Our discussion focused on ways of doing reflection in the wild by looking at reflective practices in CPD, working alone, as part of a professional group, or through the use of social networks and online communities of practice.

In all the contexts presented in this chapter, a range of tools and procedures was presented to show how reflection gets done. Of particular value is the use and sharing of video-recorded lesson segments, online blogs or discussion forums, the use of collaborative practices involving sharing of evidence and talk, and specialized, 'ad hoc' tools (such as pro-forma or frameworks) designed with a particular context in mind and for a specific purpose.

References

Alexander, R.J. (2008). *Towards dialogic teaching: rethinking classroom talk* (4th edition). York: Dialogos.

Bolam, R. and Weindling, D. (2006). *Synthesis of research and evaluation projects concerned with capacity-building through teachers' professional development.* London: General Teaching Council for England.

Borko, H., Whitcomb, J. and Liston, D. (2009). Wicked problems and other thoughts on issues of technology and teacher learning. *Journal of Teacher Education,* 60(1), 3–7.

British Council. (2015). *Continuing Professional Development (CPD) Framework for teachers.*

Bygate, M. (1987). *Speaking.* Oxford University Press.

Cordingley, P., Bell, M., Thomason, S. and Firth, A. (2005). The impact of collaborative continuing professional development (CPD) on classroom teaching and learning. *Review: how do collaborative and sustained CPD and sustained but not collaborative CPD affect teaching and learning?*

Day, C. (1999). *Developing teachers: the challenges of lifelong learning.* London: Falmer Press.

Day, C., Stobart, G., Sammons, P., Kington, A., Gu, Q., Smees, R. and Kujtaba, T. (2006). *Variations in teachers' work, lives and effectiveness. Research Report RR743.* London: Department of Education and Skills.

Haines, J. and Miller, P. (2014). VEO: Video enhanced observation.

Hargreaves, A. (1994). *Changing teachers, changing times: teachers' work and culture in the postmodern age.* Teachers College Press.

Hayes, D. (ed.). (2014). *Innovations in the continuing professional development of English language teachers.* London: British Council.

Hixon, E. and So, H.J. (2009). Technology's role in field experiences for preservice teacher training. *Educational Technology & Society,* 12(4), 294–304.

Howard, A. (2010). Is there such a thing as a typical language lesson? *Classroom Discourse*, 1(1), 82–100.

Ingvarson, L., Meiers, M. and Beavis, A. (2005). Factors affecting the impact of professional development programs on teachers' knowledge, practice, student outcomes and efficacy. *Australian Council for Educational Research*.

Johnson, K.E. (2009). *Second language teacher education: a sociocultural perspective*. London and New York: Routledge.

Kennedy, A. (2011). Collaborative continuing professional development (CPD) for teachers in Scotland: aspirations, opportunities and barriers. *European Journal of Teacher Education*, 34(1), 25–41.

Kiely, R. and Davis, M. (2010). From transmission to transformation: teacher learning in English for speakers of other languages. *Language Teaching Research*, 14(3), 277–295.

Kong, S.C. (2010). Using a web-enabled video system to support student–teachers' self-reflection in teaching practice. *Computers & Education*, 55(4), 1772–1782.

Li, D.C.S. (2008). Understanding mixed code and classroom code-switching: myths and realities. *New Horizons in Education*, 56(3), 75–87.

Marsh, B., Mitchell, N. and Adamczyk, P. (2010). Interactive video technology: enhancing professional learning in initial teacher education. *Computers & Education*, 54(3), 742–748.

Mercer, N., Dawes, L. and Kleine Staarman, J. (2009). Dialogic teaching in the primary classroom. *Language and Education*, 23(4), 353–369.

Muijs, D. and Lindsay, G. (2008). Where are we at? An empirical study of levels and methods of evaluating continuing professional development. *British Educational Research Journal*, 34(2), 195–211.

Nunan, D. and Lamb, C. (1996). *The self-directed teacher: managing the learning process*. Cambridge: Cambridge University Press.

OECD (Organisation for Economic Cooperation and Development). (2011). *Building a high quality teaching profession: lessons from around the world*. Paris: OECD.

Richards, J. (2004). Towards reflective teaching. *The Language Teacher*, 22, 2–5.

Schmidt, R. (1990). The role of consciousness in second language learning. *Applied Linguistics*, 11, 129–158.

Schwab, G. (2011). From dialogue to multilogue: a different view on participation in the English foreign-language classroom. *Classroom Discourse*, 2(1), 3–19.

Seedhouse, P. (2004). *The interactional architecture of the language classroom: a conversation analysis perspective*. Malden, MA: Blackwell Publishers.

Stannard, R. (2016). Teacher training videos. Available at www.teachertrainingvideos.com/

Walsh, S. (2011). *Exploring classroom discourse: language in action*. London and New York: Routledge.

Walsh, S. (2013). *Classroom discourse and teacher development*. Edinburgh, UK: Edinburgh University Press.

Walsh, S. and Li, L. (2013). Conversations as space for learning. *International Journal of Applied Linguistics* (INJAL), 23(2), 247–266.

Walsh, S. and Lowing, K. (2008). Talking to learn or learning to talk: PGCE students' development of interactional competence. In *British Educational Research Association Conference, Heriot-Watt University, Edinburgh*.

Zipin, L. (2002). *Too much with too little: shift and intensification in the work of ACT teachers*. Available online at www.aeuact.asn.au/info-centre/documents/WorkloadReport.pdf. (Last accessed 31 May 2016.)

6
Reflection in Writing

6.1 Introduction

Reflective Writing

In this chapter, we consider the ways in which reflection can be fostered through writing. We have argued elsewhere for a rebalancing in teacher education courses towards opportunities for spoken reflection (Mann and Walsh, 2013). However, we still believe that written forms of reflection are important, providing that opportunities for written reflection are structured in a purposeful and well-supported way. We open the chapter with a description of what written reflection is, and then consider the effect of assessment on written reflection. Finally, we offer an overview of some of the various approaches which have been used to promote reflection through writing. Subsequent sections in the chapter offer a more detailed perspective on current approaches to reflection in writing.

What is reflective writing? And why do it? According to Burton et al. (2009), there are three reasons for doing written reflection, which they see as:

- a lifelong learning resource for teachers
- a powerful tool in any form of inquiry-based teaching, such as reflective practice and action research
- a flexible process, capable of providing professional support and stimulus to teachers in any teaching circumstances.

There are, it seems, very good reasons for promoting this kind of reflective practice. In light of the many articles about written reflection, there is ample evidence that it is by far the predominant approach around the world. Most pre- and in-service teacher education courses use written reflection, while more dialogic, spoken forms are less common (see Chapters 7 and 8). There may be good reason for this. Written forms of reflection provide a permanent record of the process and can be easily shared and read by others. By definition, they also offer practitioners the time and space needed to organize and structure their reflections and make changes as they compose (Farrell, 2013). In short, there are strong parallels between the process of reflection and the process of writing;

we would even go as far as to say that writing *is* reflection. The process of writing down thoughts, comments and introspections is more than simply a record of reflection. The act of writing *about* reflection equates *with* reflection – they are one and the same thing. In sum, by writing about an experience we are reflecting on that experience and clarifying or 'shaping' our own understanding of it.

Other researchers, however, would argue that it is very easy to write about an experience *as if* it happened, in order, for example, to satisfy the requirements of a course, avoid reflecting or please the reader. Gray and Block (2012) demonstrate how written reflections may be falsified because it is often so difficult to put into writing particular reflections about an experience. They use data from a PGCE (Postgraduate Certificate in Education) programme to support this argument. In the extract below, we see how a trainee teacher struggles with the need to provide evidence of professional learning from her teaching practice:

Extract 6.1

> I spent a whole day last week writing the evidence which consists of seven sentences starting *today I realised this* and bla bla bla. But because it's evidence based actually I could very well not have done these things and written that I had anyway. They're asking you to create the evidence out of nothing but it's completely possible because it's such a long list and I told my mentor that and he said *well do it if you think by the end of the year you haven't produced evidence for everything, just fake it.*
>
> *Gray and Block, 2012: 130–131*

In Mann and Walsh (2013), we made a number of observations about this extract:

- It demonstrates how a record of reflection *is* the reflection itself. This may not be the kind of reflection that 'they' (the tutors) want, but it is still reflective writing and stands as a record of some of the challenges posed by the process.
- It highlights how difficult it is for this trainee teacher to reflect on her own practice and use evidence to demonstrate learning (which could be a useful perspective for the tutors).
- It demonstrates, through the mentor's advice, that it is relatively easy for trainee teachers to 'fake' their reflections (Hobbs, 2007), perhaps when they have not been given adequate preparation in *doing* reflective practice.
- This reflection also highlights the need for trainees to provide their own evidence for professional development rather than selecting from a list provided by the institution.

Reflection and Assessment

A possible explanation for the situation outlined in extract 6.1 is that the trainee simply had no idea how to provide evidence for every experience; she had probably never been taught how to do this. After all, how often do we see examples of people doing reflection and how often is it actually demonstrated, described or *taught*? Another explanation, and one which concerns us directly, is the fact that most written reflections are assessed. They provide the kind of evidence that course tutors need to make judgments about 'progress' and 'professional development'. However, as we have seen in extract 6.1, assessment practices may actually distort the kind of reflections which occur; trainees simply record the more positive aspects of their teaching and ignore the negative ones. Or, they simply record 'evidence' which satisfies course tutors or assessment criteria. The consequence is the same, resulting in 'inauthentic reflection' (Roberts, 1998) or even 'faking it' (Hobbs, 2007).

In a recent study which took place in Northern Ireland and Canada (McCabe et al., 2011), student teachers and their tutors were asked to define RP, say how they do it, identify specific practices and then describe what it meant for them. One of the main findings of this study was that student teachers frequently failed to see the point of repeated written reflections which were assessed. In the words of one of the Canadian student teachers:

Extract 6.2

> Sometimes I don't really see the relevancy to reflect on some of the assignments we do, and therefore, really, all I'm doing is I am writing up something that may or may not be my actual opinion, I'm just writing something up to hand something in. I find that happens more often than maybe you'd like.
>
> *McCabe et al., 2011: 276*

And, in the words of one of the Northern Irish student teachers:

Extract 6.3

> Well, I always think that there is a personal gain to doing reflective practices, but, I found myself when I was writing my reflections at night [after a day of practice teaching] that I was thinking of, okay, what did they want to see in my reflections, rather than what do I want to see in myself.
>
> *McCabe et al., 2011: 277*

Both extracts highlight the tendency of trainees to 'fake' (Hobbs, 2007) their reflections in order to conform with course or institutional requirements, or to meet expectations. The position taken in this chapter is that teacher educators need to take account of ways to demonstrate and discuss reflection and to ensure that participants have free rein in what they reflect on. With training and the use of appropriate tools which are tailored to different stages of professional development, trainees would be much better equipped to reflect honestly and openly on their practices. There is too, we suggest, a pressing need to consider more carefully the relationship between reflection and assessment with a view to modifying current practices, or even 'decoupling' assessment from reflection. Given the issues associated with assessing reflection, there is, perhaps, a case to be made for not assessing reflection and for finding alternative ways of judging professional development.

Written Reflection and Professional Development

The act of getting teachers or trainees to write about their experiences on an assessed course raises other issues (see Mann and Walsh, 2013). The first is that the act of writing about an experience may cause practitioners to focus on the writing task itself, rather than on their reflection and accurate reporting of that experience. Very often, 'writing' entails the completion of a checklist or pro-forma, a kind of 'tick-box' exercise which may not actually promote much reflection at all. Indeed, the repeated use of such instruments is likely to result in a mechanical, unthinking approach to reflection where the main concern is to 'get the task done' rather than provide evidence of critical reflection. And of course, where reflective pieces form part of the assessed coursework of a programme, they are subjected to the institutional assessment criteria of that course. This may force practitioners to demonstrate that they meet assessment criteria rather than allowing them to really express their position. As Scott (2005: 27) says, 'reflective writing, ostensibly a form of self-analysis, takes place in an institutional forum and is scrutinized according to institutional means and standards'; Bolton sees such social structures as limiting the value of personal experience and 'increasingly hemming professionals in' (2010: 1).

Another challenge for reflective writing which uses checklists and pro-formas is that the same instruments are often used repeatedly for the duration of the course. Apart from the mechanical, 'recipe-following' behaviour this may encourage (Boud, 2010: 27), reflections are likely to operate at a 'surface' rather than 'deep' level (Biggs, 2003). Put simply, this kind of reflection does little to promote long-lasting professional development, nor does it help develop understandings of local context – something which we believe to be key to effective teaching.

Repeated use of the same instrument also means that trainees are not challenged to think differently about their performance; nor are they exposed to a range of task-types which are aligned with their stage of development. It is always important to design and use reflective tools which are 'fit for purpose' and to train practitioners in reflective practice in such a way that they are able to make informed and evidence-based decisions about their teaching. (See section 6.2 below for suggestions concerning appropriate tools.)

Approaches to Written Reflection

According to Burton et al. (2009), reflective writing should be based on the kinds of writing practices which teachers typically use in their professional lives. Examples of the kinds of writing which teachers carry out include:

- Lesson planning
- Designing units of work
- Jotting down ideas
- Note-taking
- Taking messages
- Recording the gist of meetings
- Marking student assignments
- Filling in assessment sheets
- Drafting class reports
- Making journal entries
- Editing drafts of texts
- Sending emails
- Critiquing course books
- Writing up projects.

Burton et al. (2009) argue that any one of these types of writing could become reflective. To some extent, we would agree, given that each one has the potential to provide data and evidence on which to reflect. Additionally, and importantly, we would argue that reflective writing must have a clear *purpose* and be designed for a particular *audience*. In other words, reflective practitioners need to know why they are writing and who they are writing for. As with any kind of writing, reflective writing may have high or low reciprocity (audience response) and be more or less formal or informal.

In addition to understanding the importance of writing purpose, audience, interactivity and so on, we also need some sense of the various forms that written reflection can take, and of which approaches are most commonly used. Farrell (2013) tells us that there are two main approaches to reflective writing: journals and narrative. These can be further sub-divided: journals, for example, can be represented by blogs, wikis, portfolios, e-portfolios, and so on, while narrative can take the form of both spoken and written formats. In the remainder of this chapter, we consider how written reflection 'gets done', using extracts from a range of contexts.

6.2 Checklists and Forms

There are many examples of checklists, pro-formas and forms which are currently used to promote reflection on both pre- and in-service courses and for teachers working alone ('reflecting in the wild'). Indeed, it is perhaps fair to say that such instruments are the most commonly used to promote reflection in almost any teaching context, globally. As such, their design and use are clearly central to the ways in which reflection gets done and to the extent to which they promote professional learning and development.

Like most self-observation instruments, checklists and forms have both advantages and disadvantages. Their main advantages include:

- They are relatively quick and easy to administer and use.
- They enable users to collect data quickly and economically.
- They provide a 'snapshot' of a person's behaviour/performance at any given point in time.
- They serve as permanent records which can be revisited over time to ascertain whether there have been changes in practice.

Such instruments also have a number of disadvantages which include:

- They may limit reflection by forcing the user to tick boxes or make choices. Comments may be constrained by the form itself.
- They are often assessed – see above (Introduction).
- Repeated use of the same form may cause the user to reflect in the same way over time rather than develop deeper understandings.
- They facilitate 'faking it' (see above): users can easily make claims which are designed to satisfy tutors or meet assessment criteria.
- They may become rather mechanical and pointless if used excessively.
- Users' focus is often on task completion, not reflection.

While it may appear from what has been said so far that we are adopting a predominantly critical stance towards the use of forms and pro-formas, this is not necessarily the case. We would argue that such approaches to reflective writing may play a very important role in *teaching* reflection and in *integrating* reflection in professional practice. Elsewhere in this book (see, for example, Chapter 2), we have made the case for a need for reflective practices to be taught and for reflection to be embedded and integrated more fully in a teacher's professional life. Using more structured tools, changing the focus of the reflection over time and introducing techniques which train reflection are all ways of enhancing reflective writing.

By way of illustration of the kinds of approach to reflective writing we are advocating here, let's look at some examples of the kinds of tool which we believe will promote a structured, systematic and integrated approach to the use of checklists and pro-formas.

Teti Dragas uses an integrated approach to written reflection, where writing is used alongside (for example) video or some kind of visual input. Extract 6.4 below shows how this approach works in practice. Teti works with student teachers on an MA TESOL programme, who are asked to reflect on their teaching each time they teach. In extract 6.4, the students have been asked to reflect on their first teaching practice, using a two-part task:

Extract 6.4

> Post Lesson Feedback 26th October 2015 Teaching Week 2, Lesson 1: Shirley, Rosa & Abby.
>
> *Task 1*: Make sure you understand the following terms and sketch out a definition for each, which we will use to create a class 'Glossary of Terms':
>
> Elicit, Monitor
> Instruction
> Pair work, Group work
> Peer feedback, Group feedback, Open class feedback
> TTT (Teacher Talking Time), STT (Student Talking Time)
> Activating schemata, Echoing
>
> *Task 2*:
> a. Now return to the list above and pick 2 of them to focus on.
> b. Tag the video clip with the relevant title, make a comment and ask one or two questions for that clip related to the focus.
> c. Put this on the discussion board in Week 2: Lesson 1 – National Identity. For example: Tag = Monitor Clip = a teacher in the act of monitoring students; Comment = sts are busy doing a true/false activity individually; Question = how effective was the teacher's monitoring in this instance?

From these tasks, we can make a number of observations. First, trainees using this material are taken through a series of steps to guide them in their reflections. For example, they are told to write definitions of key terms (to be used later in a student-produced glossary). This stage might be considered a 'pre-reflection' phase, designed to activate knowledge and prepare students for reflection. It also ensures that students are getting used to and practising a metalanguage to talk about their teaching. Using a commonly agreed terminology is key to facilitating both reflection and discussion and something which we would advocate as an example of good practice. Second, trainees are invited to select two of the terms they have defined and identify them in the video clip. At this point, they must reflect on what they perceive to be interesting or key in the video and make comments/ask questions. Finally, the clip, commentary and questions are uploaded to a community website for other trainees to see and comment on.

This approach to written reflection has a number of merits:

- It is structured: users must follow a series of steps designed to help them reflect and share their reflections.
- It teaches reflection by highlighting key elements to reflect *on* and providing trainees with appropriate tools to reflect *with*.
- It is interactive: users share their clips and comments with other members of the community and offer further reflections.
- It allows choice: trainees are given choice in which practices to focus on from a list of 8–10; they are also given choice in what they reflect on and how they do that. Finally, they have choice in terms of which additional uploads they comment on.

Apart from MA degrees, observation forms are used extensively on PRESET and INSET programmes such as CELTA and DELTA. Extract 6.5 is taken from one such form used on a DELTA course; it shows how one of the student teachers, Dorothy, provides feedback on an observed lesson.

Extract 6.5

LESSON FOCUS: EXPRESSING FUTURE IDEAS

Observation: 1 hour – first part of 2 hour session

Key activities/stages

- Recap/aims outlined – define diff ways to express future and definitions
- Practice use using cards with key words (offer/promise/decision etc.)
- Practice using grammar exercise – on own – class feedback
- Reading about predictions followed by class discussion

What went well in the lesson?

- Students understood 'routine' of lesson – seemed comfortable
- Clear aims – ss understood what they were doing
- Friendly atmosphere although some much quieter than others

What could have been more effective?

- Very teacher-led – could ss have explained more / worked in groups more to discuss?
- Some ss dominated at times – hard for quieter ones to get involved

Comments

Traditional grammar lesson – deductive + teacher-led but ss were comfortable with this. Don't think it would work with 16–18 ss – but clearly helped some of these ss and resulted in ss knowing exactly what was expected of them in the lesson

Course participants are invited to reflect on their teaching, using comments from their tutor, feedback from peers and their own introspections. Extract 6.6 shows how Dorothy uses the feedback from her tutor in devising an action plan for future teaching:

Extract 6.6

> In terms of my teaching practices I have enjoyed the challenge of trying out new ideas in the classroom and of being more self-aware at certain times. This has helped increase my confidence in tackling pronunciation for example, as has the learner feedback on this area. I have continued to work on my language analysis and found comparing my planning to language which arose in the actual lesson very useful. Observation of a lesson in terms of error correction and learner feedback helped focus me more on this area and I can now apply this to my own teaching using methods below. Self-recording of parts of my lessons has been extremely valuable as it has allowed me to see both the positives and negatives of lessons and because I can see/hear certain changes in my practice (e.g. teacher talk/ echo) which are positive. One of the most positive aspects of learner feedback is that it makes the learners feel more involved in the process of learning as well as giving us as teachers useful information. I have also found it interesting that my learners have enjoyed being part of my learning experience.

Of interest to the present discussion is the extent to which Dorothy's action plan makes reference to changes to her practice which have been highlighted in the feedback from the tutor. Here, for example, she comments on the challenge of trying out new ideas to make her classes more student-centred. She also comments on the value of learner feedback and using self-observation (through video recordings). Note too how she values involving learners in her own professional development (*learners have enjoyed being part of my learning experience*).

There are, then, clear advantages to using written feedback as a 'springboard' for the kind of reflection presented in extract 6.6. Ideally, Dorothy's reflective comments would receive further feedback from the course tutor in order to make the process more interactive and open up a professional conversation.

We now consider alternative formats to written reflections, also taken from a diploma course.

Non-linear Formats

There are alternatives to the more traditional checklists and pro-formas which might be used. It is fair to say that not everyone 'sees' their professional practice in linear, written terms; for many people, the act of recalling an experience or event takes the form of a pictorial representation. For example, if you are asked to describe where you live or your journey to work, you 'see' it as a picture or series of pictures. The same might be said of reflecting on professional practice; for some people, reflection is best done in a non-linear way, using, for example, pictures or other visual representations.

One way of demonstrating the visualization of an event or experience is to use a kind of mind map, or concept map. Jade Blue used this technique to reflect on her teaching practice during a diploma course that she was taking. An example of her work is included in the vignette below and accompanying extract 6.7. In the vignette, Jade describes the way in which she uses mind mapping to reflect on her professional practice. This is taken from her blog, see: https://jadeblueefl. wordpress.com/2016/05/14/mind-mapping-learner-generated-visuals/.

In her blog, Jade describes three uses of mind mapping: revision mapping, reflective mapping and thought mapping. Here, we focus only on the second, reflective mapping.

JADE BLUE'S VIGNETTE (UK)

This post is largely about different types of mind maps and their value to both their creator and reader. Mind mapping has played a large part in the diploma journey for me this past year, and I'd like to just outline some of what I understand mind maps to be, and their value for learners.

At their simplest, mind maps are a means of organizing information, and I first started using them solely for this purpose, during my pre-course reading for my diploma course. Initially I used them to summarize and organize what I was reading into a more visual form to enable me to refer back and quickly locate information. What I found was that the process of organizing the information also served as a form of revision, both in re-presenting the information, and in that the time spent colouring/shading allowed me to further process and consider the information in a relaxed state. Let's call this form of mind mapping 'revision mapping'.

Taking this a step further, as opposed to just summarizing and organizing what other people were writing, I then started using mind maps as a means of answering questions and brainstorming. This is a particularly interesting process for me, in that the nature of writing in this medium seems to allow more of a stream of consciousness than formatted text, which I believe places a (subconscious?) pressure on the writer to craft the text into something more clearly (and traditionally) structured.

Mind mapping, on the other hand seems to express an internal dialogue, and the writing within it is very much a process, one thought leading to another. As this form of mind mapping begins with a question or a point for consideration/exploration, and is very much concerned with one's own reflections, let's call it 'reflective mapping'. This approach is something that I found particularly suited me in reflecting on my observed lessons during my diploma course. The format allowed me the freedom to explore my thoughts in response to the lesson at the same time as illustrate the connections and relationships between various aspects of what I was discussing. But the freedom from traditional structural restraints that this medium allows raises important questions about the relationship between writer (or creator) and reader. How lucid are reflective mind maps for the reader? Is the written text less opaque?

The gravity of the answers to these questions entirely depends upon who the mind maps are created for. Are they created for the reader in order to communicate and/or explain a concept? Or are they solely for the purpose of the creator, as a process in themselves, and/or to serve as a visual and written record of an experience?

I would say that the reflective mind maps I've created during the course – especially those that follow observed lessons – are for both myself and the reader. They are simultaneously a means of reflecting on a process and experience for my own development, and a means of communicating those reflections to the observer. My identification of the reader – the observer – is an important point. While primarily my reflections are to support and record my own development (be they in the form of mind maps or solely written text), there is always some awareness – no matter how small – that they will be read by one of my tutors. Thus, my reflective mind maps for my observed lessons assume that the reader, having observed that lesson, has more understanding of the points I discuss than an outsider might.

Reflection is about consideration; it's about thinking deeply; it's about revealing the nature of something. My reflective blog in its entirety is both a record of my journey and a part of the journey itself.

Of interest in Jade's vignette is the way in which she emphasizes a need for both structure and freedom in reflective writing, which she views as a 'stream of consciousness'. On the one hand, there is a need to structure a piece of writing so that it can be understood by the reader. On the other hand, more traditional forms of text tend to compel the writer to write in a certain way, following established conventions which might 'get in the way' of this stream of consciousness. As Jade herself says, 'Mind mapping [. . .] seems to express an internal dialogue, and the writing within it is very much a process, one thought leading to another.' The advantage of this approach, then, seems to be that it allows both freedom and structure and provides the writer with an opportunity to engage in an internal dialogue with self and an external one with the reader. Mind maps allow both reflection and the communication of that reflection.

In extract 6.7, we see an example of one such mind map, created by Jade following her fourth observed lesson on a diploma course.

Extract 6.7 (see page 141)

There are a number of features of this piece of writing which are worthy of mention:

- It has a structure, but does not follow the pattern of a linear text (organized around words, phrases, sentences, paragraphs). Here, we see how the key elements of the teaching practice give the mind map its structure, organized around three key aspects: involvement, structure, timing.
- Jade then sub-divides the three elements of her teaching into further elements such as learners, language, CPD, planning.
- The various elements which make up the mind map are linked and Jade comments on their relationships. This is especially useful when trying to 'make sense' of a teaching episode and reflect on what happened and why.
- Other elements, represented by lines and circles, are linked in a looser way, indicating that they are somehow related but that the relationships are less fully resolved and are potentially areas for future reflection.

In this section we have seen how checklists and forms can be used to capture reflections in a relatively simple and structured way. In the next section, we consider more extended writing formats using diaries, journals and portfolios.

6.3 Diaries, Journals and Portfolios

Diaries and Journals

Probably the next most commonly used form of written reflection after proforma and checklists are diaries, journals and portfolios. Farrell (2013) makes the point that journal writing has been around for a long time and was used by explorers, seafarers and even the captain of the starship *Enterprise* (from *Star Trek*). Apart from being a simple record of events, written for the author or for

Extract 6.7

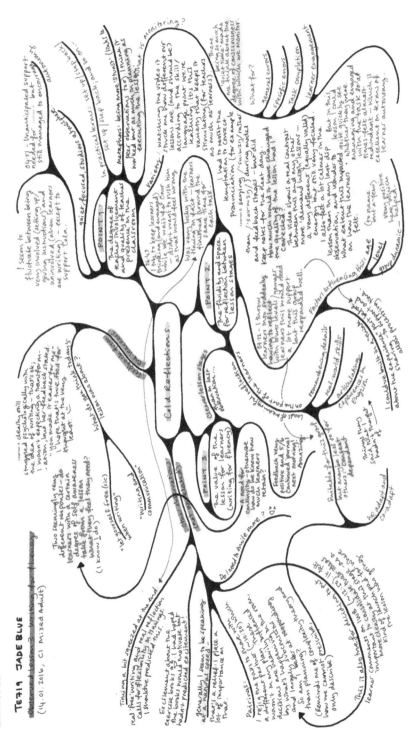

an outside audience, journal entries also have learning value; they help us, or our readers, understand a particular issue, behaviour, phenomenon or practice more fully. As Elbow (1998: 248) comments, 'as we learn to write, we write to learn'.

By writing a journal (or diary), we have an opportunity to reflect as we write and then, at a slight distance, reflect on what we have written. Written journal entries compel the writer to think about what they would like to reflect on and then provide an opportunity to learn from this writing at some later date. And of course, the process is cumulative; regular journal writing allows us to build up an understanding of our professional practice over time, perhaps changing the way we see things or modifying our behaviour in some way. After all, professional learning, or indeed any kind of learning, involves change over time: by keeping a record of our professional practice, we are more likely to change and experience the benefit of that change.

Journals may take many forms, including audio, video and online formats. We are using the term journal here to include both diaries and logs; essentially we see no difference, except perhaps that diaries are often seen as private and personal, whereas journals are regarded as being more public and professionally focused.

The basic structure of a journal entry remains the same, however, and includes a date, an introduction, some kind of commentary on 'what happened' and a reflection on that commentary. Journals may be autobiographical and use a kind of 'notes to self' format or they may be written for a teachers' group, or as part of a course. According to Bailey et al. (2001), there are four important reasons for keeping a journal:

- to articulate problems in teaching
- to vent frustrations
- to clarify certain issues
- to stretch oneself professionally.

By writing journals, we may learn to understand our teaching more fully and consider options or alternatives to current practices. Indeed, rather than focusing on 'problems' or 'issues', there is a very strong case to be made for focusing on what we do well by highlighting success as well as failure (Farrell, 2013). This is something which is often overlooked; there is perhaps a sense that journal entries should focus on problems which need solving, or issues which need to be resolved. In fact, there is much to be learnt by focusing on achievement and success. In Chapter 3, we also talked about the importance of making space for writing on intermediate, interesting, puzzling and less clear-cut issues and decisions (what Edge and Richards called 'dialogues of doubt' (1998)).

For many practitioners, it is probably fair to say that the act of writing a journal entry is, in itself, problematic. Most of us have never been trained in the use of journals and have no idea about what to say or how to say it. Add to this the trust that is required for a journal entry to be read by a colleague or 'critical friend' and we start to understand the enormity of the task. Again, perhaps the solution is to offer journal writers a more gradual, structured and integrated approach to writing, as exemplified in extract 6.8 below.

In this extract, Teti Dragas demonstrates how a series of questions can be used to structure a journal entry and make the whole process of writing much less intimidating and more straightforward. In the extract below, we see how trainee teachers (students on an MA TESOL programme) are guided to reflect on their current teaching context and one they have taught in before, potentially a very useful practice given the importance of understanding local context.

Extract 6.8

Reflective Writing Task Lesson 1 – Teachers 'Finding Differences and Similarities in Current and Previous Practice'

You are going to reflect on key differences and similarities between this teaching context and your own. In doing this, you will reflect also on the role of the teacher, the students and the learning environment. Thinking about the class you have just taught, use the following questions as prompts to write in your diary. Answer as many questions as you can. Try and write something for each question even if it is short.

1. How similar was this classroom context to the context you are most familiar with (i.e. your last teaching position)? Write a short description outlining key similarities and differences.
2. Did you do anything different in this context? If not, why? Could you have? If yes, why? What were the reasons?
3. How comfortable did you feel in this context in terms of your role as a teacher?
4. Did you feel 'different' in this context? If so, in what way? If not, what were the reasons you feel the same as always?
5. Thinking about your practice, to what extent did you change your practice in this context to what you generally do?
6. Thinking about you as a teacher, what kind of teacher persona or role do you generally adopt? (e.g. T-centred, st-centred? Friendly, strict etc.) Describe this as much as you can.
7. Now think about whether you were 'different' here. How did you feel in terms of your role as 'teacher'? Did you adopt a different role? If yes why? If no, why not?
8. Thinking about the students in the class. How similar or different were the students in this context to the one you are used to? Describe the

similarities and differences (e.g. ages; number of students/ position in classroom; level etc.).

9. To what extent did you feel comfortable teaching these students? What were you comfortable with? What were you anxious about?

10. To what extent do you think based on this reflection that context has determined your approach to teaching?

Note how the questions help teachers to focus on the key elements which make up context. The use of a series of structured questions draws their attention to teacher and learner roles, to teaching practices, to teaching style and so on. By answering the questions, trainee teachers learn how to reflect on their teaching while at the same time developing a detailed understanding of what is meant by 'context'. As we have seen elsewhere in this book, a detailed understanding of context is one of the hallmarks of effective teaching.

It is not difficult to imagine how this simple approach might be extended to journal writing more generally; by varying both the number and type of questions, writers can be given more or less guidance and have more or less 'space' to say what they really want to talk about. Over time and with practice, reflective writers using this approach will learn how to generate their own questions and identify key issues in their practice.

We should perhaps recognize that journal writing is not for everyone, no matter how much guidance and support is given. As we have shown above, most people have some difficulty writing a journal; the very act of getting started, composing and structuring complex, abstract reflections is not easy, and most of us struggle with both content and process.

In extract 6.9 below, we witness the difficulties encountered by a group of teachers of young learners in Doha, Qatar. This group, led by the researcher, Ollie Beddall (2013), underwent a process of reflective practice, using a range of techniques and instruments, including journals. In the 'implications' section of the research report Ollie outlines some of the concerns experienced by participants in relation to the use of written journals.

Extract 6.9

Evidence presented in this study suggests that RP as a teacher development tool can have some success with non-expert teachers, leading to both conceptual insights and practical classroom techniques, but [it] is likely to have considerably less impact on their expert colleagues. Findings have demonstrated that RP can make teachers feel more confident and better equipped to teach YLs by leading them to critically analyse their practice, and should therefore be considered as a component in YL teacher education initiatives.

Firstly, the process of problematising a class and developing a relevant and sufficiently focused RQ is likely to impact greatly on the reflective process undergone by a teacher. It should not be taken for granted that teachers possess the necessary skills to do this, and, consequently, the role of the tutor becomes central to the implementation of the course. Tutors looking to facilitate RP should expect to be "hands-on" in the beginning stages of a programme, particularly in helping participants through the process of defining a suitable RQ. Tutors should also consider how to deal with the fact that RP may not initially have face validity for participants and this may manifest itself in resistance. Care should therefore be taken to present the programme in an appropriate way and tutors should be prepared to guide participants into the habit of journaling. A clear definition, at the start of a course, of exactly what is meant by RP, may also help.

Tutor intervention, however, is not straightforward, and tutors should take care to allow participants to retain ownership of the process. They must take care to act as a *facilitator* rather than an *instructor* (Bailey 2006), perhaps through a strategy of asking probing questions in order to steer participants, rather than simply providing them with answers. The setting of regular "catch-up" meetings with participants in the early stages might also help to ensure the tutor is aware of any emerging issues and can respond accordingly.

Whether the reflective journal should be considered a necessary component of structured RP is less clear. Whilst there is little doubt over the importance of the RQ, the means of journaling itself is something for which I have been left with more questions than answers. Non-expert teachers experienced some difficulty with journaling and sought out other means to reflect, notably in the form of short conversations with colleagues. However, these same participants eventually appeared to regret not persisting with their journals. Providing different options for the format of journaling, such as through audio or smart phone apps, might better cater to participants with different preferences.

Ollie identifies a number of techniques which might be used to facilitate a reflective practice procedure, including setting clear objectives (as 'research questions'), getting participants 'on board' at the outset and facilitating rather than instructing reflection. With respect to the use of journals, Ollie tells us that some of the participants resisted this approach, finding other means of reflection, including dialogues with colleagues. Interestingly, those who opted out of the use of journals later regretted it; Ollie suggests that alternative forms of journal might be used in such cases, including audio or apps. Again, allowing choice in the approach to reflection seems to be very important.

Portfolios

Portfolios are often used on assessed courses as a way of enabling teachers to collect evidence over time and then reflect and comment on that evidence as a means of improving their practice. The main advantage of this approach is that writers are able to collect and use evidence and build up a portfolio of material over time. Rather than relying on journal entries, portfolio writers make use of artefacts which evidence a particular aspect of their professional practice. In an educational setting, this might include, for example, lesson plans, a piece of material, a student blog, or a video clip.

In Chapter 5, we saw how a group of university and college lecturers use portfolios as part of their professional practice. In extract 6.10, one of the members of this consortium, Audrey O'Grady, tells us how she uses the portfolio to develop her professional practice and to improve her approach to learning and teaching in higher education. Audrey works at the University of Limerick where she teaches life sciences.

Extract 6.10

> Reflective practice is vital for a good teacher to ensure that the teacher knows what works and what doesn't. For this reason I share my reflective practices of my modules with my students and encourage them to critique their own lessons just as I critique my labs and lectures. There are many aspects to consider when reflecting. Key areas include focussing on my own motivation, strengths, weaknesses and my ideas. Reflecting on skills needed in different areas of my teaching are also considered. Reflections also focus on my progress in both lectures and laboratory sessions. If my own progress is hindered in any way, I address this. As the semesters progress I reflect on knowledge and skill gaps and develop ways in which I can best work towards filling these gaps. The following are questions that I consider when reflecting on a class:
>
> – What were my intended outcomes?
> – Were these achieved?
> – What went well/didn't go well?
> – Strengths? Weaknesses?
> – How do I change in order to improve this class/student experience?
>
> Self evaluation is a routine part of my teaching and learning process. After every lecture I contribute to a reflective diary. I developed this system when I was an undergraduate pre-service teacher and have used it to date. I am now aware more than ever that it's not just novice teachers that need to reflect and improve. It is vital that I consistently aim to improve in teaching and educational standards. I have never had a lesson that

I thought was absolutely perfect. It took me a long time to come to terms with the fact that I will probably never achieve absolute perfection; however, this has led me to want and strive to achieve the absolute best I can from each class.

I recently flicked through my reflective journal from 2007 and noted that a successful class for me was one where I didn't have to over rely on 'cheat cards' to take me through a lecture. Since then I feel I have come so far. I am now much more comfortable with my subject content knowledge. I now have new challenges; for example, in order to include relevant research in my teaching I need to understand and relate to this research in the most effective way. Six years ago I could not even contemplate this as I was completely focused on the subject knowledge.

Lecture attendance was also poor when I first started teaching. It wasn't long before I realized that although I am teaching adults, they need to be stimulated just as much as young children. This has brought me to the current stage where I now incorporate as much interactive media as I can and provide a stimulus to engage in every lecture.

Self reflection has highlighted a very important aspect of my teaching – I cannot do everything on my own. Over the past five years I learned to delegate in a way that I never thought I could do. Delegating is such an important aspect of teaching and learning. For example, I ensure that teaching assistant's presence is maximized in laboratory sessions. This initially took extra time as I developed pre-laboratory briefs, but now these take much less time and the teaching assistants have a much more important role to play in teaching with me.

What is interesting about Audrey's use of portfolios is the approach adopted, which consistently uses the same five questions, focusing on what 'went well' and what might be improved or changed in the future. Note too how she has a historical dimension to reflection; she is able to look back over her notes and notice how she is developing in her practice. She also makes the interesting observation that when teachers first start, subject knowledge is more important than knowledge about teaching and learning. Through reflection, the balance can change with a focus on professional practice as well as subject knowledge, a point made by Tanner et al. (2000) who promote the idea of a 'spiral of reflection' which develops understandings of key skills and competencies.

Whatever approach is taken to portfolio-based reflection, it is apparent that some training and guidance will benefit the users no end. In particular, the historical dimension which this approach can promote is worthy of development. By revisiting previous portfolio entries, writers are able to highlight experiences which were important to their development over time and make connections between past and current experiences (see also Mansvelder-Longayroux et al., 2007).

To conclude this section, we have seen how portfolio-based reflection uses evidence, experiences and introspective commentaries to build up a picture of a person's professional development over time. For this approach to work well, there is a need for training, support and guidance in the use of portfolios and opportunities to share past experiences with other practitioners.

6.4 Narrative Enquiry

In the same way that portfolios offer a historical perspective on professional development, narratives can enable writers 'to conceptualize our own history so that we can move to a place that we control rather than a place [in which] we have been unwittingly placed' (Farrell, 2013: 101). In short, by writing a narrative of our experiences we are better able to understand and control them, enabling changes to current and past practices to be made.

In the past, of course, storytelling was used as the principal means of conveying information. According to Connelly and Clandinin (1990), narratives allow us to exchange our experiences of the world. By reflecting on these experiences, we are able to better understand the relationship between experiences and assumptions, attitudes, beliefs and actions. Teachers can therefore use written narratives to reflect on their professional experiences since these stories reveal vital information about a teacher's beliefs, identity, values, struggles and experiences. Reflections based on narratives have that important historical dimension – they provide opportunities to study accumulated experiences, acquired over a period of time.

We can say that there are as many ways to go about writing a narrative as there are to telling a story. Apart from the well-established maxim of 'beginning, middle and end', what else can narrative writers do to ensure that their 'story' actually has some professional value and helps reflection? Farrell (2013) employs the earlier work of Cortazzi (1994) to offer a four-part framework for narrative and narrative analysis:

- Orientation: background information – who, what, how, why?
- Complication: describes a problem or issue which emerged.
- Evaluation: this is the 'so what?' of the story – what does it mean for the writer? Why is it important?
- Result: outlines and explains a solution to the issue or problem.

This approach to narrative might also benefit from the use of questions or a series of questions for each of the four stages. In this way, writers are guided and supported in a task which might be alien to them and which could prove intimidating.

As we have already seen in this chapter, extended writing is not for everyone. We saw how Jade Blue uses concept mapping as an alternative to more extensive forms of writing and witnessed the benefits that this approach can bring. In a similar vein, Mark Wyatt demonstrates how poetry can capture key elements of a reflective story: in this case, he highlights the negative impact of unannounced observation, lamenting the ways in which observees are treated as objects of scientific pursuit rather than as human beings.

Extract 6.11

Hamming it up in an observed lesson

"Let's do
Cokey, woah
Cokey! Knees
stretched, ra
the front of
now feeling
ridiculously
caricature of
I lumber and
invading, are
tunnel vision.
untransparent
or just being
condescending
a wry snigger
Observers see
excessive use
no questions
stressed-out
label these
occasional

stretching larynx
a dull third-rate
croak. Observers'
upon me, subjecting
I fear being victim
checklist, murdering
casually trashed, the
luke warm gossip-praise
in the presence of the
what they expect to
of referential/
uttered in
way) and
torturous
misnomers, e.g.

the Hokey
the Hokey
bent, arms
ra ra!" At
the class,
so exposed,
and sinews,
entertainer,
eyes, space–
everything to
to a horribly
my reputation
oral feedback
provided with
head–teacher.
see (e.g. the
display, yes/
a completely
paradoxically
sessions with
'naturalistic

classroom research', which makes me sick. I really want to love research. I attended a conference once where speakers including Judith Burns, Anne Hanks, Richard Borg, and also Simon Smith were explaining exactly how research could set you free. It needs mentoring, though, or context-sensitive leadership in some way and we don't get that here. Instead there's some muppet university academic treating me like a specimen, an object or a faceless research subject fit for dissection in a laboratory, a human guinea pig, a sad case

Mark Wyatt, 2015

The poem, at 206 words, is much shorter than what we would traditionally call a written narrative. And yet, through careful choice of words, Mark Wyatt succeeds in getting his message across in a very direct and powerful way. The impact of this approach is, arguably, greater than it might have been in a more traditional story. Moreover, the actual reflection and introspection which would have been needed to create this text are likely to be deeper than more traditional reflections, culminating in the production of a scathing attack on the kinds of 'unannounced observations' which occur on a daily basis all round the world.

We summarize this section in a quote from Johnson and Golombek (2011: 235) who offer a compelling argument for the use of narrative:

> We believe that narrative inquiry tells the stories of teachers' professional development within their own professional worlds. Such inquiry is driven by teachers' inner desire to understand that experience, to reconcile that which is known with that which is hidden, to confirm and affirm, and to construct and reconstruct understandings of themselves as teachers, and of their own teaching.

There have also been several accounts of how narratives allow space for reflecting on our identity, constructing the meaning of our lives, and using narratives to make decisions about our goals and actions (e.g. Barresi and Juckes, 1997; Bruner, 1990; Carr and Kemmis, 1986). In the words of Barresi (1999: 94):

> In narrating our lives, we construct our own identities, to which we try to adhere until we are provoked to revise the story. However, because the narratives are generated at particular points in time and from particular and ever changing authorial viewpoints often the identities that we form in our self-narratives conflict with each other.

Our discussion of narrative has been necessarily brief in this section. Many of the different elements of narrative are also dealt with in Chapter 7.

6.5 Interactive Writing

In the final section of this chapter, we offer a brief account of what we refer to as interactive writing; brief, because much of what we have said about reflective writing relates to interactive writing – indeed, in an increasingly digital world, writing is far more interactive than ever before, to the extent that traditional divisions between 'speech' and 'writing' no longer apply. Essentially, as we have seen elsewhere in this book, developments in technology, the use of the internet, social media, online blogging and the like make the whole process of writing and reader response much more immediate, much faster, more contextualized and more likely to provoke a reaction.

By way of exemplification, we present Philip Saxon's vignette about online blogging.

PHILIP SAXON'S VIGNETTE (UK)

Context

Fifteen trainee English language teachers from Japan were asked to reflect on their practice experiences of teaching Japanese to secondary school pupils over a six-week period. Each week, the researcher posed a different set of structured questions on Edmodo, aimed at eliciting a personal response as well as scaffolding reflection by gradually encouraging greater specificity. Learners were drawn from years 7, 8 and 9 of a secondary school in Coventry, UK. The online platform used was Edmodo (a virtual learning environment).

Reflective Comments

Hatton and Smith (1995, cited by Moon 2006: 40) have a scale for depth of reflection:

- Level 1 – Description (essentially non-reflective)
- Level 2 – Descriptive Reflection (mostly only from one perspective)
- Level 3 – Dialogic Reflection (engages other perspectives)
- Level 4 – Critical Reflection (socio-political context is considered).

Twelve out of 15 students achieved only levels 1 and 2. Some examples of trainee teacher posts at this level of reflection now follow:

POST 1: SETTLING IN – YOUR FIRST FIVE WEEKS IN THE UK

I was often fed up with my poor English skill . . . but I overcame many difficult situations. My [host family and] friends helped me a lot . . . I appreciate it very much. Thanks to their help, I was able to come to think my situations positively . . . and I enjoy studying English now! (Student 8)

POST 3: AN ACTIVITY (1)

I think my activity was successful because through my activity, they could review 8 words about family for the exam . . . But my activity was a little difficult for them although I had thought it was good task . . . Many assistants helped them during the activity, so without them, my activity may not be successful. (Student 4)

POST 5: CLASSROOM MANAGEMENT

I think British teenagers are a little different from the same age students in Japan. In my opinion, Japanese students are more polite for teachers than British ones. Of course, some of the students in Japan behave badly to teachers . . . and I don't say that all of the British teenagers were rude or naughty, but the number of the students who behave badly to teachers in Britain seems to be larger than in Japan. (Student 4)

Three students achieved level 3 (only one was consistent) – one example of deeper reflection now follows:

POST 5: CLASSROOM MANAGEMENT

When I was a junior high school student, my English teacher had been a teacher for two years. So she was a new teacher. I think she has few experience of being a teacher, but she was a nice teacher for me. Thanks to her, I wanted to be an English teacher. She was thought to have these kinds of characteristics, so I will write her way of teaching. At first class, she introduced by herself and asked us to introduce by ourselves. For almost all of the students, it was the first time to speak English in class. Everyone looked nervous, but she kept smile, nodded during our talking and made some responses. They made me relieved. And after this class, when I met her outside of the classroom, she called my name and said something related to my hobby, club activity, or interests. I was surprised and pleased to talk with her because she remembered about me and I wanted to talk with her more. This ability, or attitude towards students makes a good impression on them, I think. (Student 13)

No one achieved level 4 – but this was not really expected from a group of young trainee teachers.

Focus Group Feedback

The following questions were discussed.

Has posting reflections and receiving feedback on Edmodo:

1. helped you make better sense of being a visitor to Britain?
2. helped you make better sense of what it means to teach in Britain?
3. made you more aware of learners' classroom needs?
4. prompted you to discuss teaching issues with peers, teacher trainers or schoolteachers?
5. made you feel comfortable sharing your thoughts about teaching with others online?
6. made you a more reflective teacher?

Sample comments from focus groups:

Yes, it gave me a chance to reflect on my experiences in Britain.

I think on Edmodo we had to analyse what we did objectively. We could think deeply and without emotion.

Sharing is one of the most important things . . . if there were no Edmodo, such a kind of sharing opportunity, we wouldn't be able to talk about our experiences face-to-face and this is an important thing.

Yes, we sometimes don't anticipate the students' level or classroom mood . . . so we can take care of each other, if the classroom level isn't what you think, through Edmodo . . .

I read the feedback of other students, and could get a lot of new ideas or new information from that.

For me, the Edmodo experience is a preparation for discussing ideas. I think without Edmodo I don't think I would be able to talk about problems in class because I wouldn't be able to say things spontaneously with native English speakers. So it was very helpful in terms of progression.

Edmodo was good. We could reflect on our own teaching practice in our own time.

Overall, 13 out of 14 participants strongly approved of using Edmodo for reflection.

Conclusions

Better methods might have yielded greater depth of reflection:

• Routinely asking what could be done better as a final structured question might have achieved results.
• Face-to-face, whole-class feedback responding to posts collectively might also serve a useful purpose.

A more tightly integrated 'blend' of online and face-to-face training might just yield optimal results. In addition, the project lasted only six weeks – we saw only *limited* gains in reflective depth! Did the students just need more time? However, whether a spirit of 'community reflection' could be *sustained* this long is open to question.

Also, Japanese are very *community-oriented*. Would students from more *individualistic* cultures feel the same way about openness? Doubts persist: but the methods used here are surely relevant to *short courses* everywhere. The case for further research appears strong.

Philip Saxon's online blogging vignette highlights a number of important features of the approach while drawing our attention to issues which could be given further consideration:

• Of considerable importance to anyone thinking about online blogging as a tool to promote reflection is the way in which the process is set up. Here, Philip highlights the importance of structured questions (like Teti Dragas') which are used to promote a personal response from the trainees while 'scaffolding' reflection; in other words, users are given space to say what they want to say, while at the same time having scaffolds (structured questions) to help them reflect more effectively.

- One of the most important elements of online blogging is the scope it provides for sharing thoughts and ideas in a relatively risk-free environment. The online community described in this study was clearly a key factor in promoting openness and honesty – key ingredients to reflection and professional development.
- The use of Edmodo was regarded as being efficient and time-saving. The VLE clearly allows users to enter their own reflective comments and reflect on the comments of others in a straightforward manner. In addition, users are able to enter their reflections in their own time, proving space for introspection and for making connections between different posts.
- The whole process is reassuring and unthreatening. Users are able to see how others are having similar experiences and explore coping strategies by considering various options to classroom practice. Users feel motivated to write posts because there is no loss of face; instead there is an atmosphere of support, guidance and respect. This has to be a real strength of the system and procedures used in this study.
- Philip comments on the extent to which such an online community could be sustained over a longer period of time and considers whether a combined online and face-to-face approach to online blogging might be more effective. There is clearly scope here for further research and experimentation with different formats.

For further examples of online blogging, see Sandra Morales' vignette in Chapter 5. See also Andy Boon's work on the use of MSN's Instant Messenger. His work investigates a real-time CMC version of cooperative development that he calls IMCD (Boon, 2005, 2007).

It would appear, then, that interactive writing has much to offer, providing it is organized in a structured and supportive way. By combining online blogging or the use of social media with the development of an online community, users have greater potential to attain a higher level of reflective capability, co-constructing new knowledge and developing professional skills through interactions with colleagues. A key advantage of the approach is that it provides a safe, secure environment where people feel safe and able to take 'risks'; in addition, interactive writing of the kind outlined here allows users to have the space and structure needed to provide honest and personal accounts of their professional experience.

6.6 Summary

In this chapter, we have provided an account of some of the more commonly found approaches to written reflection, maintaining that this medium has an important role to play in professional development, providing that opportunities for reflection are structured in a purposeful and well-supported way. As one of the most commonly found approaches, written reflection allows more time and space for practitioners to frame their thinking and present their ideas. It also enables teachers to share, question and comment on their practices in relatively unthreatening and supportive environments, especially where digital, online formats are used.

We make the point in the chapter that there are strong similarities between the process of reflection and the process of writing. The process of writing down thoughts, comments and introspections is more than simply a record of reflection. The act of writing *about* reflection equates *with* reflection; by writing about an experience we are reflecting on that experience and clarifying or 'shaping' our own understanding of it.

Written reflection is not without its challenges, a dominant one being the issue of assessment, which we address in this chapter and elsewhere in the book. A second challenge is that of eliciting genuine and meaningful reflections rather than the kind which course tutors (for example) might want to read. Promoting honesty and integrity in written reflection remains one of its major challenges and one which might best be addressed by promoting more inter-active platforms where responses and feedback can be immediate. We anti-cipate that the kinds of digital, online forms of reflection exemplified in this chapter represent a likely future direction for reflection in writing and one which is becoming increasingly straightforward with current developments in technology.

References

Bailey, K.M. (2006). *Language teacher supervision: a case-based approach*. New York: Cambridge University Press.

Bailey, K., Curtis, A. and Nunan, D. (2001). *Pursuing professional development: the self as source*. Boston: Heinle and Heinle.

Barresi, J. (1999). On becoming a person. *Philosophical Psychology*, 12(1), 79–98.

Barresi, J. and Juckes, T.J. (1997). Personology and the narrative interpretation of lives. *Journal of Personality*, 65(3), 693–719.

Beddall, O. (2013). Investigating reflective practice in a training course for young learner teachers at the British Council Doha (Unpublished MSc dissertation). Aston University, UK.

Biggs, J. (2003). *Teaching for quality learning at university – what the student does* (2nd edn). Buckingham: The Society for Research into Higher Education and Open University Press.

Bolton, G. (2010). *Reflective practice, writing and professional development* (3rd edn). London: Sage.

Boon, A. (2005). Is there anybody out there? *Essential Teacher*, 2(2), 38–41.

Boon, A. (2007). Building bridges: instant messenger cooperative development. *The Language Teacher*, 31(12), 9–13.

Boud, D. (2010). Relocating reflection in the context of practice. In H. Bradbury, N. Frost, S. Kilminster and M. Zukas (eds), *Beyond reflective practice* (pp. 25–36). London: Routledge.

Bruner, J. (1990). Vygotsky: a historical and conceptual perspective. In L.C. Moll (ed.), *Vygotsky and education: instructional implications and applications of sociohistorical psychology*. Cambridge: Cambridge University Press.

Burton, J., Quirke, P., Reichmann, C.L. and Kreeft Peyton, J. (2009). *Reflective writing: a way to lifelong professional learning*. USA: TESL-EJ Publications.

Carr, W. and Kemmis, S. (1986). *Becoming critical: education, knowledge and action research.* Lewes: The Falmer Press.

Connelly, F.M. and Clandinin, D.J. (1990). Stories of experience and narrative inquiry. *Educational Researcher,* 19(5), 2–14.

Cortazzi, M. (1994). Narrative analysis. *Language Teaching,* 27(3), 157–170.

Edge, J. and Richards, K. (1998). May I see your warrant, please?: Justifying outcomes in qualitative research. *Applied Linguistics,* 19(3), 334–356.

Elbow, P. (1998). *Writing with power.* New York: Oxford University Press.

Farrell, T.S.C. (2013). *Reflective writing for language teachers.* Sheffield: Equinox.

Gray, J. and Block, D. (2012). The marketisation of language teacher education and neoliberalism. In D. Block, J. Gray and M. Holborow (eds), *Neoliberalism and Applied Linguistics* (pp. 114–143). London: Routledge

Hatton, N. and Smith, D. (1995). Reflection in teacher education: towards definition and implementation. *Teacher and Teacher Education,* 11(1), 33–49.

Hobbs, V. (2007). Faking it or hating it: can reflective practice be forced? *Reflective Practice,* 8(3), 405–417.

Johnson, K.E. and Golombek, P.R. (2011). A sociocultural theoretical perspective on teacher professional development. In K.E. Johnson and P.R. Golombek (eds), *Research on second language teacher education. A sociocultural perspective on professional development* (pp. 1–12). New York: Routledge.

Mann, S. and Walsh, S. (2013). RP or 'RIP': a critical perspective on reflective practice. *Applied Linguistics Review,* 4(2), 291–315.

Mansvelder-Longayroux, D. D., Beijaard, D. and Verloop, N. (2007). The portfolio as a tool for stimulating reflection by student teachers. *Teaching and Teacher Education,* 23(1), 47–62.

McCabe, M., Walsh, S., Wideman, R. and Winter, E. (2011). The R word in teacher education: understanding the teaching and learning of critical reflective practice. *International Electronic Journal for Leadership in Learning,* 13(7), 271–283.

Moon, J.A. (2006). *Learning journals: a handbook for reflective practice and professional development* (6th edn). New York: Routledge: Taylor and Francis Group.

Roberts, J. (1998). *Language teacher education.* London: Arnold.

Scott, T. (2005). Creating the subject of portfolios: reflective writing and the conveyance of institutional prerogatives. *Written Communication,* 22(1), 3–35.

Tanner, R., Longayroux, D., Beijaard, D. and Verloop, N. (2000). Piloting portfolios: using portfolios in pre-service teacher education. *ELT Journal,* 54(1), 20–30.

Wyatt, M. (2015). *ELTED,* 20, www.elted.net/uploads/7/3/1/6/7316005/02_wyatt__poems_.pdf

7

Reflection in Speaking

7.1 Introduction

This chapter focuses on spoken reflection in different teacher education contexts. Creating space for spoken reflection in teacher education needs careful handling and support, and the aim of this chapter is to consider key factors that both constrain and encourage spoken reflection. In order to do this, we look at the promotion of reflection across a wide range of teacher education contexts. After this introduction, 7.2 considers the pervasive nature of evaluation and assessment in teacher education and considers how far spoken reflection is possible when evaluation and assessment of reflection are integral parts of most teacher education courses. Section 7.3 proposes a range of tools that can foster such data-led reflection – a theme that will be developed in Chapter 8. In 7.3, we concentrate on the role of video alongside other tools (e.g. screen capture software). Section 7.4 foregrounds aspects of collaboration and considers how encouraging awareness of different sorts of talk can be helpful. In particular, 7.4 introduces cooperative development as a tool for fostering collaborative reflective talk.

Written journals or diaries vary considerably in the way they are used. They are not one-off records and can involve dialogue and collaboration and, in some cases, prompt spoken reflection. Lee (2008) distinguishes between different types of journal, which vary in the degree to which they foster interaction and collaboration. However, for our purposes, they make clear that written reflection is not separate from spoken reflection. Journals provide the basis for either spoken interaction between the trainer and the novice teacher or between peers:

- Dialogue journals involve teachers and students 'writing and exchanging their writing in mutual response' (Lee, 2008: 118).
- Collaborative/interactive group journals (Ho and Richards, 1993) involve student teachers in writing and exchanging their journals to support one another as peers.
- Response journals require student teachers to record their reflection on and personal reactions to what they read, observe, listen and think.
- Teaching journals refer to reflections based on teaching experiences.

Farrell (2016) has provided an extensive review of studies that consider the nature and value of reflection, and reveals that discussion, in some form, is particularly highly valued. However, it is still the case that, on most teacher education programmes, where reflection is assessed, it is usually in written form. Writing continues to be the usual basis for assessment of reflection. Although we have two separate chapters focusing on written and spoken reflection (Chapters 6 and 7), we would not want to be understood as promoting their separation. There is a great deal of crossover. Discussion will often be prompted by written texts. Similarly, individual reflective writing often has a reflexive relationship with discussion tasks and more collaborative processes.

We have argued elsewhere (e.g. Mann and Walsh, 2013) that spoken reflection is undervalued in comparison with written reflection. However, it is also important to recognize in this book that this distinction (between spoken and written) is increasingly difficult to sustain as teacher education courses are increasingly blended and use digital formats. Nonetheless, our sense is that a lot of RP is still written in nature and does not involve interaction with another practitioner. Riordan and Murray (2010) have established the hybrid nature of CMC text and show how written online reflection shares many features of spoken reflection. Increasingly, online formats for reflection allow sharing and commenting in both written and spoken forms (e.g. Husu et al., 2007; Mirzaei et al., 2014). This is an area we have already explored in Chapter 6, where we looked at a number of online tools for encouraging interaction.

7.2 Evaluation and Feedback

Chapters 3 and 4 have already provided a thorough overview of some of the constraints and difficulties associated with fostering reflective practice in a variety of contexts. In addition, Chapter 3 has considered issues of power and the pervasive influence of evaluation in pre-service teacher education. All in all, there is a growing literature that analyzes and accounts for reflection (or lack of it) in teacher education talk, especially in POCs (post-observation conferences). This section reviews the main issues and literature related to power and evaluative talk and then considers frameworks and options for trying to make POCs more reflective in nature.

Research specific to second language teacher education (SLTE) has identified core features of POCs, including the prevalence of a transmission style and 'directive' feedback (Freeman, 1982). Against this backdrop, there has been important work raising awareness of different supervision styles (Freeman, 1982; Gebhard, 1984; Zeichner and Liston, 1985; Wallace, 1991; Brandt, 2008). There are a number of issues that stand out from this literature. The first is that there is an inequality between the supervisor/mentor/tutor figure and the novice teacher/teacher learner/student teacher: roles are asymmetrical. This inequality or power difference often results in an inherent tension. Copland argues that such tension in post-observation feedback sessions is an outcome of multiple aspects of the feedback process that include 'phases, participatory structures, and discourse practices' (2010: 471). This tension leads to a need to focus on and manage face issues in the negotiation of the POCs (Copland, 2011, 2012) rather than building up the kind of trust and openness needed for more reflective talk. The interactive space is often pressurised. It is a goal driven speech event where predictability in participants' roles usually positions the novice teacher as a deferential recipient (Copland, 2010). In other words, the power differential (where the trainer is also the assessor) can limit opportunities for reflection. It is of course the case that advice needs to be given and, if appropriate self-evaluation is not forthcoming, then teaching errors, shortcomings and gaffes might need pointing out. Two pieces of data from Copland (2011) make clear the tutor/teacher expectations and the balance that needs to be struck. In the first extract the tutor manages to sum up the desirability of self-evaluation and peer feedback but also that a tutor evaluation ('appraisal') needs to be made:

Extract 7.1

```
My function is to encourage them to make comments on each
other and to reflect on their own lessons erm (.) and also
to give my own appraisal of what they've done.
```

In the second piece of data, we can see that trainees accept (or at least have been socialized into accepting) 'negative evaluation as a necessary evil':

Extract 7.2

```
I think the most uncomfortable thing is when you're criticised
by the tutor but it's also the most useful thing, I've got to
say. I mean you might not like it while it's actually happening
but when you go back and kind of reflect on it you learn.
```

It is also interesting to note that although negative evaluation in feedback might be 'uncomfortable' at the time, it still may be useful in the more medium term ('when you go back and reflect').

POCs, especially on short CELTA type courses (often lasting four weeks) are a very challenging context to create space for spoken reflection. However, our position is that it is possible, that it is desirable and that this effort might be important in not positioning trainees as 'recipients'. Waring (2013: 104–105) has a useful section summarizing suggestions for promoting reflection in POCs including:

- talking less and being less directive (Copland et al., 2009);
- withholding value judgments or unsolicited feedback (Brandt, 2008; Zepeda, 2007);

- asking mediational questions such as 'how do you think the lesson went?' (Costa and Garmston, 2002);
- making open-ended statements about some aspects of teaching (Zepeda, 2007);
- being aware of the importance of the mentor's nonverbal behaviour when eliciting the teacher's self-disclosure;
- trying different timings of the post-observation briefing to affect the quality of reflection (Williams and Watson, 2004);
- avoiding the danger of giving advice without fully identifying the problem (Timperley, 2001).

Perhaps the most important building blocks for teacher trainers are trust and honesty. It must be possible for trainees to be honest with us (teacher educators) without feeling that we will negatively evaluate them. We come back to this point later in this chapter where we talk about the importance of safety and trust. However, at this point, it may be helpful to look at Rana and Esra's vignette (Appendix 6) as this shows a strong example of where simply talking honestly and openly to trainees may reveal interesting (and sometimes unwelcome) insights.

If we look now at a piece of data (extract 7.3) from a PRESET context in Mexico, we can see what is to be gained by encouraging such honesty and openness. Here, Luna is comparing herself unfavourably with her peer (Laura). Like Rana and Esra's data in Appendix 6, we can see the value in giving novice teachers the space to reflect on what is troubling them as they establish their identity as a 'real teacher':

Extract 7.3

```
10  I could not control the students as I thought
11  I would be able to control them . . . um . . . they
12  were talking, and standing up during the whole
13  lesson . . . I don't know . . . I mean, I realise that
14  children cannot be on their seats nor stay
15  quiet for a long period of time. I realised
16  that the type of activities I thought would
17  work, did not work at all, so . . . for the next
18  lesson I changed the activities and made them
19  more interactive, more entertaining. I also
20  created more material . . . still it was hard to
21  control the group. Yes, it is a bit . . . a lot
22  challenging. Right now I have no security or
23  confidence in myself because . . . I mean, compared
24  to Laura, who has already taught two lessons
25  too . . . the students behave better with her.
26  They are actually obedient. The students are
24  quiet and working.
```

```
[some lines omitted]
27  But it has been hard work and [sometimes] I
28  think "Well, what am I doing?" and I am
29  looking at Laura and observing what she is
30  doing that I'm not, "Why things work for her
31  and not for me?" At first I thought: "Well,
32  it's maybe the kids who were very anxious and
33  noisy". And now I'm realising that it might be
34  something I'm doing, because I've had already
35  two lessons(because I teach one lesson and
36  she [Laura] teaches the next one). So, by now,
37  I think I should already have a little more
38  control over children, but no, it isn't
39  happening that way. In contrast of what
40  happens with Laura. So, then, I start to feel
41  worried and I think: "What am I doing? Or what
42  am I not doing?" It's been really hard for me
43  and . . . . I don't know what to do . . . [giggles]
```

There are several aspects of Luna's articulation that are interesting. We get an insight into her willingness to be honest with her tutor (Flori). We also see the process of reflection: analyzing, looking for solutions, trialling, evaluating, comparing with others, and analyzing again. We can also see distinctive features of spoken reflection such as voicing questions she is asking herself ('Well, what am I doing?') as she compares negatively with Laura ('Why things work for her and not for me?'). In view of these comments on space, it is interesting to note the fact that Laura opens up space for self-improvement that she, other teachers or the tutor can occupy. The key point for us is that, in doing so, she invites not negative evaluation but positive support.

As well as building trust, openness and honesty, teacher educators can consciously adopt frameworks that help differentiate choices in giving feedback. Heron's (2001) *Six Category Intervention Analysis* has been widely used. Heron's categories help teacher educators to consider their role in shaping feedback interaction. The interventions are classed into 'authoritative interventions' ('prescriptive', 'informative' or 'confronting') and various 'facilitative interventions' ('cathartic', 'catalytic' and 'supportive'). Many others have tried to establish a less directive relationship (e.g. Baecher and McCormack, 2015). Baecher and McCormack present evidence that suggests that greater integration of video observation into the teacher training process can help establish a less directive relationship, giving novice teachers a greater voice in their POCs and fostering a less directive style of supervisor feedback. We will come back to their work in 7.3.

It can also help to consciously try to keep the focus positive in POCs where possible. Kurtoglu-Hooton (2008, 2010, 2016) uses Egan's approach to foreground 'confirmatory feedback'. In simple terms this prioritizes the 'pat on the back' and puts the focus on the positive. Kurtoglu-Hooton's approach builds on work on appreciative pedagogy (Yballe and O'Connor, 2000) which is a pedagogical adaptation of appreciative inquiry, a philosophy for change in which teacher trainers adopt the principle of focusing positively where possible (Cooperrider and Srivastva, 1987).

As well as adopting a positive focus, another conscious approach that can be adopted is to talk less and leave space for the novice teacher to articulate his or her current understanding. This inevitably means a less directive experience (see Copland et al., 2009) as the tutor backs off from giving value judgments or unsolicited feedback (Brandt, 2008). Bede McCormack's vignette shows what is possible when a tutor adopts a more back-seat approach.

BEDE MCCORMACK VIGNETTE (USA), LaGuardia Community College, CUNY

Context

This transcript is of a post-observation conversation between a teacher candidate (TC) and me after I had just observed his lesson. As the TC reflects on the lesson he has just taught, he considers it in light of what happened in previous lessons and what we have gone over in seminar discussions. He comes to several conclusions about how he might approach things differently in future classes.

BMcC: hmm right so, why don't you start, just talk about what you liked, what you didn't, stuff that you did differently from previous classes that you thought worked well and, yeah let's see where we go.

TC: ahh, this time I tried to pretty much jump right in, I've been giving them out handouts that I did a handout from the previous lesson that showed what we did last, in the previous lesson, and how that was gonna fit in. And that could take, depending on how many times I get off the track, it could take a while. So I just dispensed with that, I just . . . I think it was lesson 5 that I . . . and I had them read clippings or showing them clippings of present perfect tense that I had cut out of newspapers and magazines and that got the conversation going on about the present perfect tense which I wanted to go over with them a little bit since some of the students had missed the class, so that was . . . I don't think I'm gonna, I'm not gonna do that, I'm not gonna spend 10, 15 whatever minutes talking and tying it in with the previous class, I think . . . I realized that that wasn't really that productive, it didn't really help them hmmm . . . and the other thing

that I tried, I tried my first time which was that Bingo
game, hmm and the response was really good, I think, it
seemed that they were enjoying it and . . . they were
working in groups so I got them, you know as you
mentioned last time, to get them . . . to get me not be
the focus but to have them work with each other. And so
I felt that . . . I felt good about it I thought that
that was a good activity and I'm gonna do a similar
activity for lesson 6 only is gonna be, the theme is
gonna be health. As far as I can get through it, what
else did we do last time, and I spent . . . I really
limited the amount of vocabulary, grammar rather I'm
sorry grammar, I limited the amount of grammar, ahmm
. . . compared to the first couple of lessons I just
narrowed down to expressions of quantity, which fit
nicely to the different foods, that was, it just fit
nicely with the food theme there. Ahmm and ahmm I had a
break after we did the Bingo, then we talk, you were
there when we talked about the expressions of quantity,
yeah I took note of your comment here to organize which
sure makes sense, ahmm and then the final activity as
you left was to have them get together and I gave a
worksheet which was a worksheet here I'll just show you
what it was, it was, they worked in groups and they
each group was assigned to a dish or two that they
wanted to make and they were gonna decide on the dish,
they were gonna make a shopping list for the groceries
they needed to buy and try to include the quantities so
they could, you know re-impose the quantity thing and
then make a list of you know all the other things that
we talked about in class. Make a list of the utensils
and how they were gonna cook, you know the process of
cooking you know mashing the potatoes and chopping this
celery or you know baking versus boiling and frying
which is one of the things we talked about and so I let
them go with that for like a while right up to the end
of the class and then . . . yeah it was fun you know
they, each group made, you know planned a meal and I
went around in every single group I had time to . . .
to make plans with their . . . . One fellow in
particular, he said something like "papa" and as soon
as he said that everybody in the room was like ohh yeah
"Papa Ballerina" some type of Peruvian dish but
apparently they all knew it. There are a lot of folks
from Colombia, and Brazil, and Argentina and so forth.
So they were familiar with that dish, but he did all
the ingredients and everything in English so, I mean so
it wasn't . . . just the name was in Spanish but

idiomatic Spanish I would guess but and so basically I got through my lesson plan which is the first time I came close to . . . you know I finished it, I got through and so I really, I made a lesson plan that it was packed with group work it was only, lets see out of the four activities, three were group work and the only whole class warm-up activity was with the clippings of the newspaper articles and magazines about the present tense, present perfect tense rather. But ahmm, it really paid off, I mean ahmm, and it's not like I haven't been exposed to that idea before I mean professor T. really, really taught us all about how to do that but I, I don't know what it was I guess . . .

BMcC: taught you how to do what?

TC: you know . . . get the tension away from the teacher, and have the students communicate with each other and so forth, you know but I guess it took me a few lessons to actually make that work or put it into practice so to speak so . . .

BMcC: was there any time in the class when you realized that you needed to try that or what kind of . . . what made you move in that direction do you think . . .

TC: yeah I think two things, ahmm I think it was lesson number 2, I covered . . . I made a massive lesson plan and I covered gerunds, participles as adjectives, present perfect and I was pretty much the focus the whole time, now I got them doing things, doing exercises but, they were really exhausted and I think I was exhausted as well. So the combination of sort of seeing, just giving them too much was just flat out can't cover that much stuff and then of course your comments from that class you know . . . about you know shifting focus it wasn't new to me, is just that I didn't figure out how to do this yet, and figure out how to do that yet but is a combination of experience and being tired, seeing them being tired made me think that I should cut down on the amount of grammar focuses and do more student activities.

Commentary

As the TC talks, he paints a picture of what happened in a class – what kind of handouts he distributed, how students reacted to them, how he spent time at the beginning of class reminding them about what they did in the last class, etc. And all the while he is meta-thinking about how all this worked out – "I realized that wasn't really that productive, it didn't really help them, hmmm." He goes on to make connections between what a seminar instructor (Professor T.) covered with him and how he tried to implement the idea in class – to "get the tension away from the teacher, and have the students communicate with each other and so forth" and notes that changing one's classroom practice can take time – "I guess it took me a few lessons to actually make that work or put it into practice so to speak so . . ."

He also shows empathy with his students when he realizes how he overwhelmed them with "a massive lesson plan" that led to both he and the students being "really exhausted and I think I was exhausted as well." Through his "combination of experience and being tired", he concludes that he should "cut down on the amount of grammar focuses".

This is a particularly powerful transcription that shows how a novice teacher can realize on his own what changes need to be made to improve learning outcomes.

As we said in the introduction, one of the most striking aspects of the above extract is the amount of space that the teacher candidate has in order to articulate learning points. This allows for voicing, conjecture, realizations, emotional reactions, tentative language and decision-making. It also allows for connecting received knowledge (e.g. Professor T.'s input) to more personal and experiential knowledge (managing classroom materials and tasks). Bede deliberately restricts his role to elicitation and what might be called reflective prompts and this allows further articulation of consideration of language learner responses, the amount of target grammar, lesson timings and management, as well as orientation to previous suggestions from Bede.

By 'taking a back seat', as demonstrated in the above vignette, teacher trainers can do a lot to create the kind of space needed for teacher candidates to express their thoughts and comment on their performance. Interactional space – denoted by long turns on the part of the teacher candidate and shorter turns on the part of the tutor – enables ideas to be formulated and articulated, thoughts to be processed and new understandings to emerge. This space should be viewed as 'space for learning' (Walsh and Li, 2013): it is a key element of professional dialogues and one which should be developed and mastered by teacher educators. For example, while the candidate is speaking, the tutor needs to engage in active listening (e.g. visible attentiveness, nodding, minimal responses).

In another study, Tudor Jones (2012) focuses her research on the nature and design of her trainer questions in POCs. She produces an account of the effect that different questions have on getting trainees to talk in their POCs. In doing so, she considers the range of different questions that she uses ('hinting' questions, direct 'wh' questions, and initiating questions) and assesses how these different kinds of questions play different roles in creating different talk opportunities for trainees, especially in fostering peer-to-peer interaction. 'Hinting' questions, for example, offer an invitation (rather than transmitting knowledge). Tudor Jones calls these 'semi-collaborative' and argues that they are one way to push novice teachers 'a little bit beyond the "safe" and "known" into new, developmental areas'. More direct 'wh' questions, which attempt to elicit reflection, appeared less helpful for the interlocutors in the featured data. However, on many occasions, although the recipient of the 'wh' question did not necessarily reflect as a result of the question, 'wh' questions could prompt a collaborative response from a group of more confident trainees. Tudor Jones uses CA (conversation analysis) tools to uncover salient features of the interaction.

Section 7.2 has concentrated on some of the difficulties and tensions in POCs. However, it has also considered a number of ways in which teacher educators shape the nature of the feedback event to create space for reflection. The next section (7.3) considers the role of video and screen capture software in facilitating data-led feedback and reflective discussion.

7.3 Video and Other Tools

Section 7.3 concentrates on video and screen capture software and evaluates their importance in fostering spoken reflection. We are not suggesting that these are the only valuable tools for enabling spoken reflection. For example, the use of conversation analysis (CA) tools can help novice teachers, and we will be talking more about this in Chapter 8. Elsewhere in the book we have argued that tools such as 'rep-grids', metaphors and critical incidents can be helpful in enabling reflective talk. We begin this section by reviewing the literature on video use in language teacher education. We focus primarily on how video can be used in POCs to focus attention on concrete detail.

Almodaires (2009: 209), working in Kuwait, makes a specific argument that video has an important role in eliciting detail from classrooms and sees this as responding to a common barrier for reflective practice:

> A major barrier relates to the complexity of recalling the different details in an experience in order to describe and analyze this experience. This barrier has been highlighted in several research studies as a major obstacle in realizing the potential of the reflection approach and is also described sometimes as a major weakness in this approach.
>
> *Boud et al., 1985*

The use of video to promote reflection, especially in post-observation feedback conferences, is not a new thing (e.g. Fuller and Manning, 1973) and has been shown to help focus on teaching detail. In recent years the ease of capturing digital video, with greater online storage facilities, coupled with the availability of other tools (e.g. captioning and annotation) has meant that video has become an increasingly flexible and powerful mediating tool (Rich and Hannafin, 2009).

There is certainly evidence that video and visual media are increasingly being used in language teacher training and development (see Marsh and Mitchell, 2014) and during the last few decades there has been growing understanding of the role videos are having in contributing to teacher autonomy, engagement and development (Conole and Dyke, 2004; Grant and Kline, 2010). Tripp and Rich (2012) is a particularly useful contribution to our understanding of video use because they review a wide range of studies reporting the benefits of using video for teacher reflection. In some studies teachers reflected on their videos individually, while in others teachers reflected on their videos collaboratively. Tripp and Rich used the following criteria to review the dimensions of video use:

1. type of reflection tasks
2. the guiding or facilitation of reflection
3. individual and collaborative reflection
4. video length
5. number of reflections
6. ways of measuring reflection.

Overall, Tripp and Rich found a great deal of variety in video reflection tasks, guiding frameworks and methods used to measure the benefits of video reflection. They see video as a consistently powerful tool for teacher reflection, where teachers can 'more effectively "see" their practice' and where teachers who 'engage in video reflection report recalling prior videos of their teaching during future teaching, enabling them to more effectively, "reflect in practice"' (2012: 679). Such recall and consideration helped teachers to identify gaps between beliefs and classroom reality and also to better articulate their tacit assumptions about teaching and learning. They could notice things that they could not remember, focus on multiple aspects of classrooms, and assess strengths and weaknesses. Masats and Dooly (2011) and Baecher et al. (2013) also offer useful summaries and examples of various procedures (video-modelling, video-coaching, video-viewing and video-making). Drawing on this literature, we would emphasize the following as important aspects of video use:

A Focus on Concrete Detail

Video encourages a focus on the concrete details and events of classroom practice, taking the trainee teacher back into a teaching moment, incident, choice or decision. Helping novice teachers to locate specific aspects of their lessons makes the process of reflection more data-led (e.g. Baecher et al., 2014). A teacher might use video to look again at a moment they were conscious of at the time, but video can also enable a focus on the 'aspects of classroom life that a teacher might not notice in the midst of carrying out a lesson' (Borko et al., 2008: 418). In the following example, in a novice teacher's report, the teacher is engaged in just such a process of recalling, describing and reflecting on a teaching incident (here, reflecting on appropriate levels of silence in the classroom):

> While they (students) were answering the questions, there was a great silence in the classroom – um, a silence not ordinary for a language classroom. I gave them 10 minutes to read the text and answer the questions; during the lesson I thought that it was normal; but while I was watching the video I saw that silence period was too long. Besides, I realized that I was so quiet during the lesson; it would have been better if I had been more active and energetic.
>
> *Borko et al., 2008: 418*

Developing Sensitivity to Classroom Talk

As this data shows, it is often challenging for novice teachers to achieve an appropriate balance between their own talking time (TTT: teacher talking time) and that of their students (STT: student talking time). More importantly, as we have discussed in Chapter 5, there is a need for teachers to understand that their use of language and interaction has a profound effect on learning and learning opportunity; choices concerning the use of language may create or restrict learning opportunities (Walsh, 2002). One of the challenges for teachers is developing sensitivity to both encouraging talking and allowing silence. Giving instructions, eliciting language and asking questions are difficult practices to master, as demonstrated in the following example, where a student is grappling with this problem and coming to a possible solution (preparing questions in advance):

> While watching her own video, Esra realized that she had trouble with speaking in English. She observed that she would 'start a sentence with one structure and continue with another or say something at the end when [she was] supposed to say it at the beginning'. Her mixing of structures and sequences, especially when giving instructions, resulted in confusion among the students and diverted their attention from classwork. Similarly, Meltem noticed in her video that she paused too much while interacting with the students, and when she 'tried to construct the sentences spontaneously in the classroom, [she] wasn't successful, and the students realized it too'. She felt she lost the respect of the students as well as the control of the class due to the gaps in her speech and consequently decided to prepare her questions ahead of time.
>
> *Eröz-Tuğa, 2013: 179*

Use of Video Models

Video allows reflection on other teachers' practice. Hiebert et al. (2002) argue that video provides concrete examples of instructional practices that avoid much of the ambiguity of written descriptions (see also Masats and Dooly, 2011). A video extract is not just a 'model' but can provide a strong stimulus for discussion and associated reflective thought for viewers. Hiebert et al. (2002) also argue that the educational community lacks a shared language for describing aspects of teaching and that video has a particular role to play here. For example, key phrases such as 'problem solving' or 'language experience' often mean different things to different teachers. Videotapes of lessons therefore offer the possibility of pinning down aspects of classroom experience so that the teacher has a clearer frame of reference and can be more specific about their own actions and intentions. Video extracts also offer the possibility of co-constructing knowledge through the interpretation of and reflection on classroom practices (Sherin, 2004).

A Meditational Tool

In considering the role of video, Golombek (2011) uses a series of data extracts to show how 'dialogic video protocols' have the potential to promote more 'expert thinking' in relation to 'authentic teaching activity' (2011: 122). She talks specifically about video as a tool for mediating teacher reflection in such teacher–learner conversations focused on classroom activity. She shows examples of how the use of video helps to reconstruct teachers' perspectives on these teaching events through sharing 'intersubjectivity' (2011: 135). Lewis and Anping have a similar aim in the design of their video-viewing tasks (2002), and this dialogic element of reflection will be explored further in Chapter 8. See also our discussion on VEO (video-enhanced observation) in Chapter 5.

Supporting Novice Teachers' Voices

Kurtoglu-Hooton (2010, 2016) presents evidence suggesting that greater integration of video observation into teacher training contexts can help nudge the SLTE field away from a directive supervisory pattern, give teacher candidates a greater voice in their POCs and, in turn, foster a less 'imperator-style' approach to supervisor feedback. As we saw earlier, she favours an approach to using video which foregrounds 'confirmatory feedback'.

Video use can also help in building a longer-term sense of growth and development. In the following vignette from Teti Dragas, we see how a systematic approach to the use of video in a Masters level programme enables reflection on a particular module. We believe that the use of video as evidence, requiring a focus on concrete detail, reduces the likelihood of 'faking it' (Hobbs, 2007). This vignette offers an insight into how documenting evidence over time might produce more grounded reflection.

TETI DRAGAS VIGNETTE (DURHAM, UK)

Context

The context is a teacher development module that forms a core part of an MA in Applied Linguistics for TESOL at a British university. The key module aims are to develop teachers' 'ability to critically reflect on aspects of their teaching practice both as observers and as practitioners'. The students are a group of international teachers (with two or more years of teaching experience) from a range of different countries and contexts who, as part of the module, teach a total of nine lessons between them over a ten-week period to a group of international language learners. Each teaching practice (TP) session was recorded and placed on the VLE. Following TP, teachers were given reflective tasks to focus them on aspects of the lesson, which were discussed collaboratively in a further two-hour group feedback session. In the discussion sessions, teachers were encouraged both to draw on reading to focus on points that arose out of TP and to review videos to help them to reflect on practice. Throughout the module, pre-, during and post teaching practice and group feedback sessions, teachers were asked to record their thoughts in a reflective diary, the extracts of which formed part of the assignment, allowing teachers to remember, select and return to certain critical learning periods during the module and reflect on these further. The extract below draws on an observation the teacher made during TP, which was further developed in the group discussion session.

Data

In the lesson, the lead teacher played a revision game where a question was asked, and the student who raised their hand first was given the opportunity to answer. Following the lesson, there was a discussion on why the activity was not the most suitable form of revision. (1) We narrowed down the problem to the amount of time the teacher waited before calling on a student for a response. (2) Upon watching the video again, I calculated the teacher's average wait-time to be 1.28 seconds. In fact, a majority of the teacher's utterances (after a question was asked) happened so quickly, it was hard to measure the exact number of milliseconds. The statistic is unsurprising as Rowe (1972: 2) points out. On average, teachers allow only one second of time to start answering a question. If students do not respond, teachers either repeat the question or select another student to answer. After a response, teachers typically wait 0.9 second before either making a comment, following up with another question or changing the topic entirely. (3) Analyzing my practice to see where I stood in comparison to the research findings was a valuable exercise.

Though I had already heard of the concept of wait-time, (4) observing my teaching lessons again and reading Rowe (1972) made me re-evaluate my understanding of wait-time. I thought it to be merely the amount of time that a teacher waits for a response. (5) I had never considered rephrasing my question as a factor that impacted wait-time, neither had I included the time after a student responds to a question as an important period to allow others to process the response. (6) An analysis of the videos of my teaching showed that in no instance did I give out any answer to the students, but I often interrupted thinking time by rephrasing my question. For example in my second teaching lesson, I was clarifying an error that was made in a gap-fill exercise. I said, "Look at 'have' and look at 'need'. Can you see if they are in the right place?" 2.40 seconds later, I said "Just look at that sentence again. Are 'have' and 'need' in the right place?" Reflecting on my past experience, the habit of rephrasing may have begun because I work with young students that have relatively low attention spans . . . Working in this new context [with adult learners] has shown that rephrasing is perhaps an unnecessary interruption of thought flow.

(7) Going forward, I have two strategies to help me keep wait-time alive in my classroom. The first is to allow enough processing time before I call on a student to respond. The second is to ensure enough thinking time after a response has been given.

Reference

Rowe, Mary Budd. 'Wait-time and rewards as instructional variable, their influence in language, logic and fate control.' Paper presented at the *National Association for Research in Science Teaching*, Chicago, IL, 1972.

Commentary

The extract above comes from an assessed piece of reflective writing, which formed the summative assessment of the module and was drawn from both a reflective diary that the student wrote throughout the module, and reflections that the teacher wrote in retrospect after further reflecting on the lesson and the learning. It has been chosen for a number of reasons, the primary one being that it clearly demonstrates the development of the teacher's thinking through reflection on practice. The underlined sections and phrases from 1–7 map the process which begins at: 1) noticing the problem; 2) analyzing the evidence (based on the video of TP); 3) and 4) moving from reflection of others' practice to reflection of own practice; 5) identifying areas of practice that the teacher hadn't considered before; 6) analyzing the evidence of this in the teacher's own practice based on evidence-based analysis (video); 7) finding strategies to develop practice in the future (i.e. applying knowledge to future practice). There are a number of useful conclusions we might draw from how reflection 'happens' and/or how to encourage teacher reflection to promote individual teacher growth or, as Korthagen put it, 'growth competence' (2001) and these include: the use and importance of both individual and collaborative discussion (Walsh and Mann, 2015); writing consistently in reflective journals (Bassot, 2013; Bolton, 2014); focused video review (Bryan and Recesso, 2006; Tripp and Rich, 2012); and the importance of context in reflection on teaching (Finlay, 2008). Whilst all these measures can promote the development of reflection in teacher education, what is important to remember is that teachers need both guidance and training in order to use these tools and techniques effectively.

One of the interesting things about this vignette is the way video is used in a collaborative way (between the individual teacher and tutor and between peer teachers). The reflective tasks, following the teaching practice, require individuals to review both videos and their reading (connecting practice to theory). These individual reflections feed into collaborative reflective talk, as Teti has shown above.

Borko et al. (2008: 417) suggest that providing a reflection framework based on video enhanced the quality of teacher reflection but, at the same time, teachers reported that they preferred some element of choosing their own reflection focus. However, teachers also clearly preferred more collaborative reflection rather than individual reflection on their videos (see Chapter 8). Borko et al. (2008) share an example from a student (Ken) of just such a perspective:

> I think this [watching and discussing video clips] was the single most valuable part of the STAAR program. I have learned the most about my teaching by watching my teaching practice. Even better, though, was watching others teach a lesson that I also taught. My ideas have been sparked by others in this group. Having a safe place to watch ourselves and not feel like we were being criticized or evaluated was critical also.

It is obvious from this extract that Ken particularly values the collaborative ('others ... sparked by others in the group') and Borko et al. stress the value of the shared reflection on classroom events and interaction as it allows a space for the consideration of alternative pedagogical strategies (Brophy, 2004). This is also a further example of what we talked about earlier in the chapter: that safe spaces and trust are especially important in allowing genuine reflection. There are many other studies that provide evidence that reflection can be supported by peer group discussion and that novice teachers greatly value such interaction and discussion (Cunningham, 2002; Hepple, 2012; Nguyen, 2013; Rich and Hannafin, 2009; Wachob, 2011).

Outside teacher education programs, there is also evidence that video clubs offer an environment for collaborative reflection. Within a video club, teachers make a commitment to meet, view and discuss video recordings from participating teachers' classrooms (Sherin and van Es, 2005). Examples of the kind of learning communities that can be established within such video clubs, as well as the kinds of teaching and learning conversations that result, have been well documented (Sherin, 2004; Sherin and Han, 2004; Sherin and van Es, 2009; van Es, 2012).

Some Difficulties and Dangers

As we have explained in Chapter 1, reflective practice faces a continuing dilemma. If you give it status within a programme (especially where a programme needs to be passed or where certification is required) it will probably need to be assessed. On the one hand, assessing it can be seen as confirming its importance. However, this may cause other problems that Tony Wright talked about in his vignette in Chapter 4. Some organizations (such as the National Board for Professional Teaching Standards (NBPTS) in the USA) also require this kind of evidence of reflection for professional certification. As Verlaan and Verlaan explain, NBPTS has 'long required candidates to submit two video recordings, each supplemented by an essay, contextualizing, describing, and analyzing what is shown on the clip as evidence of reflection on their practice' (2015: 152). While we believe that reflection based on video is more likely to lead to data-led reflection, it can also be daunting and teachers may need appropriate levels of guidance. We have already argued in Chapter 3 that pre-service teachers need careful introduction to reflective practice and it needs to be properly exemplified. Teachers are 'not well served when we expect reflection to happen without careful instruction in both how and why the process is both intellectually rigorous and pedagogically and personally beneficial' (Verlaan and Verlaan, 2015: 154). In a partial answer to this dilemma, Verlaan and Verlaan offer a vision of what might be gained by adopting a more collaborative approach:

> With guidance rather than instruction as their purpose, teacher educators would also take on a more collaborative than evaluative role, freeing up the intern to focus more on analysis and revision of practice than simply the evaluation of performance, and freeing up the educator to offer additional alternatives to the intern's thinking without the risk of suggesting to the intern that she or he is performing below standard. Cultivating a deliberate and methodical habit of reflection, and being empowered to select the standards of reflective practice and procedures to achieve them, an intern's choice to reflect will become a natural response to classroom experience.
>
> *2015: 155*

Reflection can be difficult to get used to and needs appropriate support, whether with video or not. If it is compulsory and is being used for assessment purposes, it needs careful handling and teachers need to be encouraged to make their reflections data-led.

At this point you might want to read a vignette (Appendix 5). There, Jo Gakonga is illustrating the difficulties of dealing with video for the first time on a Masters level programme. Her innovation is getting more experienced teachers to 'mentor' those with no teaching experience. The novice teachers are mentored based on a video of their micro-teaching. Jo's aim is to build awareness of how to create a safe, trusting relationship where reflection and self-evaluation can happen. However, at least initially, this is difficult to achieve, as more experienced teachers tend to fall into 'judgementoring' (Hobson and Malderez, 2013) typical of mentors in schools:

> [M]y mentor in my second year [of ITP] . . . whenever I said 'this is the way we have to do things' she said . . . 'oh you shouldn't be doing that . . . you should be doing this' . . . I kind of felt 'all that work and it is worthless because I have got to do it your way' . . .
>
> *Hobson and Malderez, 2013: 96*

However, in Jo's case, the difficulty is not just a case of establishing the mentoring role; it is also getting novice teachers used to video-based feedback. As we see from the data below, there can be too much focus on the negative (from the teachers confronted with their video). Here Jo is reflecting on why the reaction to the video might have led to focusing on the negative:

Extract 7.4

```
T.   . . . because going through with them, when I was doing the
     feedback with them, it was the first time I'd ever done
     feedback video like that, at the same time, and I thought,
     yeah, this is really powerful, this is really great. And it's
     really interesting to see how, how much negative stuff they've
     taken from it. Perhaps that's something to consider, but it
     is, maybe it's too in-your-face, particularly for beginner
     teachers or maybe the sensitive teachers. You know, maybe
     the idea of it being really there, and so you can't deny it
     because it's there.
```

There are other accounts which reveal a similar problem (getting used to seeing yourself on video and using the experience for reflective purposes). For example, Crystal (in Verlaan and Verlaan, 2015) begins her first reflection by noting 'there is not much more cringe inducing than watching yourself on film' (2015: 156).

One final concern is with video and ethics. It is relatively easy to get permission from participants for micro-teaching on a Masters level course but what about when teaching practice is taking place in real schools? The account provided by Phillipson et al. (2015) demonstrates some of the problems getting permission from classroom teachers and headteachers to video-record in schools. From 'the original 166 students in this cohort, only 12 were sufficiently interested to seek permission from both their supervising teacher and the school principal'. Of these 12, four were successful in gaining permission from both their teacher and the principal.

Using SCS (Screen Capture Software)

This section talks about the value of SCS in providing reflective feedback. (Appendix 3 presents a number of options for using SCS if you are unfamiliar with this tool.) As a brief introduction, with SCS (screen capture software) you record the computer screen and your voice. You can either form a box around the section of the computer screen you wish to capture or capture the whole of your screen. Having 'boxed' the area of the screen, a record button is then pressed. From that moment, everything within the marked area is recorded as a video, including the tutor's voice. You can highlight aspects of the text with your cursor and point to specific aspects of the screen or text to which you want to draw the teacher's attention. This section concentrates particularly on the giving and receiving of feedback through SCS. We will consider how students feel about getting feedback in this form, as well as providing and evaluating a number of SCS choices.

The provision of feedback on writing tasks and assignments is an integral component of many language teaching and teacher education contexts. The advantage of SCS is that you can highlight the actual part of the text that you want to focus on (using a cursor and highlighting tools). You can simultaneously use voice comments to provide feedback. By recording your computer screen, you can also show teachers other sites and resources (websites and online tools) and even embed video extracts into the final version. Being able to simultaneously provide a visual focus and an auditory commentary has been called 'multimodal' feedback (Stannard, 2007). In the following vignette, Russell Stannard summarizes the value of SCS.

RUSSELL STANNARD VIGNETTE (UK)

Over a period of more than 5 years, I have experimented with using screen casting and video to get students and teachers to reflect on different aspects of their learning. One of my first examples was with using Screen Capture Technology. It was with a group of teachers doing an M level course around technology training. We had done a lesson using a specific technology called 'Wallwisher' and I wanted the teachers to reflect on the lesson and discuss what they had learnt and what dynamics had taken place within the group and to link these to aspects of language learning. I wanted them to think more about the actual activity and what had actually happened during it. I would usually have done this through a questionnaire, however I sometimes think that teachers find it easier to reflect orally (either in their L1 or L2 depending on the context) and wanted to experiment with the idea.

After we had done the lesson, which was a group based lesson using a technology called 'Wallwisher', I uploaded a PowerPoint slide with 5 questions I wanted the teachers to think about related to the lesson. I asked the teachers to screen cast the PowerPoint presentation and record their answers to the questions. In that way the reflections were very guided, though the questions were quite broad in nature. The questions encouraged the teachers to reflect on the lesson, how the activity was set up and how the technology was exploited.

Teachers were offered a range of possible technologies that they could use. Some chose to use Techsmith JING, some used myBrainShark and others chose Present.Me. These are all similar tools in nature and offered the chance for teachers to record their voices as they worked through the PowerPoint slides. I made the PowerPoint slides available in DropBox, so all the teachers had to do was open the slides and use whatever technology they were most comfortable with to record their answers.

Overall teachers tended to provide a lot more information than similar activities done in written form and I was quite surprized at the honesty of some of their answers. In fact, the result was that I realised that the lesson using 'Wallwisher' needed some changes to accommodate some of the issues that the teachers had raised in their reflections. Subsequently we had a classroom discussion where teachers made suggestions about improvements to the actual 'Wallwisher' lesson.

I have never sat down to code their reflections and compare them to similar activities I have done with written reflections but what immediately struck me was just how freely the teachers provided information and the detail is far more than I have ever received in written reflections we have done. I also asked the teachers informally whether they liked reflecting on the lessons this way rather than through written forms and the response was overwhelmingly positive, though they emphasised that it was something that could easily be overdone. I have used this technique many times since that initial experiment.

Example of Teacher's Reflection

www.youtube.com/watch?v=mxrcll18KmU

One observation that Russell makes is that there is far more detail in this form of feedback. This finding has been supported by Chen (2012) and Mann (2015) who report on various aspects of using SCS on an MA course. Like Russell Stannard, they found that SCS (in this case Jing) produces a more detailed and elaborate text than in written feedback. This seems to give teachers more detail to reflect on. Extract 7.5 is a comment from a teacher in an interview about the use of Jing. The tutor (I) has given feedback on an assignment called Spoken English which involves recording, transcribing and analyzing spoken data:

Extract 7.5

```
1   I   So (.) would you pick out anything that
2       is different about the Jing feedback-
3   T   you mean Issues in ELT (.) or this one?
4   I   this one
5   T   well (.) I'd say:: it there's a lot of detail
6       especially the transcript and analysis (.) you
7       gave me lots of other possibilities for looking at
8       the data (1.0) there are less general comments I
9       think (.) and more detail to think about
```

Chen (2012: 18–19) includes these two interview comments (extract 7.6) from tutors who have used Jing:

Extract 7.6

```
Michael  from the teachers' point of view I think it is
         (practical), because I think the amount of feedback that
         you can provide in such a short space of time you can
         never do that if it's written (.) it provides a lot more
         information to the student, you can elaborate more (.)

Paul     Jing is useful for the detail (.) it's for elaboration
         (.) extra extra information
```

SCS seems to offer more detail and clarification and this may be because it is 'multimodal' feedback (see Stannard, 2007; Brick and Holmes, 2008). As well as greater detail, there seems to be something significant about seeing and hearing at the same time. As another student said, 'seeing corrections on the screen and hearing the explanation makes it clear to me' (Chen, 2012: 19). In addition, feedback is more personal, perhaps because the spoken voice allows more tone and expression (Rust, 2001) and at least in some cases makes the feedback easier to take. Oral feedback tends to be more 'off-record' and more 'personally addressed to the student' (Gardner, 2004: 24). Mann (2015: 170) includes this interview extract (7.7) with a novice teacher:

Extract 7.7

```
1   I   You just said it feels more personal (.) in what way?
2   T   Because (.) it just like a personal tutorial (.) actually
3       (.) it is just one way (.) but even if it is one
4       way but still I can feel face to face tutorial (.)
5       so I prefer to receive Jing rather than written feedback
6       because it's more humanistic interaction
7   I   So (.) it feels almost like a face to face tutorial?
8   T   Yes I think so (.) this kind of feedback can help
9       the relationship
```

Part of this more personal feel is probably due to there being less distance and more humour, as well as the more colloquial and informal choices of spoken language. Written feedback may be seen as more formal and may not be as 'hedged'. Sampling both written and spoken feedback, Mann (2015) found that written texts were more 'bald-on-record'. Although there were approximately the same proportion of softeners in two samples, there are fewer questions and fewer instances of personal attribution. In relation to calls for feedback to be more 'dialogic' in nature (e.g. Attwood, 2009), SCS feedback moves away from transfer of pre-existing knowledge to a more scaffolded and dialogic process (see also Farr, 2010).

As well as SCS tools there are also tools like Kaizena which has all of the advantages of normal Word 'review' comments but can add audio and is fairly user-friendly. At the moment it is free to sign up on the site (Kaizena.com). You can have a teacher or student account and then give learners a code so that you can give feedback. When you upload the document you want to look at, you then highlight parts of the text and write comments as you would normally do. The innovative part is that you can leave audio comments in addition. The potentially dialogic part is that the other person can reply. Kaizena also sends you email notifications when feedback is updated. However, at the moment it only works on Google Chrome.

The value of both video and SCS tools is that they create more opportunities for talk to be about detail and evidence. This emphasis on detail can help talk in teacher education to be more collaborative, and the next section (7.4) takes up this theme more explicitly.

7.4 Collaborative Reflection

Section 7.4 establishes the importance of collaboration in pushing reflective practice beyond an essentially individual pursuit. In this section, we comment on the ways in which teacher education can encourage a collaborative view of teaching, where peers/colleagues can support and scaffold reflective practice and where teachers are not restricted to isolated teaching roles but see belonging to networks and communities of practice as viable and essential to their development. The section begins by reviewing the importance of teacher educators valuing and drawing on teacher experiences (developing some of the themes of Chapter 4; see also 'Collaborative CPD' in Chapter 5 and 'Dialogic Reflection' in Chapter 8) and then introduces a specific tool for fostering listening and collaborative reflection (cooperative development).

When teachers have been used to a transmission style of education, they may not be used to drawing on and referring to their own experience in explicit ways. The ultimate goal of teacher education is to help teachers to become autonomous decision-makers, able to make appropriate decisions and choices about materials, methodologies and technologies. However, this should not mean that they see this goal as an entirely individual one. Of course, the value of collaboration is not restricted to teacher education. Collaboration with colleagues is increasingly recognized as an important dimension of teaching itself; the ability to jointly construct materials, design a course, work as a team, understand and be comfortable with the rhythms and challenges of teamwork is an important dimension of independent professionalism (Leung, 2009). This dimension is sometimes referred to as 21st-century skills (i.e. communication, collaboration, team-work, creativity). Taking all this into account, an individual view of the teaching enterprise is extremely limiting. Kiely and Davis (2010: 280) make this point when they consider a number of factors contributing to potential slow progress in language teacher training:

> Teaching is often an isolated activity (Fullan, 1991), with teachers seldom discussing or exploring with colleagues what happens in their teaching. As members of an 'egg box' profession (Freeman, 1998), their teaching unfolds either intuitively (Atkinson and Claxton, 2000), or mechanically, without ever exploring or rationalizing it, i.e. without understanding their pedagogy through explaining it to others (Mann, 2005).

Socio-cultural theory (SCT), in particular, sees it as desirable that teachers learn from their own and others' practice and that teacher education should seek to maximize collaborative teacher learning opportunities (Johnson, 2006). Chapter 8 will focus more on SCT, but for now we can say that SCT values and accounts for how such scaffolded talk (experience-based elaboration of concepts and praxis) can be the central process in teacher education (rather than relying on an input-led model). In particular, notions such as the constructivist power of collaborative small groups (Bailey and Willett, 2004: 15), investment in learning (Norton, 2000), teacher identity (Richards, 2006) and communities of practice (Wenger, 1998) have cemented the value of embedding such a collaborative process within teacher education. Johnson (2009: 241) confirms that 'collaborative teacher development (CTD) is an increasingly common kind of teacher development found in a wide range of language teaching contexts'. This process is usually valued by teachers themselves. For example, Kiely and

Davis found that the participants 'were happier and perceived a greater value in the examination of their practice using subjective measures developed in discussion than they were employing the external, objective paradigms suggested by the research literature' (2010: 292).

Tsui (2009: 30) argues that teachers find 'sharing reflective writings and engaging in collaborative reflections' particularly useful. As well as the 'sharing' process they also value an element of choice in topics for spoken reflection (Wright and Bolitho, 2007). In Chapter 4, we looked closely at the approach taken by Wright and Bolitho (2007) in building a learning community with in-service teacher education. The aim for them and like-minded teacher educators is always to foster a social group that will have a life of its own for the duration of the course, where 'the eventual outcome of the course will to a considerable extent be forged in the interactions between the members of the learning group' (2007: 34). This is a humanistic view of training and the development of reflection, as there is a great deal of focus on 'teambuilding' and trust activities. This humanistic view of training aims to establish basic fundamentals of teaching first:

> Hearing everyone's voice, learning everyone's name and making 'eyeball to eyeball' contact with every other group member.
>
> *2007: 35*

The observations above are related to Masters level provision. However, the inclusion of at least some element of spoken reflection increases the potential of having a co-constructed and collaborative approach in shorter INSET training too. Wedell (2009) argues that, in doing so, the course is less likely to perpetuate a deficit model of development; including collaborative discussion is more likely to offer space for an ongoing process of assessing experiences, beliefs, goals, and learning outcomes. It is possible for a teacher education programme to have the dual aim of developing individual teacher autonomy (working with individual teachers to help them explore and reflect on their own practices) and more collaborative practices (in order to create a cooperative ecology of thinking, focusing on teaching experience, narratives and classroom data).

This next part of 7.4 concentrates on strategies and tools for establishing constructive and collaborative relationships in the group. As Hatton and Smith (1995) have argued, reflection is most likely to be demonstrated when strategies involving critical friends or collaborative discussion in a supportive and trusting environment are adopted. Such an environment is not necessarily easy to establish and it is important to be aware of pitfalls. Some students will take to collaborative and reflective discussion easily and find it enjoyable. This is the case with a teacher in Qatar, who has just completed a short INSET course. He makes clear in an interview (extract 7.8) that he particularly values working collaboratively on teaching problems:

Extract 7.8

```
. . . I think I have enjoyed talking about the problems
that faced teachers in the current context. I also enjoyed
discussing corresponding solutions to those problems
because it provided me with ways to tackle reading in my
classrooms . . .
```

However, in the next data extract (7.9) from an INSET teacher's learning log, we get a strong sense that group work can sometimes be challenging:

Extract 7.9

> We did another group work today. Why was I being harassed? I find again that group presentation is not very pleasant for me. It gets me clashing more with others. Why? I hope I get answers soon. Are they reacting to my foolishness or (...) my strength (...) are they competing with me? Adult learners are not much different from children learners. In as much as group work is (...) valuable, the teacher must (...) provide rules for communication.

The group presentation has not gone well for this student. It is positive that the teacher (in the extract above) feels able to make these comments so that the tutor might be able to respond, but the emotional reaction is strong ('harassed'/'not pleasant'/'competing'). It is also interesting that the student feels that 'rules for communication' may be necessary. In simple terms, it may be possible to get trainees to talk, but there may still be problems with establishing reflective talk within the group. Dominant students may be locked into a debate culture (see Tannen, 1998) and more comfortable with transmission styles of talk. Wright and Bolitho make the comment that some teachers dominate 'air time' in putting forward their contributions (2007: 120). The point we wish to make at this point is that some guidance or training might be necessary. This might not have to be 'rules for communication' as the teacher suggests above. However, it may be helpful to make the nature of collaborative talk a discussion point in its own right.

To establish reflective talk, some fundamentals may need to be established in the group. First and foremost is the importance of listening. McCarthy talks about 'good listenership' (2002: 49), and this is the most essential pre-requisite for collaborative reflection. Gendlin integrates a 'listening partnership' where the listener is encouraged to contribute only when they cannot follow:

> From the start I had the students in my class meet in listening partnerships during the week. They divided two hours, taking turns purely listening. 'Just listen. Only say when you don't follow,' I instructed them. 'If your

partner is working on a paper, don't tell about how YOU would write the paper.'

2004: 2

The next part of 7.4 introduces a tool (cooperative development) that we have found particularly helpful for encouraging collaborative spoken reflection. Cooperative development (CD) is a collaborative approach to professional self-development talk. It adopts a Rogerian discourse framework that builds trust, empathy and understanding (see Rogers, 1980; Rogers and Freiberg, 1994). It is explicitly based on Carl Rogers' principles of self-actualization and non-judgemental understanding. The purpose of CD is to create a collaborative reflective space where an idea can emerge and grow. This is very different from a space for reporting ideas that have already been rehearsed, presented or published. In simple terms, the idea is that reflection is facilitated through the conscious adoption of such a framework so that ideas can go through a process of 'inchoation or incubation' (Prabhu, 1990: 170) and become clearer and more fully formed.

CD offers teachers the space to develop a line of thought or argument that is quite different from the more prevalent debate styles of talk or in agenda-driven meetings (Mann, 2002). Edge (2002: 13) specifies the following enabling goals for CD to increase:

- awareness of your own strengths and skills;
- appreciation of the strengths and skills of others;
- willingness to listen carefully to others;
- ability to interact positively with changes in your teaching environment;
- capacity to identify directions for your own continuing development;
- potential to facilitate the self-development of others.

There are a number of distinct 'moves' which peers can use in the role of 'Understander' in order to support the spoken reflection of the 'Speaker'. In what follows, capitalization of roles and moves helps emphasize the deliberately different discourse. There is one Speaker in each meeting and individuals within the group take turns to be Speaker. The Speaker uses the opportunity to reflect on an idea, an issue, a puzzle or a personal concern. The resulting reflective talk is more useful to the Speaker if they have not planned the topic in advance. Understanders try to keep all evaluative aspects out of their contributions and resist the temptation to offer advice or suggestions. The main reason why this is possible is that the Understanders consciously use CD's non-judgemental moves (see Edge, 2002), particularly those termed Reflecting, Focusing and Relating:

Reflection
Offering back a version of what the Speaker has just said. It does not have to be word for word. It is not a case of 'parroting' the last thing said. Rather, the Understander is honestly trying to reflect back a version of what has just been said.

Focusing
Offering something that the Speaker has previously said as a possible topic for further articulation. It might go something like 'a few minutes ago you said X, would you like to say a little more about that?' This kind of move can also be used early on in a session to establish the scope of the topic, idea or theme being articulated.

Relating
Taking two or more aspects of the Speaker's previous talk and presenting them back. It is often a case of saying 'you've said A and you've said B, how are they related?'

Mann (2002), in a two-year study of a cooperative development group, established that Reflection can be considered the core move as elements of Reflection are usually present in both Focusing and Relating moves. Although the Understander tries to reflect as accurately as possible, it can still be helpful if the reflection is not quite right. For example, Boshell (2002) provides examples where 'inaccurate reflections' prompt him to articulate an issue more deeply. If you are interested in learning more about cognitive development, there is a useful site (http://cooperative-development.com/) run by Mariam Attia where you can find resources and activities. Here too you will find details of Andy Boon's work. He has taken Edge's face-to-face model and developed a real-time CMC version of CD using MSN's Instant Messenger (IMCD) (Boon, 2005, 2007).

7.5 Summary

This chapter has confirmed the importance of spoken reflection in the teacher education process. Teacher educators can consciously make space for collaborative spoken reflection by making their contributions less directive and by making sure there are adequate opportunities for peers to properly discuss and reflect on their teaching experiences. Such collaborative spoken reflection can be a key site for connecting received knowledge and more personal and experiential knowledge. Tools such as video and SCS can help put greater emphasis on evidence, data and classroom experiences and make spoken reflection more data-led. It can also be very helpful to talk to student teachers about their experiences on the programme. Engaging them in reflective talk about the value of the course and their experience of it can be revealing. An additional vignette on p. 236 provides another example of how this can be helpful.

Early in this chapter we talked about the inevitable asymmetry between the tutor and the teacher learners. The point for us is that the asymmetry is always there, the power is always (potentially at least) with the tutor, but what matters is how it is used. We have shown the negative effects it can have if it is used to impose the tutor's views on the teachers, to close down their opportunities to reflect, to make them feel that they are being judged, etc. However, such asymmetry can also be used positively not only to open up spaces for teachers but also to direct the talk where necessary. For example, if one teacher learner dominates group discussions or a teacher's turn strays from the point or loses focus, the tutor can steer the talk back to a more positive and productive format. The use of power can be positive as well as negative and the value of spoken interaction is that it allows subtle adjustments to be made as the talk unfolds.

It is our view that teacher education should play its part in reducing an isolating and individual view of professional growth and development. This can be done partly by emphasizing the importance of collaborative relationships as much as possible. As Leung (2009) has shown, collaboration with colleagues is a very important dimension of teaching. Teacher educators can make sure that programmes put emphasis on team processes (team-teaching; the ability to jointly construct materials; jointly planning lessons) and also raise awareness of choices we have in the way we talk to each other. Teacher educators can support spoken reflection if they demonstrate the importance of listening and more dialogic forms of talk. In other words, they might lead by example. Novice teachers' greater awareness of talk can help them consider and evaluate interaction in both language classrooms and in their future professional lives.

References

Almodaires, A.A. (2009). Technology-supported reflection: towards bridging the gap between theory and practice in teacher education (Unpublished PhD thesis). University of Twente.

Atkinson, T. and Claxton, G. (eds). (2000). *The intuitive professional*. Buckingham: OUP.

Attwood, R. (2009). 'Agenda for change' aims to combat feedback myths. *The Times Higher Education*, 15th October 2009.

Baecher, L. and McCormack, B. (2015). The impact of video review on supervisory conferencing. *Language and Education*, 29(2), 153–173.

Baecher, L.H., McCormack, B. and Kung, S.C. (2014). Supervisor use of video as a tool in teacher reflection. CUNY Academic Works. http://academicworks.cuny.edu/hc_pubs/4

Baecher, L., Kung, S.C., Jewkes, A. M. and Rosalia, C. (2013). The role of video for self-evaluation in early field experiences. *Teaching and Teacher Education*, 36, 189–197.

Bailey, F. and Willett, J. (2004). Collaborative groups in teacher education. In M. Hawkins and S. Irujo (eds), *Collaborative conversations among language teacher educators* (pp. 15–32). Alexandria, VA: TESOL.

Bassot, B. (2013). *The reflective journal*. London: Palgrave Macmillan.

Bolton, G. (2014). *Reflective practice: writing and professional development* (4th edn). Los Angeles, London and New Delhi: Sage.

Boon, A. (2005). Is there anybody out there? *Essential Teacher*, 2(2), 38–41.

Boon, A. (2007). Building bridges: instant messenger cooperative development. *The Language Teacher*, 31(12), 9–13.

Borko, H., Jacobs, J., Eiteljorg, E. and Pittman, M.E. (2008). Video as a tool for fostering productive discussions in mathematics professional development. *Teaching and Teacher Education*, 24(2), 417–436.

Boshell, M. (2002). What I learnt from giving quiet children space. Teachers' narrative inquiry as professional development. In K. Johnson and P. Golombek, *Teachers' narrative inquiry as professional development* (pp. 180–194). Cambridge: Cambridge University Press.

Boud, D., Keogh, R. and Walker, D. (1985) Promoting reflection in learning: a model Ch1. In D. Boud, R. Keogh and D. Walker (eds), *Reflection: turning experience into learning*. London: Kogan Page Ltd.

Brandt, C. (2008). Integrating feedback and reflection in teacher preparation. *ELT Journal*, 62(1), 37–46.

Brick, B. and Holmes, J. (2008). Using screen capture software for student feedback: towards a methodology. Available at https://curve.coventry.ac.uk/open/file/5baad20d-1c6f-3a98-b380-02167e5d1cd4/1/brickiadis.pdf

Brophy, J. (ed.). (2004). *Advances in research on teaching: Vol. 10. Using video in teacher education*. Oxford, UK: Elsevier.

Bryan, L. and Recesso, A. (2006). Promoting reflection with a web-based video analysis. *Journal of Computing in Teacher Education*, 23(1), 31–39.

Chen, J. (2012). Investigating spoken feedback through Jing: a study at University of Warwick (Unpublished dissertation). University of Warwick.

Conole, G. and Dyke, M. (2004). What are the affordances of information and communication technologies? *Association for Learning Technology Journal*, 12(2), 113–124.

Cooperrider, D. and Srivastva, S. (1987). Appreciative inquiry in organizational life. In W.A. Pasmore and R. Woodman (eds), *Research in organizational change and development (volume 1)*. Greenwich, CT: JAI Press.

Copland, F. (2010). Causes of tension in post-observation feedback in pre-service teacher training: an alternative view. *Teaching and Teacher Education*, 26(3), 466–472.

Copland, F. (2011). Negotiating face in the feedback conference: a linguistic ethnographic approach. *Journal of Pragmatics*, 43(15), 3832–3843.

Copland, F. (2012). Legitimate talk in feedback conferences. *Applied Linguistics*, 33(1), 1–20.

Copland, F., Ma, G. and Mann, S. (2009). Reflecting in and on post-observation feedback in initial teacher training on certificate courses. *English Language Teacher Education and Development*, 12, 14–22.

Costa, A. and Garmston, R. (2002). *Cognitive coaching*. Norwood, MA: Christopher-Gordon.

Cunningham, A. (2002). Using digital video tools to promote reflective practice. In Society for Information Technology and Teacher Education International Conference (Vol. 2002, No. 1, pp. 551–553).

Edge, J. (2002). *Continuing cooperative development: a discourse framework for individuals as colleagues*. Ann Arbor, MI: University of Michigan Press.

Eröz-Tuğa, B. (2013). Reflective feedback sessions using video recordings. *ELT Journal*, 67(2), 175–183.

Farr, F. (2010). *The discourse of teaching practice feedback: a corpus-based investigation of spoken and written modes*. London: Routledge.

Farrell, T.S.C. (2016). The practices of encouraging TESOL teachers to engage in reflective practice: an appraisal of recent research contributions. *Language Teaching Research*, 20(2), 223–247.

Finlay, B.L. (2008). Reflecting on 'reflective practice.' PBPL paper 52, (January), pp. 1–27.

Freeman, D. (1982). Observing teachers: three approaches to in-service training and development. *TESOL Quarterly*, 16(1), 21–28.

Freeman, D. (1998). *Doing teacher research: from inquiry to understanding*. Boston: Heinle and Heinle.

Fullan, M.G. (with Suzanne Stiegelbauer). (1991). *The new meaning of educational change*. London: Cassell.

Fuller, F.F. and Manning, B.A. (1973). Self-confrontation reviewed: a conceptualization for video playback in teacher education. *Review of Educational Research*, 43(4), 469–528.

Gardner, S. (2004). Knock-on effects of mode change on academic discourse. *JEAP*, 3(1), 23–38.

Gebhard, J. (1984). Models of supervision: choices. *TESOL Quarterly*, 18, 501–514.

Gendlin, E. T. (2004). Introduction to thinking at the edge. *The Folio*, 19(1), 1–8.

Golombek, P.R. (2011). Dynamic assessment in teacher education: using dialogic video protocols to intervene in teacher thinking and activity. In K.E. Johnson and P.R. Golombek (eds), *Research on second language teacher education: A sociocultural perspective on professional development* (pp. 121–135). London: Routledge.

Grant, T.J. and Kline, K. (2010). The impact of video-based lesson analysis on teachers' thinking and practice. *Teacher Development*, 14(1), 69–83.

Hatton, N. and Smith, D. (1995). Reflection in teacher education: towards definition and implementation. *Teacher and Teacher* Education, 11(1), 33–49.

Hepple, E. (2012). Questioning pedagogies: Hong Kong pre-service teachers' dialogic reflections on a transnational school experience. *Journal of Education for Teaching: International Research and Pedagogy*, 38, 309–322.

Heron, J. (2001). *Helping the client: a creative practical guide* (5th edn). London: Sage Publications Ltd.

Hiebert, J., Gallimore, R. and Stigler, J. W. (2002). A knowledge base for the teaching profession: What would it look like and how can we get one? *Educational Researcher*, 31(5), 3–15.

Ho, B. and Richards, J.C. (1993). Reflective thinking through teacher journal writing: Myths and realities. *Prospect*, 8(3), 7–24.

Hobbs, V. (2007). Examining short-term ELT teacher education: an ethnographic case study of trainees' experiences (PhD dissertation). University of Sheffield, UK.

Hobson, A. J. and Malderez, A. (2013). Judgementoring and other threats to realizing the potential of school-based mentoring in teacher education. *International Journal of Mentoring and Coaching in Education*, 2(2), 89–108.

Husu, J., Patrikainen, S. and Toom, A. (2007). Developing teachers' competencies in reflecting on teaching. In J. Butcher and L. McDonald (eds), *Making a difference: challenges for teachers, teaching and teacher education* (pp. 127–140). Amsterdam: Sense Publishers.

Johnson, K.E. (2006). The sociocultural turn and its challenges for second language teacher education. *TESOL Quarterly*, 40(1), 235–257.

Johnson, K.E. (2009). *Second language teacher education: a sociocultural perspective*. London: Routledge.

Kiely, R. and Davis, M. (2010). From transmission to transformation: teacher learning in English for speakers of other languages. *Language Teaching Research*, 14(3), 277–295.

Korthagen, F.A.J. (2001). *Linking practice and theory: the pedagogy of realistic teacher education*. Mahawah, NJ: Lawrence Erlbaum Associates.

Kurtoglu-Hooton, N. (2008). The design of post observation feedback and its impact on student teachers. In S. Garton and K. Richards (eds), *Professional encounters in TESOL: discourses of teachers in teaching*. Basingstoke: Palgrave Macmillan.

Kurtoglu-Hooton, N. (2010). Post-observation feedback as an instigator of learning and change: exploring the effect of feedback through student teachers' self-reports (Unpublished PhD thesis). Aston University, UK.

Kurtoglu-Hooton, N. (2016). From 'plodder' to 'creative': feedback in teacher education. *ELT Journal*, 70(1), 39–47.

Lee, I. (2008). Fostering preservice reflection through response journals. *Teacher Education Quarterly*, 35(1), 117–139.

Leung, C. (2009). Second language teacher professionalism. In A. Burns and J. Richards (eds), *Second Language Teacher Education* (pp. 49–58). Cambridge: Cambridge University Press.

Lewis, M. and Anping, H. (2002). Video-viewing tasks for language teacher education. *RELC Journal*, 33(1), 122–136.

Mann, S. (2002). The development of discourse in a discourse of development (Unpublished PhD thesis). Aston University, UK.

Mann S. (2005). The language teacher's development. *Language Teaching*, 38, 103–18.

Mann, S. (2015). Using screen capture software to improve the value of feedback on academic assignments in teacher education. In T. Farrell, *International perspectives on English language teacher education* (pp. 160–180). London: Palgrave Macmillan.

Mann, S. and Walsh, S. (2013). RP or 'RIP': a critical perspective on reflective practice. *Applied Linguistics Review*, 4(2), 291–315.

Marsh, B. and Mitchell, N. (2014). The role of video in teacher professional development. *Teacher Development*, 18(3), 403–417.

Masats, D. and Dooly, M. (2011). Rethinking the use of video in teacher education: a holistic approach. *Teaching and Teacher Education*, 27(7), 1151–1162.

McCarthy, M.J. (2002). Good listenership made plain: British and American nonminimal response tokens in everyday conversation. In R. Reppen, S. Fitzmaurice and D. Biber (eds), *Using corpora to explore linguistic variation* (pp. 49–71). Amsterdam: Benjamins.

Mirzaei, F., Phang, F.A. and Kashefi, H. (2014). Assessing and improving reflective thinking of experienced and inexperienced teachers. *Procedia-Social and Behavioral Sciences*, 141, 633–639.

Nguyen, H.T.M. (2013). Peer mentoring: a way forward for supporting preservice EFL teachers psychosocially during the practicum. *Australian Journal of Teacher Education*, 38, 30–44.

Norton, B. (2000). Identity and language learning: gender, ethnicity and educational change. London: Longman.

Phillipson, S.N., Cooper, D.G. and Phillipson, S. (2015). Flip, feedback and fly: using LOOP to enhance the professional experience of initial teacher education. *Australian Journal of Teacher Education*, 40(8), 7.

Prabhu, N.S. (1990). There is no best method – Why? *TESOL Quarterly*, 24(1) 161–176.

Rich, P. J. and Hannafin, M. (2009). Video annotation tools technologies to scaffold, structure, and transform teacher reflection. *Journal of Teacher Education*, 60(1), 52–67.

Richards, K. (2006). 'Being the teacher': identity and classroom conversation. *Applied Linguistics*, 27, 51–77.

Riordan, E. and Murray, L. (2010). A corpus-based analysis of online synchronous and asynchronous modes of communication within language teacher education. *Classroom Discourse*, 1(2), 181–198.

Rogers, C. (1980). *A Way of Being*. New York: Houghton Mifflin Company.

Rogers, C.R. and Freiberg, H.J. (1994). *Freedom to learn*. Columbus: Merrill Publishing.

Rowe, M.B. (1972). Wait-time and rewards as instructional variable, their influence in language, logic and fate control. Paper presented at the National Association for Research in Science Teaching, Chicago, IL.

Rust, C. (2001). A briefing on assessment of large groups, www.bioscience.heacademy.ac.uk/ftp/Resources/gc/assess12largeGroups.pdf (Accessed 12.09.07).

Sherin, M.G. (2004). New perspectives on the role of video in teacher education. In J. Brophy (ed.), *Advances in research on teaching: Vol. 10: Using video in teacher education* (pp. 1–27). Oxford, UK: Elsevier.

Sherin, M.G. and Han, S.Y. (2004). Teacher learning in the context of a video club. *Teaching and Teacher Education*, 20(2), 163–183.

Sherin, M.G., and van Es, E.A. (2005). Using video to support teachers' ability to notice classroom interactions. *Journal of Technology and Teacher Education*, 13(3), 475.

Sherin, M.G., and van Es, E.A. (2009). Effects of video club participation on teachers' professional vision. *Journal of Teacher Education*, 60(1), 20–37.

Stannard, R. (2007). Using screen capture software in student feedback. HEA English Subject Centre Commissioned Case Studies. Available at www.english.heacademy.ac.uk/explore/publications/casestudies/technology/camtasia.php (Accessed 12.08.15).

Tannen, D. (1998). *The argument culture: moving from debate to dialogue*. New York: Time–Life Books.

Timperley, H. (2001). Mentoring conversations designed to promote student teacher learning. *Asia-Pacific Journal of Teacher Education*, 29(2), 111–123.

Tripp, T. and Rich, P. (2012). Using video to analyze one's own teaching. *British Journal of Educational Technology*, 43(4), 678–704.

Tsui, A.B.M. (2009). Teaching expertise: Approaches, perspectives and characterizations. In A. Burns and J. C. Richards (eds), *The Cambridge guide to second language teacher education* (pp. 190–197). Cambridge: Cambridge University Press.

Tudor Jones, C. 2012. A reflective inquiry into post-observation multiparty feedback (Unpublished dissertation). University of Warwick.

van Es, E.A. (2012). Examining the development of a teacher learning community: the case of a video club. *Teaching and Teacher Education*, 28(2), 182–192.

Verlaan, W. and Verlaan, S. (2015). Using video-reflection with pre-service teachers: a cautionary tale. In E. Ortlieb, M. McVee and L. Shanahan (eds), *Video reflection in literacy teacher education and development: lessons from research and practice* (pp. 151–171). Bingley, UK: Emerald Group Publishing Limited.

Wachob, P. (2011). Critical friendship circles: the cultural challenge of cool feedback. *Professional Development in Education*, 37, 353–372.

Wallace, M. (1991). *Training foreign language teachers*. Cambridge: Cambridge University Press.

Walsh, S. (2002). Construction or obstruction: teacher talk and learner involvement in the EFL classroom. *Language Teaching Research*, 6(1), 1–23.

Walsh, S. and Li, L. (2013). Conversations as space for learning. *International Journal of Applied Linguistics*, 23(2), 247–266.

Walsh, S. and Mann, S. (2015). Doing reflective practice: a data-led way forward. *ELT Journal*, 69(4), 351–362.

Waring, H.Z. (2013). Two mentor practices that generate teacher reflection without explicit solicitations: some preliminary considerations. *RELC Journal*, 44(1), 103–119.

Wedell, M. (2009). *Planning for educational change: putting people and their contexts first*. London: Bloomsbury Publishing.

Wenger, E. (1998). *Communities of practice: learning, meaning, and identity*. Cambridge, MA: Cambridge University Press.

Williams, J. and Watson, T. (2004). Post-lesson debriefing: immediate or delayed? An investigation of student–teacher talk. *Journal of Education for Teaching*, 30(2), 85–96.

Wright, T. and Bolitho, R. (2007). *Trainer development*. Lulu.com.

Yballe, L. and D. O'Connor. (2000). Appreciative pedagogy: constructing positive models for learning. *Journal of Management Education*, 24(4), 474–483.

Zeichner, K.M. and Liston, D. (1985). Varieties of discourse in supervisory conferences. *Teaching and Teacher Education*, 1, 155–174.

Zepeda, S.J. (2007). *Instructional supervision: applying tools and concepts*. Larchmont, NY: Eye on Education.

8
Dialogic Reflection

8.1 Introduction

This chapter adopts a social view of learning and professional development, taking the position that learning is a dialogic process in which meanings are mediated by language. Dialogue allows meanings to be co-constructed, new understandings to emerge and professional learning to develop. Dialogic processes can either be intrapersonal or interpersonal (private or public), entailing interactions between individuals or between an individual and an artefact or tool. Building on some of the work on spoken reflection that we covered in Chapter 7, our concern here is to show how dialogic reflection – a bottom-up, teacher-led, collaborative process entailing interaction, discussion and debate with another professional – can lead to professional learning.

A key element of a dialogic, mediated approach to reflection is the way in which tools and artefacts can act as a catalyst (e.g. metaphors, critical incidents, video) and help promote more systematic and focused professional dialogue. We focus in particular on the use of transcripts and recordings of classroom talk, developing and extending Harfitt's (2007) argument for the inclusion of lesson transcripts in the process of learning to teach and developing ways of thinking reflectively. At the same time, we demonstrate how there are alternatives to transcribed lesson extracts and advocate the use of 'snapshot' lesson excerpts: short 10–15 minute recordings which are then analyzed without transcription. We conclude the chapter with the argument that this kind of dialogic approach to reflection can promote shared understandings and result in 'deep' rather than 'surface' awareness of pedagogy. (Please note: while stimulated recall is not dealt with in this chapter (see Chapter 5), it is clearly of considerable relevance to any discussion on dialogic reflection.)

Micro-analysis

Why do we attach so much importance to dialogue and mediation? Our main argument is that learning, including professional development, is a dialogic process in which language, in particular, plays a key role. Put simply, almost everything we learn (or learn to do better) entails the use of language and frequently requires interaction with another person. Talking to and collaborating with others are often key elements of any reflective process, allowing new understandings to emerge, current practices to be questioned and alternatives to be explored. The very act of 'talking through' a recent experience, such as a segment of teaching, facilitates reflection and may ultimately result in changes to practice.

'Dialogic reflection', as we shall now refer to this process, is often an important element of teacher education programmes and may also be an important process in less structured contexts where teachers are working with colleagues in some kind of CPD environment. In order to understand how dialogic reflection 'gets done', we adopt a micro-analytic approach to transcripts, following the principles and theoretical underpinnings of conversation analysis (CA). Using CA, we are interested in the ways in which interactants achieve intersubjectivity (or shared understanding). In order to gain an *emic* (insider) perspective on a particular interaction, we try to capture as much of the detail as possible, following a turn by turn analysis in order to ask the key question which CA poses: 'why this, why now?' In other words, we, as analysts, approach the encounter in much the same way as the original participants do, as if we were present, setting out to explain why a particular social action is performed at a particular point in time. Put simply, and using the words of Heritage (1984), each utterance is both 'context shaped and context renewing'; one utterance both establishes a context and determines what may follow.

By way of exemplification of dialogic reflection, we present extract 8.1 below, taken from a pre-service teacher education programme: a CELTA course in Thailand. CELTA (Certificate in English Language Teaching to Adults), is an initial teacher training course aimed at pre-experience teachers. The course is often offered in an intensive format over a period of 4 to 5 weeks. Trainees must undertake 6 hours of supervised teaching practice and engage in a structured group feedback session after each lesson they teach.

In extract 8.1, a group of three trainees (D, S, A) are discussing a recent class with their trainer (I). This is day 13 of a 20-day course, with most trainees by now having taught 4 to 5 hours. The extract opens with a question by the trainer, Irene (I), about 'good openers' and is followed by an attempt by Scott (S) to offer his explanation. Note that Scott is commenting on the teaching of one of the other trainees, Anginette (A), rather than self-evaluating his own teaching:

Extract 8.1(a)

```
1  I: Wh- What do you mea::n by tha:t (.) Scott good opener (.) °like° (.)
2     >what does< it do:,
3     (0.6)
```

```
4  S: [Well]
5  I: [W- why] is it good
6  S: Fi:rst it breaks the (.) >Monday morning< i::ce (.)
7     [huh huh hh]
8  I: [Yes       ] (.) ye:s=
9  S: =It kinda gets everybody's attention you kno:w looking up, (0.6) to
10    he:r
11 I: Yep
12    (0.6)
13 S: U::m
14    (0.8)
15 S: A:ND you know she ha:d a good mind map going on the boa:rd (0.4) >good
16    use of< the boa:rd (.) and mind ma:p and u:::m (1.0) GOOD job of
17    keeping their attention throughou:t I think cos they're I've I've
18    noticed that this (.) cla:ss is (.) very difficu:lt in getting their
19    (.) keeping their attention
20 I: ↑Anything that you think he::lped (.) the:re that Angin- that Anginette
21    did
22    (0.4)
23 S: Well I mean (0.4) definitely (.) >and this has been said a million<
24    times befo:re just her persona::lity
25 I: Hmm mm
26 S: A::nd (.) the way that she prese:nts an- she ki:nd of (.) she's just
27    out there (.) you kno:w she's just out there (0.8) °and e:r°
28    (1.2)
```

Harris, 2013

There are a number of elements in this extract which demonstrate the value of dialogue in helping participants reflect on a recent experience and co-construct understanding. The opening question asked by the trainer, Irene, is to some extent a rather hesitant one, indicated by the frequent pausing, the use of vague category markers (like, said quietly) and stretching (mea::n by tha:t). Note too that Irene uses alternative forms of the question so that Scott has a chance to really understand what she is getting at (What do you mea::n by tha:t; what does< it do; why is it good?). After a 0.6-second pause, Scott responds to Irene's opening question with a hesitation device (well) which is followed by a clarification from Irene, said in overlap ([W- why] is it good).

In lines 6–14, and following the clarification from Irene, Scott offers a number of reasons as to why the opener was good. Using a combination of pausing and minimal response tokens, the trainer ensures that Scott retains hold of the floor, providing some space for further reflection and indicating she would like him to continue. This might also suggest, given the role asymmetry of this institutional discourse setting, that Scott has still not yet produced the response she is looking for.

In lines 15–19, Scott produces an extended response and offers a number of reasons why the opener was good (A:ND you know she ha:d a good mind map going on the boa:rd (0.4) >good use of< the boa:rd (.) and mind ma:p and u:::m (1.0) GOOD job of keeping their attention throughou:t I think cos they're I've I've noticed that this (.) cla:ss is (.) very difficu:lt in getting their (.) keeping their attention). At the end of this extended turn, which is marked by hesitations (indicated by micro and longer pauses and the use of stretching), the trainer (I) seeks clarification, offering the floor back to Scott in lines 20–21. Here, the high rise at the opening of the turn and use of stretching (↑Anything that you think he::lped (.) the:re) suggest that Irene is still not quite satisfied with Scott's response, as further evidenced in line 25 through the use of the continuer (Hmm mm).

There is further evidence that Scott is not entirely sure what Irene is looking for in lines 26–28. Does the use of stretching, hesitation devices (er) and repetitions, together with frequent pausing, suggest that Scott is struggling to really answer Irene's opening question, 'what's a good opener?'

In the second part of this extract, we see how the talk becomes more dialogic, with greater co-construction of meaning and negotiated understandings of professional practices.

Extract 8.1(b)

```
29 I: ANY ↑thi:ng that (.) anything else that (.) helped (.) keep the
30    students attention or maybe focused the students attention (.) at times
31    (0.4) °(wheneve:r)° (0.4) ↑because I mean (.) .hh I I do agree that
32    pa::rtly it's personali:ty, but ↑that go only goes that fa::r (.) it's
33    it's no:t, (.) just the pe:rsonality that gets things happening
34 S: .tch (.) well I mean part of it too is to do with he:::r (0.6) really
35    good (.) ability of (.) monito:ring (0.4) and just being there
36 I: Yes (.) ye:s
37 S: You know I've seen what they're do:ing (.) a:nd (.) probing °o::n an°
38 I: ↑Yeah
39    (1.0)
40 D: Yeah yeah they are (pretty clo:se) I mean they they are (close) which
41    we are teaching
42 I: Hmm mm
43    (0.4)
44 D: °Yeah° (.) you can see that (.) otherwise maybe (.) they start their own
45    talking (0.4) that is normally happen (0.4) if they are no:t (0.4) you
46    know focused (on what you sa:y) (0.6) but (.) they are the:re (.) you
47    (.) when you: (.) give infor↑mation, about (.) what are you going to
48    say they just (.) listen to you (0.6) <tha:t's good>
49    (1.0)
50 A: °It's my loud voice°
```

```
51 D: Yeah focus
52 S: Huh huh [huh huh]
53 A:       [.hhhh hhh]
```

Harris, 2013

In lines 29–33, Irene re-launches the topic and introduces a dis-preferred response to Scott's earlier suggestion (lines 23–24) that the success of an opener in class largely depends on a teacher's personality. Here, in lines 29–33, we see Irene disagreeing (it's no:t, (.) just the pe:rsonality that gets things happening), provoking an immediate response by Scott (lines 34–35), who introduces the idea of monitoring and the importance of 'probing' (line 37). Scott's responses are met by enthusiastic responses from Irene, in the form of continuers (yeah, yeah and yes). It seems, from the reaction of Irene, that she has finally got what she was looking for: monitoring and checking are key elements in effective teaching.

After a one-second pause, the floor is taken by Diane (D) in lines 40–41. She picks up the comments made by Scott in lines 34–37, and develops this in a long turn in lines 44–49. This turn is punctuated by both micro pauses and longer pauses as Diane tries to articulate her intended meaning, an example of 'reflection-in-action'. It appears from lines 44–48 that Diane is literally constructing her understanding of the importance of monitoring through her own talk; having an opportunity to engage in dialogue with the trainers and her peers enables her to reflect openly and actively on a key classroom practice: monitoring. Note too that Irene, the trainer, has now withdrawn from the interaction, allowing others (Scott and Anginette) to show their affirmation of what Diane has said (lines 52–53).

To summarize the analysis of this piece of data, we can observe the ways in which understandings of new practices are gained through dialogue and discussion. We note the importance of the 'give-and-take' in the dialogue, where interactants seek clarification, demonstrate understanding or approval, and even disagree. Dialogic reflection, as evidenced in this extract, has enormous potential, since it allows reflections to be co-constructed through talk; put simply, professional learning is enhanced through interactions with both peers and more experienced professionals.

Having demonstrated the value of dialogic reflection and its importance for professional learning, in the next section we offer a more detailed consideration of the relationship between reflection and learning.

8.2 Reflective Practice and Socio-cultural Theories of Learning

In this section, we review some of the more current perspectives on learning and relate them to reflective practice. The main argument is that if the goal of reflection is professional development, we need to have some sense of how theories of learning might inform development through reflection. We adopt an essentially socio-cultural position on learning and demonstrate its relevance and application to dialogic reflection.

Learning as a Social Process

Since the late 1990s, there have been a number of significant developments to challenge traditional and long-standing views of both the nature of language and the nature of learning. One of the key influences of recent theories of language was the seminal paper by Firth and Wagner (1997 and revisited in 2007) which challenged the prevalent (and largely cognitive) theories of second language acquisition (SLA) which had existed up until that time. The Firth and Wagner paper argues that learning should be seen as a social process and that language should be viewed as a complex, dynamic system which is locally managed by interactants in response to emerging communicative needs. According to this view, learning can be traced in the moment-by-moment co-construction of meanings and by using conversation analysis (CA). The relatively new, emergent field known as 'CA-for-SLA' quite clearly views learning as participation and collaboration and maintains that we can measure and track learning through the interactions which take place (see, for example, Markee, 2008; Hall et al., 2011).

Despite this relatively recent re-positioning of language learning theory, social psychological perspectives on learning and human development have actually existed for much longer. Within socio-cultural theory (SCT), learning is viewed very much as a social process whereby learners interact with 'expert' teachers 'in a context of social interactions leading to understanding' (Röhler and Cantlon, 1996: 2). Learning, under this perspective, entails dialogue, discussion and debate as learners collectively and actively construct their own understandings through interactions with others who may be more experienced. This view of learning owes its origins to the influential work of the Russian philosopher Lev Vygotsky (1978), whose theories on human development and L1 acquisition have been applied to L2 learning by researchers like Lantolf (2000), Lantolf and Thorne (2006), and van Compernolle (2015); as far as teacher education is concerned, Karen Johnson has written extensively on the value of SCT (see, for example, Johnson (2009) and Johnson and Golombek (2011)).

By emphasizing the social, dynamic and collaborative dimensions of learning, proponents of SCT stress its 'transactional' nature: learning occurs in the first instance through interaction with others, who are more experienced and in a position to guide and support the actions of the novice. During this part of the process, language is used as a 'symbolic tool' to clarify and make sense of new knowledge, with learners relying heavily on discussions with the 'expert knower'. As new ideas and new knowledge are internalized, learners use language to comment on what they have learnt; spoken interactions are used to both transmit and clarify new information and then to reflect on and rationalize what has been learnt.

Our discussion continues with a necessarily brief overview of some of the main constructs which underpin a SCT perspective on learning. The discussion of this section concludes with an outline of the importance and relevance of SCT to reflective practice.

The Zone of Proximal Development (ZPD) and Co-construction

According to Lantolf (2000: 17), the ZPD should be regarded as 'a metaphor for observing and understanding how mediated means are appropriated and internalized'. Lantolf goes on to offer his own definition of the ZPD:

> The collaborative construction of opportunities [..] for individuals to develop their mental abilities.

A number of key terms emerge from the work of Vygotsky and Lantolf, including 'collaboration', 'construction', 'opportunities' and 'development'. Other writers use a similar terminology: van Lier (2000: 252), for example, refers to opportunities for learning as 'affordances', while Swain and Lapkin (1998: 320) talk about 'occasions for learning'. Ohta (2001: 9) talks about learners' '. . . level of potential development as determined through language produced collaboratively with a teacher or peer'. As a construct in reflective practice, the value of the ZPD lies in its potential for understanding the 'give and take' in the professional development process. The 'collaborative construction' of opportunities for learning is examined through the ways in which teachers, interacting with peers or more experienced mentors, collectively construct meaning and develop new understandings. Put simply, new understandings do not simply happen – they are jointly created through dialogue.

In extract 8.2 below, we encounter Lidia, an experienced English teacher working in Brazil. In a study conducted by Maristela Silva, Lidia was asked about moments in her teaching which triggered reflection. Here is her response:

Extract 8.2

> There are many [moments] that I can say. They are likely to occur . . . even of course these days. I'm learning all the time, it's a . . . It occurs when I record myself in class and then I revisit it and I see things that shouldn't be there or why they happen and I reflect a lot upon them. I can

tell you for example that the most recent one was a case in which I checked that I am quite repetitive in my delivery of instruction. I say something, I try to ... it doesn't matter the level, I try to cut it up in small chunks anyways. So that the procedures are very clear, step by step clear. So I noticed that I am quite repetitive in the instruction. I say for example, just an example 'OK, guys, now I need you to get these slips of paper and you're going to write, I don't know, three sentences, OK? You're going to write three sentences, OK? In the slip of paper, OK?' Yeah. I think I repeat this like four or five times and I go ... why? It's quite disturbing. I mean, I shouldn't be doing this. Then, on the next class I tried not to do .... Tried to do it in a different way. I mean, this is one that I can say, there are many, many ... I don't know. Another one it was like a big moment I have to say. It was a moment ... you know ... I was ... I ... I used to touch students.

Lidia, interview 1

In this extract, there are many examples of Lidia's professional knowledge which are co-constructed and articulated through the prompt question ('Tell me about moments in your teaching which trigger reflection'). For example, she tells us about the need to be less repetitive when giving instructions and her 'big moment' about the importance of not touching students. There is also evidence of what we might call a 'light-bulb moment' where she describes how she repeats the same instruction several times and then asks why: 'I think I repeat this like four or five times and I go ... why? It's quite disturbing. I mean, I shouldn't be doing this.' Arguably, it is through dialogue with a more experienced peer that Lidia has had an opportunity not only to reflect on her instruction-giving practices, but also to articulate those reflections more fully.

In language classroom interactions, we experience co-construction very frequently; it is one of the most important strategies for creating intersubjectivity, or joint meaning-making. Extract 8.3 has been selected to illustrate the importance of collaborative meaning-making and the need to allow interactional space so that teachers and learners can create opportunities for language acquisition; these same principles apply in teacher education settings (see Chapter 7). In extract 8.3, a group of upper-intermediate students on a UK university in-sessional English language course is discussing ways of regulating their lives.

Extract 8.3

```
1   T    =so it's eh . . . I . . . from a skeptical point of view what you
2        have is a way of regulating your life =
3   L1   =yes=
4   T    =and eh giving you direction =
```

```
 5  L1  =yeah=
 6  T   =and goals and meaning [and]
 7  L4                          [so] do you think ((6))? . . .
 8  L1  no I think that eh for example that my argument is that if
 9      I take alcohol I'm culpable I get sick=
10  T   =everybody does=
11  L1  =but I think for me it's like a sign stop doing this=
12  T   =me too ((3))=
13  L1  =or take take ((2)) for yourself and you won't feel sick
14      you'll be like high?=
15  T   =yes=
16  L1  like yes ((4)) . . .
17  T   so it's good for you as far as being good?=
18  L1  =yes I think so
```

Walsh, 2011

Rather than acting as a 'facilitator', a role which is so often advocated under more decentralized teaching methodologies such as CLT and TBLT, the teacher here plays a focal role, guiding, clarifying, supporting and 'shaping' contributions (Walsh, 2013) so that learners have opportunities to reflect on and learn from the unfolding interaction. Here, for example, in lines 1, 4 and 6, the teacher paraphrases and summarizes L1's previous contributions as a means of offering support and enabling other students to follow the dialogue. While the dialogue is mainly between the teacher and L1, this strategy of summarizing, checking and negotiating is important if all class members are to understand and contribute to the discussion. Essentially, any dialogue between a teacher and an individual student is directed at the whole class as a 'multilogue' (see Schwab, 2011); that is, the focus and content of the interaction has potential relevance for everyone in that classroom. The same could be said of many PRESET courses, where post TP feedback conferences are held for the benefit of the entire teaching practice group, not only for those who have taught. Interactions between trainer and trainee are designed to help the professional development of all present, a kind of 'multilogue'.

The rapid turn-taking in the extract (indicated by latching, marked =) identifies it as being almost conversational in nature, with one big difference: the teacher participates in the dialogue but, more importantly, ensures that messages are understood and refined for the other listeners, the other students. This extract illustrates very nicely a process of co-construction, where one more 'expert' person leads another (individual or group) through a process of development and shared understanding (see also Copland, 2010).

Scaffolding

A key construct in SCT is that of 'scaffolding', used to refer to the ways in which linguistic support is first given by a tutor and then removed (Bruner, 1990).

Central to the notion are the important polar concepts of *challenge* and *support*. Learners are led to an understanding of a task or concept by, on the one hand, a teacher's provision of appropriate amounts of challenge to maintain interest and involvement, and, on the other, support to ensure understanding. Support typically involves segmentation and ritualization so that learners have, in the first instance, limited choice in how they go about a task which is broken down into manageable component parts (Bruner, 1990: 29). Once a task has been mastered, scaffolds are removed and the learner is left to reflect and comment on the task.

Clearly, the amount of scaffolded support given will depend very much on the perceived evaluation by the 'expert' of what is needed by the 'novice'. In a professional development setting, it may be difficult for more experienced practitioners to 'lead' a discussion while at the same time allowing the other participants an opportunity to express their views. One approach which might facilitate dialogic reflection was put forward by Mercer (2004) as *exploratory talk*. In Mike Chick's vignette below, we see how this works in practice.

MIKE CHICK'S VIGNETTE (UK)

As a teacher educator, I have been involved in exploring how organization of discussions on teaching can improve the effectiveness of reflective practice. One dialogic approach to learning that has become particularly interesting to me was put forward by Mercer (2004), who introduced the idea of *exploratory talk*. This is a type of talk that is characterized by the encouragement of constructive engagement with each other's ideas; by an atmosphere of trust; and where suggestions can be offered for joint consideration and opinions treated with respect. In the context of a post-teaching feedback discussion, it is a type of talk in which peer contributions and interactions, *as well as* educator-guided mediation, are seen to be advantageous in facilitating learning. To be clear, a more dialogic approach to feedback conferences represents my attempt to move away from the traditional, transmissive or evaluative approach that tends to occur in post-teaching discussions.

The text discussed below stems from research that was conducted on a course of second language teacher education (SLTE) that is embedded in a three-year BA degree programme at a British university. The participants were final-year undergraduates studying TESOL modules as part of a degree in the Faculty of Humanities. All were women, British, native English speakers, and ranged from 20 to 24 years of age.

The extract provides a representative example of the shape of the interactions and type of turn-taking that can emerge in discussions set up on a more exploratory basis. The conversation involves the educator (myself) and four learner teachers. One of the teachers (LT 2) had just taught a 60-minute lesson to a class of eight, mixed-nationality, upper-intermediate level, adult students. The lesson involved a language focus on vocabulary for personal description and directed the learners' attention to the use of adjectives such as *conscientious*, *considerate*, *diligent* and so on. The participants in the feedback discussion are jointly discussing the merits and efficacy of the materials that LT 2 chose to include in the lesson and also the methodology within which the class tasks and activities were carried out. Observation notes record that the language learners did not seem particularly engaged or challenged and that the class was a little monotonous.

Extract 1 (TP Wed 22nd Nov)

1. Educator: How could we have set it up in order to get them a bit more steamed up to complete the task?
2. LT 1: Could you get them to describe each other or . . . ?
3. Educator: Get them to describe each other . . . possibly. There is no 'one' right answer in my head.
4. LT 2: Is that possible with adjectives like 'arrogant' and 'possessive'?
5. Educator: Why are they used then?
6. LT 2: It's English, they are upper-intermediate and they are meant to be learning English (*laughs*).
7. Educator: Yeah – I mean to what end? In what context will they hear them? Do we use them ever then?
8. LT 2: Of course we use them – they're common words . . .
9. Educator: Ah, ok – in what context are they used?
10. LT 2: . . . to describe people
11. LT 3: It could be in a conversation, couldn't it?
12. Educator: So if they are used and we create the realisation that '*ah these are useful*'' then they are more
13. likely to be motivated to take part. Could it be up to us to create that need . . . ?
14. LT 2: It could be yeah, I guess, I know what you mean.
15. Educator: . . . rather than say, you know, '*Fill in this out-of-context gap fill*''.
16. LT 2: Maybe, but do you have to make everything you do, you know, that engaging?
17. Educator: Maybe I'm being overly . . .]
18. LT 3: [It's selling the task.
19. LT 4: And it's talking about people – which is what people talk about most of the time so I think . . .
20. LT 2: So what would you do then to . . . to create a more . . . (*pause*)?]
21. LT 1: [Make it more interesting?
22. LT 3: Have less of them or make it '*my* gap fill'.
23. LT 2: Having fewer of them doesn't change it though.

```
24.LT 1:    Could you just use flash cards with the adjectives or
            something and get the students to work-out
25.         together which ones go goes where or something?
```

The discussion may be justifiably described as exploratory rather than one-sided or educator-dominated for a number of reasons. Firstly, the extract contains many examples of idea-sharing, challenging and contributing from the learner teachers. The topics discussed concern language, language use and the learners' interests, rather than the teachers' timeline skills or utilization of concept check questions. All the participants are involved, rather than simply waiting for an evaluative comment from the educator.

Secondly, it reveals how the participants feel empowered to challenge, contribute and make suggestions. There is the opportunity, in effect, for what is described by Maggioli (2012) as reciprocal scaffolding, i.e. learning from one another. For instance, LT 2 (line 20), asks for clarification of what alternatives to the approach taken the others are heading towards. LT 1 (line 24) makes a suggestion and justifies it by explaining how her approach would "get the students to work together". These are important insights for learner teachers who are at the very beginning of their professional development.

Finally, the exploratory nature of the interaction suggests that the participants realize that their ideas are respected, welcomed and valued. Although LT 2 (line 23) appears to doubt the others' suggestions, it is evident that all are absorbed in the issues surrounding student motivation and engagement.

The importance of creating the right conditions for the type of interactions that facilitate truly exploratory talk is, of course, central to the success of inculcating a dialogic pedagogy. In a formal setting, where learner teachers are concerned about their grades as much as their personal development (Holland and Adams, 2002), creating an appropriate atmosphere may indeed be a challenge. Nevertheless, as Kurtoglu-Hooton (2010) argues, development is more likely, despite the asymmetrical roles of the participants, in contexts where LTs feel free to express their own beliefs and ideas about teaching and learning.

In sum, feedback sessions which share the type of characteristics described above as exploratory talk, can indeed be beneficial to promoting *dialogic reflective practice* (Walsh and Mann, 2015: 365). Such carefully organized discussions, that involve moments of both teacher mediated dialogue as well as more symmetrical exploratory talk, can indeed help to bring about a stronger appreciation of many aspects of language teaching. As Edge (2011: 18) reminds us, although increased awareness is unlikely to result in immediate changes in teacher behaviour, it nevertheless ". . . multiplies the opportunities on which development might be based".

Mike Chick's vignette strongly supports a less directed, more open approach to post-lesson conferences which allows all participants to feel valued and respected. The roles of educator (or more experienced 'knower') and student teachers are more symmetrical and there are equal opportunities to contribute to the discussion. Throughout the discussion, there is a strong sense that participants are working things out together in a spirit of shared responsibility and a desire to find answers to the problems which have been raised. Note how the educator takes more and more of a 'back seat' as the discussion progresses, allowing the student teachers to negotiate their own understandings. It is this approach to dialogic reflection which we are advocating here. Key elements, as mentioned by Mike Chick, include creating an atmosphere of trust and respect where risk-taking is valued; maximizing the involvement of all partici-pants; sharing and debating ideas; allowing space for ideas to be challenged; scaffolding, by both the tutor and peers; and enabling learner teachers to express their own ideas about teaching rather than following a prescribed 'set text'. (See also Wayne Trotman's vignette in Appendix 7 for a discussion on peer–peer observation.)

Mediation, Appropriation and Affordance

A central component of SCT is *mediation*, or the ways in which learning is influ-enced by artefacts and tools. According to Vygotsky, language is one such artefact and all learning is mediated by language, a 'symbolic tool'. Essentially, everything we learn or learn to do is mediated by something: often language. Advocates of SCT argue that in order to understand learning, we need to study what people do and say, rather than what is going on in their heads. Very often, this entails the study of language and interaction. Van Lier's work on ecological approaches to learning (see, for example, 2000) has resonance here. An ecological view of learning emphasizes its emergent nature and attempts to explain learning in terms of the verbal and nonverbal processes in which learners engage. That is, rather than trying to understand processes which take place in the head, we should view learning in terms of the interactions which take place between learners and other learners and between learners and teachers; here, of course, this equally applies to interactions between peers.

A central feature of this theory is what van Lier terms 'affordance': the relationship between learners and particular features in their environment which have relevance to the learning process. Affordances may be viewed as opportunities which create 'space for learning' (Walsh and Li, 2013). In a lan-guage classroom, affordances may be created through the use of technology, through a teacher's questioning techniques or approach to error correction, or even simply through the use of a particular course-book. In a reflective practice context, affordances may be created through, for example, the use of stimulated recall, a conversation with a colleague or the use of an online blog (see sections 8.3 and 8.4).

By emphasizing the social, dynamic and collaborative dimensions of learning, proponents of socio-cultural theories of learning stress its 'transactional' nature: learning occurs in the first instance through interaction with others, who are more experienced and in a position to guide and support the actions of the novice. During this part of the process, language is used as a 'symbolic tool' to clarify and make sense of new knowledge, with learners relying heavily on discussions with the 'expert knower'. As new ideas and knowledge are internalized, learners use language to comment on what they have learnt; spoken interactions are used to both transmit and clarify new information and then to reflect on and rationalize new knowledge.

Rather than seeing learning as 'having', social theories emphasize learning as 'doing' (see Sfard, 1998; Larsen-Freeman, 2010) and regard learning as a process, an activity, something we take part in, perform. Learning is not something we have or own; it is something which entails encounters with others, where participation is central to the process. There is plenty of evidence to show that learning and participation are closely connected and that participation can support learning (see, for example, Mori, 2004; van Lier, 2000). It is through participation and interaction with others that we gain access to new understandings. New knowledge is typically gained 'publicly' and our understandings of, for example, monitoring (see extract 8.1) are often derived through dialogue with others. Once we have gained some sense of understanding, we need to make it our own, we need to internalize it and find ways of both remembering and using it. This process is known as *appropriation*: the individual and private internalization of new knowledge. Staying with our example of 'monitoring', appropriation may entail any number of things including: trying out new ways of monitoring; being more/less active when monitoring; observing the monitoring practices of colleagues; taking a 'back seat' and not monitoring at all; self-observation of monitoring, and so on. Appropriation acknowledges that we all learn in different ways and have different ways of remembering and using new knowledge, skills and understandings.

SCT and Reflective Practice

There are a number of reasons why SCT has potential in an RP context. In the first instance, the emphasis on the importance of social interaction is in tune with what is currently considered to be 'good practice' in professional learning: an emphasis on discovery-based learning through problem-solving; the value of 'talk' in promoting new understandings; and the importance of publicly derived knowledge becoming privately internalized or appropriated.

According to van Lier (2000), in a language learning context, social development can only become language acquisition when the quality of the interaction is maximized. Collaboration with the teacher, less able learners, more able learners and the individual's own resources can facilitate interaction which is both meaningful and productive. Arguably, the quality of that interaction is very much dependent on the teacher's ability to manage complex interactional processes and 'correctly' interpret the learning environment. We are suggesting here that much of this argument applies to professional development contexts, where practitioners interact with peers or more experienced colleagues and where the quality of that interaction is important in influencing how new understandings are derived and internalized. Put simply, the value of dialogic reflection is inextricably linked to the quality of the interaction which underpins it.

A key aspect of SCT is dialogue, the ways in which learning is mediated by language. Throughout this section, we have demonstrated how valuable this notion is in an RP setting. Dialogue facilitates understanding by allowing interactants space and support to express their ideas and arrive at new or different takes on a particular practice, issue or concern. Opportunities for reflection and learning are maximized when new concepts, or the metalanguage used to realize them, can be both understood and verbalized. However, the centrality of speech to learning has another, more significant dimension in that consciousness, considered by Vygotsky as being central to learning, is developed through social interaction. Learners become more aware, through participation in social activity, of themselves as learners. Dialogic reflection, we suggest, may lead to deeper, longer-lasting professional development and can facilitate the appropriation of good practice.

A second key element of SCT which is of high relevance to RP is collaboration, which has already been mentioned in this section and elsewhere in the book. While for some, the process of reflection may be seen as a solitary practice (see, for example, Osterman and Kottcamp, 1993; Larrivee, 2000), it is not always easy to be critical when reflecting on one's own behaviour or practice. As Osterman and Kottcamp put it, 'analysis occurring in a collaborative and cooperative environment is likely to lead to greater learning' (1993: 6).

There are a number of ways in which collaborative reflection might be fostered. Finlay, for example, states that 'practitioners gain from working in a dialogical team context that enables them to hear the alternative perspectives so vital for reflective practice'. Note here the importance of dialogue to collaboration, a point made above and again below. In their framework of collaborative reflective practices, Cooper and Boyd list learning buddies, mentoring, peer-coaching, work-exchange or shadowing, action research, study group, peer support groups and professional dialogue groups among others (1998). Farrell (2008: 3) talks about teacher groups for professional development and identifies three types of groups – peer groups within the school, teacher groups that operate out of the school and within a school district, and virtual groups that can be formed anywhere on the internet.

In Farrell's 2012 essay on revisiting reflective practice, he states that:

> A reexamination of both Dewey's and Schon's work has reinforced the idea that reflective practice is not isolated introspection; rather, it is evidence based, in that teachers need to systematically collect evidence (or data) about their work and then make decisions (instructional and otherwise) based on this information.
>
> *2012: 40*

This section has presented a necessarily brief review of the relevance of SCT to RP. In the next section (8.3), we consider alternative tools and procedures for facilitating dialogic reflection.

8.3 Tools and Procedures for Dialogic Reflection

In Mann and Walsh (2013), we comment on the pressing need for appropriate tools for reflection, a theme which we have developed throughout this book. Our main concerns are that tools are not always sufficiently oriented to a particular stage of development; the same tools are often used throughout a course rather than being tailored to a particular context or moment; different reflective tools should be introduced slowly and should be varied to suit progression. We have already highlighted the value of video-based observation (see Chapter 7), the relevance of 'snapshot' episodes (short and untranscribed recordings) and the importance of having data as a focus for reflection or springboard for discussion. In this section, we present a number of alternative tools and procedures which we consider to be appropriate for dialogic reflection:

- *ad hoc* self-observation
- online discussion forums
- critical incident analysis
- structured reflection
- video and dialogic reflection.

Ad hoc *Self-observation*

While we do not favour the more general, 'tick-box' type of observation instrument which was so prevalent in the 1980s, there is much to be gained from the use of *ad hoc* self-observation instruments, designed for specific tasks in specific contexts (Wallace, 1998). The idea behind this is that there is a focus on one practice which is studied in detail, as opposed to a more general approach to observation. *Ad hoc* implies that the instrument is designed by and for teachers for use in a particular context and with a particular goal in mind.

One example of such an instrument was devised by Walsh (2006) and presented in Chapter 5. The SETT (self-evaluation of teacher talk) framework (Walsh, 2013) was designed in collaboration with a group of university TESOL teachers and used to help teachers gain closer understandings of the complex relationship between language, interaction and learning. The reader is referred to Chapter 5 for a full description.

In extract 8.4 below (which we first encountered in Chapter 2), the teacher, Joy, has analyzed her teaching using the SETT framework and is talking about her evaluation with a colleague, Mike. The focus of the reflection is scaffolding.

Extract 8.4

Mike: Is scaffolding something you think you do more of in that
       type of mode for example you're in a skills and systems
       mode here? Do you think it's something that happens more
       in some modes than others or is it maybe too difficult to
       say at this stage?

Joy: My first feeling would be yes because it's so focused on
       language that anything they give me that might not be
       correct and not clear then I'm going to re-formulate it or
       anything they don't understand I'm going to give them a
       lot of examples so that's all scaffolding isn't it?

Joy's comments suggest that she is trying to both understand for herself and explain to Mike how scaffolding occurs in practice (*I'm going to re-formulate it [. . .] I'm going to give them a lot of examples so that's all scaffolding isn't it?*). She explains that scaffolding occurs more in some micro-contexts than others (skills and systems mode), whereas Mike plays a key role in this extract in helping Joy to clarify her own reflections, understand when a particular practice occurs, and explain why.

Through dialogue and the use of data, Joy is able to reach an understanding of scaffolding, explain how it 'works' and why she does it, and evaluate its usefulness in a particular lesson context. In sum, we can see that *ad hoc* self-observation is a relatively easy and quick means of promoting co-constructed understanding.

Online Discussion Forums

Elsewhere in this book, we have shown how dialogic reflection can be fostered through the use of online blogs and discussion forums (see Chapter 5). Here, to illustrate how this tool can mediate dialogic reflection and help participants reflect together to achieve a collective understanding of an issue or puzzle, we present an example taken from a university course in Chile and described in Sandra Morales' vignette below.

SANDRA MORALES' VIGNETTE (CHILE)

Context

The following extract is taken from the interactions of eight English language teachers from Chile and Easter Island talking in discussion forums and blogs that were part of an online teacher training and development course implemented on the virtual learning environment Moodle. The aim of the online course was to develop teachers' technological and pedagogical skills to use technology with language learners. The duration of the course was 8 weeks and the developmental cycle included theoretical aspects of technology for L2 teaching, practical activities and reflection both individual (blogs) and collaborative (discussion forum). (Individual blogs were presented in Chapter 5.)

Data

MEG. TUESDAY, *18 JUNE 2013, 10:24 PM*

I agree that adapting course book materials to make them relevant for students is crucial to even begin to connect with students. As Frank said, even changing the names of the places mentioned in textbooks so they are familiar (places in Chile) is a start. We are always trying to make language the most relevant for students. How can we make language more relevant than negotiating meaning with a real human being in the target language? Telecollaboration is the communicative approach at its best. I was reading the Robert O'Dowd article on the Moodle on teachers designing telecollaboration tasks for post-secondary students. Telecollaborative exchanges between students in different parts of the world, in the context of a language course, certainly take a lot of work. However, I can't think of a better way to make the contents of a textbook leap off the page and onto a computer screen in the form of a real person!

CECE. MONDAY, *24 JUNE 2013, 03:55 AM*

In some ways course-books are good for teaching culture but it is not the best way to accomplish that task, they try to cover some interesting topics and they engage students in some activities related to culture but with technology you can go further, they get closer to the target language and they have more options to get to know the new culture they are studying. Through technology, students can get in touch with native speakers, they can search information if they have questions and they can practice in real-time different life situations.

Neko. Tuesday, 25 June 2013, 12:44 AM

Completely agree with you. Since technology is really close to students' lives, why not using it for productive reasons? Kids use their mobiles way more often than computers now, so we as teachers should take advantage of all that! I think that's the key, we can use any tool at hand and achieve the established goals (just by knowing how to adapt the contents and so on).

Easter. Monday, 24 June 2013, 08:33 PM

Most of the textbooks should be designed at promoting exposure and practice of the target language. However, I have some doubts that I would like to set up. Are the topics interesting for language learners? Are the tasks appropriate and effective for encouraging productive skills? Do they have activities that promote long and short term learning? How do teachers participate in selecting textbooks? Are textbooks organized to cause an impact on students? Are they created to engage them cognitively and affectively? Do textbooks consider local cultures? I have more questions than answers. I have been working with the course-books provided by the Ministry of Education for state schools and I don't like them. For example, many of my students can't participate in the listening comprehension since it is confusing and boring. The topics of the reading section are even worse. My students would love read something related to sports (surfing, body boarding, rugby), music, stories from the island, traditional parties or computer games. I think this island is still 3700 kms far away from Chile where the need for contextualization is not understood. Most of the time I have to adapt texts according to learner's age, level of proficiency in English , students' interests and attitude to learning. This is definitely a time-consuming activity. Beside the adaptation or creation of texts might have certain degree of linguistic errors, that's why, I consider online resources as a good way of fostering not only intercultural communication but also providing language learners with linguistic authentic materials that can be used to engage students in challenging tasks. These motivating activities can be used to support language exposure and practice as well.

Commentary

Reflection in the online course was usually initiated by the online tutor (this researcher), but the teachers had the opportunity to do so as well. In the extracts above from the discussion forum about teaching materials and using technology to teach culture, it is possible to observe how teachers use their experience, prior knowledge and the input they received in the course in order to construct new knowledge in collaboration.

> For instance, Meg reacted to a suggestion made by one of her col-
> leagues in the community (Frank) and at the same time provided infor-
> mation and questions about an article that she had read as part of
> the course. Andy as well talked about her experience in a conference
> about technology and shared that with her colleagues. This can be
> considered as relevant in professional development in online commu-
> nities, as it may mean that as teachers bring their experiences from
> the 'outside world' into the community, they can also exchange this
> knowledge from the community to their colleagues in their educational
> institutions.
>
> Additionally in this discussion, Cece, Neko and Easter discuss their
> views and teaching contexts which show how different these can be,
> even in the same country, and how technology can support how they
> teach culture in diverse settings (Easter Island vs continental Chile).
> This collaborative reflection around pedagogical practices opens the
> discussion for finding techniques and give/receive suggestions on
> how to improve them. As a result, teachers feel supported and feelings
> of isolation decreased. The teachers' constant dialogue during the
> online course was essential to promote reflection which, in turn, helped
> them to better understand the different strategies to use technology
> effectively with L2 students.

Of interest in Sandra's vignette is her use of the term 'collaborative reflection' (see also Chapter 7) and the ways in which collaborative reflection gets done. She makes the point that teachers use a variety of sources to collaboratively reflect on technology integration, exploring different options and sharing ways of achieving common goals. In their commentaries, for example, participating teachers discuss a number of key topics, including telecollaboration ('the communicative approach at its best'); the use of mobile phones to integrate technology and learning; and the importance of topics which are relevant to context. In her commentary, Sandra also highlights the extent to which collaborative/dialogic reflection can help foster closer understandings of context and reduce the feelings of isolation or anxiety which can be found in almost any educational setting.

The use of an online discussion forum has much to recommend it. It is relatively easy to set up, promotes collective reflections around common themes and actually helps teachers understand their practices more fully.

Critical Incident Analysis

In a similar vein to Sandra Morales, Mark Brooke used an online VLE (virtual learning environment) as a means of collecting and sharing the reflections of third year pre-service (BEd) ESOL teacher trainees during a period of teaching practice. In this study, it was found that reflections are improved significantly through online discussions, collaboration and asynchronous communication. Participants were asked to use critical incidents to prompt reflection and discussion with peers through online posts. As Mark Brooke says:

> The VLE was selected because of the potential benefits of the asynchronous, collaborative discussion forums as a platform on which reflections could be posted and shared. Using action research methodology over eighteen months, three case studies were conducted and a model which could scaffold trainee online reflections constructed.
>
> *2014: 1*

In extract 8.5, we see an example of one of the threads from the VLE (Blackboard). The pre-service teachers have selected critical incidents – events in their professional practice that they felt to be worthy of discussion or sharing. Here, we see three consecutive posts by Jennifer, Candy and Scarlet, discussing a discipline-related issue in a Hong Kong secondary classroom:

Extract 8.5

> *9. Thread: A critical incident by Jennifer. Posted: February 27, 2010 5:23 PM.*
> My critical incident is the first English lesson I observed in a Hong Kong secondary school. I was really surprised by the boring and demotivating classroom atmosphere. The teacher simply analyzed the text in the textbook and then asked students to do exercises. As students were quite bored with the lesson, there were quite a lot of discipline problems and the teacher had to shout at students for a number of times. At the end of the lesson, the teacher gave students lots of homework and also asked students to prepare for the dictation for the next lesson. Actually the teacher knew that her lesson was boring when she talked with me, but she said she had to do so because the students she taught needed to take HKCEE (Hong Kong College Entrance Examination) and she had to prepare them by using the more traditional teaching style. What do you think?

> *10. Thread: Candy's critical incident Post: RE: Candy's critical incident Posted Date: February 27, 2010 5:30 PM.*
> I think the first step is to separate the two students and make them calm down. Then the teacher can talk with each student, ask him to explain the reason for this incident and help him to use a better approach to solve this kind of problem. The teacher needs to be patient and kind when he/she talks with each student, and tries to help him rather than blame what he has done.

> 11. *Thread: Scarlet's Critical Incident Post: RE: Scarlet's Critical Incident Posted Date: February 27, 2010 5:30 PM.*
> In my view, the first thing teachers can do it to identify why the boy can't concentrate on the class and always make noise. I think this is the first also the hardest step. Then, you can reinforce the importance of keep classroom discipline by announcing class rules at the beginning of the class. Also, you can make your learning materials more interesting to attract the students' interest.

What is interesting about this thread of online posts is that they all respond to an actual incident and suggest alternative ways of dealing with the issue. Class management and discipline are always a concern for pre-service teachers during the early stages of their practicum. What we witness in extract 8.5 is a kind of online self-help session where trainees offer advice and share alternative ways of approaching this problem. Both Scarlet and Candy suggest sensible ways of dealing with the issue and their advice might be the kind of suggestion a more experienced teacher would offer. There is clear evidence in the tone of the posts that respondents both trust and respect each other and feel able to offer advice. This kind of online support, where teachers ask for and offer advice, is certainly something we would advocate; it allows issues to be raised and alternatives to be discussed in a safe, non-threatening environment.

Structured Reflection

One of the issues we have raised in this chapter and elsewhere is the need for reflective tools which are appropriate to a particular context and to a particular stage of development – either while following a pre- or in-service course or when engaging in RP 'in the wild'. The need for the use of tools which are appropriate to a practitioner's stage of development is of paramount importance, as is the need for tools which are appropriate to context and which challenge users to think and address key issues.

In extract 8.6, we see examples of tools which we consider to be extremely appropriate for RP in general and for dialogic reflection more specifically. Teti Dragas works on an MA TESOL programme in the UK and her students undergo a period of teaching practice, lasting around seven weeks. The tasks below are used in week 4 of the practicum and get student teachers to focus on one learner using videotaped recordings of a class.

Extract 8.6

Task 1: Focus on the Student

Look through the video recording of the lesson. Pick one student you'd like to focus on and watch the video back concentrating on this one student. Make comments on the following:

How engaged was the student throughout the lesson? At what point was the student most engaged and least engaged? (What were they doing?)

How often did the student get to 'talk'? Was this with others/ to the teacher/ both?

How was the student feeling throughout the lesson? (e.g. confused/ interested/ on task/ happy/ bored etc. . . .) Which of these was the most dominant overall?

Anything else you'd like to comment on?

What implications does this have for the class as a whole? What can you take from this for future lessons? (Think about this in terms of advice for the group).

Task 2: Materials

Look at the materials used in the lesson and also think/look back at how they were used in the lesson (i.e. the tasks associated with them). (You might want to watch the video back).

Pick **one piece of material** and identify two issues with the materials and tasks and suggest adaptations to materials and or tasks which would have led to improvements in their use and effectiveness for students

Materials used:

- Fei's Materials: listening on equal rights; crossword; matching words
- Iris's Materials: reading materials (extracts)
- J.'s Materials: video clip from YouTube.

The advantage of this structured approach to reflection is that participants are given specific areas to focus on in relation to learners and materials. By asking guiding questions, student teachers on this programme are trained to become more reflective about their own practice. The advantage of using a video of another teacher (rather than looking at oneself) is that the focus of attention is taken away from one's own pre-occupations and concerns (c.f Paul's vignette above). Instead, student teachers completing these tasks are free to try and understand what is actually happening, explain why and provide alternatives – all key elements of 'online decision-making' when teachers have to make decisions about their practice in the moment, while teaching.

Note too that although the task is undertaken individually, all the comments, responses to questions and so on are posted online and shared with the rest of the group. From an SCT perspective, this allows learning to progress from the group or collective (intrapsychological) to the individual (interpsychological); in sum, learners gain ownership of their own professional development through, initially, dialogue with others and then, at a slight distance, through individual reflection and introspection.

Video and Dialogic Reflection

In Chapter 7, and throughout the book, we have looked at a number of ways in which video can be used to promote more engaged reflection. Video has the advantage of immediacy: a segment of teaching can be recorded with little need for state-of-the-art technology; it can then be used as a springboard for discussion or in order to facilitate group or individual refection. In sum, it is probably the most flexible, readily available and useful tool for dialogic reflection.

In Paul Slater's vignette below, Paul is conducting a final post-teaching feedback session with a student teacher, Jade Blue, who is taking a TESOL Diploma course. Jade has opted to use a mind map to present her reflections on the lesson and the discussion which follows centres on the relative merits of this approach to reflection. (An example of one of Jade's mind maps is presented in Chapter 6.)

PAUL SLATER'S VIGNETTE (UK)

Context

The participant, Jade Blue, attended a nine-month TESOL Diploma course delivered at the University of Brighton. Jade is an experienced teacher who completed a CELTA prior to taking the Diploma. The data below comes from a discussion which Jade had with the observer of her final observed lesson on the Diploma course. Prior to this discussion Jade had already talked to the observer about the lesson immediately after it had been given, had watched a video recording of the lesson, and had submitted her reflection on the lesson in the form of a mind map. In the full discussion Jade talked through her reflections on the lesson using the mind map, but in the extract below the focus is on why she chose to use mind mapping to capture her reflection.

Data

```
PS: You've chosen to do your reflection in a mind map.
JB: Yes
PS: Why?
JB: Okay. What I like about the mind map, as opposed to one
    piece of text on screen or printed out, is that you can
    bring this (points to sections of the mind map) back to
    here, this connects to here, and this goes in three
    directions and you can choose what you read first, so you can
    see it in its entirety, whereas when you read something,
    when you read a piece of linear text, you're never really
    seeing it in its entirety. Perhaps you are after you've
    finished it, when you've got time to think about it but you
    don't necessarily see the relationship between the different
    parts.
```

PS: Okay, so what you're raising, one of the issues you're raising for me now, is this almost seems like a perfect launchpad for a discussion.

JB: Yes, it's a good starting point for discussion, but I think it's also reflective of a discussion. It would be interesting to get loads of, loads of little Post-it notes and write down thoughts, but for both the teacher and observer to do that and then together to work out how those map out. So then this (the mind map) is then a dialogue. In some ways it already is. I've got references to things you've said in here, and it looks more like a dialogue to me in its structure and its form, it feels more like a dialogue, it's more of stream-of-consciousness whereas as soon as you ask me to put that (the mind map) in one body of text I feel an obligation to make it more crafted and structured and that's where it loses something, something honest, something, something reflective. Because a crafted piece of writing, is one step beyond a reflection, it's a conclusion. It's conclusive, none of this (the mind map) is conclusive, this is all questions.

PS: What's jumping out at me is that this, as a vehicle, is a really good vehicle for reflection. Now, I don't think this would work with people who haven't got a background in mind mapping, but it's interesting that this acts, this is almost like a garden, isn't it? It's almost like a garden with all these different flowers, I mean and you can say "When did you plant this? And why did you plant this? And why did you plant this here?"

JB: Yeah, I want to disagree though, because I don't have a background in mind mapping. I, the first mind map I did was last summer when I was doing some pre-course reading and I wanted to formulate notes that I'd made in the margins as a summary, if you like, of what I'd read, bulletpoints of what I'd read, and I wanted to formulate that into something that I could follow more easily and I did it in a mind map. So that was a revision mind map. And from that, I mean, learning to do a mind map is learning to draw lines and connect them actually. There's no formula, there's no, a mind map is whatever comes out of your mind it can go in any direction you want so if you can draw a line you can do a mind map. So I dispute that it wouldn't work for people without a background in mind maps.

PS: Oh, I'm not, ah . . .

JB: I think it wouldn't work for everybody because I think some people don't think in that way, but I think we should be encouraging people to think in that way.

PS: Okay

JB: It's complex, it's a complex system, isn't it? But it's interesting what you said earlier about transparency because, yeah, you could take a series of photos, you could do an interpretive dance.

```
PS:    That's exactly what I was thinking, you could act it out.
JB:    But how transparent is it and how transparent does it need
       to be? And the thing about mind mapping, as opposed to you
       know writing a song or doing a dance is, it's more,
       hopefully, transparent enough.
PS:    You've got to exactly the point that I was trying to get to
       about what you've got on the blog which is this issue of
       transparency and when I talk about modes rescuing each
       other, it's the argument about the functionality of the text
       and to what degree the text has to rescue the imagery. The
       imagery actually doesn't have enough "yeah but what exactly
       do you mean?"
JB:    This text doesn't work without them the images, whatever you
       want to call them, the map.
PS:    Uh-huh
JB:    The, the, you take the text out of there and it doesn't
       work, but they're both supporting each other. There's a word
       for that but I can't remember what it is. There's a
       relationship between the two.
PS:    Multimodality?
JB:    Maybe.
```

Mode, Multimodality and Reflection

Some years ago the TESOL Diploma course team at the University of Brighton started to video all the participating teachers' observed lessons. After each observation the teacher is given a recording of the lesson and asked to identify aspects of their teaching in the lesson for reflection and comment. The remit is very open with teachers asked to look at any areas which they would like to develop in their future teaching, or consider any points in the lesson which they believe deserve comment. Most teachers opt to use a written pro-forma to record their reflections which they then return to the observer. The observer provides a written response to the teacher's reflections, adds additional comments on the lesson, and grades the lesson.

Prior to the introduction of video recordings into the observation process, there had always been opportunities for dialogue between the observer and the teacher. There could be some discussion in a 'hot feedback' session immediately after the lesson, or in a meeting between the observer and the teacher after the teacher had received written feedback and a grade from the observer. With the introduction of the video recordings the opportunities for observer/teacher dialogue were retained, but with the added advantage for teachers that they could now observe and reflect on their teaching using the lesson recording prior to any discussion with the observer. This was empowering for teachers as they had the experience of teaching the lesson and observing it.

Following the introduction of the lesson recordings, the course team began to consider the role of mode and multimodality in the reflective process. With digital technologies so accessible to the teachers the potential to use different modes to record, share and promote reflection opened up. Instead of restricting a teacher's post-observation reflection to the written form, teachers can now record their reflection on a lesson in an audio or video file and then send this to the observer. Some of the teachers have opted for this approach and, for example, use their smartphones to record and send feedback. Listening to and viewing these recordings it has become apparent that the mode that a teacher uses to record their reflections can affect reflection. While more research is needed, there is some evidence that the audio and video recordings promoted a more circuitous and discursive approach than writing, but for some teachers this seems to promote more sustained reflection than writing.

Coming to the dialogue above, Jade Blue is the first student taking the TESOL Diploma at Brighton who has decided to record their reflections using a mind map. Jade's use of mind maps is interesting for a variety of reasons. Given that a mode is a specific communication channel, examples being writing, images, video or gesture, the different modes that the mind mapper can use makes the mind map multimodal. This multimodality gives the creator of the map different ways in which to represent, record, and develop their reflections using text but they can also present ideas, concepts, and interrelationships visually using colour, shape, line, proximity, alignment, repetition and contrast. In addition, the speed at which the teacher can record ideas when mind mapping allows them to rapidly capture the flood of ideas that can come to mind when recalling everything associated with a given lesson.

While a mind map may be a highly effective way of exploring and capturing ideas for the person who creates the map, it is debatable how readable one person's mind map is to someone else. However, Jade used her mind maps in ways which allowed her to continue her process of reflection and communicate her reflections to others. In some cases, Jade's maps were a precursor to written reflections on her lessons which she then posted on a blog which each student writes as one of the assessed elements of their course. Following some of her observed lessons, as in the extract above, Jade also shared her mind map in a face-to-face meeting with the lesson observer and it was used to trigger discussions about the lesson as the tutor asked Jade to explain or clarify elements on the map and how they related to the lesson and her reflections on it.

Paul's vignette is packed with comments and observations which chime with so much of what has been said in this chapter, summarized below:

1. Why use mind maps for reflection? Jade's main argument is that, in addition to being a springboard for discussion ('a launchpad'), a mind map is actually a representation of the reflection itself, as a kind of dialogue (*it looks more like a dialogue to me in its structure and its form, it feels more like a dialogue, it's more of stream-of-consciousness*). Jade also comments on the fact that a mind map captures the process of reflection better than a written text, which seems more complete, more final. Her comments are very pertinent in relation to the observations we have made in this chapter about the transitory and collaborative nature of dialogic reflection: understandings do not simply happen; they emerge through co-construction and perhaps a mind map is one way of capturing that process.

2. A mind map helps to make connections. One of the advantages of a mind map, which is clearly of value to any reflective process, is the potential it has to help the user make connections, to link ideas and to relate one feature or one practice to another. As Jade puts it: *What I like about the mind map, as opposed to one piece of text on screen or printed out, is that you can bring this* (points to sections of the mind map) *back to here, this connects to here, and this goes in three directions and you can choose what you read first, so you can see it in its entirety, whereas when you read something, when you read a piece of linear text, you're never really seeing it in its entirety.* The ability to make connections, to see how different elements of a complex process like teaching fit together, is surely one of the fundamental reasons for any reflective practice; put simply, our understandings are enhanced when we see how things fit together, when we are able to link ideas or relate one classroom practice to another. Mind maps go a long way in helping practitioners make connections, perhaps even more so than a linear text.

3. You don't have to be an expert in drawing mind maps. In response to Paul's comments about the need to have experience in using mind maps, Jade suggest that this is not the case at all, making the point that there is no one way of drawing a mind map, that it is basically down to the individual, who has complete freedom: *There's no formula, there's no, a mind map is whatever comes out of your mind it can go in any direction you want so if you can draw a line you can do a mind map.* And in a sense, this is the beauty of the approach; we are not restricted by forms, checklists or pro-formas – we simply reflect and use a mind map to represent our reflections, something which we should all do, at least some of the time.

4. Transparency. Both Paul and Jade comment on the extent to which a mind map has the potential to be more transparent than a written, linear text. In essence, the images and words work in a symbiotic way, where one reinforces the other, making the process of reflection more transparent and

more accessible. This observation might be especially true in dialogic reflection where images may convey an idea to the listener more easily and more accurately than words.

5. Multimodality. In the final section of the vignette, Paul highlights the importance of the modality of text, observing that the mode of reflection (spoken, written, dialogic, pictorial, etc.) impacts on and influences the reflection itself. Interestingly, Paul suggests that reflections which make use of audio and video recordings may be more sustained than those which make use of written reflections. While more research is needed, there is some evidence that the audio and video recordings promoted a more circuitous and discursive approach than writing, but for some teachers this seems to promote more sustained reflection than writing. Paul's comments echo much of what we have presented throughout this book and underline the need for spoken, collaborative and dialogic reflections to be used alongside more traditional (written, individual) approaches. Indeed, as others have argued (see, for example, Teti Dragas' work), there is perhaps a case to be made for using more than one mode to re-present reflection; video, for example, could be used as a precursor to written reflection, or a mind map might precede a conversation with a colleague. There is, we suggest, much to be valued in combining different modes of reflection.

8.4 Summary

In this chapter, which builds on the arguments put forward in Chapter 7, we have introduced and exemplified a number of approaches to dialogic reflection, adopting the position that learning is a dialogic process in which meanings are mediated by language. Using examples from a range of contexts, we set out to demonstrate the ways in which understandings are co-constructed, allowing new understandings and professional development to emerge. Of central importance to this process are spoken interaction and artefacts which act as a mediating force. Talk is central to all learning; our aim in this chapter was to show how dialogic reflection – a bottom-up, teacher-led, collaborative process entailing interaction, discussion and debate with another professional – can lead to professional learning. Similarly, we commented on the importance of using appropriate artefacts to mediate the learning process; in particular, we explored the ways in which recordings and the use of video can promote more systematic and focused professional dialogue. In the final section of the chapter, we looked at the value of combining modes of reflection such as video followed by dialogue, or mind map plus written reflection. Through the use of dialogue, tools or artefacts and multimodal forms of reflection, practitioners have the potential to acquire deep, sustained understandings of their pedagogy.

References

Brooke, M. (2014). *Enhancing pre-service teacher training: the construction of an online model to develop reflective practice* (Doctoral dissertation). Durham University.

Bruner, J. (1990). Vygotsky: a historical and conceptual perspective. In L.C. Moll (ed.), *Vygotsky and education: instructional implications and applications of sociohistorical psychology*. Cambridge: Cambridge University Press.

Cooper, C. and Boyd, J. (1998). Creating sustained professional development. In C. Brody and N. Davidson (eds), *Professional development for cooperative learning: Issues and approaches* (pp. 49–62). Albany, NY: State University of New York Press.

Copland, F. (2010). Causes of tension in post-observation feedback in pre-service teacher training: an alternative view. *Teaching and Teacher Education*, 26(3), 466–472.

Edge, J. (2011). *The reflexive teacher educator in TESOL: roots and wings*. New York: Routledge.

Farrell, T.S. (2008). Reflective practice in the professional development of teachers of adult English language learners. CAELA Network Brief. *Center for Adult English Language Acquisition*.

Farrell, T.S. (2012). Reflecting on reflective practice: (re)visiting Dewey and Schön. *TESOL Journal*, 3(1), 7–16.

Firth, A. and Wagner, J. (1997). On discourse, communication, and (some) fundamental concepts in SLA research. *The Modern Language Journal*, 81(3), 285–300.

Firth, A. and Wagner, J. (2007). On discourse, communication, and (some) fundamental concepts in SLA research. *The Modern Language Journal*, 91(s1), 757–772.

Hall, J.K., Hellermann, J. and Doehler, S.P. (eds). (2011). *L2 interactional competence and development* (Vol. 56). Bristol, Buffalo and Toronto: Multilingual Matters.

Harfitt, G.J. (2007). Research reports on 'Examining the teaching-and-learning differences in whole class and reduced class size English language classrooms in Hong Kong: a sociocultural perspective'. In *Postgraduate Research Conference 2007, Faculty of Education, The University of Hong Kong*.

Harris, A.R. (2013). *Professionals developing professionalism: the interactional organisation of reflective practice* (Unpublished PhD thesis). University of Newcastle. Downloaded 10.10.15 at https://theses.ncl.ac.uk/dspace/bitstream/10443/2354/1/Harris,%20A.%2013.pdf

Heritage, J. (1984). A change-of-state token and aspects of its sequential placement. In J.M. Atkinson and J. Heritage (eds), *Structures of social action: Studies in conversation analysis* (pp. 299–345). Cambridge: Cambridge University Press.

Holland, P. and Adams, P. (2002). Through the horns of a dilemma between instructional supervision and the summative evaluation of teaching. *International Journal of Leadership in Education*, 5(3), 227–247.

Johnson, K.E. (2009). *Second language teacher education: a sociocultural perspective*. London: Routledge.

Johnson, K.E. and Golombek, P.R. (eds). (2011). *Research on second language teacher education: a sociocultural perspective on professional development*. London and New York: Routledge.

Kurtoglu-Hooton, N. (2010). *Post-observation feedback as an instigator of learning and change: exploring the effect of feedback through student teachers' self-reports* (Unpublished PhD thesis). Aston University, UK.

Lantolf, J.P. (2000). *Sociocultural Theory and Second Language Learning*. Oxford: Oxford University Press.

Lantolf, J.P. and Thorne, S. (2006). *Sociocultural theory and the genesis of second language development*. Oxford: Oxford University Press.

Larrivee, B. (2000). Transforming teaching practice: becoming the critically reflective teacher. *Reflective Practice: International and Multidisciplinary Perspectives*, 1(3), 293–307.

Larsen-Freeman, D. (2010). Having and doing: learning from a complexity theory perspective. In P. Seedhouse, S. Walsh and C. Jenks (eds), *Conceptualising 'learning' in applied linguistics* (pp. 52–68). Palgrave Macmillan UK.

Maggioli, G.D. (2012). *Teaching language teachers: scaffolding professional learning*. New York: R&L Education.

Mann, S. and Walsh, S. (2013). RP or 'RIP': a critical perspective on reflective practice. *Applied Linguistics Review*, 4(2) 291–315

Markee, N. (2008). Toward a learning behavior tracking methodology for CA-for-SLA. *Applied Linguistics*, 29(3), 404–427.

Mercer, N. (2004). Sociocultural discourse analysis. *Journal of Applied Linguistics*, 1(2), 137–168.

Mori, J. (2004). Negotiating sequential boundaries and learning opportunities: a case from a Japanese language classroom. *The Modern Language Journal*, 88(4), 536–550.

Ohta, A.S. (2001). Second language acquisition processes in the classroom: learning Japanese. London and New York: Routledge.

Osterman, K.F. and Kottkamp, R.B. (1993). *Reflective practice for educators*. Newbury Park eCL CL: Corwin Press.

Röhler, R.L. and Cantlon, J.D. (1996). Scaffolding, a powerful tool in social constructivist classrooms. Master of Arts. Literacy and Language Instruction, Michigan State University.

Schwab, G. (2011). From dialogue to multilogue: a different view on participation in the English foreign-language classroom. *Classroom Discourse*, 2(1), 3–19.

Sfard, A. (1998). On two metaphors for learning and the dangers of choosing just one. *Educational Researcher*, 27(2), 4–13.

Swain, M. and Lapkin, S. (1998). Interaction and second language learning: two adolescent French immersion students working together. *The Modern Language Journal*, 82(3), 320–337.

van Compernolle, R.A. (2015). *Interaction and second language development: a Vygotskian perspective*. Amsterdam: John Benjamins Publishing Company.

van Lier, L. (2000). From input to affordance: social-interactive learning from an ecological perspective. In J.P. Lantolf (ed.), *Sociocultural theory and second language learning*. Oxford: Oxford University Press.

Vygotsky, L.S. (1978). *Mind in society: the development of higher psychological processes*. Cambridge, MA: Harvard University Press.

Wallace, M.J. (1998). Action research for language teachers. Cambridge: Cambridge University Press.

Walsh, S. (2006). *Investigating classroom discourse*. London: Routledge.

Walsh, S. (2011). *Exploring classroom discourse: language in action*. London and New York: Routledge.

Walsh, S. (2013). *Classroom discourse and teacher development*. Edinburgh, UK: Edinburgh University Press.

Walsh, S. and Li, L. (2013). Conversations as space for learning. *International Journal of Applied Linguistics (INJAL)*, 23(2), 247–266.

Walsh, S. and Mann, S. (2015). Doing reflective practice: a data-led way forward. *ELT Journal*, 69(4), 351–362.

9

Practitioner Research

9.1 Introduction

The next two chapters consider the most important elements of the relationship between reflection and research. Chapter 9 focuses on practitioner research (i.e. research which is conducted by the teacher herself/himself.) Chapter 10 evaluates current research on reflection and then looks at possible future research directions. In Chapter 9 we are interested in all forms of practitioner research, but we will concentrate mainly on action research (AR). This is partly because most accounts of AR include a specific step or stage called reflection (e.g. observation-*reflection*-planning-action), but also because AR is the most well known and widely adopted form of practitioner research (Burns, 2005). However, in discussing aspects of the relationship between reflection and research, the themes developed will be relevant to all forms of practitioner research.

Before looking more closely at AR, we should explore the relationship between reflection and research. It is widely recognized that reflection has a key role in developing teaching skills and that reflection helps teachers to build self-awareness, but what is its relationship to research? It can be helpful to see them as a continuum:

> ... there is a continuum between, at one end, what Wallace (1991: 56) calls 'normal reflective practice of many teachers' or what 'caring teachers have always done' (Bailey 1997: 1) and, at the other end, the more structured and rigorous forms of teachers' research which include action research. The shorthand for this continuum would be reflection and research where reflection is a pre-requisite of development and research is a desirable option for development.
>
> *Mann, 2005: 108*

When Wallace talks about action research (1991: 56), he sees it as an extension of teachers' normal reflective practice but 'slightly more rigorous'. Others might make a sharper distinction. For example, when Borg (2010: 393) distinguishes between teacher research and reflective practice, he quotes Cochran-Smith and Lytle (1999: 22) when they define teacher research as encompassing:

... all forms of practitioner inquiry that involve systematic, intentional, and self-critical inquiry about one's work in K–12, higher education, or continuing education classrooms, schools, programs, and other formal educational settings. This definition ... does not necessarily include reflection or other terms that refer to being thoughtful about one's educational work in ways that are not necessarily systematic or intentional.

Borg argues that this distinction (between reflective practice and teacher research) is helpful because 'while teacher research is necessarily reflective, reflecting on one's practice does not automatically constitute teacher research' (2010: 394).

So a continuum might look like this:

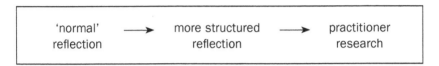

A number of organizations, conferences and publications have consolidated the importance and value of practitioner research and these are summarized in Appendix 9. However, practitioner research is not only an academic matter. There is a more mainstream sense of its worth and importance. As an example, the following appeared in a newspaper article endorsing the importance of engaging in research for teachers (Sherrington, 2013) with the title 'Teachers as researchers: the ultimate form of professional development'.

> For several years my school has branded itself as a 'research-engaged learning community'. A touch grand perhaps but it captures the essence of the culture we are trying to engender throughout the school. We encourage teachers to engage with research – to read journals, articles, blogs and books about teaching and learning, and leadership. We want teachers to engage in research – to contribute to developing our collective understanding of how to maximise the richness and depth of our students' educational experience.
>
> Action research of this kind is a superb form of continuing professional development (CPD). At the heart of any good CPD is a process of reflection whereby teachers adapt their practice in the light of new information, ideas or feedback. Engaging in research is an excellent way to do this. Firstly, because of the rigour of the approach and, secondly, because of the level of commitment secured as teachers select a topic of special interest to them; action research affords a high level of autonomy which teachers thrive on.

This is a particularly evangelical account of teacher research, but it captures both the potential autonomy of the practice and also the range of activities that might constitute a research culture within an organization. We might wonder in passing whether all the teachers in the school are equally enthusiastic about this 'excellent way to go about CPD'. In what follows, we consider both the advantages and also some constraints and problems associated with AR.

9.2 Action Research

Although practitioner research is recognized as the best umbrella term (see Zeichner and Noffke, 2001), there are various terms that have emerged during the last 20 years (e.g. action research, action enquiry, exploratory practice, collaborative inquiry, critical inquiry, practitioner inquiry and teacher research). This section establishes the importance of action research, as it is the most common and widely used form of practitioner research (Burns, 2009). We do not wish to undervalue the other forms of practitioner research that have emerged since the 1990s. However, space dictates that we can only do justice to one form of practitioner research here, in exploring its relationship with reflective practice.

Dörnyei (2007: 191) tells us that there 'is one big problem with action research', that there is 'too little of it'. He says that the TESOL/TEFL teaching profession increasingly values both the process and outcomes of action research. Barnes was one of the first to recognize the importance of action research, particularly in bringing tacit understandings to a more conscious level. He also argued that the process of reflection (whether in written or spoken form) could help uncover aspects of teaching that have become either 'unconscious or invisible' (Barnes, 1975: 13). In this book we are promoting reflective tools, lenses and procedures that might reveal such invisible knowledge. In this chapter we are concentrating on the role of reflection within the context of action research. We believe that with appropriate support, good reflective practice can develop into worthwhile action research. Once teachers feel engaged and more conscious of these research choices, they will be in a better position to frame appropriate research questions and procedures to explore them. As has been demonstrated elsewhere in this book, current advances in technology facilitate RP and allow it to be shared easily through online forums, blogs and so on. It would be fair to say that such advances also make action research – both the doing and the sharing of research – easier, quicker and much more feasible, especially when practitioners are working collaboratively.

The value of all forms of practitioner research is that the research is conducted by the practitioner and not by an outsider: the practitioner can see their classroom with an 'outsider's eye, but an insider's knowledge' (Barnes, 1975). Nunan (1990) was one of the first to make the argument that research in ELT is only valuable if teachers themselves engage with it. He argued for a closer relationship between teaching and research and between teachers and researchers. In general terms, action research (AR) takes the position that teachers need to be not only 'involved' in the research process, but at the heart of it. The importance of AR for the teaching profession is that it both values and encourages the 'insider' view of reflection and research. Rather than leaving the research field to those who trumpet the importance of objectivity, control groups and hypothesis testing, AR creates a research space where teachers can develop and sustain their own projects without feeling inferior in terms of scale and scope of what they are attempting to achieve. Indeed, Edge (2001) and others have argued that in many ways the reflective teacher is in the ideal position to articulate and uncover the complexities of the classroom.

There have been a number of influential contributions in shaping our current understanding of how teachers might investigate their practice through AR. Altrichter et al. (1993) provided an important early impetus to the ideas put forward by Nunan (1990). Later, Wallace (1998) provided an influential guide for teachers and this book was widely used on Masters programmes worldwide. Burns (1999) also provided a comprehensive introduction to the conceptual and practical aspects of conducting action research and has continued to do important work in making action research accessible and understandable. Burns (2009) summarizes the purposes of action research in L2 teacher education as being to:

*   address specific issues in teaching or learning situations;
*   investigate curriculum innovation and the change processes;
*   facilitate teachers' professional development;
*   enhance teachers' knowledge of conducting research and to equip them with research skills;
*   enhance the development of their personal practical theories; and
*   provide a vehicle for reducing the gap between research and practice.

A later section in this chapter provides plenty of resources and gives examples of how to conduct action research. However, although guides and examples can give reassurance to reflective practitioners who want to take a further step into practitioner research, too much reading and background information (endless models and frameworks) can also be off-putting. We would suggest jumping in at the deep end and getting on with it. Models (be they cycles, steps or spirals) may provide a useful conceptual metaphor, but they should not be seen as linear and fixed. It is hard to conceive of practitioner research that is not based on the elements of observation, reflection, planning and action, but there is no necessary 'right order'.

Getting Started with AR

Action research is practical in nature: Wallace (1991: 56) says that action research should focus on 'practical problems and should have practical outcomes'. The first point to make is that you should not be too ambitious; choose a challenge, issue or problem that has a realistic chance of being addressed. Mann (1999) discusses the topic of getting started on a process of action research (AR) and developing a sustained focus on an aspect of teaching. The first step is usually identifying an idea, puzzle or problem. For many teachers it may be more useful to make their AR focus on a puzzle. Indeed Allwright and Bailey (1991) and Allwright and Hanks (2009) see concentrating on a puzzle as a particularly productive way of integrating research and pedagogy. Once you have arrived at research focus, it may start out as a general idea. So, you might start with something like 'My students don't seem very interested in learning outside the classroom' as a general focus. The movement to a more narrow focus, for instance, on showing them how to use specific web resources (e.g. lyricstrainer, lyricstraining.com; brainshark, www.brainshark.com;), helps to take the AR into something particular and achievable.

The challenge facing teachers in conducting AR should not be underestimated (i.e. lack of time, expertise and support). Nunan (1993), while generally positive about the possible benefits of AR, addresses the major problems that face teachers. In response to the more general problems, Nunan sees possible solutions as:

1. having individuals with training in research methods available to provide assistance;
2. requesting release time from face-to-face teaching;
3. setting up collaborative focus teams.

He also mentions the fear of being revealed as an incompetent teacher as a potential problem. This may be a further reason why working collaboratively with a teacher from outside your teaching context is worth considering. See also Burns (1999: 45–52) who has a useful section on constraints and how to work with them. In particular, Nunan (ibid.) points out that there can be a requirement to produce a public account of the research and this is off-putting. In terms of possible solutions, it is not necessary to produce a full-scale academic article about the research. The kinds of reflective writing we have highlighted in Chapter 6 are usually more suitable in terms of sharing. We highlighted the importance of interactive writing, where, for example, the use of online blogs and discussion fora can facilitate a reader response. We also talked about the extent to which 'digital discourse' makes the whole process of writing more collaborative and interactive. At this point, it is worth making clear that our position is that the more accounts of AR that are published either in print or online the better, especially those which promote accounts and innovation that are practical and usable and those that foreground practical steps and procedures (see Mann and Edge, 2013).

Narrowing the Focus

Burns (1999) claims that practitioners new to AR comment that finding a focus and developing a research question is one of the most difficult parts of the research process. Allwright and Bailey (1991) say that starting with a general issue, thinking about the issue, then deciding what data is needed is the best start. Wallace suggests (1998: 27) that the next important challenge is to narrow the focus. In other words, it is important to consider how a general issue can be made more manageable. There are lots of possible general areas. Here is a short list of examples:

- increasing learner autonomy
- adapting and supplementing materials
- increasing use of VLEs (virtual learning environments)
- language awareness raising
- increasing student motivation
- developing writing skills
- involving learners in more task-based learning
- developing metacognitive awareness
- making use of students' iPads and smart phones
- helping students to develop self-study techniques.

Mann (1997) advises the complementary use of focusing circles (Edge, 1992) and mind mapping (Buzan and Buzan, 1996) to narrow the focus. Many teachers can quickly decide on a general issue, but find this issue overwhelming. Focusing circles and mind mapping can be used in complementary ways to find a focus that is small enough to manage, but also see connections and relationships:

> *Focusing circles.* This is a technique from Edge (1992: 37–38) through which you can narrow your focus. First you draw a small circle. The issue, topic or problem is written in the small circle and the circle is divided into four segments (like a cake). In each of these segments an aspect of the topic is written. You then choose one of these four segments to become the topic of the next circle and so on until you cannot think of ways of dividing down. The thinking involved in 'focusing circles' is selective. At each stage you need to make choices and justify them.
>
> *Mind maps.* Most teachers have, at some time, used mind maps or spider webs. Probably the most comprehensive guide to the use of mind mapping is provided by Buzan and Buzan (1996). Here the issue is written at the centre of a piece of paper and related factors branch out from the centre. See also the mind map from Jade Blue that is featured on p. 141. With mind maps, the main thinking goes into making connections, one thing leads to another, and relationships can become evident.

There can be dialogic relationship between the narrowing process and the widening/connecting process. As the focus narrows and then develops, it can be tracked within the bigger picture. Teachers have reported that this back and forth process has helped them both form and reflect on a developing AR focus.

Drawing on Edge (1992), Wallace (1998) and Burns (1999), we can add the following advice in terms of starting out:

- Narrow your focus and limit the scope and duration of your research.
- Avoid topics or questions which are essentially unanswerable.
- Choose a research focus which is contextually relevant (perhaps to your language learners or other teachers) or research that is of direct relevance and interest to yourself and to your school circumstances.
- Avoid a research focus where you have little wiggle room or scope for even small changes.
- Try to plan achievable steps and focus on one issue at a time.

Questions and Statements

Wallace (1998: 21) provides some basic questions that are worth asking early on in the AR process, but teachers should not be put off if they cannot answer them. They are only useful if they help you move on. If they do put you off, ignore them. Teachers may only be ready to provide answers nearer the end of the AR process:

- Why are you engaging in this action research? (Purpose)
- What area are you going to investigate? (Topic)
- What is the precise question you are going to ask yourself within that area? (Focus)
- What is the likely outcome of the research, as you intend it? (Product)
- How are you going to conduct the research? (Mode)
- How long have you got to do the research? Is there a deadline for its completion? (Timing)
- What are the resources, both human and material, that you can call upon to help you complete the research? (Resources)
- As you proceed with your research, are you prepared to rethink your original question? (Fine tuning)

Another way of making a start is by making a series of statements, as Kemmis and McTaggart (1988: 18) suggest. For example:

- I would like to improve . . .
- Some people are unhappy about . . .
- What can I do to change the situation?
- I have an idea I would like to try out in my class.

Talking Out Your Ideas

Once teachers have narrowed their focus, it is ideal if they can talk over ideas with a colleague or another interested teacher. Teachers working on AR projects often report the value of having the space to articulate their ideas. We have suggested a number of ways to do this in Chapter 7 (pp. 182–183).

After having set out some basic practical steps for getting started on AR, the next comment from Julian Edge clarifies some key aspects of the relationship between reflection and action research.

JULIAN EDGE COMMENT (UK)

Reflection and Action Research

My aim is to address briefly what I see as the most important elements of the relationship between reflection and action research. In what follows, therefore, the focus will move through: the AR cycle, reflection as stage and process, praxis and theorization, stepping back and stepping up, reflection-in-action, constraints and affordances, and reflexivity.

Action research is typically characterized in terms of a cycle along the following lines. In the midst of action, observation leads to the identification of a focus for attention (whether problem, goal, need or something else). Reflection on that focus leads to the formulation of a plan of action. The plan is implemented and further observation leads to evaluation as to whether the cycle should be repeated. Action-Observation-Reflection-Planning-Action . . .

Reflection, then, is the type of cognitive process that creates awareness from experience via the analysis of experience, the diagnosis of need, and the summoning of relevant information (intellectual, emotional, socio-cultural, etc.). That awareness is then invested in the formulation of response. The larger-scale outcome is the development of *praxis*: informed, principled, sensitive, socially just and culturally appropriate practice.

One element that distinguishes action research from reflective practice is the articulation and communication of what has been learned, above and beyond the improvement of praxis itself. The role of reflection here includes the summoning of relevant information from various written, spoken or interactive sources and their amalgamation towards a coherent statement. As reflection feeds planning in the action cycle, reflection also feeds planning in the theorization process. In both cases, reflection involves stepping back from direct involvement, while action and articulation involve stepping up to re-involvement again, mediated by a stage of planning.

At this point, we must note that as well as being seen as a stage in the action research process (Schön's (1983) *reflection-on-action*), reflection is also required in the midst of action (Schön's *reflection-in-action*). (I am reminded of the tenor saxophonist Wayne Shorter describing improvisation as composing-at-speed.) Action researchers need to be adept in both modes, reflecting on their feet as well as at their desk. In this sense, just as the whole action research cycle should not be seen as a set of insulated steps, there is no time at which the power of reflection (creating awareness from experience in order to direct future experience) is not required.

A defining aspect of action research is that it seeks to generate its responses by drawing on the nature of the context being investigated. In other words, it aims not to import previously formulated theoretical solutions to be applied in practice, but to theorize practice in ways that will establish praxis and generate theoretical insight. In ecological terms, therefore, the unit of analysis is always a holistic one of organism-in-context. A particular task of reflection, from this perspective, is to distinguish between what we can call *constraints* and *affordances*. Constraints are those elements of the perceived context that the organism can see no opportunity to influence or escape. Affordances are those elements of the context that are seen to allow for direct agentive action by the organism. To be plain, I may have to teach the prescribed textbook. That is a constraint. If I wish to address that issue, I have to rank-shift my actions up the power hierarchy to where such decisions are made. Exactly *how* I use this textbook, however, may offer a number of affordances that I can explore directly in my classroom environment.

If action research is to be the kind of whole-person endeavour to which some of us aspire, it will also acknowledge personal outcomes beyond professional results. That is to say, reflection will have a reflexive element: I am not the same person when I complete the action research project as I was when I entered into it. In what ways is this true? What is its significance? The role of reflection here is to (re)cognize the observations of introspection (and perhaps the commentaries of others) so as to be able to articulate what changes have taken place. Reflection will also recognize that this process of gathering and articulation is itself developmental and needs to be monitored in a reflection-in-action kind of way.

Julian Edge has had 30 years of experience in working with teachers developing their AR projects. His vignette captures the cyclic and iterative nature of AR and the importance of reflection in creating awareness from experience and consolidating 'praxis'. What we found powerful about this vignette is that reflection is central and necessary and that it has an iterative relationship with AR: reflection informs AR and vice versa, in much the same way that the relationship between theory and practice (see above) can and should be an iterative one.

There are a number of important observations which can be gleaned from Edge's thought-provoking vignette. In the first instance, we work through an example:

1. Observation (of self and others) is a key element of the AR/RP cycle. Linking back to some of the other themes in this book, this point once again highlights the important role of video, probably the most important tool in developing observational skills.
2. From initial observation(s), an issue, puzzle or, indeed, problem may emerge, which might be formulated, through reflection.
3. Identifying a clear focus will result in further reflection and a plan of action. Continuing with the example of student writing, our plan might involve trying out some new writing materials, introducing process writing or getting students writing together in small groups.
4. Following a phase of evaluation, data collection, further reflection and modification, the outcome of this process might be the development of a new approach to teaching writing involving a number of elements and stages.

From this example and Julian's vignette, it is clear that reflection is firmly embedded in any action research cycle, occurring at various times within a cycle. Reflection heightens awareness, facilitates the formulation of a response and, ultimately, leads to the emergence of a new practice or praxis. Implicit in the process is the need for information to reflect on data – which may be spoken or written. And note too, as mentioned in the vignette, that reflection occurs both 'in the moment' (while teaching, during a conversation with a colleague, etc.) and after the event, at a slight distance.

Of interest here is the importance Julian attaches to context; any context offers both opportunities (affordances) and constraints. One of the attractions of action research is that it is bottom-up and teacher/learner led, rather than top-down and imposed. As Julian emphasizes, it is important in any action research project to understand the constraints as a way of identifying opportunities. This observation resonates very strongly with the position taken on context throughout this book: action research entails both being sensitive to context and developing new understandings of it.

Working Collaboratively

Individual practitioners often undertake AR projects. However, it is also possible to undertake AR as a group. Earlier in this chapter we talked about the challenges of AR and mentioned the possible advantages of working collaboratively. There are several publications that provide support to the notion that working collaboratively on action research projects can be productive (Thorne and Qiang, 1996; Valeri, 1997; Mathew, 2000; Tinker Sachs, 2002; Wang and Zhang, 2014). Even if the teacher works individually, support from other teachers can be helpful (Rochsantiningsih, 2004). In Chapters 5 and 6 we have looked at different and complementary ways of using written and spoken reflection. As we have said, they often feed each other; face-to-face talk might feed into some kind of email or online exchange and vice versa. Collaboration has many advantages (see Burns, 1999, 2010), not least providing a more supportive environment. Of course, working in groups is not necessarily easy and brings its own interpersonal challenges. The following vignette gives us an insight into two phases of an AR practitioner's career trajectory and development. In both phases we get a strong sense of the support and excitement that derives from working collaboratively.

DARIO BANEGAS VIGNETTE (ARGENTINA)

Reflection is at the heart of teaching. Our dynamic teaching practices act as interpellators in our professional development because they challenge our routines; they help us denaturalize and deconstruct what we do. When we teachers engage in systematic reflection and start to develop an ethnography of language education it is because we are curious about what happens; we want to know why we do what we do. We also want to understand our teaching reality to make changes, to improve our practices and to become the best possible version of ourselves as teachers. It is at this intersection that I locate collaborative action research. I'm a firm believer (but I also have proofs!) that we need to encourage collaborative action research to strengthen teachers' in-service professional development.

Let me tell you two stories.

Story One: Between 2010 and 2013, I set out a project to implement CLIL (Content and Language Integrated Learning) at a secondary school in Esquel, Argentina. I didn't do this alone. I managed to work together with three colleagues because I wanted four of the teachers at this school to implement CLIL through collaborative action research. The research included regular meetings, journal keeping, group and individual interviews and peer observation. Such an experience helped understand and implement CLIL, but, above all, became a catalyst of reflection with others. Through different paths, we developed professionally as collaborative action research allowed us to systematize reflection, frame our discussions, ideas and concerns, and act cohesively as a group who wished to change our teaching landscape. Besides enjoying and learning through this process, we also achieved a wonderful research-driven product: the publication of our story (Banegas et al., 2013).

Story Two: It's 2016 and I am now more involved in initial English language teacher education at a tertiary institution. I started noticing that very few teacher educators engage in/with research (it's not part of their role anyway). Those who do it's because they've submitted a proposal to different calls in our province. However, their research tends to focus on descriptive-exploratory account in primary or secondary education. So I asked myself, "What if we start looking into our formative practices in higher education? Now, with other teacher educators we've set up a collaborative action research group to examine and improve the links between subject-matter knowledge (modules such as Syntax or English and Interculturality) and the Professional Practice and Practicum modules in our programme. It's not easy. Sometimes we say that we look like a self-help group because of all our cathartic moments when we get together. However, what we value is this opportunity to reflect and act as a group because we see that through reflection, research and the sharing of our professional biographies, we are co-constructing knowledge and developing professionally.

Dario's vignette reminds us of the challenges of engaging in action research. It is difficult to get teachers engaged in research. However, his vignette confirms how important collaboration has been in both setting up and sustaining research projects. This collaboration has been important in both developing CLIL at the secondary level and then later linking subject-matter knowledge with more practice-based modules at the tertiary level. This collaboration has been important in his personal career trajectory. The development of knowledge is co-constructed and very closely tied to the kinds of constraints and affordances that Julian Edge talked about above.

Of interest too is the way in which action research may result in the setting up of a self-help group, or, indeed how a self-help group may engage in AR. Such groups were discussed in Chapter 5 and it is perhaps worth reminding the reader of their potential. In terms of the position we are adopting on RP, such groups 'tick all the boxes': they promote collaboration and generate dialogue; they facilitate longer, more sustained action research projects of the kind described by Dario; they allow the sharing and analysis of data from specific contexts.

9.3 Working with Language Learners

Talking about EP (exploratory practice), Allwright (1993) suggests that a good place to start may be simply getting students to discuss an issue related to teaching and learning in class rather than starting with a questionnaire survey in the traditional academic way. This section considers the value of both talking to and involving learners in teacher research.

Burns (2010: 56) includes the following example of how simply talking to students can be revealing. This group had low morale because the class contained a number of 'failed' or 'repeat' students:

> With 15 minutes left at the end of the fourth class session, I asked the students about their problems in English and why they were multiple repeaters ... There was some hesitation ... but then one student asked if she could reply in Arabic ... therefore many more were encouraged to take part in the conversation. I had to allocate turns ... What the students said in this session convinced me that I needed to allocate more than just a 15-minute chat ... I then asked their permission to interview them [individually] for 15 minutes after class (Troudi, 2007: 164).

Here talking to students (a 'group chat') leads to later interviews and then to a viable action research plan. It is also useful to note the apparently simple but important decision to encourage the learners to talk and reflect in their L1 (Arabic). There are plenty of other useful accounts of how talking to learners leads to changes in methodology and curriculum. For example, Gulyamova et al. (2014: 50) show how talking to and involving learners 'kick-started' the project:

> Designing the third and fourth years of the curriculum involved the team in rethinking the approach to research that future English teachers might usefully take. Instead of persisting with the longstanding tradition of knowledge-oriented research into literary and linguistic topics, we agreed to incorporate courses in classroom investigation, thereby encouraging students to look into aspects of their teaching during their school-based teaching experience in Year 4. This, in turn, kick-started the process of reflection on practice. The result has been a different kind of final research paper, which teachers and students in all participating institutions have now bought into.

The following vignette also shows the value of taking account of learner voices as they reflect on their learning in 'learner diaries'. These learner reflections provide an important form of evidence for developing an appropriate methodology (in this case developing learners' metacognitive skills):

BUSHRA AHMED KHURRAM (PAKISTAN)

Context

The participant in the data below was a first year Bachelor of Arts (BA) student studying a compulsory English course at a public sector university of Pakistan. She took part in the first cycle of an action research study undertaken to investigate how metacognition of reading strategies could be promoted in university level ESL students in Pakistan. The first cycle spanned a period of four months. The main data sources of the study were interviews, think-aloud protocols, a researcher journal, and also learner diaries. The latter were especially important in gaining a reflective perspective on the learners' meta-cognitive development. The extracts below are taken from one student's learner diary. The first extract was written by the student a month after the start of the study, the second two months into the study and the third towards the end of the study.

Data

EXTRACT ONE

After filling the questionnaire to analyze the techniques we know and don't know that help in reading, I actually realized that "Oh My God! Was I dead all this time?" There were so many about which I never heard of. I didn't know that prediction and activating prior knowledge existed, forget the use. In my mind there was a little concept of being attentive while reading, but the concept of paying attention to the title, or thinking before reading was something very new . . . After knowing that my average was 2.1, I was amazed how much there is to reading and how little I knew.

EXTRACT TWO

There are certain strategies which are new to me like prediction of title, using prior knowledge etc. since they are new, I don't have a command over them and because of lack of time-phase most of the time I forget to use it.

EXTRACT THREE

I used my prior knowledge and prediction that if climate change is talked upon, usually global warming will be focused on as previously we were asked to evaluate changes in weather if any and changes are because of global warming. Secondly, if conflict is mentioned then maybe lack of resources and fight over resources is discussed in the text as I know that it is proposed that the third world war is supposed to break out on scarcity of water. Thirdly, if cooperation is discussed then it must be regarding achieving sustainability. I want to find out what are the risks of conflict and advantages of cooperation so that I can frame my mind.

Comment

In the extracts above the student is reflecting on her awareness and use of reading strategies. Her accounts illustrate the changes that occurred in her awareness and use of the reading strategies during the course of the study. There are some interesting features about her description and reflection on the learning process.

The first extract shows that the student explicitly reflected on the gap in her knowledge with respect to the reading strategies. Her self-conscious evaluation of the gap she noticed in her prior knowledge of reading strategies is evident from the phrases she used in her diary: 'Oh my God! Was I dead all this time?', 'I did not know . . . forget the use' and 'was something very new.' It seems that she gained awareness of some of the strategies of reading such as prediction and activating prior knowledge on filling in a reading questionnaire during one of the lessons. She also seems to have realized that there is a lot in the domain of reading that she was unaware of. In a typical Pakistani reading class it is often the case that the students passively 'receive' instructions and do not develop a sense of self 'as an active cognitive agent'. Consequently, they do not reflect on their own learning and performance. The first extract suggests that the student initiated reflection on her knowledge of reading strategies and that she valued gaining awareness of the reading strategies she could employ during reading.

The second extract shows the student consciously reflecting on the experience of forgetting to use newly introduced reading strategies. She is becoming more familiar with the strategies that can be used during reading. However, this awareness is not yet translating into actual use. This kind of reflection on the current state of her metacognitive awareness was helpful for me (the teacher researcher) in realizing that she and perhaps other students needed further time and practice in becoming more familiar with the introduced strategies.

In the third extract the student reports her reading process. The extract reveals students' active participation in the reading process as she explicitly related the text she was to read with her prior knowledge on the topic. On the basis of this, it seems that the student generated a prediction that the text might discuss the issues of 'global warming', 'lack of resources and fight over resources' and 'sustainability'. Her reflection on her reading process shows that she was aware of her purpose of reading as she reported what she wanted to get out of the reading. This suggests that the student used the input on reading strategies provided in the lessons during her reading.

Overall, the extracts suggest the value of making students aware of and reflect on the reading strategies they use or could use during reading. The extracts also suggest the value of using learner diaries as a pedagogical tool as it could raise students' awareness and help them reflect and understand better the learning process or their progress.

In this vignette we can see the close connection between the students' reflections and the teacher-researchers' decisions (e.g. whether to push on and introduce more reading strategies or to reinforce those metacognitive strategies already introduced). Involving the learners in the research and focusing on their reflections feeds into making the intervention more appropriate (in the class-by-class process). This reflective data also forms the basis of what claims can be made about this topic (what the practitioner can say about how best to develop learners' metacognitive strategies) in the wider research project.

In this next piece of data, the learners are adults in South Korea. The researcher (George Skuse) is drawing on the work of Brookfield and Preskill (1999) in encouraging adult students to come up with ground rules for talk in the classroom. Brookfield and Preskill (1999: 44) point out that 'we cannot assume that students possess the social and communicative skills necessary for collaboration' and that sometimes 'these need to be taught'. In the following extract the students are in the process of generating their ground rules for talk and offering reasons why the rules are important. The following excerpt shows A, E and S generating the rule 'respect each other' and discussing why respect is important:

Extract 9.1

```
225. A:  I think we need to respect about each other.
226. E:  Mm, so [inaudible] not like discussion, like
227.     debate haha, so you can respect each other, so
228.     show respect
229. S:  Mm, yes so what to write down?
230. E:  Show respect.
231. A:  If you don't respect each other, I don't remember
232.     word.
233. E:  Maybe I think it uh make the discussion poor. Uh
234.     what do you think, the reason for show respect?
235. S:  respect, uh, natural thing I think. Natural
236. E:  Oh yeah
237. S:  Without respect, we can't hear freely our ideas
238.     because without respect, patience, uh respect, it
239.     can be a little thick atmosphere, thick
240.     atmosphere, and um [inaudible]
```

The excerpt above demonstrates how students were able to talk together, reflect on the rules and express their opinions. It is also worth noting the collaborative nature of this talk (as they build on each other's turns). This generates a list of 'ground rules' (e.g. that ideas may be challenged and that they should ask many questions, listen actively, give reasons, participate actively and seek agreement).

So far, in Bushra's vignette we have seen the value and impact of involving learners in reflecting on their progress within an AR research project. In George's data, we can see the value of getting learners to talk about and reflect on their learning (as part of a wider practitioner research project). In the following vignette, Ian Nakamura explores the value of switching roles (in an interview with a student at a university in Japan) and its effect in making space for reflection. More specifically, he allows space for the interviewee (the student) to ask questions and lead the talk. As well as integrating reflective journalling into the programme, Ian encourages teachers to focus on the nature and value of classroom interaction.

IAN NAKAMURA VIGNETTE (JAPAN)

Context: Interview Between a Tutor and an In-service Teacher Learner

This account explores the surrounding discourse environment of a decision-making moment when the interviewer (T) shifts the focus of the talk away from his questions to the teacher learner (TL). The excerpts to be discussed come from an ongoing collection of talks between a teacher trainer and several MA in TESOL TLs who are in-service teachers. They meet at the end of each semester. All of the TLs have taken a course on analyzing classroom interactions which includes reflective journalling.

Data: Interview in Three Phases

The interviews usually last for 20–25 minutes. This particular interview is the third time that they have met. The opening lines of each phase of a single talk are discussed.

PHASE 1: OPENING QUESTION BY THE TEACHER-INTERVIEWER

After greetings and small talk, the main question of the interview is asked by the teacher (T). The TL explains some changes that she has noticed since they last met. The discussion is organized in question-answer pairs: T's questions and TL's answers.

```
T:    And ah (.) how how has it been going this semester. Ah
      has anything changed from the past when you teach (.)
      in the second semester (.) reading or translation?
TL:   Uhm (1.0) I think well that uh in the same freshman
      class uhm students were more interested in (.) reading
      literature than other years.
```

PHASE 2: TRANSITION FROM THE INTERVIEWER'S QUESTIONS TO THE INTERVIEWEE'S QUESTIONS

After about 15 minutes of talking about her classroom teaching, there seems to be little else to say on this topic. Instead of shifting to another of his planned topics, T makes a move to create space for the TL to talk about what she is interested in.

```
T:   So let's switch a little bit and ah last few minutes um
     do you have any do you have some questions?
TL:  Ah for my research
```

PHASE 3: STUDENT ASKS A QUESTION

Here is an opportunity for the student to nominate a topic of immediate concern. After all, she is not only expected (in the programme) to reflect on her teaching, but also to start collecting data for her thesis. This new phase starts with a question about procedure.

```
S:   Oh. . . . Can I uh . . . do you usually . . . let
     students write their names down?
TL:  Um . . . nowadays um . . . it seems questionnaires
     . . . um one type of questionnaires they do write their
     names down (NB: He goes on to mention anonymous
     questionnaires are commonly used for large-scale
     studies).
```

The talk continues and delves deeper into what the TL is thinking of doing. T minimizes his responses and gives the floor to her to explain.

```
TL:  Oh. (.) Can I uh (.) do you usually (.) let students
     write their names down?
TL:  If I know the names so some students study very hard
T:   Right right
TL:  I want to know what they tho[ught
T:                              [Yeah yeah]
TL:  because they
T:   Yeah
TL:  made efforts in this cla[ss
T:                           [Yeah]
TL:  so I want to know what they're thinking about my class
```

Commentary: Co-accomplishment of Knowledge and Action

The organization and direction of the interview change to meet the need for a new topic to keep the interaction going. By creating space for the student to nominate the next topic, she supplies valuable insights that might not have been mentioned otherwise.

Working with the student's thoughts about teaching and research is beneficial to both parties. The student receives information, formulates a plan of action, and justifies it. The teacher sees how his role has expanded beyond asking questions. His actions include: (1) Find out how the student has changed her teaching. (2) Find out what concerns

> her. (3) Provide relevant information. (4) Create an opportunity to talk about what she wants to do (without giving judgmental comments).
>
> How different the talk would have been if it stuck solely to the teacher's questions and the student's answers to them. In the end, what seemed to fit this interaction was not necessarily what the teacher wanted to know, but what the student needed to know.

Talking to learners is always a good idea (whether they are language learners or TLs), whether you are engaging in what Wallace calls 'normal reflective practice' (1991: 56) or whether you are engaged in full-scale research. In terms of the latter, Zandian (2016) is an excellent example of a thesis which researches *with* language learners and makes sure that they are both involved in and informed about the research. There is detail (p. 91ff) of follow-up sessions where she shows how children were encouraged to reflect on the research they took part in. In the findings section (pp. 234–257) she also shares the findings from children's reflection on the process of the research as well as on the pedagogic tasks (see also Pinter and Zandian, 2015). In addition, Appendix 1 provides a task that gets learners to reflect. It can be used with language learners or trainee teachers.

9.4 Options and Tools

This last section furthers our understanding of what specific types of reflection and what type of *tools* might help encourage reflection for research purposes. We consider various kinds of tools, such as prompts for reflection, repertory grids and reflective tasks. In the first vignette of this section, George Skuse is talking about a form of practitioner research called design-based research. We featured some of his data in 9.3 above. Here, he is talking about four different kinds of reflection that he uses to engage with the research process:

GEORGE SKUSE VIGNETTE (SOUTH KOREA)

Context

I am using a form of design-based research (DBR) based on the work of McKenney and Reeves (2013). The focus of my research is the design of a pedagogic intervention aimed at improving L2 learner discussion by helping learners to achieve exploratory talk for language learning (ETLL). It is hoped that the adoption of such exploratory talk will help make the students more effective and resourceful in their L2 discussion. An important part of my DBR process has been to include reflection on my classroom methodology (as practitioner) as well as my data collection and analysis (research methodology). McKenney and

Reeves offer a method of reflection that has been helpful for me. They differentiate four different triggers for reflection: point, line, triangle and circle reflection.

POINT, LINE, TRIANGLE AND CIRCLE REFLECTION

In point reflection, I reflect on a particular data extract and look for unplanned insight. To give you an example, as part of my research, I designed an activity in which students practise disagreeing (a characteristic of ETLL) and used classroom transcripts to analyze whether revision of the activity was needed. By revisiting the transcript, I was able to gain further insight. Specifically, I found that the language produced during the activity contained more of the characteristics of quality discussion than disagreeing alone; students were also able to give opinions, offer reasons and scaffold each other's language, meaning the activity offered more benefit than the stated aim of simply practising disagreeing.

Line reflection involves investigating a particular instance during the intervention and considering the likely social norms, related to 'actor, process and product' in order to improve the intervention. As part of my intervention, I asked my adult students to make discussion ground rules. I was worried that students would consider the concept of making rules somewhat elementary and, therefore, not take the activity seriously. To remedy this, as the teacher, I pointed out that I wanted students not to include rules that start with 'don't' and instead focus on things that students can 'do' in order to have quality discussions. Line reflection allowed me to pinpoint this as a critical moment, as by writing only 'do' rules, students avoided more arbitrary actions they should 'not do' and focused instead on rules that reflected conduct they would hope to embody in a high standard of L2 academic discussion.

Triangle reflection requires considering an issue by looking at it from the perspective of different participants and reflecting on what can be learned from those different perspectives. My intervention includes eight strategy training 'sessions' and I used triangle reflection to focus on the issue of how many and how often strategy sessions should be taught over a ten-week course. During the first iteration the eight strategy sessions were taught simply at points that felt appropriate. However, as the research developed, by using triangle reflection, I considered student suggestions (e.g. having a longer time for some design elements). Getting student insight into the sequence and timing of sessions was helpful. For example, one student felt that while the strategy training sessions were useful, she emphasized the need for book work in class, saying 'Yes activity is ok, but I like writing, I think using the book is very useful'. My field notes suggested that having the sessions once a week, run over one lesson at the end of a textbook unit provided a point that was not overly intrusive. While the interview and field notes data is by no means conclusive evidence,

> this reflection allowed me to further consider how I integrate strategy training sessions into the course.
>
> Finally, circle reflection represents <u>consideration of the research methods used</u> in order to identify and address issues. I was somewhat disappointed with my field notes, as they rarely gave much insight into the success or failure of any part of the intervention. Notes were often overly general, for example, 'students were engaged in the activities quite a lot', and needed to be ethnographically richer. Circle reflection made me aware that I needed to try and note more specific and detailed points of interest that arise throughout the sessions.

This vignette reveals detail of a process of structured reflection. Point, line, triangle and circle reflections help this researcher to sustain a more focused and critical thinking approach to reflection during his research process. These four triggers for reflection are among other possible choices. Each practitioner/ researcher will make decisions about the selection and timing of such triggers, lenses or tools. We want to make the argument here that the conscious adoption of different forms of reflection can produce insights that fuel further changes in either practitioner methodology or research methodology. By adopting different kinds of reflection at different times (here 'point', 'line', 'triangle' and 'circle' reflective lens), George is able to gain insight into different aspects of his developing practitioner research. Point and line reflection encourage a close look at evidence and data. Triangle reflection encourages a wider angle on social processes, recognizing that different participants have multiple perspectives on the classroom. We are reminded here of the kind of thinking skills that de Bono promotes (see de Bono, 1992). For example, triangle reflection is rather like de Bono's OPV (Other People's Views). See also de Bono's six coloured thinking hats in Appendix 2.

In the pre-service teaching context, Korthagen (1992) was one of the first to argue that reflection was dealt with in a rather vague way and that there needed to be more detailed information about tasks and tools designed to encourage reflection. The following (Table 9.1) is a summary of three reflective task types (from Korthagen, 1992: 266) which we have found a helpful catalyst for different forms of reflection:

TABLE 9.1

The wall	• The wall is where relationships between educational goals and values are explored. This technique aims at promoting reflection on the relationships between educational goals and values.
	• Each student teacher in the group receives a number of paper 'bricks' with statements about educational goals or values. Some of the bricks are blank and have to be filled in by the prospective teacher.

- The task is to build your own 'teaching wall', placing the bricks with the most important principles at the bottom, and the others on top. The wall is glued onto a piece of paper.
- The student teacher can also draw a 'waste-paper basket' in which useless bricks are deposited.

Columns

- Columns helps teachers explore the relationships between educational goals and actual teaching behaviour.
- Each student teacher chooses one class in which he or she teaches. Four columns are drawn on a large sheet of paper. In the first column the student teacher enters a general goal he or she thinks is important in education (perhaps selected from the 'wall').
- In the second column the student teacher enters a specific goal for the next series of lessons with that class, derived from the general goal in the first column. In the third column the student teacher puts down a further specification of the goal to be reached in the next lesson.
- The fourth and last column is filled in after the lesson, and based on, for example, an audio recording of the lesson, the student teacher comments on achieving the goal.
- In seminar sessions, the student teachers show their columns to each other, discuss them and make further columns.

Arrows

- Arrows also helps raise awareness of goals, pupil characteristics and teaching strategies.
- A pupil characteristic (e.g. 'dependent') is linked to an educational goal (e.g. 'seeing relationships between the subject matter and everyday life'). Both are written down on separate cards. Then a paper arrow is placed between the two cards and the student teacher has to fill in the strategy he or she would use in order to attain that goal in the case of a student with that specific characteristic.
- Group discussions on the strategies promote further reflection. This tool is useful to highlight the role of subjective theories in teacher behaviour. Asking questions about the how and why of the strategies written on the arrows enables sharing and discussing subjective theories among participating students. This often leads to the restructuring of the student teachers' subjective theories.

These techniques work well with pre-service teachers who are engaged in teaching practice (TP) and can reveal conflict between, for example, goals, beliefs and actual teaching. This in turn can lead student teachers to change their views, beliefs and practices. The exchanges among teachers often lead to interesting discussion as they begin to connect and relate classroom actions and outcomes to beliefs.

One final tool is the repertory grid ('rep-grid'). It is particularly helpful in bringing tacit expert knowledge to the surface. Originally proposed by Kelly in the 1950s as a methodological component of his 'Personal Construct Theory', the rep-grid provides the basis for a reflective conversation and allows a practitioner to distinguish one experience from another. The repertory grid procedure involves several stages, beginning with a development stage, where the parameters of the research and the grid are decided. There then follows an administration stage, where 'elements' and 'constructs' are rated by the interviewer. In the final stages the grid data are analyzed and interpreted by the researcher.

The grid usually has four parts and, once completed, looks like a matrix/table with rows, columns and 'boxes' for ratings. This might include the topic, elements (instances, examples or pieces of data related to the topic), constructs (terms interviewee uses to make sense of the elements) and a set of ratings of elements on the constructs. In Korthagen's version, each student teacher writes three individual pupil names on three different cards. The teacher chooses one of the three pupils and explains how they think they are different from the other two. The teacher then formulates a construct that adequately describes the perceived difference (in a word or phrase). Over several iterations, a list of personal constructs is generated. We would recommend Easterby-Smith (1980) and Tan and Hunter (2002) as good initial guides. In more sustained research, the rep-grid can be completed during a speech event resembling a conversational interview, where the practitioner construes and interprets his or her experience of a chosen focus (topic). See Mann (2016: 110–113) for a fuller account of the use of a rep-grid by Ceren Oztabay in North Cyprus.

9.5 Conclusion

This chapter has explored the relationship between reflection and research. We can make a distinction (see Borg above) between the two but in fact they are often very closely related. Reflection may lead to teacher research; it is always part of teacher research, and teacher-researchers find different tools and triggers to shape their own reflections and also the reflections of research participants.

We have focused particularly on AR in this chapter as one of the most important forms of teacher research. Despite the possible problems listed above, most teachers find action research stimulating and rewarding:

> Action research is intended to support practitioner researchers in coping with the challenges and problems of practice and carrying through innovations in a reflective way. Experience with action research over more than 30 years has shown that teachers are able to do this successfully and can achieve remarkable results when given opportunities and support.
>
> *Altrichter et al., 2013: 6*

It is not always easy to get started and find a viable focus, but there is a strong sense of ownership and renewed professional purpose. As we have said, reading about AR helps, but we shouldn't become too entrenched in simply reading. There is no substitute for getting started. Perhaps begin by talking to learners or other teachers, or begin with using a recording or video of a class to establish a possible focus. You will then be in a position to narrow that focus and devise a series of steps or stages in order to begin the investigation.

Collaboration can certainly help to sustain research, as Dario Banegas's vignette shows. Consider who you are able to collaborate with and how this might practically be organized. Collaboration is possible with teachers in your institution, but also within professional organizations and online communities of practice. In other words, it is increasingly possible to work collaboratively with people further afield (indeed in different countries). It is always important to see language learners as possible collaborators, and involving and talking to them is often the first stepping stone to AR.

Those of us who have roles to play in language teacher education often started our research and teacher education careers with small-scale pieces of teacher research on Masters programmes. Indeed MA programmes often include a module on AR or at least on teacher research (see Pennington, 1996). Programmes may also require, or at least encourage, teachers to engage in AR for one of the assignments or assessments on the course. One caveat is that there is not much evidence that this is sustained after the programme itself. As Tsui comments, many studies 'were conducted in the context of a teacher education program, in which student teachers were required to conduct an action research project as partial fulfilment of the program requirements' (2009: 31). In other words, teachers often complete AR projects for assessed work but when they return to their teaching contexts, AR may not be possible for the reasons outlined above. Burns (2009) includes an overview of the way action research is promoted in teacher education programmes.

More positively perhaps, AR at MA level can sometimes lead to valuable PhD research. We read this account recently, where Emily Edwards, who has been part of an AR programme, reflects on her trajectory from first encounters with action research to publishing and then a PhD application:

> Reflecting on how I have been enabled to pursue these opportunities, I think much can be attributed to the development of my research, writing and presentation skills during my participation in the AR programme. When I reported on my research, I wrote: 'I have had an invaluable induction into classroom-based research methods, equipping me with useful skills to continue my postgraduate studies.' ... Indeed, having collected and analyzed my data and experienced the report drafting process as part of the AR programme, I was then able to attempt a longer peer-reviewed article, which was accepted for publication in the *English Australia Journal*. In turn, my publications provided very valuable support for my research degree application.
>
> *Burns, 2013: 78*

The next chapter looks more specifically at the 'what, why and how' of doing research on reflective practice, considering the content and methodology of some of the more recent studies, before looking to the future with suggestions for projects which may be of interest to both research students and early career researchers.

References

Allwright, D. (1993). Integrating 'research' and 'pedagogy': appropriate criteria and practical possibilities. In J. Edge and K. Richards (eds), *Teachers Develop Teachers Research* (pp. 125–135). Oxford: Heinemann.

Allwright, D. and Bailey, K.M. (1991). *Focus on the language classroom: an introduction to classroom research for language teachers.* New York: Cambridge University Press.

Allwright, D. and Hanks, J. (2009). *The developing language learner: an introduction to exploratory practice.* Basingstoke: Palgrave Macmillan.

Altrichter, H., Feldman, A., Posch, P. and Somekh, B. (2013). *Teachers investigate their work: an introduction to action research across the professions.* London: Routledge.

Altrichter, H., Posch, P. and Somekh, B. (1993). *Teachers investigate their work: an introduction to the methods of action research.* London: Routledge.

Bailey, K.M. (1997). Reflective teaching: situating our stories. *Asian Journal of English Language Teaching*, 7, 1–19.

Banegas, D., Pavese, A., Velázquez, A. and Vélez, S. M. (2013). Teacher professional development through collaborative action research: impact on foreign English-language teaching and learning. *Educational Action Research*, 21(2), 185–201.

Barnes, D. (1975). *From communication to curriculum.* Harmondsworth: Penguin.

Borg, S. (2010). State-of-the-Art Article. Language Teacher Research Engagement. *Language Teaching*, 43(4), 391–429.

Brookfield, S.D. and Preskill, S. (1999). *Discussion as a way of teaching* (Vol. 85). San Francisco: Jossey-Bass.

Burns, A. (1999). *Collaborative action research for English language teachers.* Cambridge: Cambridge University Press.

Burns, A. (2005). Action research: an evolving paradigm? *Language Teaching*, 38(2), 57–74.

Burns, A. (2009). Action research in second language teacher education. In A. Burns and J. Richards (eds), *The Cambridge guide to second language teacher education* (pp. 289–297). New York: Cambridge University Press.

Burns, A. (2010). *Doing action research in English language teaching: a guide for practitioners.* New York: Routledge.

Burns, A. (2013). Innovation through action research and teacher-initiated change. In K. Hyland and L.L.C. Wong (eds). *Innovation and change in English language education* (pp. 90–105). Abingdon: Routledge.

Buzan, T. and Buzan, B. (1996). *The mind map book: how to use radiant thinking to maximise your brain's untapped potential.* London: Plume.

Cochran-Smith, M. and Lytle, S.L. (1999). Relationships of knowledge and practice: teacher learning in communities. *Review of Research in Education*, 24, 249–305.

De Bono, E. (1992). *Serious creativity: using the power of lateral thinking to create new ideas.* New York: Harper Collins.

Dörnyei, Z. (2007). *Research methods in applied linguistics.* Oxford University Press.

Easterby-Smith, M. (1980). How to use repertory grids in HRD. *Journal of European Industrial Training*, 4(2), 2–32.

Edge, J. (1992). *Cooperative development.* Harlow: Longman.

Edge, J. (ed.). (2001). *Action research.* Alexandria, VA: TESOL.

Gulyamova, J., Irgasheva, S. and Bolitho, R. (2014). Professional development through curriculum reform: the Uzbekistan experience. In D. Hayes (ed.), *Innovations in the continuing professional development of English language teachers* (pp. 45–64). London: British Council.

Kemmis, S. and McTaggart, R. (1988). *The action research planner* (3rd edn). Geelong, Victoria: Deakin University Press.

Korthagen, F.A. (1992). Techniques for stimulating reflection in teacher education seminars. *Teaching and Teacher Education*, 8(3), 265–274.

Mann, S. (1997). Focusing circles and mind mapping. *IATEFL Newsletter*, 136, 18–19.

Mann, S. (1999). Opening the insider's eye: starting action research. *The Language Teacher*, 23(12), 11–13.

Mann, S. (2005). The language teacher's development. *Language Teaching*, 38(3), 103–118.

Mann, S. (2016). *The research interview: reflexivity and reflective practice in research processes.* London: Palgrave Macmillan.

Mann, S. and Edge. J. (2013). Innovation as action new-in-context: an introduction to the PRESETT collection. In J. Edge and S. Mann (eds), *Innovation in pre-service teacher education and training* (pp. 8–22). London: British Council.

Mathew, R. (2000). Teacher-research approach to curriculum renewal and teacher development. In R. Mathew, R. L. Eapen and J. Tharu (eds), *The language curriculum: dynamics of change. Volume I: The outsider perspective* (pp. 6–21). Hyderabad: Orient Longman.

McKenney, S. and Reeves, T. C. (2013). *Conducting educational design research.* London: Routledge.

Nunan, D. (1990). Action research in the language classroom. In J. Richards and D. Nunan (eds), *Second language teacher education* (pp. 62–81). New York: Cambridge University Press.

Nunan, D. (1993). Action research in language education. In J. Edge and K. Richards (eds), *Teachers develop teachers research: papers on classroom research and teacher development* (pp. 39–50). Oxford: Heinemann International.

Pennington, M. (1996). When input becomes intake: tracing the sources of teachers' attitude change. In D. Freeman and J. Richards (eds), *Teacher learning in language teaching* (pp. 320–350). Cambridge: Cambridge University Press.

Pinter, A. and Zandian, S. (2015). 'I thought it would be tiny little one phrase that we said, in a huge big pile of papers': children's reflections on their involvement in participatory research. *Qualitative Research*, 15(2), 235–250.

Rochsantiningsih, D. (2004). *Enhancing professional development of Indonesian high school teachers through action research* (Doctoral dissertation). Macquarie University.

Schön, D.A. (1983). *The reflective practitioner: how professionals think in action.* Aldershot: Ashgate Publishing.

Sherrington, T. (2013). Teachers as researchers: the ultimate form of professional development. *The Guardian*, downloaded 12. 12. 2013 at www.theguardian.com/teacher-network/teacher-blog/2013/feb/22/action-research-teaching-education-professional-development

Tan, F.B. and Hunter, M.G. (2002). The repertory grid technique: a method for the study of cognition in information systems. *MIS Quarterly*, 39–57.

Thorne, C. and Qiang, W. (1996). Action research in language teacher education. *ELT Journal*, 50(3), 254–262.

Tinker Sachs, G.T. (ed.). (2002). *Action research in English language teaching.* Department of English and Communication, City University of Hong Kong.

Troudi, S. (2007). Negotiating with multiple repeaters. In C. Coombe and L. Barlow (eds), *ELT teacher research in the Middle East* (pp. 161–172). Alexandria, Virginia: TESOL Publications.

Tsui, A.B.M. (2009). Teaching expertise: approaches, perspectives and characterizations. In A. Burns and J.C. Richards (eds), *The Cambridge guide to second language teacher education* (pp. 190–197). Cambridge: Cambridge University Press.

Valeri, L. (1997). What do students think of group work? In A. Burns and S. Hood (eds), *Teachers' voices 2: teaching disparate learner groups* (pp. 37–39). Sydney: NCELTR, Macquarie University.

Wallace, M. (1991). *Training foreign language teachers.* Cambridge: Cambridge University Press.

Wallace, M. (1998). *Action research for language teachers.* Cambridge: Cambridge University Press.

Wang, Q. and Zhang, H. (2014). Promoting teacher autonomy through university–school collaborative action research. *Language Teaching Research*, 18(2), 222–241.

Zandian, S. (2016). *Children's perceptions of intercultural issues: an exploration into an Iranian context* (Unpublished PhD thesis). University of Warwick. Available at http://wrap.warwick.ac.uk/77629/ (Accessed 1.12.16).

Zeichner K.M. and Noffke, S.E. (2001). Practitioner research. In V. Richardson (ed.), *Handbook of research on teaching* (4th ed., pp. 298–330). Washington: American Educational Research Association.

10
Researching Reflective Practice

10.1 Introduction

In this chapter we consider some of the current trends which have emerged in RP research and then look towards future possibilities. We are interested in both the focus of research and the methodologies which have been used, and which are likely to be developed in the future. Our aim in Chapter 10 is to give readers a sense of 'where we are at' in reflective practice research, develop a perspective on how research might inform other aspects of teacher education and professional development, and give suggestions for possible future projects in areas where, for example, there is a paucity of research or a need for more research. In particular, we suggest areas for future research which might be of benefit to, for example, doctoral students and early career researchers.

In section 10.1, we present a summary of the main themes of this book; 10.2 offers a brief overview of current research, while 10.3 makes some predictions concerning future research on reflective practice. In 10.4, we provide some concluding remarks.

We open the chapter with a summary of the main ideas which we have presented in this book as a means of providing a backdrop for the chapter and to position our work with other research in the field. We present this summary as a list of the main themes which we have covered and which have reoccurred in various chapters.

Theme 1: How Does Reflection 'Get Done'?

One of the starting-points for this book is the position we adopted on the current orthodoxy concerning reflection. In Chapter 1, we demonstrated that there is no shortage of articles and books highlighting how important reflection is for teachers. This is the (widely) accepted position among teacher educators and course providers. Our concern is that there is insufficient evidence of how reflection gets done and a lack of evidence of how to do it. Theme 1, then, has two elements: (a) we need to see evidence of practitioners doing reflection by collecting samples of reflective practice from as many different contexts as possible; (b) we need to embed reflection in teacher education by showing student teachers and practitioners how to do it: reflection needs to be taught.

In Chapter 4, we went to some lengths to demonstrate how reflection might be operationalized in teacher education. This process entails improving understandings of reflection, devising methods and approaches of sharing reflective commentaries, and making the whole experience of reflection more deliberate and conscious. Of paramount importance in this theme has been the use of technology to promote reflection (see, for example, Sandra Morales' use of online blogs; Paul Slater's use of an online discussion forum; Phil Saxon's use of Edmodo).

Theme 2: Reflection Needs to be Data-led and Evidence-based

A key argument running through the book, and one which is linked to theme 1, is that we need better evidence of how reflection gets done. There are two aspects to this: (a) data showing how reflection gets done is essential to promoting deeper understandings of reflective processes and for enhancing research on reflection; (b) data are necessary so that practitioners have something to reflect *on*.

Every chapter in the book presents data in the form of vignettes or extracts demonstrating reflective processes from around the world. Many of the extracts are from online sources, once again highlighting the importance of technology in reflection. By data, we mean anything which shows evidence of reflection or which helps professionals do reflection. Examples include online blog posts, extracts of classroom interaction, interviews, conversations with students and journal entries.

Theme 3: Reflection Can Promote Detailed Understandings Of Context

One of the hallmarks of effective teaching is an understanding of local context. Effective teachers use their detailed knowledge of context in, for example, their choice of materials, adaptation of tasks and choice of feedback strategy. In Chapter 5, we discussed 'reflection in the wild' and considered how teachers working alone or as part of an informal or professional network might generate detailed understandings of context. Through reflection and dialogue with others in the same context, we explored how professional development can be informed and influenced by local understandings of context.

Theme 4: There is a Case for Having More Spoken, Dialogic Reflection

One of the central themes of the book is the need for more spoken, dialogic reflection (see Chapters 7 and 8), an argument made not only by ourselves, but by many others as referenced throughout the book. There are several reasons for making the case for spoken, dialogic reflection. First, we note that most teacher education courses use written reflection, which is then assessed (see theme 7 below). We question the reliance on this practice, since it is often seen as an assessment criterion, something which has to be done to pass a course. It rarely, we suggest, promotes deep, interactive reflection – the kind of reflection needed to promote learning. Second, we present evidence which highlights the ways in which spoken reflection opens up space, allows alternatives to be discussed and results in deeper understandings. Third, spoken reflection allows the use of a much wider range of reflective tools (such as video) which can be tailored to local context. Fourth, using socio-cultural theories of learning and development, we demonstrate how professional learning can be enhanced though dialogues which are mediated by language and other artefacts, such as technology. Dialogue allows meanings to be co-constructed and new understandings to emerge; it also allows ideas, issues and puzzles to be shared and discussed.

Theme 5: Collaboration With Peers is Important for Effective Reflection

Related to theme 4 is the importance of collaboration, seen here as a key element of reflective processes. In Chapter 1, we observed that reflection is often a solitary process, especially when it is assessed. We advocated the use of professional collaboration through online discussion forums, chat rooms, blogs and face-to-face interactions. In 7.4, we introduced the notion of cooperative development as a tool for fostering reflective talk. In Chapters 5 and 8, we demonstrated how teacher self-help groups can work together to develop closer understandings of their context and identify issues which are of common concern. A key element of collaboration is the way in which tools and artefacts can act as a catalyst and help promote more systematic and focused professional dialogue. Of particular value to collaboration and a more dialogic approach to reflection in general is the use of video, transcripts and recordings, though we also commend the use of 'snapshot' recordings – short, untranscribed teaching moments which can be used for collaborative talking-points.

Theme 6: We Need Appropriate Tools for Reflection

In Mann and Walsh (2013) – and throughout this book – we make the case for the need for and use of appropriate tools for reflection. By 'appropriate' we mean fit for purpose; tools which are fit for purpose enable practitioners to collect evidence appropriate to their stage of development. For example, we would normally expect the reflective tools used in week 4 of a CELTA course to be different from those used in week 1 because trainees are more aware and have a better sense of what constitutes good practice. Similarly, teachers with many years of experience would be using tools which differ from the ones used by those just starting out.

By using the term 'appropriate tools', we are also implying that they must be suited to the context in which they are used. Much in the same way that materials are adapted to local contexts, tools should also be tailored to the context they are being used in. Perhaps the most important consideration when tailoring tools to local context is the extent to which tools generate data; the whole point of having appropriate tools is to collect evidence on which to reflect.

Throughout the book, we have highlighted a range of tools including journals, diaries, the use of narrative, video recordings, stimulated recall and screen capture software and self-evaluation frameworks. For a full list, the reader is referred to Appendix 3.

Theme 7: The Relationship Between the Assessment of Teaching and Reflection Needs to be Better Understood

Without wishing to dwell too much on this theme since it has been given a very thorough treatment in various places throughout the book, we would like to emphasize our concern over the extent to which reflection has become synonymous with assessment on many teacher education programmes. For anyone following a pre- or in-service teacher education course, showing evidence of reflection is a *sine qua non* for passing that course. Course tutors typically look for evidence of reflection in written assignments which are assessed. Students may use a range of strategies to satisfy this course require-ment, including 'faking it' (Hobbs, 2007), tailoring their reflection to the course tutor who is assessing the assignment, or even writing reflective commentaries before teaching (Delaney, 2015). Further research is needed on the impact of assessment on reflection and on identifying alternative approaches to assessing teacher development.

There is a clear and pressing need for the relationship between reflection and assessment to be more fully understood. The question which immediately comes to mind is: should reflection be assessed at all? And if so, to what extent? And how? Without wishing to suggest that reflection should not be assessed at all, we do highlight the significance of the issue and raise it as something for further discussion and debate. This is especially true of courses which lead to certification such as CELTA and DELTA, but applies equally to, for example, BA and MA degrees which have a teaching practicum. Essentially, there is a strong and pressing need for the assessment of reflection to be problematized, debated and possibly modified.

10.2 RP Research: What, Why and How?

In this section we review the current state of play regarding research on reflective practice, before turning, in 10.3, to a consideration of possible future research directions. The section is organized into three sub-sections, following the questions which are typically asked at the outset of any research project:

- **What** is the focus of the research (which research questions does it set out to answer)?
- **Why** is the research needed, what is its rationale (what gaps exist in the current body of research)?
- **How** will data be collected and analyzed (what methodology will be used and why)?

One of the most recent surveys of reflective practice research was conducted by Tom Farrell (2016). In his article, 116 published studies were surveyed between 2009 and 2014. In each of the studies surveyed, TESOL teachers were encouraged to reflect on their practice. Farrell's overall findings suggest that teachers on both pre- and in-service courses were interested in and benefited from reflecting on their practice. In addition, reflection was found to increase awareness and motivation, and led to existing practices being challenged, especially when teachers noted tensions between their 'philosophy, principles, theory and practice both inside and outside the language classroom' (Farrell, 2016: 241).

We now consider examples of what research on RP might be undertaken, why it is needed and how it could be done.

Research on Reflection: What?

Supervision. Given that for most teachers, the most important training they receive is their initial preparation course, it is hardly surprising that there have been a huge number of studies focusing on pre-service teacher education (see Chapter 3). Recent estimates suggest that there are more than 11,000 participants taking the most popular TESOL certificate courses: CELTA and Trinity Certificate (Brandt, 2008). For most participants, this will be the only training they receive and one which will have a huge impact on their future professional development, beliefs, cognitions and practices. Needless to say, and perhaps most importantly, the training they receive will also have an enormous impact on the thousands of learners around the world studying English.

It is, then, more than a little surprising that reflective practice on pre-service certificate teacher education courses has received so little attention. Of the 116 studies surveyed by Farrell (2016 – see above), only 23 focused on certificate courses in 2014, an increase from six in 2009. It would appear therefore that there is a need for more research in this context (see, however, Delaney, 2015). Further, very few of the existing studies look at one of the most important elements of the certificate course: teaching practice supervision. In 2003, Ferguson and Donno claimed that there was a 'dearth of published research into the phenomena' (2003: 147). More recently, there have been studies which have looked at supervisory practices on certificate courses (see, for example, Copland et al., 2009; Copland, 2008, 2010, 2011; Garton and Richards, 2008).

One of the most important practices on certificate and initial teacher education courses is the post-observation conference (POC) session, where trainees give and receive feedback on their teaching to and from each other and to and from their tutor. Clearly, this is a highly sensitive and potentially confrontational situation (Delaney, 2015), where trainee teachers' performances are evaluated and assessed. Typically, trainees give and receive feedback to and from each other before tutors offer their evaluation and assessment. Given the high stakes nature of these meetings, it would be logical to expect that they have already received much attention and been heavily researched. This is not the case at all; indeed, it would be fair to say that there has been relatively little research in this area. As long ago as 1971, Weller told us:

> Volumes have been written on the subject [supervision], but research on the effects and on the processes of supervision is virtually non-existent. Supervision is rarely observed except by those who are actually involved in the process . . . In reality, very little is known about what actually happens in instructional supervision . . . the need for research on supervision is obvious.
>
> *Weller, 1971: 1*

Such research that has existed, up until recent years, has taken the form of theoretical approaches to supervisory practices and offered, in its findings, prescriptive approaches to supervision (see, for example, Sergiovanni and Starratt, 2002). In other words, there has been, until comparatively recently, little empirical research into what actually happens in these POC sessions.

Since the 1990s, a small number of researchers have studied POCs, using a range of qualitative, empirical research methodologies, including conversation analysis (Arcario, 1994; Waite, 1995), linguistic ethnography (Copland, 2008, 2010, 2011), corpus linguistics (Farr, 2011), and mixed method approaches (Copland et al., 2009; Vasquez and Reppen, 2007). These studies have looked in detail at supervisory practices and resultant reflections and have generated findings concerning the use of different questioning strategies, the importance of topic choice and management, the structure of feedback sessions and the roles of tutor and trainees. Harris (2013) offers perhaps one of the most detailed accounts of POCs, though there have been more recent studies which have followed a similar micro-analytic methodology (see below and see also Sert, 2015, and Waring, 2013).

Of concern to Paul Slater, and an area for future research, is the need to rebalance the relationship between the teacher trainee and the mentor. The issue is that if the mentor is an authority figure (as is often the case), then there is little 'real' dialogue; to what extent do power relationships inhibit reflection?

This is especially problematic when the mentor is not only responsible for providing feedback, but also for grading the trainee teacher.

Language. Following on from the work which has been done on supervisory meetings, some researchers have focused more specifically on the use of language in reflection. As we have claimed throughout this book, our understandings of reflection are rooted in the ways in which people interact and the language choices they make. For example, the use of vague language (O'Keeffe et al., 2008) can have profound effects on the pragmatic features of any social encounter: degrees of formality and informality, directness and indirectness, role symmetry and asymmetry may all be influenced by the use of vague language. A piece of critical feedback, for example, can be greatly softened in this way, allowing spaces to be opened and options to be explored.

In a similar vein, the use of modality as a softening and hedging device has been studied as a means of mitigating feedback and potential face threatening acts (FTAs) (Copland 2011, 2012). Corpus-based approaches which employ quantitative, statistical tools to analyze data have a huge role to play in studies which focus on the language of reflection (see below, Farr, 2007, and Murphy, 2012). In much the same way that there has been a focus on learner corpora in recent years in order to understand what language is actually used between learners, there is much work to be done using corpus-based approaches in the study of the language of reflective practice.

In Chapters 7 and 8 we highlighted the importance of spoken and dialogic reflection, arguing that much professional development occurs through talk, especially talk between peers who jointly create understandings of complex phenomena. In such cases, the talk itself is more than simply evidence of reflection: it is the reflection itself. Through talk we often air new thinking, try out new ideas or simply comment on each other's thought processes. The give and take which takes place through interaction, the ways in which new understandings are co-constructed and the ways in which space is created so that options can be explored all entail careful management of language. Studying the language of reflection tells us much about what reflection actually looks like in practice; so, for example, understanding different questioning strategies or pronoun choices can tell us much about the process of reflection (see, for example, Tudor Jones, 2012). Similarly, 'light-bulb moments', where understandings are reached or new ideas are aired, are represented in language. We need to understand how language, interaction and social actions combine to foster these important developmental moments.

Culture. Closely aligned with language is culture. There are almost certainly different approaches to and beliefs about reflective practice according to the culture you identify with. A Chinese student recently asked one of us (Steve Mann) if uptake of reflective practice was dependent on culture. He replied that it probably was but that assumptions should not be made because there are other dimensions to whether any individual finds RP helpful or not. For one thing there is bound to be some intra-cultural variation and also aspects of gender probably need to be taken into account in such judgments. As an example, he referred him to two articles that take very different views on whether reflective practice is incompatible with 'Arab-Islamic' culture. Richardson argued (2004) that reflective practice was incongruent with the values of 'Arab-Islamic' culture and is therefore not an appropriate approach to promote in teacher education in the UAE. Clarke and Otaky (2006) take issue with this position, arguing both that the view is based on selective reading of available literature and also that their student teachers' experience 'far from endorsing the inappropriateness of reflective practice in the UAE context, shows Emirati women wholeheartedly embracing – and doing – reflective practice' (2006: 111). Gender is not an area we have focused on in this book but may well be an area for useful further work (see, for example, Zwozdiak-Myers (2009: 267), who also calls for more exploration in this area).

This is by no means an exhaustive list; it merely exemplifies a number of key areas where research has been conducted and where there is scope for future research.

Research on Reflection: Why?

To see how reflection gets done. While we have made the case for much more evidence of how reflection gets done, there is clearly a need for much more research in this area. We need to understand how reflective processes may lead to co-constructed understandings of new phenomena; in short, we need to understand in much more detail the *process* of reflection.

To understand the place of technology in reflective practices. This point has been made several times so we will not dwell on it here. It is clear from the vignettes and references we have presented throughout the book that technology has already become an integral part of reflective practice. We might even say that the use of technology in reflection has attained almost the same orthodoxy as reflective practice itself. This said, we still need to develop closer understandings of the place of technology in RP: to what extent does it create opportunities for professional development? And, by the same token, does it prevent or impede reflection in certain contexts? Which tools offer the most potential? How does technology create opportunities for sharing and comparing reflective practices on a local or international scale? There is clearly much potential in future research around the use of technology in reflective practice.

To compare alternative approaches to reflection. Comparative research studies have much to offer in terms of their potential for developing close understandings of local practices. Consider, for example, the benefits of comparing a teaching approach used in one context with one used in another. This approach to research has much to commend it. In the same way, our understandings of reflective practice could be greatly enhanced by comparing alternative approaches; this might be across contexts or through the use of alternative approaches, practices or procedures. We need to know much more about how some approaches are better-suited to certain contexts than others and consider ways of evaluating each approach. In the same way that teaching approaches need to be adapted to local context, we can make a similar case for reflection.

To develop theories and models of reflection. In view of the many approaches to studying second language teacher education and professional development (including, for example, teacher cognition, teacher learning, professional learning and inquiry), there is a need for research which theorizes reflection and which improves understandings of the relationship between reflection and other forms of professional development. As Tom Morton comments (see below), there is a need for research which enhances our understanding of the impact of reflection on, for example, student teachers. Studies which look at perceptions of and attitudes towards reflection would help to both generate models of reflection and inform our understandings of what actually works, what helps professional development and what does not.

Research on Reflection: How?

Micro-analysis. There has been a call in recent years for more micro-analytic studies of the interactions and dialogues which take place between teachers and their peers. A number of researchers have advanced this argument by using discourse analytic research methodologies in their work (see, for example, Sert, 2015; Hazel, 2012).

Andy Harris (2013) makes a strong case for studying 'doing reflection' by looking at the talk which takes place between teacher educators and trainee teachers. Pointing to the plethora of studies on reflective practice, the existence of a journal dedicated to research on RP and the many studies which position RP as the dominant model within language teacher education (Wallace, 1991), Harris questions the paucity of studies which have looked at RP from an empirical, data-driven perspective. Harris then highlights the value of studying RP as a spoken phenomenon:

> Another aspect of these critiques is that there have been a very limited number of studies that have looked at RP from an empirical, data-driven perspective. This is particularly true of research into RP as a spoken phenomenon, where, to date, there has not been a single empirical study that has

taken a systematic approach to studying the interactional organisation of reflective practice or the phenomena of 'doing reflective practice as an interactional activity'. This is a surprising omission in the research literature, particularly given the dominance of RP as a model in the field and the simple fact, as any teacher-training professional would attest to, that much of the business of 'doing' teacher-education occurs dialogically, through the medium of talk. This study takes the first steps towards filling this research niche by engaging directly with the question: what happens when practitioners attempt to implement a process of RP through talk?

Harris, 2013

Harris goes on to look at the supervisory feedback meetings which occur after teaching practice on a CELTA course in Thailand. His findings confirm that post-teaching feedback conferences have a clear structure and are organized in a number of phases, each focusing on different types of feedback: individual, group, critical and positive. Harris's study uncovers the interactional organization of feedback meetings and offers a systematic description of 'reflective practice as an interactional activity'. Clearly, there are many implications for this study for teacher educators and trainee teachers in terms of how the process of doing feedback might be enhanced, roles of participants and understandings of the importance of professional talk in learning. Again, there is scope for further research using discourse analytic methodologies.

More recently, other researchers have used micro-analysis to produce 'up-close' descriptions of the social interactions of teachers in training and their mentors or supervisors. In the vignette below, Olcay Sert, who runs teacher education programmes at Hacettepe University, Ankara, Turkey, outlines the value of this approach for the study of reflection.

OLCAY SERT'S VIGNETTE (TURKEY)

Context

This extract comes from a peer feedback session of two intern Turkish EFL teachers, based on a class that the female teacher (T1) taught in May 2015 in a secondary school in Ankara. The peer feedback session after each teacher finishes a class is a part of the teacher education programme. In this particular episode, before the beginning of the extract, T1 has been talking about the brainstorming activity that she used in the class and has reflected on the positive aspects of what she has done. In line 1, she assesses her performance positively, and in line 3, she asks for feedback from a colleague (T2) who had been observing T1's class.

Data

```
01  T1:    . . . brainstorming bence iyiydi.
           brainstorming was good I think.
02  T2:    hmm
03  T1:    bununla ilgili bi düşüncen var mı?
           do you have any thoughts on this?
04  T2:    brainstorming iyiydi canım er bakayım bir saniye
           brainstorming was good my dear, let me check
05         ((checks notes)) er brainstorming iyiydi ama benim
           brainstorming was good but what I think is . . .
06         düşüncem şey . . . giriş iyi oldu warm up kısmı,
           the warm up part was good
07         ama brainstorming yaparken böyle
           but during your brainstorming activity
08         çocuklar brainstorming yaptığını pek anlamadılar
           the kids did not understand that you are doing a
           brainstorming activity
09         yani [böyle şey yapmak lazım
           well you need to do kind of . . .
10  T1:         [bence anlamaları gerekmiyordu ama
           I think they did not have to understand it but . . .
11  T2:    yani böyle bir bilgilendirme olsa güzel olurdu hani
12         er girişte orientation tarzı
           it would have been nice if they had been informed on
           it . . . like an orientation ,
13  T1:    hmm [çocuklar yaptıkları aktivitelerin ne
               do the kids know what the activities that
14  T2:        [hani şunu yapçaz bunu yapçaz sonra
               "we're gonna do this we're gonna do that"
15  T1:    olduklarını biliyorlar mı ki yani?
           they are doing are anyway?
16         bilmiyorum (.) gerek duyma[dım]
           I don't know, I didn't feel the need.
17  T2:                            [işte] bunu işlicez demek
18         iyi oluyo bence (.)bugün bunu işlicez tarzı bir
19         konuşma falan ya da öyle bir orientation.
           I think saying "we will work on this activity" is good
           (.) an instruction like "today we will do this" or a
           kind of orientation like that.
20  T1:    huh huh
21  T2:    ama onun dışında iyidi brainstorming
           but apart from that I think your brainstorming
           activity was good
```

Commentary

Olcay Sert (the supervisor) comments:

I think we see a variety of things related to teacher cognition here. One thing that first struck to my mind after listening to this recording is how one of the teachers (T2) thinks that teaching should be explicit and the learners should be aware of it. He also emphasizes the value of signposting and clear instructions. There is clear evidence to what he thinks in lines 11 to 14 and 17 to 19. In lines 11 to 14, T2 thinks that the students should be explicitly directed to the forthcoming activity (*we're gonna do this we're gonna do that*) and they should know that it is a 'brainstorming activity' for instance. He further elaborates on this in lines 17 to 19, claiming that it is better to attract students' attention to the forthcoming activity using metalanguage. T1, on the other hand, thinks that learners do not necessarily need to be 'aware' of the activity type, but they should just be engaged in talk. Evidence to her position comes between lines 10 to 15, where she overlaps T2's talk and counter argues T2, in a way that shows us that she is a kind of teacher that prioritizes meaning over institutional norms and obligations, like instructions and activity metalanguage.

Of course there are many other things happening here too, but what is good for me as a teacher trainer is to be able to see how the teachers that I am training can spot moments in classroom interaction that they can talk about, and can argue and counter argue creating a constructive dialogue that can help them develop language awareness and classroom interactional competence. I know, by experience, that the next class that these teachers will be teaching, they will remember this interaction and will consider:

- how and when instructions should be done
- whether they need to use 'metalanguage' about activities that they are carrying out
- if they clarified the forthcoming and ongoing activities using appropriate 'managerial' language
- whether learning should be more meaning-focused, with less classroom language etc.

The point is that there is no reason for trying to figure out which teacher is right. They are both right and wrong. This is definitely not the point. The point is that by reflecting on their own and each other's classroom activities, they are creating room for development, and development is not a linear, straightforward phenomenon. They are creating room for what I can call 'try-outs': this extract may or may not lead to better teaching experiences in the future, but it will encourage them to try different things, and be less subjective in what they believe is 'right' in teaching. What is better than looking in the mirror is helping someone else look in the mirror by holding the mirror, and receiving the same favour from that person simultaneously, face to face, in interaction, in action.

There are a number of aspects of this vignette which are of relevance to the present discussion:

1. It is immediately obvious that there is considerable value in recording the interactions of student teachers. This transcript highlights the ways in which new understandings emerge and how teachers in training do not necessarily agree on what is the 'right way' to perform a particular practice: here, giving instructions. Further research on the 'talk' of teachers in training would be particularly valuable, especially studies which compare different subject areas or look at trainee teacher talk in, for example, two or more locations.
2. As Olcay points out in his commentary, the use of recordings and transcripts allows trainee teachers to have multiple 'try-outs' and to learn from their dialogue and actions. By studying their interactions, we see how, through talk, reflection gets done. Here, the metaphor of not only looking in the mirror but of holding the mirror is used to demonstrate the importance of this dialogic collaboration.
3. Olcay also suggests that this kind of approach can lead to enhanced CIC (classroom interactional competence, Walsh (2013)) and help trainee teachers acquire the kind of metalanguage they need to reflect on and talk about their practice. Being able to use a commonly agreed metalanguage is an important element of reflective practice and one which can only be fully developed by studying spoken interactions.

Longitudinal studies. There is huge potential for studies which track reflection over time, demonstrating how professional learning emerges through reflection. Longitudinal studies would provide us with much more detailed understandings of the various stages that professionals pass through in any reflective process. They would also help to promote better understandings of the kinds of tools which might be appropriate at different stages of development. While there have been some such longitudinal studies (see, for example, Dzay Chulim (2015), a longitudinal study which tracked growth in reflection on undergraduate programmes; Wyatt (2008), who looked at the development of RP over a longer BA course), there is clearly scope for more work in this area. Such studies might also make more extensive use of technology in tracking reflection over time. An example of one such study is Brooke (2014), who presents an account of an action research process into the use and development of an online virtual learning environment. It shows evidence of novice teachers using the blackboard platform for reflection during their school 'block' placements. His study highlights the need for more studies which look at the use and impact of different VLE platforms (i.e. the extent to which they promote collaboration and how reflection changes over time).

Greater use of video. We have already highlighted the immense value of video in reflective processes and as a tool in teacher education more generally. There is scope for studies which look at the extent to which video promotes more dialogic, collaborative reflection. Almodaires (2009), for example, looks at the ways in which the gap between theory and practice can be bridged through technology-supported reflection. We need more accounts of how video and visual media are being used in language teacher training and development, building on the work of, for example, Marsh and Mitchell (2014) and Baecher and McCormack (2015). There would also be huge value in more studies which carry out intertextual research on the relation between reflective pieces of writing and video data to demonstrate 'evidence of reflection on their practice' (Verlaan and Verlaan, 2015: 151).

Again, the examples quoted here are just some of the ways in which reflection research could be conducted. In light of current trends in social science research more generally, it is likely that future research on reflection will employ mixed methods and may entail the production of larger data-sets, accompanied by smaller, detailed case studies. The use of video, technology and software packages are all likely to feature prominently in future research on reflective practice – the focus of the next section in this chapter.

10.3 Future Directions

In considering future directions for reflective practice research, we solicited the views of a number of teacher educators engaged in research with, for and by teachers. The selection included below is intended to provide a cross-section of opinions, including the views of professionals who are actively engaged in reflective practice research, as well as those who are less committed to RP or, indeed, who are less favourably disposed towards reflection. Respondents were asked to predict likely future research directions and corresponding research methodologies related to RP.

Tom Morton works as a teacher and teacher educator in Madrid. He questions the pragmatic and theoretical underpinnings of reflection vis-à-vis alternative approaches to professional development and learning.

TOM MORTON ON TEACHER EDUCATION AND
PROFESSIONAL DEVELOPMENT

Along with the work in the current volume, which seeks to make reflection more effective by providing participants with adequate tools, it is worthwhile critically examining how 'reflection' is used (and abused) in teacher education and professional development, and from a more theoretical perspective, subjecting the construct itself to a rigorous examination. Research on reflective practice is needed to examine the construct both theoretically and practically. What is reflection as a form of conscious deliberation? What role does reflection (i.e. conscious deliberation) play in relation to more implicit (tacit) forms of teacher learning and development? Is reflection a type of metacognitive strategy? There is also work to be done on exploring reflection as discursive practice. Is the discourse of 'reflection' a window into underlying cognitive processes expressed *through* language, or is the discourse itself 'where it's at'? Also, reflection has been critiqued in the wider field of education as being too individually centred and asocial, and for playing down the contextual constraints on teachers' practices and the importance of power differences. It may be interesting to explore participants' (student teachers and teacher educators) experiences of 'reflection' and the extent to which they perceive these experiences as helpful to their development. Another crucial question (and perhaps the most important one) is what effect does reflection (in whichever guise) have on learners' achievement of learning outcomes? This reflects current critiques of teacher cognition research in general that it doesn't do enough to examine the effect of whatever mental activity teachers get up to on their students' learning achievements.

Research methodologies to pursue these issues could include think-aloud protocols, stimulated recall based on video clips (e.g. VEO), discourse analysis of reflection sessions, and ethnographic research into 'cultures' of reflection in teacher education and professional development settings. This would be of benefit to teacher educators in planning and designing the curriculum for pre- and in-service language teacher education, especially for the practicum, and its attendant 'reflective' activities.

Tom's comments chime with much of what has been said in this book and add some new perspectives on reflection. His comments concerning the ways in which reflection 'is used and abused' are especially pertinent to some of the concerns laid out in Chapter 1, highlighting a need for research which shows us how reflection gets done. Tom goes further, suggesting that we need to better understand reflection in relation to other forms of professional development, such as teacher learning and teacher cognition. Of huge importance too is research which reveals what practitioners actually think of reflection and the extent to which it facilitates professional development. And quite rightly, Tom highlights a need to study reflection in relation to the 'end-users' of the whole process: the students. In what ways might RP benefit learners? What could be done to make learners more reflective and where is the evidence? These are certainly tough questions to answer, but they are, at the same time, worthy of study in any endeavour to enhance understandings of RP.

In terms of methodology, Tom also highlights the importance of technology, especially video, in promoting reflection and teacher development more generally. His views are shared by Brona Murphy, whose comments below echo much of what has been said in this book.

BRONA MURPHY ON THE USE OF TECHNOLOGY

Working with TESOL postgraduate pre-service teachers, I find they seem more enthused about reflecting when technology is involved. They tend to enjoy blogging and producing e-portfolios which can be shared and used in an interactive way. I find that this also appears to produce more genuine reflective engagement than more solitary work where students, in the past, have said that they don't really mind what they write as they're usually the only ones to see it. Future directions for RP would benefit from allowing teachers to experiment with reflection online and in a more interactive way drawing on insights from social media and using photos, quotes and other tools to support collaboration and sharing around reflection.

Brona stresses the value of technology both in terms of engaging student teachers and in the potential it has for promoting interactivity. Interestingly, she makes the point that student teachers are more likely to provide genuine reflections if they are shared with their peers through, for example, an online forum or the use of blogs. Of interest too are her comments concerning the use of alternative formats of reflection, including more visual elements and the use of social media. These comments echo Jade Blue's ideas on the use of mind maps, presented in Chapter 6.

Our third respondent, Fiona Farr, works as a teacher educator in Ireland. Her predictions highlight the need for more interdisciplinary research and a greater use of methods which help us to understand the cognitive processes of reflection.

FIONA FARR ON INTERDISCIPLINARY RESEARCH

I would like to make two predictions, which, if they evolve in the following order, have the potential to have an enormous impact on the future development of good teaching practices:

– increased inter- and multi-disciplinary research approaches
– a better balance and integration between research which focuses on the 'reflective' and the 'practice' components of RP.

Calls for more evidence around the processes and impact of RP have resulted in increased data-based research accounts using methodologies such as discourse analysis (some corpus-based), surveys, focus groups and interviews. Much of this has been qualitative and often ethnographic in nature, and has provided some genuine insights and understandings. However, such approaches are limited in that they only afford a recounted linguistic narrative and leave researchers using professional and emic understandings in order to reach plausible conclusions. We know little of the cognitive processing and affective impact which happens during teacher-oriented RP activities, and I predict that this will soon change. There are now some established interdisciplinary frameworks which examine real-time brain patterns and reactions, such as those used to examine cognitive processing during vocabulary acquisition, or motivation in language learning. These will soon further find their way into the research approaches in RP and will provide another invaluable source of evidence for a more scientific understanding of what effective RP looks like from emotional and neurological perspectives. Researcher practitioners will then be in a position to examine the complex relationship between 'good RP' and real classroom contexts, moving us closer to the still elusive question of the impact of RP on teaching practices.

Fiona's predictions point towards the use of technology to develop closer understandings of cognitive activity during reflection. She makes a compelling argument for the use of 'interdisciplinary frameworks' which are currently being used to study brain activity during vocabulary acquisition, or to study from a neurological and emotional perspective. In sum, her argument is that we need to actually *see* what happens when professionals are engaged in reflection by studying brain activity and looking at emotional behaviour. Current advances in technology are making this increasingly possible.

Our final respondent, Fiona Copland, makes a compelling case for the use of linguistic ethnography (LE) as a means of researching RP. Her comments highlight the enormous value of this approach, which combines linguistic analysis (of spoken or written texts) with ethnographic approaches, such as observation and interview.

FIONA COPLAND ON REFLECTIVE PRACTICE AND LINGUISTIC ETHNOGRAPHY

Linguistic ethnography (LE) is an approach to research which, crudely put, brings together tools of linguistic and ethnographic data collection and analysis (for a full discussion, see Copland and Creese, 2015). LE has been adopted by researchers exploring very different topics, from throat cancer surgeries (Collins, 2015) to hip hop (Madsen and Karrebæk, 2015). It has also been used to provide a detailed and nuanced exploration of oral reflective practice in post observation feedback conferences (Copland, 2010, 2011; Donaghue, 2016).

In this regard, LE provides particular affordances in terms of under-standing the contextual features of feedback conferences. For example, Donaghue (2016) showed in her study that experienced teachers could successfully 'perform' being reflective to their super-visors despite having no intention of making the changes to their prac-tice that this reflection identified. The performance of reflective practice was evidenced in the micro-analysis of recordings of feed-back; the teacher's attitude to change was revealed in ethnographic interviews. In my work, I have suggested that a novice teacher's lack of engagement with providing reflective comment in feedback confer-ences seemed to be the result of misunderstanding the generic features of feedback conferences rather than a wilful rejection of reflection or an inability to reflect (Copland, 2010). It was evident through a microanalysis of the feedback recordings that the novice teacher did not provide the expected reflective comments; her reasons for doing so emerged through observations of feedback, written up as fieldnotes, and group interviews. In both cases, neither linguistic data and analysis nor ethnographic data and analysis were sufficient in themselves to uncover the complexity of doing reflective practice. The strength of the analytical points came from bringing linguistics and ethnography together.

As this book has shown, there is still a great deal of work to be done in researching reflective practice and as the authors have also argued, this research should be based on empirical data. I would like to suggest that researchers consider using LE in carrying out this work. It seems to me that LE would be particularly suitable for developing understandings of how experienced teachers' reflections are manifested in changes to practice. Observations of teachers reflecting on their practice and of teachers implementing change could be combined with recordings of both activities. LE could also help researchers to focus on how reflection can be encouraged by supervisors/mentors within assessment regimes such as certificates and diplomas. Again, feedback conferences could be observed and recorded and both teachers and supervisors could be interviewed to gain their perspectives of how talk was designed and perceived to be reflective.

As Fiona rightly points out, there is huge value to be gained from a methodology which combines an analysis of texts (linguistic) with methods which provide more detailed understandings of actions, behaviour and thinking (ethnography). Essentially, the advantage of this approach is that it engages with both practice and reflections on that practice, something which future research on RP is likely to attend to. Deeper and more comprehensive understandings of an issue can be fostered when different data-sets are used, and LE also offers opportunities to include a longitudinal dimension to a study. Of particular value is the extent to which an approach such as linguistic ethnography is capable of comparing actual practices with perceptions of those practices; as Fiona suggests, only by a close micro-analysis of, for example, interview data is it possible to check perceptions of what is really happening.

In this section, we have provided a necessarily brief overview of likely future research on reflective practice. In the final section, 10.4, we summarize the main arguments of this chapter.

10.4 Summary

In this chapter, we have summarized the main components of the book under seven interrelated themes. We then went on to consider the current 'state of play' in research on reflection; presenting a discussion of the what, why and how of current research. We noted that there has been and continues to be a need for research on supervision and supervisory practices, especially in view of the fact that roles are asymmetrical and assessment still features heavily.

Increasingly, the language of reflection has attracted much attention and is likely to do so in the future. There is, for example, much to be gained from research which uncovers the dialogic nature of reflective talk, or research which helps further understandings of what reflection looks like in practice. We have also seen that we not only need to understand the language of reflection but the mental processes from which reflection originates. Micro-analytic research methods (such as conversation analysis or linguistic ethnography) have much to offer in promoting understandings of the language of reflection.

Technology impacts almost everything we do; reflection is no exception. We have seen in this chapter how technology can be harnessed in the doing of reflection research; it is also a very rich source for research. We need studies which look at the ways in which technology can be integrated into professional development practices, as well as studies which tell us what professionals think of technology as a tool for reflection. The use of video, social media and software packages all provide us with means of conducting research into reflective practice in addition to providing a research focus.

The future, then, offers multifarious opportunities for conducting research on reflective practice. Advances in technology, combined with multi-disciplinary and cross-disciplinary research, together with new approaches to mixed-methods research, collectively mean that there is enormous scope for enhancing understandings of reflective practice and for making it more accessible to professionals around the world. Future research should embrace these opportunities and develop closer networks of teachers, teacher educators and researchers in an attempt to ensure a more inclusive and more representative approach to professional development.

References

Almodaires, A.A. (2009). *Technology-supported reflection: towards bridging the gap between theory and practice in teacher education.* University of Twente.

Arcario, P. (1994). *Post-observation conferences in TESOL teacher education programs* (Unpublished doctoral dissertation). Teachers College, Columbia University, New York.

Baecher, L. and McCormack, B. (2015). The impact of video review on supervisory conferencing. *Language and Education*, 29(2), 153–173.

Brandt, C. (2008). Integrating feedback and reflection in teacher preparation. *ELT Journal*, 62, 37–46.

Brooke, M. (2014). *Enhancing pre-service teacher training: the construction of an online model to develop reflective practice* (Doctoral dissertation). Durham University.

Clarke, M.A. and Otaky, D. (2006). Reflection 'on' and 'in' teacher education in the United Arab Emirates. *International Journal of Educational Development*, 26, 111–122.

Collins, S. (2015). The geography of communication and the expression of patients' concerns. In J. Snell, S. Shaw and F. Copland (eds), *Linguistic ethnography: interdisciplinary explorations*. London: Sage.

Copland, F. (2008). Deconstructing the discourse: understanding the feedback event. In S. Garton and K. Richards (eds), *Professional encounters in TESOL: discourse of teachers in teaching* (pp. 5–23). Basingstoke: Palgrave Macmillan.

Copland, F. (2010). Causes of tension in post-observation feedback in pre-service teacher training: an alternative view. *Teaching and Teacher Education*, 26(3), 466–472.

Copland, F. (2011). Negotiating face in the feedback conference: a linguistic ethnographic approach. *Journal of Pragmatics*, 43(15), 3832–3843.

Copland, F. (2012). Legitimate talk in feedback conferences. *Applied Linguistics*, 33(1), 1–20.

Copland, F. and Creese, A. (2015). *Linguistic ethnography: collecting, analysing and presenting data*. London: Sage.

Copland, F., Ma, G. and Mann, S. (2009). Reflecting in and on post-observation feedback in initial teacher training on certificate courses. *English Language Teacher Education and Development*, 12, 14–23.

Delaney, J. (2015). The 'dirty mirror' of reflective practice: Assessing self- and peer- evaluation on a CELTA course. In R. Wilson and M. Poulter (eds), *Assessing language teachers' professional skills and knowledge*. Cambridge: Cambridge University Press.

Donaghue, H. (2016). *The construction and negotiation of identity and face in post observation feedback* (Unpublished PhD thesis). Aston University.

Dzay Chulim, F.D. (2015). *Pre-service teachers reflecting on their teaching practice: an action research study in a Mexican context* (Unpublished doctoral dissertation). University of Warwick. Downloaded 10.10.15 at http://wrap.warwick.ac.uk/77716/.

Farr, F. (2007). Spoken language as an aid to reflective practice in language teacher education: using a specialised corpus to establish a generic fingerprint. In M.-C. Campoy and M.-J. Luzón (eds), *Spoken corpora in applied linguistics* (pp. 235–258). Bern: Peter Lang.

Farr F. (2011). *The discourse of teaching practice feedback: a corpus-based investigation of spoken and written modes*. New York: Routledge.

Farrell, T.S.C. (2016). The practices of encouraging TESOL teachers to engage in reflective practice: an appraisal of recent research contributions. *Language Teaching Research*, 20(2), 223–247.

Ferguson, G. and Donno, S. (2003). One-month teacher training courses: time for a change? *ELT Journal*, 57, 26–33.

Garton, S. and Richards, K. (eds). (2008). *Professional encounters in TESOL: discourses of teachers in teaching*. Basingstoke: Palgrave Macmillan.

Harris, A.R. (2013). *Professionals developing professionalism: the interactional organisation of reflective practice* (Unpublished PhD thesis). University of Newcastle. Downloaded 10.10.15 at https://theses.ncl.ac.uk/dspace/bitstream/10443/2354/1/Harris,%20A.%2013.pdf.

Hazel, S. (2012). Interactional competence in the institutional setting of the international university – talk and embodied action as multimodal aggregates in institutional interaction. Roskilde, Denmark.

Hobbs, V. (2007). *Examining short-term ELT teacher education: an ethnographic case study of trainees' experiences* (PhD dissertation). University of Sheffield, UK.

Madsen, L.M. and Karrebæk, M.S. (2015). Urban classrooms, polycentricity and sociolinguistic resources. In F. Copland, S. Shaw and J. Snell, *Linguistic ethnography: interdisciplinary explorations*. London: Palgrave.

Mann, S. and Walsh, S. (2013). RP or 'RIP': a critical perspective on reflective practice. *Applied Linguistics Review*, 4(2), 291–315.

Marsh, B. and Mitchell, N. (2014). The role of video in teacher professional development. *Teacher Development*, 18(3), 403–417.

Murphy, B. (2012). *I know I have got it in me I just need to bring it out: exploring the discourse of reflective practice in teacher education*. Talk given at the University of Newcastle.

O'Keeffe, A., McCarthy, M. and Walsh, S. (2008). . . . post-colonialism, multi-culturalism, structuralism, feminism, post-modernism and so on and so forth. *Corpora and discourse: the challenges of different settings*, 31, 9.cop

Richardson, P.M. (2004). Possible influences of Arabic-Islamic culture on the reflective practices proposed for an education degree at the Higher Colleges of Technology in the United Arab Emirates. *International Journal of Educational Development*, 24(4), 429–436.

Sergiovanni, T.J. and Starratt, R.J. (2002). *Supervision: A redefinition* (7th edn). Boston: McGraw-Hill.

Sert, O. (2015). *Social interaction and L2 classroom discourse*. Edinburgh: Edinburgh University Press.

Tudor Jones, C. (2012). *A reflective inquiry into post-observation multiparty feedback* (Unpublished dissertation). University of Warwick.

Vasquez, C. and Reppen, R. (2007). Transforming practice: changing patterns of participation in post observation meetings. *Language Awareness*, 16(3), 153–172.

Verlaan, W. and Verlaan, S. (2015). Using video-reflection with pre-service teachers: a cautionary tale. In E. Ortlieb, M.B. Mcvee and L.E. Shanahan (eds), *Video reflection in literacy teacher education and development: lessons from research and practice* (pp. 151–171). Published online: 6 May 2015. Permanent link to this document: http://dx.doi.org/10.1108/S2048-045820150000005014

Waite, D. (1995). Teacher resistance in a supervision conference. In D. Corson (ed.), *Discourse and power in educational organizations* (pp. 71–86). Cresskill, NJ: Hampton Press.

Wallace, M.J. (1991). *Training foreign language teachers; a reflective approach*. Cambridge: Cambridge University Press.

Walsh, S. (2013). *Classroom discourse and teacher development*. Edinburgh, UK: Edinburgh University Press.

Waring, H.Z. (2013). Two mentor practices that generate teacher reflection without explicit solicitations: some preliminary considerations. *RELC Journal*, 44(1), 103–119.

Weller, R.H. (1971). *Verbal communication in instructional supervision*. New York: Teachers College Press.

Wyatt, M. (2008). *Growth in practical knowledge and teachers' self-efficacy during an in-service BA (TESOL) Programme* (Doctoral dissertation). University of Leeds. Downloaded on 11.11.15 from http://etheses.whiterose.ac.uk/11337/1/666548.pdf

Zwozdiak-Myers, P. (2009). *An analysis of the concept reflective practice and an investigation into the development of student teachers' reflective practice within the context of action research* (Unpublished PhD thesis). Brunel University.

Appendix 1
'Getting Learners to Reflect'

Task – Getting learners to reflect (Briony Beaven)

This task is useful for either a group of trainee teachers or a group of language learners. Participants consider the statements in italics. Each one features a different way that learners can reflect. There is one example provided and participants are encouraged to think of at least one more example themselves.

In our experience, this works best if you give individuals a chance to reflect and then they work in pairs or small groups to tell each other which example activities they have used with their classes and if they have used or know about other ways to encourage learners to reflect.

The activity can additionally or alternatively be used for teachers to reflect on their own learning within their teacher education course, in which case the statements should be changed to, e.g. 'Teachers can reflect on their own personal needs', or 'Teachers can reflect on the training session they have just had'. Time is then provided in the training course for teachers to reflect as per the statements. Such reflections can be shared orally or written up in a reflective journal.

Complete the list with further examples and then share the ideas with the whole group.

- *Learners can reflect on their personal language needs*
  Examples
  1) Completing a questionnaire about their needs in English.
  2) ....

- *Learners can reflect on the lesson they have just had*
  Examples
  1) Remembering all the activities they have done in the lesson.
  2) ....

- *Learners can reflect on their whole course*
  Examples
  1) A questionnaire asking the learners to reflect on their course and look to future plans.
  2) ....

- *Learners can reflect on their own participation in the course*
  Examples
  1) In group work, one group member is an observer, who counts the number of times the other group members contribute.
  2) ....

- *Learners can reflect on how they can best learn*
  Examples
  1) Learners meet the idea of a word network, they try one out, they compare with other word learning techniques they have used.
  2) ....

- *Learners can reflect to assess their own communicative skills*
  Examples
  1) Learners get a list of "can do" statements. They decide which already apply to them.
  2) ....

- *Learners can reflect on areas they need to work on by themselves*
  Examples
  1) The teacher suggests three 'homework' activities and elicits the purpose of each. The learners choose which is the most appropriate activity for each of them to do.
  2) ....

Beaven, B. Recognising and Creating 'Good' Materials for Teacher Education, Munich Adult Education Institute, Germany. Available at https://www.matsda.org/folio-sample-beaven.pdf

Appendix 2
'Six Coloured Hats' (de Bono, 1992)

This activity can help a group consider different aspects of thinking. Each of the six coloured hats represents a different way of thinking.

De Bono suggests getting used to and switching 'hats'. In this way, you can bring different thinking processes and conversations to tasks or meetings.

White hat	The White Hat concentrates on information and data. It concentrates on collecting information, facts and figures. It asks what I need to find out and how can I get the information I need. This kind of thinking is neutral and objective.
Yellow hat	The Yellow Hat concentrates on thinking about an idea optimistically. It emphasizes the positives, the strengths and the plus points of an idea. Concentrating on the positive value of an idea, you explain why an idea is useful and provide reasons for this view. This hat is rather like 'strengths' and 'opportunities' in SWOT analysis (strengths, weaknesses, opportunities and threats).
Black hat	The Black Hat concentrates on negative evaluation. It focuses on why things may not work. It considers the difficulties, problems and constraints. Rather like 'threats' and 'weaknesses' in SWOT analysis (strengths, weaknesses, opportunities and threats), it concentrates on articulating risks and challenges.
Red hat	The Red Hat allows space for gut instinct. It concentrates on emotions, intuition and feelings. You might think about hopes and fears.
Green hat	The Green Hat focuses on creatively considering alternatives and innovations. In allowing space for new ideas, the green hat can concentrate on finding solutions to black hat problems.
Blue hat	The Blue Hat works at the metacognitive level. In other words, it manages the thinking process. It asks questions like: What thinking is needed? How can I organize my thinking better?

Appendix 3
'Screen Capture Software Options'

Camtasia Studio	Expensive PC option. Hard to use but can produce very professional results if you have a lot of time.
Adobe Captivate	Very expensive and really only for professionals. Most teachers would find it hard to use.
Camtasia:Mac	Less expensive than Studio (above) but takes some getting used to. If you are comfortable on a Mac, a good option.
Tapes	A quick and easy way to make a screencast. Has a limit of 3 minutes. It requires a one-time payment which gives you 60 minutes of recording per month.
Screenr	This is a web-based, Java tool so you don't need to download anything on your computer. The drawback is that it is slow (waiting for the video to upload).
Screenflow	Expensive but powerful – another good Mac option.
Jing	Free tool and easy to use. However, it doesn't have many features. Videos are limited to 5 minutes.
Skitch	Skitch is a screen capture tool with many of the same features as Jing.
SnagIt	You do have to pay for SnagIt but it has no limit on time and you can publish in MP4 format.
Collaaj	This works on both Mac and PC. It is also available as an iPad app. You can integrate webcam. The free version has a limit of 2 minutes. Worth considering.
Screencast-O-Matic	This is the best free option. It is easy to use and can record both webcam and screen. It is available for both Mac and PC. It will limit you to 15 minutes and places a 'Screencast-O-Matic' watermark in the corner of the published video. You can download as a file or publish to YouTube.
Apple QuickTime	This has a screen recording function and so is a good starting point for Mac first timers.

Movenote	This presents your documents with video. Movenote works within Google docs and provides a fast way to add audio content to presentation slides. You can add your favourite content from your computer. Free, but you can remove ads for a small charge.
Quicktime player	(Mac version ONLY) has the option to record the screen, and the resulting footage can be edited in iMovie.
Apowersoft	Apowersoft allows you to record both video and audio on Windows or Mac computers. Fairly simple to use. Has the choice of Full-Screen mode, Custom-Screen mode or Webcam Capture mode.
FastStone Capture	Allows you to record all screen activities. It has editing tools, including annotating and cropping.

Appendix 4
'Establishing a Collaborative Style of Feedback'

ESTABLISHING A COLLABORATIVE STYLE OF FEEDBACK
(BASED ON WALLACE AND WOOLGER, 1991)

A *Four Stage Process:*

Wallace and Woolger (1991) provide a four-stage process for establishing a more collaborative style of feedback:

- Establishing the facts: what happened?
- Objectives and achievements. Focuses on the objectives that the teacher had in mind, concentrating on evaluating student learning.
- Generating alternatives: the novice teacher considers the strengths and weaknesses of alternatives.
- Self-evaluation: the trainer listens carefully to help the trainee reflect on what has been learned from the observed lesson.

Establishing a Collaborative Style of Feedback. Intervention Types.

We have also found the distinction Wallace and Woolger (1991) make about different *levels of authority* in intervention types to be helpful. They distinguish between:

- 'prescriptive' (observees take the role of the receiver);
- 'informative' (sharing the trainer's knowledge about the teaching situation);
- 'confronting' (challenging the teacher about aspects of their teaching performance).

In addition, they talk about more *facilitative* intervention types:

- 'cathartic' (giving the trainee the chance to talk about feelings and emotions);
- 'catalytic' (encouraging teacher self-discovery and leading teachers to their own self-evaluation);
- 'supportive' (affirming the value of the observee's qualities, attitudes and actions).

Wallace, M. and Woolger, D. (1991). Improving the ELT supervisory dialogue: the Sri Lankan experience. *ELT Journal*, 45(4), 320–327.

Appendix 5

This vignette features data from a mentoring project. Jo Gakonga is a teacher educator at the University of Warwick, UK.

JO GAKONGA VIGNETTE (UK)

Context

The extract below is, for me, an illustration of the fact that reflection is subjective and personal but that it is also ongoing and constructed over time in the light of different experience. In this case, my reflections built on my own initial impressions, mediated and given new perspectives by discussion with others and revised again subsequently with access to new information.

It is quite rare that more than one person gives feedback on the same lesson but the situation in my context is that both the tutor (T), myself in this case, and a trainee mentor (TM) observe and give feedback (independently and sequentially) to a novice teacher after peer teaching. The purpose of this is primarily for the trainee mentor's development and as part of this, they reflect on this process with a critical friend (CF) and the tutor. Although this is designed to enable reflection on the part of the trainee mentor, in this case it also provided an opportunity for my own reflection.

In the feedback I gave to the novice teacher, I had made use of video stimulated recall for the first time and felt that this had enormous potential for increasing the awareness of trainee teachers. However, when discussing this with the trainee mentor, who saw them after me, she voiced the opinion that the teachers had seen their lessons in a very negative light because of the use of the video and this excerpt shows my reconsideration of the methodology:

Extract

T.   Something I did with them, and it's interesting because I found it very powerful but I wonder if that's why it came across as so negative, was that I did their feedback from the video. We actually looked at the video, we looked at parts of it and looked at where it was, you know, good and bad.

But I wonder if it was, and I thought that was really great. I really liked doing it that way. But I wonder, it's interesting that their feedback was obviously so focused on the negative.

TM. They focus on themselves, they focused on

CF. They focus on themselves?

TM. They'd taken, they didn't really come up with anything positive and they told me lots of negatives and they told me what they'd seen in the video of themselves. Emily said she looked really stiff and didn't move, which was (.) true (.) but it was the first time she'd ever taught. And I was saying to her, there were all these people, you know. I was sitting there watching, the video and Jo so I said, you know that's quite daunting really. I was trying to say to her, you know you did really well just to get up there and teach. With all these people watching. You were a bit stiff. But that will change..

T.... With confidence

TM. XX was talking about how she used her hands, and she seemed to think that was a negative thing and I was saying, no, no it's not negative. I think maybe if you're watching a video and you're in it, and you watch yourself, so . . .

T. And we not used to seeing ourselves so I think 'do I really look like that?', you know fat, or 'do I look that?', you know 'what does my hair look like?', all that sort of stuff going on and probably 'do I use my hands like that?', and all that sort of thing

TM. And do I really sound like that?

CF.... I clapped about 10 times!
(All laugh)

TM. I think it's a good way of showing different parts of the lesson. So you're not talking about something, and they think 'oh no, that didn't really happen', or 'oh yes, all the students were engaged' and you're saying they're not. If you show them on the video, 'look, two people are working but the other two weren't', it's there in front of them. Yeah, I didn't notice that. I think video can be good, once you get over, 'oh that's really me'.

T. It's interesting because, it's an interesting thought for me because going through with them, when I was doing the feedback with them, it was the first time I'd ever done feedback video like that, at the same time, and I thought, yeah, this is really powerful, this is really great. And it's really interesting to see how, how much negative stuff they've taken from it. Perhaps that's

something to consider, but it is, maybe it's too
in-your-face, particularly for beginner teachers or
maybe the sensitive teachers. You know, maybe the idea
of it being really there, and so you can't deny it
because it's there. You can't deny it in your head,
and think 'she doesn't really know what she was talking'
about because it's there in front of you. It's
interesting, isn't it? Because your own truth isn't
necessarily . . .

CF.   And it means you can, and they will know now what to
focus on next time, because they've seen it.

TM.   Yeah! (Laughs)

T.   But maybe it's . . .

CF.   But maybe with time?

TM.   Maybe it was too early? Maybe . . .

CF.   And also . . .

TM.   . . . after five or 10 lessons . . .

CF.   Yeah.

T.   So I mean, these things are quite interesting for me to
think about, too. Because I did it as someone who is
giving feedback, and the first time I did it I thought it
was really powerful, really good, you know, I really
enjoyed doing it that way. But it's quite interesting
that it's not necessarily, you know, that there is that
negative side that you don't necessarily see, isn't it?
Interesting. Very interesting.

Comment

I see in this extract evidence of my own defensiveness in places in not
allowing the trainee mentor to speak without taking the floor, labelling
my assessment of the talk consistently as 'interesting' and laughing
to diffuse the inherent criticism, but it did lead me to question my
previous judgments about the value of stimulated recall.

As a final addendum to this, again highlighting the inherently subjective nature of the act of reflection, I had access to a recording of the
feedback conducted by the trainee mentor and listening to it, my perception of the teacher's comments was not as wholly or damningly
negative as the trainee mentor's had been. This, again, changed my
perception of the potential for this approach, and at the least, has
given me a desire to continue to experiment with it.

This vignette features data from a post-observation meeting during a teaching practice module. Rana Yildirim and Esra Orsdemir are teacher educators at Çukurova University, Turkey.

RANA YILDIRIM AND ESRA ORSDEMIR VIGNETTE (TURKEY)

Context

The reflection featured below took place between a university supervisor (S) and an ELT student teacher after a post-observation feedback session which was carried out during the 10-week practicum experience of the student teacher (ST). In this context, each student teacher is observed twice, by the mentor at practicum school and the supervisor, and later post-observation feedback sessions are carried out. The reflection below was carried out in order to see how the student teacher felt about the feedback s/he received and to what extent it was valuable for his/her future practice.

Data

(Supervisor: S, Student-Teacher: ST)

S: *How did you find the feedback you received? How do you feel about what I said?*

ST: *For sure, you observe us very carefully. You catch and jot down many things which I am not aware of as I teach . . . and later on your sharing these points with us increases our awareness. Otherwise, we won't be able to see our mistakes. One important thing . . . I heard that some supervisors sometimes criticize harshly but you are constructive. For example, you did not directly tell me that there were problems in my instruction-giving instead you first reminded me of what I did and then gave a better example and asked me to tell the difference. I believe this was very effective. If it was the other way round, it would not have been comprehensible enough for me . . . I would not have wanted to accept what you said. But in this way, I think it is more effective.*

S: Ok . . . Now I have carried out two detailed feedback
       sessions with you, have you found any aspects that you can
       reflect on your future teaching?

ST: I would really like to reflect every aspect that you
       articulated on my future teaching but to be honest, I feel
       as though when I go to my own classroom I would teach in
       the way I was once taught. In the faculty courses, always
       the ideal was taught to us but the school, here, is really
       different as my mentor always says . . . Also, we did
       not learn English as you explained to us, yet we learned
       it effectively. That's why I think I would choose the
       deductive approach in my teaching instead of inductive.
       Because like I said, that is how I was taught.

S: This is sad, ok, . . . let's put deductive and inductive
       aside but I also gave you some other feedback related to
       your tone of voice, instructions, activity sequencing
       . . . Do you also think that it is no good?

ST: No, of course I benefited from it. These are different,
       I think. These are techniques. Techniques which come with
       experience. And you are more experienced than us and are
       sharing and suggesting these to us and I acknowledge you to
       be right. However I think the issue of being deductive or
       inductive is a belief. For example, you suggested that my
       instructions should be more clear and specific and I took
       this into consideration in my next teaching. And it worked
       better therefore I will keep doing so. I mean in my first
       teaching I did not use clear and specific instructions it
       caused a complete chaos in the classroom, yet I do not see
       any problems in using deductive approach, on the contrary
       I do feel I am doing the right thing when I use it.

Commentary

In the extract above, the student teacher appreciates the supervisor's feedback in several aspects. The most remarkable aspects of the feedback received were articulated to be that the supervisor was meticulous during the observation, was constructive, and had a way of directing the student teacher to think about his own actions (instruction-giving example).

One dominant, interesting and important point in the student teacher's reflection concerns his way of valuing the supervisor's feedback but at the same time his desire to stick to the way of language teaching he himself has been exposed to. He believes his own experience of learning EFL taught him a lot because he 'learned English effectively' through deductive approach, though he does not deny that the feedback as a whole is contributory. The influence of past experiences in his instructional behaviour is clearly seen in his reflection. This would suggest a cliché used to describe what supposedly happens during teacher education programmes: student teachers often teach as they were taught, not as they were taught to teach (e.g. McMillan, 1985; Bennett, 1991).

Adding to this, the student teacher's belief is also supported by his school mentor that the reality is so different from the 'ideal' envisaged in the teacher education programme at the university. This would suggest the split between theory and practice in pre-service teacher education. He believes that 'experience' in teaching/practice is important in determining what works well in the classroom. Thus, he reflects on being selective in what advice of the supervisor he should take and follow. For example, he accepts the supervisor's advice on his instruction-giving, but not on using an inductive approach to teaching because he strongly believes it would not work in the 'real' classroom. This would suggest, at least in this case, that pre-service teacher education has little effect on teachers' ultimate teaching behaviour in schools.

This vignette features a novice teacher talking about her classroom choices and trying to relate a classroom observation to her own students' learning. Wayne Trotman is a teacher educator at Izmir Katip Çelebi University, Turkey.

WAYNE TROTMAN VIGNETTE (TURKEY)

Context

As a teacher educator, part of my role in the Professional Development Unit (PDU) is to help set up peer observations for recently qualified novice teachers working on the preparatory year English programme in a state university in Turkey. Peer observations are carried out on a voluntary basis, but are encouraged by the PDU as a vital means of teacher development. I have a professional interest in observing the impact of such observations on novice teachers' future classroom performance. My analysis of a corpus of twelve reflective accounts of lessons observed appears in Howard and Donaghue (2015); this outlines who novice teachers opted to observe and their reasons for doing so, along with perceived developmental outcomes. In the extract below I (WT) am interviewing a teacher (MO) who is in her first year of the programme. We are talking about the impact of her observation of a lesson given by an experienced teacher.

Data

1	WT:	which topic did you choose to focus on in the lesson with (Teacher X) and could you explain
2	MO:	. . . giving instructions . . . I thought my students sometimes failed to understand the ones I gave
3	WT:	could you please explain that in more detail for me
4	MO	. . . I've had difficulties (in giving students instructions) and made a lot of effort to get them to comprehend but I wasn't sure if they understood
5	WT:	and what did you get out of this observation
6	MO:	I wrote down eleven examples of when Teacher X instructed the students..I'll use some in my own lessons

```
7    WT:    can you tell me one example
8    MO:    yes.. she told the class "you don't need to write it
            now..I'll give you time later.."
9    WT:    it'll be interesting to see if they work with you..
            I hope I can come and observe your own instructions
            later
```

Analysis

The extract consists of nine moves, during which I firstly probe MO's reasons for her topic of focus. In her first response (line 2) she indicates a realization based on earlier classroom experience that she has a shortcoming in her knowledge base. In the extract this realization is part one of a problem–solution pattern. Following further probing, in line 4, MO opens up and expands upon her uncertainty. My two questions (lines 5 and 7) lead to her illustration of a potential solution, as they elicit from her the insights she has gained from observing a more experienced colleague.

MO's primary concern was – unsurprisingly for a novice teacher – classroom management. More unexpected, though, was how she was trying to see things not only from her own, but also from the students' perspective. In this respect, I noticed how she herself was thus reflecting upon two levels of developmental challenges (Fuller and Brown, 1975; Johnson, 1992; Tsui, 2003): the first concerned survival and mastery, the second the impact of her teaching on learning. This, I felt, was in contrast to Fuller and Brown (1975), who indicate how concern for the impact of lessons on students tends to come much later.

MO's comment on how she had picked up eleven different examples of instruction confirmed my belief that peer observations carried out by novice teachers, and in fact teachers at all levels of their development, when given more of a concrete pedagogical focus, may result in clearly identifiable acquisitions to a teacher's classroom management knowledge base. Furthermore, and perhaps in contrast to more affective factors teachers tend to observe, such measurable learning outcomes noted by this teacher could be, and indeed were, assessed in a follow-up observation during which she displayed variations on the instructions she had earlier acquired.

References

Fuller, F.F. and Brown, O.H. (1975). Becoming a teacher. In K. Ryan (ed.), *Teacher education: the seventy-fourth yearbook of the National Society for the Study of Education* (pp. 25–51). Chicago: National Society for the Study of Education.

Howard, A. and Donaghue, H. (2015). *Teacher evaluation in second language education*. Bloomsbury, UK.

Johnson, K.E. (1992). Learning to teach: instructional actions and decisions of pre-service ESL teachers. *TESOL Quarterly*, 26(3), 507–535.

Trotman, W. (2015). Reflective peer observation accounts: what do they reveal? In Howard and Donaghue (2015).

Tsui, A. (2003). *Understanding expertise in teaching: case studies of ESL teachers*. New York: Cambridge University Press.

This vignette features a student teacher talking about an incident in a micro-teaching class. Although the tutor attempts to put the student teacher's mind at rest, the student teacher's self image (as a competent teacher and knowledge source) is clearly under threat. Li Li is a teacher educator at University of Exeter, UK.

LI LI VIGNETTE (UK)

Context

This data extract comes from a research project on language teacher cognition in EFL classrooms (Li, 2017). The student teacher (Paula = P) here is a Chinese pre-service teacher who is on an MA TESOL course in the UK. The context of this piece of reflective interaction was a post-teaching reflection led by her tutor (T), in which the teacher participants were asked to reflect on their own micro-teaching, in particular focusing on their strengths and weaknesses.

Data

```
1   STP   this is bad (.) isn't it? (.)
2   Tu    don't worry about that (.) that happens=
3   P     =I should have checked it but I thought I knew it (.)
4   Tu    it's ok and you corrected it quickly=
5   STP   =yeah but really it's <they CORRECTED ME > (.)
6   Tu    [hmmm
7   STP   [and I am the teacher and er I was teaching them some
8         cultural knowledge but (.) °it didn't go this way.
```

Analysis

The extract had been chosen because the teacher (ST: Paula) had displayed her understanding and beliefs about the role of teachers and learners in a learning activity. Such understanding is managed through the jointly constructed interactional work between Paula and her tutor. In the lesson, Paula had asked students to talk about making travel plans by eliciting information from them. She was using musician Chopin as a lead-in question to introduce Poland, but mispronounced the word. Students displayed confusion and one student 'corrected' Paula's mistake.

In the reflection, Paula evaluates this classroom moment as 'bad', as she has mispronounced the word (turn 1). The tutor produces a relevant second pair part to ease Paula's concern (turn 2). However, for Paula, being corrected by a student seems a big deal and, in turn 3, she blames herself for not having checked the pronunciation before the class and taking her knowledge for granted. Another attempt to turn a negative evaluation into a more positive one by the tutor (turn 4) only prompts further negative beliefs about being corrected by her student (turn 5); note that Paula emphasizes this point by a slower speed and louder voice. Paula then reinforces this with an expression of her belief that the teacher needs to be a 'knowledge authority' and that passing knowledge to students lies in her responsibility (turn 7).

In this extract, although Paula does not explicitly express her authoritative role in the class, her interaction displays such beliefs since she is not happy and comfortable with challenges or correction from students. Perceived insufficient subject knowledge exerts a strong impact on Paula's confidence. Research suggests that teacher knowledge influences teachers' decision-making and pedagogical effectiveness (Li, 2013; Tsui, 2003) and here we see the expression of concern about what the teacher sees as unacceptable consequences of gaps in such knowledge.

References

Li, L. (2017). *Social interaction and teacher cognition*. Edinburgh: Edinburgh University Press.

Li, L. (2013). The complexity of language teachers' beliefs and practice: one EFL teacher's theories. *Language Learning Journal,* 41(2), 175–191.

Tsui, A.A.M. (2003). *Understanding expertise in teaching*. New York: Cambridge University Press.

Appendix 9
Practitioner Research Resources

This appendix summarizes a number of key organizations and publications that have helped establish practitioner research. In this appendix we concentrate mainly on action research (AR).

ORGANIZATIONS AND CONFERENCES WHICH HAVE CONSOLIDATED THE IMPORTANCE AND VALUE OF PRACTITIONER RESEARCH

The Teachers Develop Teachers Research (TDTR) series from 1992 to 2005 was particularly influential in building on the reflective teaching movement (e.g. Schön, 1987; Zeichner and Liston, 1996) and was closely aligned with the philosophy of action research (see Altrichter et al., 1993). The TDTR series (Edge and Richards, 1993; Field et al., 1997; Head, 1998; De Decker and Vanderheiden, 1999) aimed to bridge what Clark (1994) conceptualized as the theory–practice dysfunction. There is an intentional ambiguity in the title (TDTR) so that it can be read in two ways:

1. It is teachers who should develop teachers' research.
2. Teachers develop through engaging with teachers' research.

The rationale of TDTR was to make a move to reverse the normal trajectory of knowledge most commonly found in the applied science model where theories generated in universities are supposedly applied by teachers in their practice (see Wallace, 1998). TDTR is part of a response to this 'theory-practice dysfunction' aiming to turn 'the hierarchy on its head' and put 'teachers on the top' of an array of 'pundits, professors, administrators, researchers' (Clarke, 1994: 18). This is an ambitious aim and perhaps it is more realistic to say that movement at least helped to establish the value and importance of teachers' research (see Julian Edge's Vignette on pp. 227–228) and created a space and impetus for more exposure and appreciation of teacher research. The view taken by TDTR is that practitioner research can support teachers' professional self-development, but that the scope of teacher research does not need to be large-scale; it should be focused on small-scale improvements and innovation.

More recently, work arising from IATEFL's ReSig (Research Special Interest Group) from 2011 has built on the spirit and philosophy of the TDTR series. Bullock and Smith (2014) have produced a summary of how teacher research can be an important aspect of continuing professional development (CPD). Two other notable contributions that also follow this spirit supported by The British Council and IATEFL are Dikilitaş et al. (2015), which offers a range of contributions from teachers engaging in research projects, and Rebolledo et al. (2016) showcasing teacher accounts of their research in Chile.

Other important work has been done by IATEFL (e.g. Mitchell-Schuitevoerder and Mourão, 2006). The 'Teachers' Voices' series (e.g. Burns and Hood, 1995, 1997; de Silva Joyce, 2000) also provided a platform for teacher accounts of research, and in the USA, TESOL commissioned the 'Language Teacher Research' series which achieved global coverage (Borg, 2006; Farrell, 2006; Burns and Burton, 2007; Coombe and Barlow, 2007; McGarrell, 2007; Makalela, 2009).

Informative Overviews

There are a number of informative overviews that include procedures, data collection examples and advice (e.g. Nunan, 1990; Brindley, 1991; Elliott, 1991; Crookes, 1993; Wallace, 1998; Thorne and Qiang, 1996; Freeman, 1998; Burns, 1999, 2010; Crookes and Chandler, 2001; Edge, 2001; McNiff and Whitehead, 2002; Gebhard, 2005; Somekh, 2006; Reis-Jorge, 2007; Altrichter et al., 2008; Atay, 2008).
If you are completely unfamiliar with AR, then it might be best to start with a basic overview chapter (e.g. Bailey et al., 2001). Of the available books, Burns (2009) is probably the best bet.

Useful Websites (Resources and Links)

Action Research and Action Learning is one of the largest collections of links and resources and is maintained by Bob Dick: www.scu.edu.au/schools/gcm/ar/arp/books.html
Action Research Resources is maintained by Vron Leslie. It includes a good number of guidelines and resources as well as links to on-line journals: www2.warwick.ac.uk/study/cll/courses/professional development/wmcett/researchprojects/action/resources/
The Canadian Journal of Action Research maintains a comprehensive links page at http://journals.nipissingu.ca/index.php/cjar/pages/view/links
ActionResearch.net is maintained by Jack Whitehead and contains information regarding the process of action research, along with a selection of extracts from theses that have used action research as their methodology www.actionresearch.net/

Useful web-based guides

Action Research: A Guide for Associate Lecturers (Open University) available at www.open.ac.uk/cobe/docs/AR-Guide-final.pdf
Action Research Guide. Provided by The Alberta Teachers' Association is available from www.teachers.ab.ca/SiteCollectionDocuments/ATA/Publications/Professional-Development/ActionResearch.pdf

Examples of Particular AR Projects

We would also recommend the following because they have examples of particular AR projects (rather than more general guides). Edge (2001) provides a range of action research reports from different TESOL contexts. Edwards and Willis (2005) include some AR accounts in their collection on task-based learning. Most of the contributions to Tinker Sachs (2002) and Hadley (2003) are also framed as AR projects. Gallagher and Bashir-Ali (2007) focus on AR in pre-service teacher education and Bartels (2005) includes AR studies from those delivering teacher education. The TESOL edited collections have also provided a platform for AR across the globe (Borg, 2006; Farrell, 2006; Burns and Burton, 2007; Coombe and Barlow, 2007; McGarrell, 2007; Makalela, 2009).

Journals Which Regularly Include AR Contributions

*   *Action in Teacher Education*
*   *Action Learning: Research and Practice*
*   *Action Research*
*   *Canadian Journal of Action Research*
*   *Education Research for Social Change*
*   *Educational Action Research*
*   *ELT Journal*
*   *English Teaching Forum*
*   *European Journal of Teacher Education*
*   *Inquiry in Education*
*   *Journal of Reflective Practice*
*   *Language Teaching Research*
*   *Teaching and Teacher Education*
*   *TESOL Journal*

References

Altrichter, H., Feldman, A., Posch, P. and Somekh, B. (2008). *Teachers investigate their work: an introduction to action research across the professions* (2nd edn). London: Routledge.
Altrichter, H., Posch, P. and Somekh, B. (1993). *Teachers investigate their work: an introduction to the methods of action research*. London: Routledge.

Atay, D. (2008). Teacher research for professional development. *ELT Journal*, 62(2), 139–147.

Bailey, K.M., Curtis, A., Nunan, D. and Fan, D. (2001). *Pursuing professional development: the self as source*. Boston, MA: Heinle & Heinle.

Bartels, N. (ed.) (2005). *Researching applied linguistics in language teacher education*. Springer US.

Borg, S. (2006). Research engagement in English language teaching. *Teaching and Teacher Education*, 23(5), 731–747.

Brindley, G. (1991). Becoming a researcher: teacher-conducted research and professional growth. In E. Sadtono (ed.), *Issues in language teacher education* (pp. 89–105). Singapore: Regional Language Centre.

Bullock, D. and Smith, R. (eds) (2014). *Teachers Research!* Faversham: IATEFL Research SIG. Online (Open Access).

Burns, A. (1999). *Collaborative action research for English language teachers*. Cambridge: Cambridge University Press.

Burns, A. (2009). Action research in second language teacher education. In A. Burns and J.C. Richards (eds), *The Cambridge guide to second language teacher education* (pp. 289–297). Cambridge: Cambridge University Press.

Burns, A. (2010). *Doing action research in English language teaching: a guide for practitioners*. New York: Routledge.

Burns, A. and Burton, J. (eds) (2007). *Language teacher research in Australia and New Zealand*. Alexandria, VA: TESOL.

Burns, A. and Hood, S. (eds) (1995). *Teachers' voices: exploring course design in a changing curriculum*. Sydney: National Centre for English Language Teaching and Research.

Burns, A. and Hood, S. (eds) (1997). *Teachers' voices 2: teaching disparate learner groups*. Sydney: National Centre for English Language Teaching and Research.

Clarke, M.A. (1994). The dysfunctions of the theory/practice discourse. *TESOL Quarterly*, 28(1), 9–26.

Coombe, C. and Barlow, L. (eds) (2007). *Language teacher research in the Middle East*. Alexandria, VA: TESOL.

Crookes, G. (1993). Action research for second language teachers: going beyond teacher research. *Applied Linguistics*, 14(2), 130–144.

Crookes, G. and Chandler, P. (2001). Introducing action research into the education of postsecondary foreign language teachers. *Foreign Language Annals*, 34(2), 131–140.

De Decker, B. and Vanderheiden, M. (eds) (1999). In *Proceedings of the TDTR4 conference*. CD-ROM, available from Centrum voor Levende Talen, Dekenstraat, B-3000 Leuven, Belgium.

de Silva Joyce, H. (ed.) (2000). *Teachers' voices 6: teaching casual conversation*. Sydney: National Centre for English Language Teaching and Research.

Dikilitaş, K., Smith, R. and Trotman, W. (2015). *Teacher-researchers in action*. Kent: IATEFL.

Edge, J. (ed.) (2001). *Action research*. Alexandria, VA: TESOL.

Edge, J. and Richards, K. (eds) (1993). *Teachers develop teachers research*. Oxford: Heinemann.

Edwards, C. and Willis, J. (eds) (2005). *Teachers exploring tasks in English language teaching*. Basingstoke: Palgrave Macmillan.

Elliott, J. (1991). *Action research for educational change*. Milton Keynes: Open University Press.

Farrell, T.S.C. (ed.) (2006). *Language teacher research in Asia*. Alexandria, VA: TESOL.

Field, J., Graham, A., Griffiths, E. and Head, K. (eds) (1997). *Teachers develop teachers research 2*. Whitstable, Kent: IATEFL.

Freeman, D. (1998). *Doing teacher research*. Boston: Heinle and Heinle.

Gallagher, K. and Bashir-Ali, K. (eds) (2007). *Action research and initial teacher education in the UAE. Perspectives from teacher education at the Higher Colleges of Technology*. Abu Dhabi: HCT Press.

Gebhard, J.G. (2005). Awareness of teaching through action research: examples, benefits and limitations. *JALT Journal*, 27(1), 53–69.

Hadley, G. (ed.) (2003). *Action research in action*. Singapore: Regional Language Centre.

Head, K. (ed.) (1998). *Teachers develop teachers research 3*. Whitstable: International Association of Teachers of English as a Foreign Language.

Makalela, L. (ed.) (2009). *Language teacher research in Africa*. Alexandria, VA: TESOL.

McGarrell, H.M. (ed.) (2007). *Language teacher research in the Americas*. Alexandria, VA: TESOL.

McNiff, J. and Whitehead, J. (2002). *Action research: principles and practice* (2nd edn). London: RoutledgeFalmer.

Mitchell-Schuitevoerder, R. and Mourão, S. (eds) (2006). *Teachers and young learners: research in our classrooms*. Canterbury: IATEFL.

Nunan, D. (1990). Action research in the language classroom. In J. Richards and D. Nunan (eds), *Second language teacher education* (pp. 62–81). New York: Cambridge University Press.

Rebolledo, P., Smith, R. and Bullock, D. (2016). *Champion teachers: stories of exploratory action research*. London: British Council.

Reis-Jorge, J.M. (2007). Teachers' conceptions of teacher-research and self-perceptions as enquiring practitioners – a longitudinal case study. *Teaching and Teacher Education*, 23(4), 402–417.

Schön, D.A. (1987). *Educating the reflective practitioner: toward a new design for teaching and learning in the professions*. San Francisco: Jossey-Bass Inc.

Somekh, B. (2006) *Action research*. Maidenhead: Open University.

Thorne, C. and Qiang, W. (1996). Action research in language teacher education. *ELT Journal*, 50(3), 254–262.

Tinker Sachs, G. (ed.) (2002). *Action research in English language teaching*. Hong Kong: City University of Hong Kong.

Wallace, M.J. (1998). *Action research for language teachers*. Cambridge: Cambridge University Press.

Zeichner, K.M. and Liston, D.P. (1996). *Reflective teaching: an introduction*. Mahwah, NJ: Lawrence Erlbaum Associates.

Appendix 10
Online Resources

CEFcult

www.cefcult.eu/index.html
An enjoyable learning environment for assessing your intercultural communicative competence!

As employees increasingly work in international, multi-cultural settings, success in intercultural professional communication requires not only language skills, but also the ability to understand and deal with cultural and linguistic diversity. CEFcult aims to increase the language and intercultural skills of the (future) labour force in Europe.

The CEFcult platform should be viewed as a vehicle in which assessees and assessors can apply their interests, critical thinking and creative ideas to self-selected areas of interest. It is a safe environment for helping language learners refine and improve their speech performance and communicative skills.

Learners are able to record themselves and make annotations to peer review their assessments in social networks. The learner is in charge, but experts can be called in to feed the assessment from a professional perspective. As such, a résumé of a student online might be validated by means of a peer and an expert review, with a recording, imported from CEFcult.

SACODEYL

www.um.es/sacodeyl/
SACODEYL is a web-based system for the assisted compilation and open distribution of European teen talk in the context of language education.

The project includes the collection and distribution of English, French, German, Italian, Lithuanian, Romanian and Spanish teen talk.

SACODEYL sees itself as a pedagogical mediator in the language learning process of young Europeans, exploiting web multimedia resources to deliver learning experiences based on data driven, constructivist approaches to language acquisition.

If you want to learn more from SACODEYL click here.

Index